ᴛʜᴇEXPENDABLE

THE TRUE STORY OF PATROL WING 10, PT SQUADRON 3, AND A NAVY CORPSMAN WHO REFUSED TO SURRENDER WHEN THE PHILIPPINE ISLANDS FELL TO JAPAN

John Lewis Floyd

Trou de Lapin

Tucson, Arizona

This book is typeset in Minion Pro, Futura Book, and American Typewriter.

Editing, cover and interior design, maps, and production by Wynne Brown LLC. The cover design incorporates a photograph of Charles Beckner's uniform shoulder patch worn during the period he was a Chief Petty Officer.

Photographs 1-3, 7, 9-10, and 18-21 are from the private collection of Barbara Beckner Floyd. The remaining are U.S. Navy Archive or National Archive photographs in the public domain.

Trou de Lapin Press
Tucson, Arizona
USA

ISBNs:

978-1-7345421-0-3 (softcover)
978-1-7345421-2-7 (hardcover)
978-1-7345421-1-0 (ebook)
978-1-7345421-3-4 (audiobook)

Dedication

For Barbara

My best friend and partner in all things good for a half-century.

For John Matthew, Karen Christine, and Elizabeth Anne

I was your father, but you were my teachers.

To the memory of Charles Conrad Beckner, CWO4 USN

and "The Greatest Generation"

I would say that I am a stubborn, opinionated, somewhat difficult individual with an average sense of humor. I firmly believe that any opinion, even wrong, is better than no opinion at all. It is better to be occasionally wrong than to be right all the time and have a weak, vacillating opinion to adjust to fit the situation in question. My errors are principally errors of commission and not of omission.

— Charles Conrad Beckner
Essay on Character Analysis

I am no stranger to death. I have seen it many times in my regular occupation and as a combatant in several campaigns in World War II. It is not a dashing, noble, welcome thing in ninety-nine percent of the cases. Tragic is a better description generally. As for me, dying is not my "cup of tea" and I intend to postpone it as long as possible.

— Charles Conrad Beckner
Essay on *Thanatopsis* by W. C. Bryant

Contents

PART I

Part II

Part III

Part IV

PART V

PART VI

List of Photographs

Maps

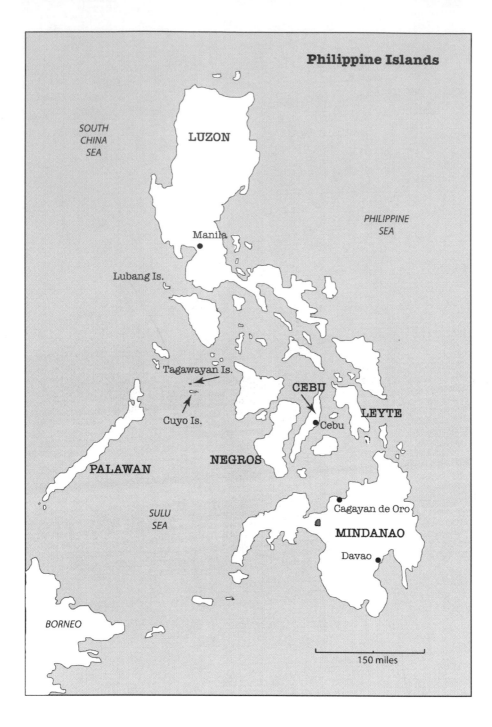

Philippine Islands

SOUTH
CHINA
SEA

LUZON

PHILIPPINE
SEA

Manila

Lubang Is.

Tagawayan Is.

CEBU

LEYTE

Cuyo Is.

Cebu

PALAWAN

NEGROS

SULU
SEA

Cagayan de Oro

MINDANAO

Davao

BORNEO

150 miles

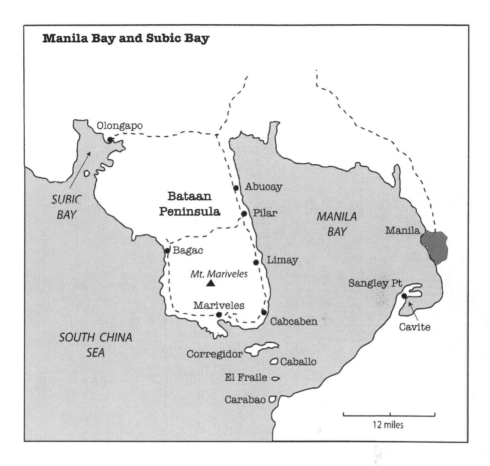

Manila Bay and Subic Bay

Olongapo

SUBIC
BAY

Bataan
Peninsula

Abucay

Pilar

MANILA
BAY

Manila

Bagac

Limay

Mt. Mariveles

Sangley Pt

SOUTH CHINA
SEA

Mariveles

Cabcaben

Cavite

Corregidor

Caballo

El Fraile

Carabao

12 miles

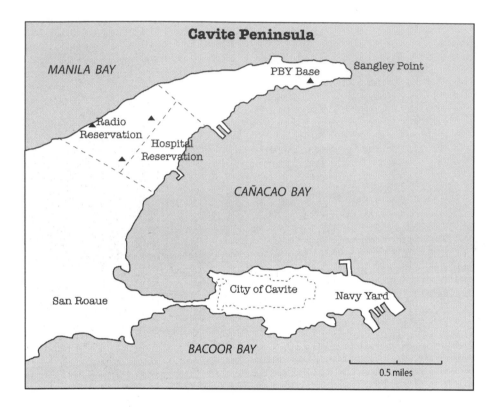

Cavite Peninsula

MANILA BAY

PBY Base

Sangley Point

▲Radio
Reservation

▲

Hospital
Reservation

▲

CAÑACAO BAY

City of Cavite

Navy Yard

San Roaue

BACOOR BAY

0.5 miles

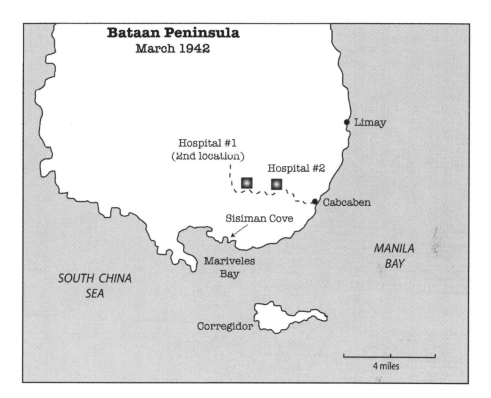

Bataan Peninsula
March 1942

Limay

Hospital #1
(2nd location)

Hospital #2

Cabcaben

Sisiman Cove

MANILA
BAY

Mariveles
Bay

SOUTH CHINA
SEA

Corregidor

4 miles

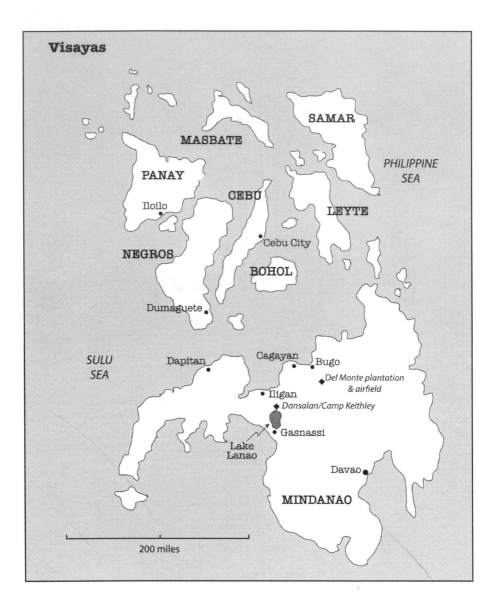

Visayas

MASBATE

SAMAR

PANAY

PHILIPPINE
SEA

Iloilo

CEBU

LEYTE

NEGROS

Cebu City

BOHOL

Dumaguete

SULU
SEA

Cagayan

Bugo

Dapitan

Del Monte plantation
& airfield

Iligan

Dansalan/Camp Keithley

Gasnassi

Lake
Lanao

Davao

MINDANAO

200 miles

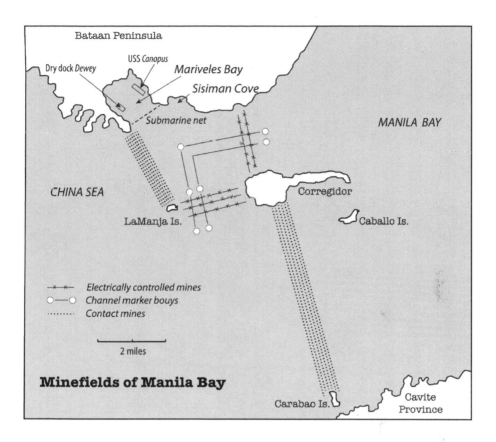

Bataan Peninsula

USS *Canopus*

Dry dock *Dewey*

Mariveles Bay

Sisiman Cove

Submarine net

MANILA BAY

CHINA SEA

Corregidor

Caballo Is.

LaManja Is.

×—×— *Electrically controlled mines*

○—○ *Channel marker bouys*

········· *Contact mines*

2 miles

Minefields of Manila Bay

Carabao Is.

Cavite
Province

Foreword

I came to this story through marriage. Finishing medical school as the Vietnam conflict peaked in 1970, I was assigned to the large USAF hospital in San Antonio. There I met a nurse, Lieutenant Barbara Beckner, who turned down my first request for a date. Fifty years later we're still a pair.

When the time came for me to buy an engagement ring, Barbara suggested I contact her Uncle Jim Beckner, a Master Jeweler in Princeton, Indiana. He was more than pleased to design a custom ring for his niece, personally selecting a flawless, blue-white, pear-shaped diamond and donating it to the cause.

I asked Jim not to tell his brother Charles about the engagement until I'd had time to call and ask Charles's permission to marry his daughter. Jim laughed, "Don't worry about that, son. I'm not about to say anything to him. You're going to have to face that man all by yourself!"

He then broke out in laughter again.

After Jim's comment, it was with some trepidation that I prepared to speak with Barbara's father for the first time. I telephoned his San Diego home in early 1971. "Mr. Beckner, this is John Floyd. I'm an Air Force Medical Corps Captain, a physician, calling from San Antonio, Texas. I'd like to marry your daughter, and I hope you'll give us your blessing."

The prolonged silence that followed cast doubt on how the conversation might end. Eventually both he and Barbara's mother, Mary Carolyn Beckner, overcame their shock and graciously embraced our union.

From our first meeting through his interment with Full Military Honors in Arlington National Cemetery in 2009, I never thought to address Charles Beckner CWO4 (Ret) in any way other than "Mr. Beckner." Even when I was promoted to Colonel, he was still, for me, "Mr. Beckner."

In truth I could never outrank this hero of WW II.

The events narrated in *The Expendable* were not shared by Mr. Beckner as a chronological story. The process was more like pulling teeth. He preferred to live in the now and let the past remain exactly where it lay.

The story began during one of our many visits to the Beckners' San Diego home. I picked up a picture of him in uniform in his later career and commented on the many ribbons on his uniform.

He nodded, "There's a couple."

I thought I recognized several of the ribbons. "This is the Silver Star?"

"It is."

At the time, I was more focused on the academic ladder than the military career ladder. Even so, I knew that the Silver Star was the military's third-highest award for bravery in combat. "And this is the Bronze Star, with two oak leaf clusters, and this is a Purple Heart. Where and how did you get that?"

"Okinawa. They got me three times. The first two, I patched myself up. The third time they carried me off and sent me to the hospital on Guam. Someone there must have filed paperwork for the Purple Heart."

"How did that happen? Were you shot?"

"Sniper. My leg. Took me three weeks to get back to Okinawa. Still got some metal in there, and it aches now and then. Want more coffee? Let's go see what the girls want for lunch. I might need to make a trip to the commissary. Want to come?"

I looked skyward in frustration but knew better than to pursue the matter. If I hadn't been in uniform myself, Mr. Beckner might not have told me as much as he did over the years. During one visit he shared a two-sentence description of the carnage on an Okinawa battlefield. The next visit, I listened to a board-by-board, nail-by-nail, description of his conversion of an airplane engine shipping crate into a cold-smoke curing house for salmon behind the Navy Hospital in Kodiak, Alaska.

Over time these diverse and unrelated vignettes coalesced into a coherent story.

Mr. Beckner and I often talked while barbecuing chicken "low and slow" at his grill. Yielding to Mary Carolyn's rule of no hard liquor, we normally enjoyed a beer or two (or three) over the course of an afternoon's grilling. I learned to ask general, tangential questions about his war years if I wanted more than one-word answers. "How big were the tunnels on Corregidor?" or "You said yours was the only PT boat with three officers. How did that happen?" or "Did you have any encounters with Moros?" or "Did you see any Japanese ships on the run with MacArthur and Rockwell?"

Sometimes he would reminisce and discuss the question. Just as often the only reply concerned the adequacy of seasoning on the chicken or the possibility of more beer in the refrigerator.

Around 2003, faced with Mr. Beckner's growing physical and mental frailty, I decided to write a brief narrative of his World War II experience in the Philippines. I'd simply type up the story as a short vignette, along with some Beckner family photos, and print a thin, center-stapled pamphlet to share with his family.

I'd read *In the Hands of Fate,* a history of Patrol Wing 10 during 1941-42. I followed that with Iliff Richardson's fascinating story of MTB 3 typed during his first months in the guerrilla resistance on the island of Leyte. Among Mr. Beckner's personal papers I found letters from Bill Johnson, Tom Pollock, Tom Mitsos, and others. One thing led to another. I researched several archives and made visits to the Navy Memorial, the Pensacola Naval Air Museum, the PT Boat Museum, and the PT 658 Heritage Museum and Education Center.

I had fallen down the rabbit hole.

The Expendable is Creative Nonfiction. It uses literary styles and techniques to create a factually accurate narrative. Lee Gutkind, editor of *Creative Nonfiction* magazine and author of *You Can't Make This Stuff Up* explains:

The mission of creative nonfiction is to communicate ideas and information in a cinematic way using the literary techniques employed by fiction writers—dialogue, description, detail, action, scenes, to introduce the characters behind the facts with action and excitement in a more compelling story-oriented way than with straight exposition or traditional journalism. But unlike fiction, the story is true, the characters real, the facts accurate.

Within these parameters, I employed extensive dialogue as a literary element. I was faithful to Mr. Beckner's story but added invented dialogue to complete narrative scenes. The men of Patrol Wing 10 and Motor Torpedo Boat Squadron 3 are genuine. I made use of original or copies of letters some of them wrote to Mr. Beckner after the war. Stories of the Paradies and Aboitiz families come directly from Barbara (Paradies) King, who was born in Cagayan de Oro. It was she who first told me of their family friend, Father Haggerty, and his memoir *Guerrilla Padre*.

No invented dialogue was assigned to either General MacArthur or Admiral Rockwell. Their words were directly quoted from firsthand accounts and documents without alteration or addition. Even General MacArthur's talk with Father Haggerty in General Sharpe's headquarters is quoted directly from the priest's memoir.

Lieutenant Mary Tallulah Finian and the other nurses are composite characters. Their journey is derived from personal stories of Navy nurses shared by Mr. Beckner, research of specific events, and study of personal narratives and oral histories of Army and Navy nurses from this time and place. Barbara (Beckner) Floyd RN, a Vietnam-era USAF infectious disease nurse, provided character insight into the remarkable women who volunteer and perform military service in wartime. Many of the nurses in the Philippine Islands on 8 December 1941 ultimately became Japanese prisoners of war. The role these Navy and Army nurses accepted in the defense of the Philippine Islands in WW II was far too important to exclude from this story.

They also were among the expendables.

John Lewis Floyd

May 2020

Prologue

Lake Lanao, Philippine Island of Mindanao

1 May 1942

Charles Conrad Beckner, a young US Navy corpsman known to most simply as Doc, looked from the starboard gun blister of a US Navy PBY seaplane skimming a few feet above the dark waters of Lake Lanao. He noted how beautiful were the deep green mountains surrounding the lake. *So that's my final view of this world? In a minute or less I'll be dead. I'll be one of the thousands already lying in unmarked graves on Bataan, Cavite, or some unnamed place in the Philippine Archipelago.*

The Pacific war began at 0753 on 7 December 1941, with the attack on Pearl Harbor. Six hours later Japanese planes bombed and strafed US Army airfields on the northern Philippine island of Luzon, destroying MacArthur's squadrons of bombers and fighters. On Christmas Eve Japanese troops swarmed across the beaches of Lingayen Gulf north of Manila, overwhelming the underequipped and undertrained American soldiers and Filipino Scouts. Four months later, backed against the sea on a small strip of land at the tip of the Bataan peninsula, riddled with malaria and dysentery, and out of ammunition, 76,000 American and Filipino troops surrendered to the Japanese Army.

A small American force still held out in the complex of tunnels on the tiny island of Corregidor. On Leyte, Mindanao, and other southern Philippine Islands, small groups of American soldiers and sailors retreated into mountain jungles as guerrillas rather than follow orders to lay down arms and surrender.

At Lake Lanao in the mountains of Mindanao a young corpsman, Charles Beckner, had no intention of following those orders. Joining other sailors and soldiers, he assembled medicines that, along with guns and ammunition, would allow them to mount a guerrilla resistance. Most importantly, they were taking

1

radios with which they could provide information to the Allies on Japanese troop and ship movements.

In a final allied effort to evacuate critical personnel, two US Navy PBY seaplanes flew from Australia to Mindanao, landing and refueling on Lake Lanao. Both then flew on to Corregidor, offloaded critical supplies, and took aboard dozens of passengers, including twenty military nurses. Both planes returned to Lake Lanao to be refueled for the final leg back to Australia.

The first seaplane took off from the lake and banked toward Australia. By a quirk of circumstance, Charles Beckner was on the second PBY. When being towed from its mooring by a native boat that seaplane struck a shelf of underwater rocks, ripping multiple holes in the hull. Knowing the added weight of inrushing water would prevent takeoff, the pilot gunned the engines and beached his aircraft at the shore. With one last look at the half-submerged plane, the passengers moved to the nearby Del Monte Plantation airfield, hoping against odds that an American bomber would penetrate the Japanese blockade and fly them out.

Overnight, a desperate and resourceful crew drew a wool Army blanket under the hull, fixing it in place with rope while men attempted a crude repair of the hull. With a column of armored Japanese troops minutes away, the men had no time to test their repairs. It would be do or die.

The plane carried only its nine crewmen plus seven passengers, two Navy officers and five sailors. The pilot, Lieutenant Tom Pollock, taxied from shore, planning to set up a long takeoff into the wind. The aluminum hull reverberated with the pounding of small waves as their speed increased. Without warning, the blanket covering the damaged hull lost suction and blew loose. Charles watched it fly past the gun blister. Tethered by the rope, the blanket flapped against the tail control surfaces. *My feet are wet!* Charles looked down. Water rose over his ankles in only a few seconds.

"We're filling with water back here!" he shouted towards the cockpit.

How ironic. After dodging Japanese bombs and bullets for the last five months, I'm going down in a goddamn lake. I don't want to die by drowning.

Hearing the shouts and glancing back to see water rising in the navigation compartment, Tom Pollock faced an urgent decision; attempt a difficult downwind takeoff or once again beach the plane on the shore. Even if he could get full power from the cold engines, there might already be so much water on board it would be impossible to get the craft airborne.

Pollock wasted no time consciously considering those variables. Immediately pushing the controls to full throttle, he began what might be the longest take-off ever attempted by a PBY. With more than two thousand horsepower from the radial engines vibrating the plane and waves pounding against the aluminum hull, the plane rose only partially from the lake water. Charles, every muscled tensed, willed the plane to rise. Everyone aboard knew it was literally do or die.

Finally, he felt the PBY transition from boat plowing through waves to a hydroplane skimming on the surface. The banging from pounding waves stopped, vibration lessened, and water stopped rising in the compartment. It felt more like flying, but the aircraft was still skimming the waves. Gaining more speed, the PBY finally rose a few feet into the air. Between water sloshing in the hull and a blanket flopping on the tail, all Pollock could manage was to keep the big plane airborne and flying straight. Bill Johnson, a sailor watching from his machine gun position on a nearby hill, later commented that the plane looked like a wounded duck making for the shore.

Pollock struggled against low altitude, water in the hull, and the blanket playing havoc with the tail control surfaces. Looking to the cockpit, Charles saw the pilot staring forward as he fought for control of his aircraft. He leaned through the Plexiglass gun blister, squinting into the airstream to see what held Pollock's attention. He stared at the onrushing forested mountains straight ahead.

Charles knew there would come a time when events beyond his control would determine his fate. *Well, I've never been a fan of drowning. At least crashing into that mountain will be a quick death.*

Part I

1

The Lesson

Princeton, Indiana

May 1933

<small>Nine Years Earlier</small>

Charles, a tall, lanky twelve-year-old, sat on four sacks of seed stacked in a wagon outside the farm store on the outskirts of Princeton, Indiana. His dark hair was short and neatly combed. His sister Mary cut his hair as well as or better than the town barber. More importantly in the deep Depression year of 1933, Mary's haircuts were free.

After Charles and his father, Lee, loaded their seed and other supplies onto the wagon, Lee returned to the store to pay with a combination of cash and credit.

A man named Frank leaned against a post in the shade of the nearby stable, as if hiding in the darkness. This was interesting since it was not yet the sticky hot weather of summer and the sun in the clear sky was still something to enjoy, not escape. Frank's pockmarked face was covered by dark stubble from inattention to shaving rather than any effort to grow a real beard. He was of good height and exceptional girth. Frank was known around town for tormenting animals and intimidating people—and he made the young boy nervous. Every time Charles chanced a glance, Frank glared back at him. When Lee emerged from the store, Frank walked from the shade, paused for a Model T to sputter past, and took a stance between Lee and the wagon.

Lee stopped, but said nothing, letting Frank speak first. "Lee, you got them four bags of seed. That's more than you can plant right now, so I'm taking one of them. I'll pay you later."

Lee Beckner was a slight but sinewy man with piercing blue eyes. As the Depression deepened, Lee had managed to keep the family fed, if barely, on rented farmland just outside Princeton. He would not easily give up a single seed, much less a sack full.

Before replying to Frank, Lee stepped closer, refusing to wince at Frank's fetid breath. Unblinking, he stared up at Frank. "I've already signed a note for these, so I think I'll have to keep 'em. But Feed and Farm has more seed, so just go buy what you need. That is unless you've got no money and no credit. In that case you've got a problem."

"No, Lee. You see, it's you with the problem. I'm taking that bag with me now, and you ain't big enough to stop me." Frank took a step towards the wagon, but Lee quickly sidestepped to stay between Frank and the seed. Frank leaned forward, his face almost touching Lee's nose. "Don't be foolish, Lee, you're going to need a doctor if you don't step aside right now!"

Despite Frank's rotted breath and spittle, Lee did not back down. Glancing at the young boy who was shifting closer to the confrontation, Lee said, "Charles, stay there." The boy was already taller than his father and had established reasonable credibility as a schoolyard fighter. His instinct told him to jump from the wagon and stand beside his father, but he knew better than to disobey him.

Lee stared up at the larger man for a moment, then came to a decision. "I tell you what, Frank, the street's no place for us to tangle, so let's you and me just go into the stable and take care of things in private." Not waiting for Frank to respond, Lee turned and walked purposefully through the stable doors calling over his shoulder just before disappearing into the darkness of the building, "You coming or not?"

Frank hesitated for a moment and then followed Lee through the doors.

The boy looked up and down the empty street. Seeing no one else, he jumped from the wagon and ran after the men. Rounding the open door he stopped in his tracks, taken aback by the tableau in the center of the stable. His dad stood to Charles's right, his face in shadow, holding a hayfork in each hand. Frank stood to Charles's left, squinting in the shaft of sunlight from the open doors.

"Here, Frank," Lee said, tossing the pitchfork in his left hand at Frank's feet. "You're a big man, but I think these are pretty good equalizers. Have you worked with one of these before? No? It doesn't matter. Pick it up so we can settle this thing. I don't think the doctor's going to be much help when it's over."

Frank looked down. The pitchfork's three long, steel tines glinted in the sunlight. He left it on the ground.

"You might want to pick that thing up," Lee said again, leveling his hay fork and stepping forward from the shadow.

"You crazy bastard, Lee! You ready to get killed over a sack of seed?" Frank's eyes focused on Lee's pitchfork, but he still made no movement to pick up the one at his feet.

"Your choice, Frank. You should know me. I could kill you right here and have not one shred of regret." Lee spoke in a rock-steady, measured tone. "Like I said, the store's got lots of seed. Get yourself some money or credit and buy your own. I really don't care, but you're not taking mine."

The men stood, staring at each other in silence broken only when a horse nervously snorted from the back of the stable.

Finally, Frank turned for the stable door, leaving the hay fork on the ground. "Go to hell, Lee. I don't want to have to explain to the sheriff why I killed a little turd like you. Keep the goddamn seed."

The boy was silent as they made their way home. His dad, seemingly undisturbed by the events of the afternoon, left the reins slack, knowing the horses would find their way back to the farm. Charles eventually formulated the question he had been working on since the face-off in the stable.

"Dad, would you have killed him? *Could* you have killed him?"

Lee continued looking ahead for a moment before responding, "Charlie, I don't know for sure how the fight would have ended, but with the pitchforks, I at least had an equal chance. Thing was, I was pretty sure I wouldn't have to fight him."

"Really? Why were you so sure?"

"You see, Charles, the world is full of bullies, and they're not always as obvious as Frank. They can be workmen, store clerks, bankers. Even doctors and preachers, I suppose. Thing is, they're all the same when it comes to a fight. If you can just give them the *idea*, the *possibility*, that you'll hurt them, or worse, they'll back down. They'll never admit it of course. They tell themselves a different story and soon believe their own lie instead of the truth."

"But what if that doesn't work, and they don't back down?"

"That would be unlikely because bullies, maybe except for the extra-stupid ones, don't take chances. They only attack weaker people. But if they don't back down, and you think you can win, then you take to the fight with every bit of strength, cunning, and skill you've got. On the other hand, when it's clear that the situation is impossible and you're going to lose that fight, then you must avoid the confrontation or put it off by any means you can."

"You mean, run away?"

"So to speak. You need to survive. Most often you'll get a chance to even the score later."

On the ride back to the farm Charles looked at the sacks of seed for which Lee had stood his ground, and he thought about his father's advice. In the middle of the night, he awoke with images of pitchforks and his father's words replaying in the darkness.

Charles Conrad Beckner, Princeton, Indiana, around 1938.

2

Leaving

Indiana

Spring 1939

Sharecropping through the leanest years of the Depression kept food on the Beckner table, but little else. Charles's mother had survived an abusive home before she married Lee and was incapable of providing much emotional warmth for the children. Otherwise, she kept the family in clean clothes and well fed.

Survival was a group effort. Charles delivered bread his mother baked for her regular customers and tended a small truck farm close to the house. On summer weekends Charles, his brother Jim, and his sister Mary loaded vegetables and melons onto the wagon to sell in Princeton. None of the children held an idyllic view of farm life.

Jim worked after school as an apprentice in the jewelry store on the square in Princeton. "I'm going to own that store someday," he confidently told his brother and sister.

"What do you know about watches and jewelry?" Mary challenged. "You just sweep the floors."

"I do more than that," Jim retorted, "and I'm learning how to run a business."

"Exactly how do you run a business, Jim?" Charles was genuinely interested.

"It's more than buying stuff and putting it out for sale. Most of his business comes from repeat customers because they know he treats them fair and square. He has customers he's never even met. They heard about him and write to ask for something special, trusting him to send it to them through the mail. How about you? You must have some plans." Jim was of course talking to Charles, not Mary. For poor rural girls, anything beyond getting married and raising their own family was almost beyond imagination.

"I don't know, Jim," Charles looked to the horizon. "I'll find a way out of here first. Then I'll see what's over the hill and past the next bend in the road."

"Dad, I applied for enlistment. In the Navy."

"Charles! Charles! You're eighteen and can make your own choices, but I assumed you would stay around at least long enough to finish high school." Lee did not hide his surprise or disapproval. "You didn't think to talk to me about this before you applied?"

Charles shrugged.

"Will they accept you?" Lee pressed.

"The recruiter said that because I'm in the High School Navy Guard, there's a good chance they'll take me. It's regular pay, and you know I'll send some, probably most of it, home. That should help, don't you think?"

"And, it gets you away from this farm. Is that why you did it?"

"Maybe." Charles shrugged again. "I'd like to see what's out there."

"I guess it could be good if the Navy gave you some skills or education. We never really talked about it much, but I've always hoped you kids would grow up to a better life than sharecropping."

"The Navy has all sorts of training programs. Who knows, Dad, maybe I'll stay in for a career."

"Some of the newspaper people think Germany is getting ready to start another Great War. You might have to go over and fight them in the trenches like we did twenty years ago."

"Dad, it's the Navy. Ships don't have trenches."

The letter arrived two weeks later.

To: Charles Conrad Beckner
Subj: Application for Enlistment, US Navy
Your application for enlistment has been accepted. You have
been scheduled for an enlistment medical exam at . . .

ᔓ ᔓ ᔓ

"Shit! Goddamn son of a bitch!"

Lee heard his son yell. *I'm going to have to teach that boy a lesson this time.* "Don't cuss like that, Charles! Everyone in the county heard you!" Lee stopped in his tracks when he saw Charles limping to the house, dripping blood from a ripped trouser leg. "What the hell happened?" he asked, ignoring his own use of profanity.

"The ax bounced off a knothole and hit my leg, Dad."

Mary heard the commotion and came from the house. "Damn, Charles, you're supposed to hit the log with the ax, not your own leg." Mixed with sarcasm, even her use of profanity seemed acceptable in the moment. She grabbed a towel and pushed it against the dripping wound.

Lee shook his head. "Let's get you to the doc and see what he can do."

The young family doctor examined the injury thoroughly before announcing, "It's not as bad as it looks. Though it's a good-sized flap of flesh there, I don't think there's any bone or tendon injury. We'll clean it up and put in some stitches. Stay off it for a week or two. If it doesn't get infected, you'll be fine."

"My enlistment physical for the Navy is in ten days," Charles told the doctor, gritting his teeth from the pain.

"I can't do anything about that, son. I need to check the wound in three days. I've cleaned it up as well as I can, but if you get a fever, if it starts draining pus, or if you see red streaks going up your leg, get back here right away."

The stitches came out ten days later. "Looks good, Charles. It's going to heal completely," the doctor announced. "But it'll take a while."

That week the Navy confirmed Charles's fears. The injury rendered him "not qualified" for duty. They had plenty of other young men waiting, also seeking to escape the deprivations of the Great Depression through military enlistment. They did leave the door open though. If Charles's leg completely healed, his doctor should send the Navy a letter to that effect. If another military medical exam also found him fit, his enlistment could go forward.

Charles chose not to sit and wait.

A week later, he talked to Lee while they were washing up for supper. "Dad? Since the Navy was never a sure thing, I applied at the same time for a place in the Civilian Conservation Corps." *I'll let you absorb that before I tell you I've been accepted.* "I know you need my help on the farm, but we also need cash. It's part of Roosevelt's New Deal. Along with a job, I'll get housing, clothing, and food. It comes with a monthly wage of $30, but they'll hold back $25 for

13

you and Mom. It's not a lot, but it's more than I can make selling tomatoes in town."

Resigned to his boy leaving one way or another, Lee only said, "Let's go eat."

At the supper table, Charles pulled out the just-arrived letter from the CCC and passed it around. "I was accepted. They're sending me to a camp in Twin Falls, Idaho."

Mary grabbed the letter. "Idaho? You're not going to stay and graduate?"

"Why should I? We need the money now, and I already know more than my teachers."

"Says you." Mary rolled her eyes, then turned serious. "Will you stay in Idaho, or will you come back here someday?"

"The Navy said I could reapply after July 1st if my leg's completely healed, so I'll be back by then."

Mary tossed the letter back at Charles. "You're going to miss me."

The Idaho CCC camp was not a military unit, but in many ways operated as one. The days began early with reveille, roll call, calisthenics, and breakfast. The men worked through the day, returning to their tents for a good and plentiful supper. After the evening meal, they traded tales of their lives and travels. The common background was poverty, and most had little formal education. Southern and Yankee accents mixed with dialects from European homelands. All in all, it was a worldly education for a curious Indiana farm boy.

Charles returned to Princeton the first week of July. Mary, sooner than others, realized she had a new, more mature brother. Not only was he taller and more muscled, but he moved with greater economy and spoke slower. She eagerly listened to his stories from Idaho. "It sounds like you didn't miss us a bit," Mary teased.

"I did miss you, Mary. On the other hand, I missed this farm like a toothache. I found it good, being on my own."

"You're about to leave again, aren't you?"

"Probably. Yes."

"That looks nice and clean. I would say that your leg is completely healed,"

the Princeton doctor announced.

"Will you give me a letter I can give to the Navy saying that?"

"Of course."

"Can I have it right now? I'll take it there myself."

The Navy doctors agreed with the Princeton doctor. Charles's enlistment would go forward.

ʕ๑ ʕ๑ ʕ๑

Two weeks later, with orders for Great Lakes Navy Training Center in hand, Charles stood at the bus stop in Princeton. Lee waited with him. The bus was already there, having stopped long enough for the passengers to have a comfort break.

Lee stood straight, proud that his son would be serving his country in uniform. At the same time, he couldn't hide the sadness in his voice. "Our town's coming back to life just as you're leaving. The Depression's not been a good time for us, but there's finally some daylight at the end of the tunnel. I think it'll all be behind us soon. In the meantime, it might be a little boring around here without you and your sister pulling your pranks day and night."

"Mary and I stayed up until three this morning, talking mostly about our good times here."

"Yes. I overheard some of that." Lee chuckled. "That story about your brother Jim and his pet chicken? I really knew all about it at the time, just pretended not to. I did overhear a thing or two I didn't already know about."

"Now you do." Charles laughed, and then turned serious. "I did tell Jim and Mom goodbye this morning."

Lee couldn't think of much more to say and waited with his son in silence. Charles took a final look at the small town and nearby fields, the stage setting of his boyhood. *Jim says he's happy here. Thinks he can learn the jewelry trade and open his own shop. After seeing Idaho, I lost any urge to stay around here, or for that matter any desire to ever return. I'll miss the family though, especially Mary.*

As he stood, lost in memories, the driver and passengers re-boarded the bus. Charles was startled when the driver called through the open door, "If you're going with us, you better get on board now!"

There was no hug, but the handshake was firm and long. Charles was sure his voice would break if he tried to speak. He nodded once to Lee and boarded the bus.

He waved to his dad as the bus pulled away.

3

Basic Training

Indiana

Summer 1939

Charles's trip to Great Lakes Navy Training Base required a series of bus/train transfers, beginning in Indianapolis. The massive, three-story granite and red brick Indianapolis Union Station dwarfed any building in Princeton. People crowded in and out the main doors, like bees swarming about their hive entrance. Mouth agape, Charles craned his neck upward, looking from the giant rose window to the 185-foot tall clock tower.

"Do you know where you're going, young man?" The well-dressed older woman looking at Charles was smiling.

"Yes, ma'am," Charles closed his mouth. "I'm on my way to Chicago."

"Do you have relatives there?"

"No. My actual destination is the Great Lakes Navy Base. I've just enlisted."

She heard the pride in his voice. "Then go on now. You work hard. Do your best." She paused a moment and then added, "Live your life in a way that when you look back on it after forty or fifty years, you will be proud of the decisions you made."

"Yes ma'am," Charles replied, nodding. "I'll do that."

The trip was tedious, with a long overnight transfer in Chicago. Charles

16

finally stepped down from the morning train at the small Great Lakes train station south of Waukegan. A waiting sailor gathered a group of other newly arrived boys and young men for a short bus ride to the old stone entrance to the base. He guided his small group through the gate and led them to a giant reception hall where dozens of other young men waited. The new arrivals signed in at a series of desks.

"Name. Last, first, middle initial, home city and state."

"Beckner, Charles C. Princeton, Indiana."

"Go stand with that group," the clerk pointed with his pencil.

Eventually a chief petty officer, dressed in a uniform so sharp he might have stepped out of a men's fashion magazine led Charles's group outside.

"Listen up," he said without shouting. His quiet voice forced the men to stop talking so they could hear. "I'm Chief Petty Officer Dixon. In the coming weeks we will come to know each other well. To be successful in this training, as well as during the rest of your time in the Navy, it is important for you to always give your best effort, to be honest at all times, and to demonstrate respect to me and to every other sailor and officer in the United States Navy." He paused, looking the boys over. "Enough formality. Time to get started."

"It's almost noon," one of the group asked, "When do we eat?"

Dixon simply answered, "Later," then efficiently, if roughly, the drill instructor aligned the boys into rows and columns, alphabetically by last name. Taking a position in front of his company, he began with short-burst instructions spoken matter-of-factly but laced with profanity. Next to Dixon was a junior enlisted sailor who demonstrated each movement as it was described.

"This is the position you assume on the command 'At Ease.'" Dixon went up and down the rows using his hands and feet to push arms and legs into proper position.

"You don't have to shove!" one of the recruits protested, fatally misinterpreting the quiet voice.

Dixon was instantly in the recruit's face, their noses less than an inch apart. He no longer spoke softly. "This is the fucking Navy, you worm," he spit out with disdain. "The Navy owns you, and I'm in charge of Navy property. That's you! Talk to me like that again, and you'll find yourself punished, discharged, and kicked out the front gate to find your own way back to your mommy." He stopped talking but stayed in the recruit's face. The recruit, too shocked and scared to respond, stood silent.

Charles and the others, thankful Dixon had not attacked them, did not move a muscle.

Dixon stepped away from the petrified recruit and resumed his instruction. "This is 'Attention.' 'Dress left.' 'Right face.' 'Left face.' 'About face.'"

They practiced until all were turning the same direction more or less in unison. Leaving the group at attention, Dixon moved on to the elemental activity common to any military unit. "Armies have efficiently moved by marching as a unit since the Roman Legions. Marching is a company, not individual, exercise. We will march in the morning, in the afternoon, and sometimes in the middle of the night. For those who successfully complete this training, your last day as a recruit will be spent marching. You start with your left foot first. OK, know which is your left foot? Follow me. Left–right–left–right. Halt–two–three!"

Dixon walked up and down the lines. "You are worthless. Every one of you. I ought to send each one of you back to your mommy, but I'm sure she's happy to be rid of you. Dress left! NO! Look left, and straighten your goddamn line, city boy!" Dixon walked to the front, shaking his head. "I know this is going to be a disaster, but now I'm going to try to march you to the barber and the dry goods store."

Aligning in formation and marching in step were the beginnings of the transformation of individual young men into a cohesive Navy unit. Uniformity in dress and appearance would be added before nightfall.

In what looked more like a sheep-shearing barn than a barber shop, each recruit's head was in seconds clipped to less than one-sixteenth inch.

Dixon then marched his bare-headed group to the clothing stores.

Each recruit received a sea bag on which they stenciled their last name. For many, this sea bag would carry their most important possessions throughout their years in the Navy. The recruits passed tables stacked with uniform items while holding their bags open. From behind the counter, using a combination of questions and eyeball guesstimates, sailors dropped uniform combinations into each bag. "Here you go, skivvies, blues, whites, and shoes." One-size-fits-all leggings, towels, handkerchiefs, socks and a ditty bag for personal items completed their wardrobe.

Unexpectedly each also received bed linens; two mattress covers, one pillow, two pillow covers, and two blankets. Then came the bigger surprise. Each recruit was given a mattress and a hammock.

The new recruits were ordered to strip completely and put their civilian clothes in boxes to be shipped home. After brief instruction on wearing the uniform, each had a photo taken in their blue jumper for identification cards and records.

Reassembling his company, Dixon demonstrated how to properly repack the sea bag, wrap the mattress within the hammock bag, and tie the hammock around the sea bag.

Taking position to the left of his company, Dixon marched the men to their barracks. "Platoon! For'ard … harch! Left … Left–right–left." Between counting cadences, he continued berating the boys. "It's not a goddamn stroll to Grandma's, freckle-face! Stay in line!"

Dixon marched his company in a series of dogleg turns, finally halting them in front of a large, plain barracks building. "Enter from the front row, and line up alphabetically on the right side. Lean your sea bag under the marks on the wall. You now have five minutes for the toilet. Return and stand at ease in front of your bag."

Exactly five minutes later Dixon called his company to attention. "Right now, we're marching, if you can call it that, to the chow hall for your first Navy meal."

In keeping with long-standing Navy tradition, the food was excellent and plentiful. Twenty minutes after entering the chow hall, they were being marched back to the barracks. "Why can't we just walk there?" a voice complained.

"Who said that?" Dixon demanded, while continuing to march his company.

Silence.

"You will open your mouth only when I ask a question. Otherwise you will wait for my instruction and then your life might be less miserable. Left–right–left. Farm boy! Your goddamn LEFT FOOT! *Left* … left, left–right–left."

Once lined up in their barracks, Dixon explained the sleeping arrangements in this particular barracks building, "I know you were expecting a bunk, but the Navy still has many ships in which sailors, and even officers, sleep in hammocks. For both historical and practical purposes, there is one way, and only one way, to set up, to take down, and to store your hammock."

It was not as simple as one would have thought. There was little space between hammocks, and Dixon demanded they be adjusted so that each one hung the exact same distance above the floor. It was not only for uniformity. If the hammock were hung too low, it would form a most uncomfortable U-shape that would make sleep impossible. Similarly, if too tight and high it would be stiff, straight as a board, and put the occupant's nose against the beam or ceiling.

The company required another half hour of instruction and practice before everyone was able to enter and exit their hammocks without help. Being one of the tallest in the company gave Charles an advantage in this maneuver.

One more toilet break, and then lights went off at 2200 hours. It had been a long day and the men, most of them only schoolboys, lay quietly in the dark. Some were too excited to sleep, others too afraid. Much had happened in the two days since Charles said his goodbyes to Lee.

Seconds later, he was in deep, sound sleep and did not wake when a sleeping recruit, rolling from his right to his left side, fell out of his hammock.

At 4 a.m. bright lights and a blowing whistle roused the men from sleep. *The Navy day starts as early as farm chores in July.*

The few who tried to ignore the light and whistles were forced out by cursing and rude prodding. Eventually all stood in a row under the hammocks. Each gave his own interpretation of "Attention!" while surreptitiously glancing at the others for guidance.

Dixon began, "Nothing adds more to the positive appearance of a barracks or a ship of war than neat stowage of hammocks. I will demonstrate, and then each of you will roll your hammock and bedding in an exact, uniform manner. Remember, seven turns at equal distance is the required number for hammock-lashing."

A few minutes later, Dixon glared each recruit into silence as he inspected the rolled hammocks. It was time to strip more individuality from his company. He stepped to the first in line, "And what's your name, sonny?"

"Adams."

"Adams what?

"Billy Adams?"

"You don't even know your fucking name." Dixon stepped to the next recruit. "And your name?"

The second recruit was already confused. "Baldwin?" he said unsurely.

"Baldwin what?" the Dixon demanded. After a moment with no response, he shook his head and stepped in front of Charles. "What's your name?" Dixon's previously quiet speech rose with anger and spittle.

"Beckner."

"Beckner what?"

Charles had no idea what this most unpleasant man wanted but gave it one more try. "Beckner, sir."

"Hear that?" the Dixon yelled to the rest of the recruits. "Always address me as either 'Chief' or 'sir.' Not that it will make your life any easier, but it makes me smile in my sleep." He turned back to Charles. "Do you know what your name really is?"

Charles had no idea what the Dixon wanted, so he simply again said, "Beckner, sir."

An asymmetric grin appeared on the DI's face, now only an inch from Charles's nose. "Your name is Maggot!" He moved on to stand in the next recruit's face. "And your name is Maggot!"

Then Dixon turned to the entire room. "Every one of you is 'Maggot.' You don't deserve your own name. You don't even rate as a blowfly. You are no more than a group of lowly worms, crawling around in a lump of horse shit on the ground. You are nothing! You are not even a tiny cog in the wheel that makes this Navy run. You are only a fleck of rust that needs to be scraped and painted over. Do you understand that?"

Silence.

"Do you understand that?"

Scattered "yesses" and "yes, sirs" came from the room.

"DO YOU UNDERSTAND THAT?"

Finally comprehending the required response, the recruits yelled in unison, "YES, SIR!"

"As of this minute, there is no individual 'you.' There is only this platoon and the United States Navy. You will dress the same, talk the same, and act the same. You will together do everything I tell you to do, and you will do nothing unless I tell you to. Do you understand?"

"YES, SIR!"

Uniformity. Look the same, march the same, eat the same, shower the same, etc. etc. While accepting their role as only one piece of a larger machine, the recruits needed to learn and accept that Navy hierarchy was historically well defined and strictly preserved. One did not have to understand the reason for an order from a senior officer. One did have to obey it.

Dixon continued, "You have five minutes to piss and crap. First squad first. Then return to this formation."

Ten minutes later, stripped and holding only soap and towel, they stood in line, waiting their turn for the shower.

"Okay, Maggots. This is a Navy shower. Enter and leave the shower room by squad. You will have water on for fifteen seconds to soap up, water off for thirty seconds to scrub, and water back on for thirty seconds to rinse off. Before you ask, cold water is good for you. Immediately exit for the next group, and proceed to the sinks and shave the fuzz from your face. Do not shave your head. Do not get used to this. The Navy cannot guarantee you such luxury in the future. When finished shaving, wait at ease in front of your rolled hammock for morning calisthenics."

The sun had not yet broken the eastern horizon when Dixon marched his irregular group to the dining hall for breakfast. After scraping and stacking trays, they marched to the parade ground for the raising of the United States of America Flag at 0800. From there the company marched to a long, wood-frame classroom building.

Inside, an unsmiling warrant officer walked to the front and addressed the company. Without preamble he launched into his speech, "Welcome to Great Lakes Naval Training Center. In the coming weeks you will drill in the customary Navy manner. You will undergo endurance and strength training you cannot now imagine."

He paused to let that vision sink in before continuing less threateningly. "You will have daily classroom study to accompany the physical training. You will learn the proud history of the United States Navy and the behaviors and mannerisms expected of a sailor. There will be shipboard instruction from which you will learn that 'port' is a direction, not a place to spend your money on overpriced booze and underpriced women. Marines will give you weapons instruction and practice. Navy firefighters will give instruction in managing ship fires."

He paused again to look them over. "You are well on the way to *looking* like sailors. Those of you who finish this course *will be* a U.S. Navy Sailor. I will be proud of you. Your mother will be proud of you. Most importantly, *you* will be proud of you."

Medical, dental, eye, and hearing exams took the remainder of the morning. Every recruit had undergone some type of physical exam near their hometown, but now a second general examination would search for something not noted, or perhaps purposefully overlooked, on the earlier examination.

Beginning with the dental station, Charles leaned back in the chair with his mouth wide while the technician poked and prodded his gums and teeth. "Good, you have perfect teeth. No requirement to be seen by the dentist."

Charles rotated next to the eye and hearing stations. "Beckner, Charles. Your hearing is excellent, and you are not color blind. You are very slightly nearsighted, correctable to 20/15. The Navy will supply you with primary and backup pairs of glasses."

"I prefer wire frames."

"It's the Navy. You can have anything you want," said the technician, as if he actually believed it.

At the medical station, twenty recruits at a time took positions around the periphery of a large, empty room. "Face me in the center!" A petty officer with a red cross on his shoulder insignia, followed by a Navy lieutenant with a caduceus on his collar, walked to the middle of the circled recruits. The lieutenant, a physician, let his petty officer run the show.

"I am a corpsman. Never, ever, call me a medic. Lieutenant Jones here is our doctor today and will proceed with his physical exam. Strip to your shorts, and place your clothes in a neat pile behind you. Now, all together, hop up and down on your right foot."

With a thunderous noise, the recruits hopped while the doctor turned to see each recruit jumping up and down. "Now, hop on the other foot. OK, stop hopping. Close your eyes and keep them shut."

When no one fell or lost their balance, the corpsman continued, "Keeping your eyes closed, touch your nose with your right index finger. Same thing with your left finger. Open your eyes, lift your left foot and stand only on your right foot."

One young man wobbled but did not fall. "OK. Do it again, this time standing on your left foot."

The same young man again wobbled and fell against the man to his left.

"Name?" the corpsman asked the unsteady recruit.

"Mason, sir."

The corpsman returned to giving group instructions. "Turn around, drop your shorts, bend over, and spread your cheeks so we can see your anus." The doctor pirouetted in the center of the room, examining each bared bottom from twenty feet away. Apparently satisfied that no one had disabling external hemorrhoids, he nodded at the corpsman to continue.

"Now stand up and turn around. The lieutenant is going to check each of you for hernia."

The doctor put a latex glove on his right hand, went to the first recruit, and pushed his index finger upward through the recruit's left scrotum, high enough to feel the inguinal canal. "Turn your head to the right, and cough." He moved his finger to the other side. "Now turn your head to the left, and cough again."

Without changing his glove, the physician moved down the line, repeating the procedure on each recruit. Charles started to blurt out, "You're not changing your glove!" but the words died in his throat as he coughed to the right and then to the left.

The physician next listened to each recruit's chest with his stethoscope for three heartbeats. He turned to the corpsman and whispered something before disappearing into his small adjacent office.

The corpsman ordered, "Mason, stay here to see the doctor. Everyone else, put your pants and shoes on, but carry your shirt. Vaccination is next."

ᔚ ᔚ ᔚ

Charles looked around, comparing himself to the other recruits. They were of all body types, but skin color was uniform. His eyes paused on two or three with olive or light brown skin, but there was no black skin.

I thought there were Negros serving in the Navy, but I sure don't see any around here. Do they train somewhere else?

Charles' concerns extended beyond body build and skin color. Most in his company had graduated from high school, and one or two probably had some college education. *I can handle whatever they demand as far as physical performance goes. But what if Dixon or some other officer prejudges me to be a dumb country hick? I might not have a high school diploma, but I'll have to prove to them that doesn't matter.*

ᔚ ᔚ ᔚ

In addition to suppressing individuality and forcing the recruits to bond with each other, it was critical each learned to accept orders from superiors without question. "Brainwashing" the impressionable young men might be too harsh a term, but it wasn't far from the truth, and it was reinforced by the rigid schedule: Lights on at 0400, calisthenics, chow hall, marching, physical exercises, classroom lectures, skills courses, and more marching.

All were required to pass a basic swimming test. Marines ran the rifle range. Considerable time was devoted to firefighting drills, culminating with the challenge of a major blaze belching acrid, black smoke in a simulated ship superstructure. Corpsmen gave first-aid instruction oriented to battle wounds. Introductory lectures and demonstrations informed the recruits of specialty skills available through additional training, including electronics, aviation, marine and engine maintenance, general machinists, communications, medical technologies, and many others. Opportunities abounded for the qualified and interested.

And they marched to the obstacle course, and they marched to meals, and, sometimes, they marched in loops for no reason beyond marching itself. With increasing frequency, they marched carrying heavy packs. Sports teams organized and competed with other companies in softball, football, and boxing.

Time, paper, and stamps accompanied orders to write letters home.

On Sunday mornings every recruit attended religious service. Following Protestant, Catholic, and Jewish services, recruits were free for afternoon visits with family, civilian buddies, or girlfriends.

Charles was among the many who never had a visitor.

At six weeks into training, every recruit received aptitude interviews and tests. These carried much weight when the Navy considered its needs versus a recruit's request.

A few days later, they all received a form on which they were to list their preference for additional, specialized training. The recruits had fifteen minutes to complete and return the forms.

Charles stared at the paper. *What kind of job training would be useful when I leave the Navy? With the Depression ending, more people will have cars, trucks and tractors. They'll need mechanics to keep them running. People are also going to buy more radios and appliances for their homes.* He listed "machinist" and "electronics" as his first two choices.

Instructed to leave no line blank, without much additional thought he recalled the doctor deferring to the corpsman during the group physical exam, and scribbled "medical" in the third line.

Four days later Charles received orders to report to the Hospital Corps School in San Diego, California, for training as "Hospital Assistant." *What the hell? This must be a mistake. I need to ask Chief Dixon what's going on.*

"Pardon me, sir, but Hospital Assistant was not my choice. I asked for machinist or electronics school. I just put 'medical' on the third line because I was told not leave any lines blank. I want to get this changed."

Dixon took the orders and studied them. Then he grinned at Charles, "Nope. Like it says, 'Beckner. Hospital School.'" His voice turned normal, almost sympathetic. "I'm tempted to tell you that the Navy must have thought you were too dumb to fix radios or engines, so they're going to let you change bedpans. I know better than that though. You're anything but dumb. Fact is, it takes a lot of smarts to be a Navy corpsman, and the Navy's needs have precedence over your wants. Instead of complaining, why don't you just make the most of it."

Charles reconsidered the orders.

It's not what I asked for, but it should be indoor work with regular hours.

And after all, no one drops bombs on a hospital. I'll get training and experience. In fact, after the Navy I could go back to school and become a doctor or dentist. Yes, I can do this.

Charles's orders allowed six days for travel. Plenty of time to get to San Diego, but not enough time for a detour to Princeton without using his personal leave time. *I only left home a few weeks ago. I think it's OK if I wait and go back for a longer visit after I finish Hospital School. I'll send Mary a postcard. She can let the others know where I'm going.*

I'm excited and ready for this adventure to begin. Fixing people should be at least as interesting as fixing radios or cars.

Charles, Basic Training, Great Lakes Naval Training Center, July-October 1939.

4

Coffee

Chicago

3 September 1939

In 1939, the Atchison, Topeka and Santa Fe Railway's *Super Chief* passenger train was the premier transportation for the privileged to travel from Chicago to Los Angeles. It included luxury Pullman sleeper cars and a formal dining car with silver, crystal, and fine china. The Navy *did not* authorize junior enlisted sailors a ticket on the *Super Chief.*

The Santa Fe's lightweight *El Capitan* train ran the same route as the *Chief.* It was pulled by the same E1 diesel-electric engine, and it took the same thirty-nine-and-a-half hours for the trip. Unlike the *Chief*, the *El Capitan* was for the masses. Instead of a formal dining car, it pulled a stand-up grill car. Rather than sleeping in luxury Pullman sleeper cars, passengers dozed sitting or leaning against the window on bench seats. The Navy *did* pay for junior enlisted sailors to ride the *El Capitan.*

Only a few sailors were scattered among the many passengers waiting on the platform for the train to Los Angeles. Charles recognized none of them, and decided he was content to embark on this next adventure in solitude. He noticed a small group of passengers engaged in serious, even somber, conversation. *They don't seem happy. Maybe they're traveling to a funeral.* At 6:30 p.m., the train doors opened. Porters stepped down from the rail cars, announcing, "All aboard!" Charles scooped up an abandoned newspaper from a bench and joined the line of boarding passengers.

He found an empty seat in a car with no other sailors—which was fine, as he hadn't found anyone waiting on the platform particularly interesting. *I wonder if it's them or me? Maybe I'm the one that's different. I seem to be a loner. I'm OK with that.* He put his duffel bag on the overhead luggage rack, dropped into the seat, and opened his gleaned newspaper. The single headline spread under the *Chicago Tribune* banner explained the somber attitude of the group on the platform.

WAR! BOMB WARSAW!
NAZI ARMY ORDER

Berlin, Sep. 1 (Friday) (AP) Adolf Hitler today ordered the German army to meet force with force. "The Polish state has rejected my efforts to establish neighborly relations and instead has appealed to weapons . . . a series of border violations . . . fight of honor. . . I expect every soldier . . . duty to the last . . . Long live our people and our Reich."

Further down the front page was a smaller headline:

1.5 MILLION GERMAN TROOPS WITH AIR SUPPORT
FLOOD ACROSS POLISH BORDER

And near the bottom of the front page:

FRANCE AND BRITAIN SAY INVASION UNPROVOKED
LIKELY TO DECLARE WAR AGAINST GERMANY

In March 1935 Adolf Hitler announced Germany would rearm, in violation of the Treaty of Versailles. In 1936, the Führer began assisting Franco's Nationalist forces in Spain, seeing an opportunity to test Germany's newest weapons. Other countries nervously watched Germany rise from the ashes of defeat in a surge of nationalism, led by their dynamic fascist leader. Germany actually invading its neighbor was earthshaking news to Americans, even though they should have expected it.

I guess Dad was right. We're probably going to find ourselves fighting the Germans again. The world has barely survived a great depression, and now we're having another war?

Charles watched through the window as the train pulled from the station.

When his car passed beyond the streetlights of the platform, he was startled to see a young man with a shadowed face and wearing a sailor's uniform outside the coach window. The sailor kept pace with the train and stared at Charles as the train gathered speed. *Did a sailor miss the train?* He had a moment of disorientation, before realizing there was no sailor outside the train, only himself, darkly mirrored in the train window.

The train wound out of Chicago, and vignettes of the city flashed by as rapidly as Charles's thoughts. *It took two years for the United States to join the Allies against Germany in the Great War. If we again join England and France in another war, when will it happen? Will we send a fleet to Europe? Will I even still be in the Navy?*

In the last purple light of evening, the great city disappeared into the darkness and into Charles's past.

In the overnight hours after leaving Chicago, Charles remained restless. Unable to sleep on the bench seat, he walked through partially darkened cars. Occasionally he met and acknowledged other insomniacs. At 0222 hours the train stopped in Kansas City long enough for Charles to briefly stretch his legs on the platform. Passengers would not be allowed to take another platform break until the train reached Barstow, California. Until then, stops would last only five minutes, enough time to change crews.

Returning to his car, Charles stood aside in the narrow passage between cars, allowing a porter carrying a stack of saucers and cups to pass. "You go ahead, sir," the black man said as he stepped back to let Charles go first, "I've got to get these to the grill car."

As the porter stepped aside, the train car rocked, and his stack of cups tilted towards the floor.

"I've got them!" Charles steadied and then took the stack of cups. "Just keep going—I'll follow you with these."

They reached the grill car and set the dishes down behind the bar. The porter turned to Charles with a wide smile. "Thank you, sir. If those cups had hit the floor, we'd have had some disappointed coffee drinkers all the way from here to California."

Charles angled the shoulder of his uniform to the porter, demonstrating the absence of rank or other insignia. "No need to call me 'sir.' Hell, I'm just barely out of basic training, and I call everyone else 'sir.'"

"In that case, you and me in the same boat," the porter flashed his large eyes and grinned. "If you want, you can call me Thomas. If not 'sir,' how might I address you?"

"Charles."

"Okay, Mister Charles. If you can stand right here for a few minutes, I'll give you a cup of the world's best coffee."

Grill service was not yet opened for passengers, so the two chatted. While Thomas prepared coffee in a chrome urn he explained to Charles that his father, two uncles, and two brothers also worked as train porters. "Of course, we can't ride as passengers in the coach cars with you white folk, but there's a rule—don't know if it's a written rule though—that all Santa Fe train porters have to be colored. In fact, one of my uncles helped form the Brotherhood of Sleeping Car Porters," Thomas puffed his chest and grinned. "Did you know that was the very first all-Negro union?"

"No, but in all honesty, I don't know a lot about unions," Charles realized he didn't know much about Negroes either, but did not say so.

"Well, in my family, we men grew up assuming we were going to join the union and become a railway porter soon as we reached the age. I have a young son. He's sharp, mind you. Between you and me, I hope he'll find some way to be a teacher, or maybe even a doctor. If not though, I'll be proud if he's a porter like me. Look here, I think this coffee's ready, and just in time."

Two men entered the car, and each bought a cup of coffee. They stood at the far end of the bar talking with each other.

"Here's coffee for you," Thomas said, placing a full cup and saucer on the counter.

Charles pulled change from his pocket, asking, "How much?"

Thomas gave a barely perceptible shake of head, "Thanks for the help, Mister Charles. Enjoy it." He then turned to serve a third man who had joined the first two.

Charles inspected his cup of coffee. This was not chow hall coffee. It was a deep mahogany color that could have been liquid chocolate. He held the cup in front of his nose. Indeed, there was a hint of chocolate, but also something floral and maybe something nutty. He tested its temperature. *Hot, but not too hot to sip.* He closed his eyes and timed a sip with the rocking of the train. There was a very slight bitter flavor, but so different from what he expected, smooth and almost sweet. *I've never had coffee like this.* A pleasant taste remained after he swallowed the sip.

He opened his eyes to find Thomas standing in front of him, eyebrow raised in question. "What you think about my coffee?"

"It's good! It's more than good. It's the best coffee I've ever had. What did you put in it?"

"Nothing but coffee. I use more than most, so it's strong. The other thing is Mr. Engel, he runs the Santa Fe Railroad company, he started buying nothing but those special Arabica coffee beans for all the trains last summer."

"Arabica," Charles repeated the word. "Like I said, it's wonderful."

Several times before they reached Los Angeles, Charles visited the grill car. Each time, with a wink, Thomas discretely handed him a cup without charge. It was their secret bond, and for Charles, the experience was an education. Thomas proved to "Mister Charles" that Negroes, like anyone else, could hold respected positions in a company. Second, a relationship based on respect and equality was possible, even normal, between a white man and a Negro. Finally, Charles learned that coffee could be more than a source of caffeine. While usually "hot, strong, and generous," open mess Navy coffee was little else. Coffee for the enlisted mess was brewed in large vats, using the cheapest Robusta coffee bean available under government contract. It had caffeine, but never that smooth sweet flavor Charles first experienced with Thomas's coffee.

I'll never again be content with a cup of bad, bitter coffee.

The dawn and Dodge City, Kansas, materialized together, shortly after 0600. The sun passed its zenith and lunch service in the grill car ended by the time they pulled out of Las Vegas, New Mexico at 1335. Night was upon them when the train changed crew and engines in Winslow, Arizona, at 2120.

At 0530 Pacific Standard Time the *El Capitan* stopped for twenty minutes in Barstow, California. Charles was groggy from lack of sleep and restless as a caged chicken. On the platform, he stretched and took a few deep breaths of fresh air. "Not much to see here," one of the passengers commented. "Be in Los Angeles in four hours though."

"True," Charles agreed. *I wonder what it will look like, that city famous for sunshine, movie stars, and fancy cars.*

5

The Librarian

Southern California

6 September 1939

Los Angeles overwhelmed Charles with its modern buildings and lush Southern California landscape. Under a cloudless blue sky, palm trees and colorful blooming foliage moved gently with the breeze. Opened only four months earlier, Union Station in Los Angeles was a statement of modern progressivism. Its lower main hall was covered by travertine marble. The upper wall surface was a new type of acoustical tile that absorbed sound and dampened echoes. It was intended to give an "elegant acoustical ambiance" to the station. Enclosed gardens graced both sides of the waiting area. Pulsing with prosperity and promise, it contrasted sharply to the farm towns of southern Indiana during the Depression.

Once settled onto the connecting train to San Diego, Charles watched seemingly endless groves of trees passing in geometrical array. Sitting opposite him was a thin, older man who was as tan as a Midwest farmer in August but dressed in a business suit.

Charles's curiosity overcame his usual reticence. "Are you from around here?"

"Yes. In fact, I'm on my way home after doing some business in LA. And you?"

"Indiana."

"That's a long way from here. I've been to Chicago, but never Indiana. Are you just passing through? Or are you assigned here?"

"I'll be in San Diego for a few weeks. After that, I don't know." Charles looked back out the window to the passing groves. "I've never been to California before. What kind of trees are those?"

"Orange." Then, realizing that this young sailor was genuinely interested, the man added, "Of course, there are different varieties of oranges. Those you're looking at now are navel oranges. They'll be ready to pick in a month or so. Later, we'll pass trees that are all green, fruit already picked. Those will be Valencia orange trees."

"Which ones are better?" Charles inquired.

"They're both good. If you want to make juice though, the Valencia is a pure orange juice machine," the gentleman smiled.

While the train wound its way toward San Diego they talked, with Charles mostly listening, about southern California agriculture, weather, and the economy. By the time they arrived in San Diego, Charles was convinced Southern California was the most wonderful place on earth. *This is where I want to live.*

San Diego's Santa Fe Depot was small compared to Los Angeles, but he was impressed by its classic Spanish Mission architecture. Across the street from the train station, Charles boarded the trolley to Balboa Park and the nearby Navy hospital.

Balboa Naval Hospital was no less stunning than any other building he had seen in Southern California. White-walled with red tile roofs, it sprawled across a hill. Manicured hospital grounds merged with the lush foliage of Balboa Park. So eager was he to begin this next adventure, only self-control kept Charles from shouldering his bag and running to the main building.

Following instructions and signs, Charles found the administrative offices for the Naval Hospital Corps School, on the campus of the Balboa Naval Hospital. After a short wait, a clerk showed him through to a rough-looking but smooth-talking warrant officer, the administrative chief of the school.

"Welcome aboard, Charles."

He didn't call me Maggot. So far, so good. "Thank you, sir. I'm eager to get started."

"Great. I know your orders have you reporting today, but someone fucked up. Your class doesn't officially start until October."

"Yes, sir." DI Patterson had been Charles's introduction to the fine art of swearing. He was gradually getting used to the incessant profanity littering everyone's speech in the military milieu. In fact, he found it contagious. "So, what do I do until then?"

"Report every morning to the enlisted chief's office. Until classes begin, he will assign you general duty as needed. Any questions?"

"Yes, sir. San Diego and the Hospital are beautiful. Have you been here long?"

"For a couple of years. I hope they'll keep me here a few more. My wife already told me that if the Navy gives me a new assignment, I might as well volunteer for sea duty. She's never going to leave San Diego."

"How did the Navy get to put the hospital up here on a hill, in a park? I expected it to be down by the docks and the Navy Yard."

"The story, as I heard it, is that the 4th Marine Field Hospital was first set up here to support the 1915 Panama-California Exposition in what is now Balboa Park. By the time the exposition closed the Great War was underway in Europe, so the Navy built a fifty-bed dispensary. They replaced it with a large, six-story hospital in 1922. The Navy Secretary at that time personally chose this site. It was known as 'Inspiration Point.' The Secretary wanted convalescent sailors to be able to sit on the lawn and look out past Point Loma to see the ships sailing in and out of San Diego Bay."

"Then I'm thankful for that Secretary."

"So are we all."

Charles reported for general duty on the morning of Friday, September 7, only to be granted an immediate weekend pass and an opportunity to explore his new home. In Balboa Park, only a five-minute walk from the hospital, the San Diego Zoo offered free admission to active duty military personnel. Minutes later, along with a half-dozen other visitors, Charles watched giraffes feeding from greenery in boxes fastened high on the enclosure's wall.

The staff worker who had just put up food for the giraffes exited the enclosure door and walked by the visitors. Charles fell in step with him, "Pardon me. Do you have time for questions?".

"Sure, if you can walk back to the service building with me. What do you want to know?"

"I guess first, how long has the zoo been here?"

"They had some animal displays at the 1914 exposition. I think that's where it started. It's had its ups and downs since then—and was pretty much bankrupt at one point. You want to hear a story about that?" he said with a wink.

Maintaining an air of conspiracy, Charles said in a lowered voice "Of course!"

"For the first ten or fifteen years, a lot of the animals here came from Navy ships. They brought the animals aboard as pets in foreign ports. By the time they dropped anchor here in San Diego Bay, the animals were grown and more difficult to manage. Rather than kill them, they gave them to the zoo. Bears were the favorite mascot, and the zoo soon had so many bears there was no place to put them. The manager found a way to kill two birds with one stone, so to speak." He looked at Charles with eyebrows raised above a big grin.

"OK," said Charles. "Go ahead and tell me the rest of the story."

"That manager sold some fancy hotels downtown on the idea of serving bear meat in their restaurants. It was put on the menu as an exotic food, and they charged several times more than for regular beef. The zoo made enough from selling bear meat to stay afloat until the park recovered financially. It's not a story we tell the kids these days, but at the time it seemed reasonable enough. I have to do some other feedings now, but if you come back another day, I can share more stories we don't generally tell the public."

"What does bear meat taste like?"

"Never tasted it myself, but someone who did said it was like beef steak, only a lot tougher."

ॐ ॐ ॐ

The enlisted ranks chief found no need to make up busy work for Charles. It was the Navy's mistake to send him to San Diego early. As long as Charles remained on base, he was otherwise free to wander around, shop at the base exchange, or explore the hospital. On the third day Charles discovered the hospital library, identified by a simple sign on the wall:

GENERAL LIBRARY

FOR PATIENTS AND STAFF

(MEDICAL STAFF LIBRARY IS ON THE 2ND FLOOR
OF THE MAIN BUILDING.)

Peeking through the glass window of the library door, he could see shelf after shelf of books with multicolored covers. *I don't have a high school diploma, but I'm smart. I just need some knowledge to go with that smart.*

He walked in.

It was large, bigger than the public library back in Princeton, consisting of two rooms, with a small separate office for the full-time librarian. Two girls of high school age wearing volunteer name tags sorted and returned books to the shelves. Both avoided direct eye contact with Charles, perhaps sternly warned by mothers against engaging with sailors.

He wandered through the shelves, pulling out books with interesting titles or covers. Well-worn adventure novels, mostly westerns and detective crime stories, dominated the fiction section. The dime novels helped convalescing sailors pass time, but Charles looked for something more. He passed through the stacks to an alcove ringed with periodicals. The newspaper and magazine display encircled two desks and several chairs. He pulled two newspapers from their rack and claimed a desk and chair. When he finished those, he perused the rest of the newspapers. Finishing those, he flipped through some magazines until the library closed.

Charles returned to the library the next day and the next, and every day for the next two weeks.

He began each visit with the newspapers. Headlines and stories described the war in which Britain and France were now fully engaged against Germany. Quickly overwhelmed, Poland officially surrendered to Germany on 27 September. Russia's Joseph Stalin signed a pact with Adolf Hitler, allowing them to share the conquered land. In mid-October German troops paused to consolidate their occupation. French troops settled in at the Maginot Line, the concrete fortifications, tunnels, and trenches recently constructed to deter invasion by Germany. The British arrived and quickly built complex trenches to close the gap between the Maginot Line and the English Channel.

As in the first years of the Great War, sentiment in the United States tilted heavily towards neutrality. Most Americans were not mentally prepared to engage in another war. "Let Europe sort out their own problems this time."

"What's happening?" the librarian casually asked Charles one afternoon. When she came to his desk, Charles stood to be polite. Feeling awkward towering over the short librarian, he quickly sat back down. It was the first time she had spoken to him. She was older than him, perhaps mid-twenties, but not so old that he would mind the company of this good-looking woman—were she not wearing a wedding ring. "The *men* in Washington keep talking about Europe. Are those *men* going to put us into that mess in Europe?" she asked, her intonations suggesting women might make better decisions.

"I can't answer that question myself," Charles replied. "Most of the editorials say it's Europe's problem to sort out, and we should stay neutral. There's the occasional editorial or letter saying that if we don't help the British right now, we'll end up fighting the Germans over here, and by then there'll be no Britain or France left to help us."

The librarian only shook her head before returning to her office.

In the editorials Charles repeatedly came across unfamiliar words like *recalcitrant, imbued*, and *vexatious*. He also had difficulty forming a clear geographic picture of places described in the reports. *What's the difference between Baltic and Balkan? What countries besides Germany share borders with Poland? Where is the Maginot Line?*

After tiring of the back and forth to the reference book section, he finally started each session at the library by pulling the *Collier's World Atlas and Gazetteer* and the massive *Webster's Twentieth Century Dictionary* from the reference stacks and lugging them to his usual desk. Both books were heavy and unwieldy, but it was worth his effort for the definitions of greater depth and the more detailed maps. With the references ready, he retrieved the first of the newspapers. When reading of battles in Europe or Japanese invasions in China, Charles referred to the *Colliers*. Likewise, if he came across a strange word, or a familiar word in unexpected grammatical context, he checked *Webster's*. Occasionally he went to the long shelf holding the *Encyclopedia Britannica* and, below it, the *World Book Encyclopedia* to explore specific subjects.

Each day before leaving Charles religiously re-shelved each reference book.

Late one afternoon, shortly before closing time, the librarian came once more to stand by his desk. As always, she was well dressed, this day in a colorful print mid-length dress with short puff sleeves. Fashionable glasses complimented brown eyes. Her oval face was graced by brunette hair, done in the current fashion of medium length with soft curls just at her ears.

She sat down in the adjacent chair. Charles had not spoken to her since that first short interchange about the editorials, but it was obvious she was ready for a longer conversation. She moved some loose strands of hair to behind her ear and flashed a pleasant smile at the tall sailor with dark hair and handsome, if still boyish, features. She waited for his attention before speaking.

"Hello, Seaman," she looked at the slash on his cuff signifying the rank of Seaman Apprentice. "I'm Susan. I see you pulling reference books every day and taking them to the newspaper desk. If you have a special project for some technical school or class, maybe I can help you find some sources."

What I want to tell her is that I feel this need to be able to discuss current world events, with a vocabulary as big as any college graduate would use, and thus armed, converse with my senior NCOs and officers from a position of intellectual, if not social, equality. I'm even hoping to lose my mid-west country accent. Dad lectured us on the importance of giving a good first impression. I'm going to look sharp, and I'll keep that impression going after I open my mouth.

"No, ma'am. I'm just spending time here waiting for my school to start next week. I read the papers and use the atlas to find where things are happening. That's mostly in Europe, but things are going on in Asia too."

"And checking to make sure the reporters are using the right words?" Susan ran her finger down the dictionary with a raised eyebrow, as if looking for a specific entry. Her manner was honest and friendly. "Yes," she observed. "Words and places. Both important to understanding this world."

Charles again took note of the wedding band on her ring finger, sensed she was only trying to be helpful, and lowered his guard. "Well, truth is, I'm not sure of all the words, and some of them have multiple meanings. Really though, I'm just killing time until my Hospital Corps class starts in a couple of weeks."

"Killing time?" Susan asked, with a mock quizzical grin. "Not the usual way for most sailors passing through this port to spend their spare hours. It's good to know there are still young men who appreciate libraries. Anything you need, you come and ask me." She patted his arm.

"Thank you, ma'am. I was a little concerned when you came over. I thought you might be angry at me for taking over the reference books when I read the papers. So, it's OK if I keep using them? I always return them to the shelf."

"Of course! I mainly wanted to come over and meet the sailor who 'kills time' reading newspapers and checking dictionaries."

Two days later Charles was at his usual desk when he looked up to see Susan standing in front of him.

"How's the world today?" she asked.

Charles stood. With the desk between them, he didn't have to look almost straight down at Susan. "No better. From the newspaper stories, Europe is spiraling downward. Hitler's army is perfectly synchronized with his ambition to control all of Europe. The news is only slightly better on the other side of the world. Either Nationalists or Communists hold the rural parts of Manchuria, blocking Japanese troops from moving into the interior. The Japanese still control the coastal cities though, and they keep expanding their occupation southward."

"Depressing. Could you check with me before you leave the library?"

"Sure. I'll probably be here until you close."

"Perfect," Susan said and returned to her small office.

At closing time, Charles returned the reference books to their shelves, went to Susan's open office door, and knocked softly. When she looked up, he said, "You told me to check with you?"

"Come with me," she instructed.

He followed Susan through the empty library to a small room near the back door. *She's smiling. What's happening here?*

Shelves, partially filled with books, lined the walls. Susan began searching the rows, occasionally extracting a book and passing it to Charles to hold.

She has nothing illicit in mind. I'm relieved—and disappointed.

"We periodically need to make room for new books," she said, as the pile in his arms grew taller. "This room holds the discards. Some have been damaged and are falling apart. Others are considered out of date, or simply aren't being used anymore."

Charles let his fingers glide over the books in his hand. "These are all in pretty good shape."

"Since we talked the other day, I decided some of these so-called discards could be checked out long term. By that, I mean you shouldn't worry about ever returning them. I chose those books you're holding because of the content, but also because they're compact and easy to carry in a pocket or sea bag."

She paused to be certain he understood. "I'm giving them to you, as long as I know you'll either keep them or pass them on. Just promise me you won't throw them in a trash can."

"No, ma'am! No trash cans."

"These I know you will use." She withdrew two books from his stack.

Charles looked at the covers. The first was *New Popular Pocket Webster Dictionary (Self-Pronouncing)*. The second was a *Rand McNally Pocket World Atlas*.

Susan explained, "I know they're not as complete as *Colliers* and *Webster's*, but both are small enough that you can always carry them, no matter where the Navy sends you."

"Thank you!" Charles ran his fingers across the titles.

She indicated the remaining four books. "These I think you'll enjoy reading—they're also yours to keep, but if you want to read them and then pass them on to a friend, that's fine with me."

Charles read out loud each cover. "*As I Lay Dying* by Faulkner, *Brave New World* by Huxley, *All Quiet on the Western Front* by Remarque, *A Farewell to Arms* by Hemingway."

Susan then handed him one last book. "This one, *Meditations* by Marcus

Aurelius, is a little different. It's not really a story like the others."

"Marcus Aurelius? Wasn't he a Roman Emperor?" Charles asked.

"Yes, that's right. He was having troubles in his empire around the middle of the second century. As he traveled with his army, he regularly recorded his thoughts. This journal became a discourse of his philosophy. To be honest, I've only read an entry here and there, but an admiral who used to come to this library told me it was the best book ever written by a military man. That admiral said he carries it on every posting, reading some of the entries over and over."

"You have more than a high school degree, don't you?" Charles blurted.

Susan looked down, unsuccessfully hiding a blush. "It's nice of you to notice. I do have a degree in history from San Diego State. I was accepted to graduate school in Los Angeles, but then along came this gorgeous man and, well, the masters in history fell through the cracks. I taught high school history until this position came available. I like the library. It suits me better than teaching."

Now past closing time, Susan walked Charles through the library to the door, turning out the lights as they went.

At the door, she turned and abruptly hugged him. "You're a few years younger, but you remind me so much of my brother. I worry about him, and I say a prayer for him every night. He ferries supply ships across the Atlantic with the Merchant Marine."

She looked at Charles directly. "I hope you keep coming here as long as you can."

That evening in the barracks, Charles stowed the gift of books, holding back the dictionary. *There are so many words here I don't know. Will I ever learn them all, the way I'm doing it now, looking up one by one as I come across them in the papers or magazines? Can anyone learn them all?*

He stared at the dictionary for a moment, then opened it to the first page:

Aardvark
> ˈärdˌvärk
>
> *plural noun: aardvarks A nocturnal burrowing mammal with long ears, a tubular snout, and a long extendable tongue, feeding on ants and termites.*
>
> *Origin: late 18th century: from South African Dutch, from aarde 'earth' + vark 'pig.'*

A tiny drawing of an aardvark accompanied the definition. *That's helpful.*

He skipped a few pages and found a word he had been thinking about since the train ride from Chicago:

Arabica
arab·i·ca
\ə- ˈra-bə-kə\
An evergreen shrub or tree (Coffea arabica) growing above 2,000 feet elevation and yielding seeds that produce a high-quality coffee.

Propping his pillow against the wall, Charles sat across his bunk and got comfortable. *This could be interesting.*

Charles and friend, Naval Hospital Corps School, San Diego
October 1939-January 1940.

41

6

The Student

Naval Hospital Corps School, San Diego, California

16 October 1939

"Good morning!"

The administrative chief of the Naval Hospital Corps School in San Diego, California, strode to the front of the classroom. He had gained a pound or two over the years, and his balding crown was trimmed by white sidewalls. Contrasting with his mundane features, his impeccable uniform displayed an impressive array of ribbons.

He stood straight, giving his introductory speech without benefit of notes. "Medical care of the ill and wounded of our military forces is a heavy responsibility. You will find the material in this course challenging. However, each of you is here because the Navy believes you possess the ability to successfully master that material. It is important to the Navy that you complete the program, because without your able assistance the doctors and the nurses of the US Navy cannot provide the best medical care possible to our members. Also, without Navy Corpsmen US Marines will have no medical care in the heat of battle. Our country will find itself at war again, and yes, I said 'will,' not 'might,' and it will be you, on the front lines of battle, saving the lives of your fellow sailors and soldiers. To that end I expect from you, and you must give in return, your very best efforts."

He paused for emphasis before resuming, "At Basic, you learned to salute, march, shoot, tell starboard from port, and follow orders. This will be different.

Starting today, you are joining a 160-year-old tradition. The Continental Congress in 1775 provided for Surgeon's Mates to care for Navy crews and any Marines in their ship's complement. These surgeons' mates fed, washed, and shaved the sick and the wounded, disposed of amputated limbs, prepared hot tar and irons for cauterizing stumps, and spread sand on the decks to keep men from slipping in the blood. The details have changed, but our goal of saving lives is the same. You will work in hospitals and clinics. Some of you will be assigned independent duty at small bases, on ships or boats, or with Marines in frontline combat. What you learn here will determine how many lives you save—or lose. If we join the conflagration in Europe, you will be glad you worked hard during these coming months."

Two sailors passed out books to the students as the introduction speech continued. "What we are giving you is the *Handbook of the Hospital Corps United States Navy*. This is the brand-new 1939 edition, freshly minted by the Government Printing Office. There are a thousand pages consisting of twelve chapters covering everything from anatomy to X-ray, submarine duty to shore patrol, and pharmacy to venereal disease. You will know it all, cover to cover. Read it. Protect it."

Charles flipped through the pages. Sure enough, there were 1,015 pages of depressingly small type and scattered illustrations and tables. It sported a quality binding and looked more like a reference text than a "handbook." *My leisurely afternoons in the library are over.*

Classroom training for the Hospital Assistant course consisted of six weeks of intensive lectures, demonstrations, and observation trips through Balboa Naval Hospital. The volume of material mandated an intense pace of learning. Every evening and weekend found the students, individually and in small groups, studying and reviewing anatomy, physiology, illness, injury and medical therapy.

Four weeks into the intensive course, all were rewarded with a weekend pass and encouragement to take a break from studying, perhaps spending time with family or friends. Only a couple of sailors' homes were close enough for them to visit. Other students made plans to explore the inexpensive and guilt-free entertainment of Balboa Park or one of the several sandy beaches reachable by local buses.

A few hoped for more excitement. A long existing attraction, the old

Chinatown, the Stingaree district, with its streets of saloons and brothels, thrived by separating young sailors from their meager wages. Visiting there was officially discouraged, but the Navy had not declared it to be strictly off limits.

"Charles," Joe, a classmate, asked, "You have plans for the weekend?"

"I need to study the section on parasites. The life-cycle of malaria is fascinating."

"For you maybe. I've got a better offer. A group is going downtown tonight. We have it on good authority that the bars there are lax about enforcing California's drinking age of twenty-one, especially for anyone with a little cash in hand."

"I suspect you want to get something more than cash in your hand," Charles suggested.

"I do hear there are a lot of ladies down there."

"So you hear."

"So I hear, and I plan to find out firsthand."

"Be careful," Charles said.

"No problem!" Joe pulled three condoms from his pocket. "I'm ready."

"That's ambitious, but not what I meant," Charles shook his head. "You know you're going to lose all your money, one way or the other. What should concern you more is knowing a sailor or two gets mugged down there every weekend. The local police couldn't care less about sailors, and the shore patrol only shows up after it's all over to throw the survivors in the brig."

Joe persisted, "Sure you won't come with us? You're going to get tired of the books, get lonely, and change your mind. It'll be too late by then."

"No, thanks," Charles smiled, shook his head, and waved Joe on his way.

On Sunday morning of the free weekend Charles sat at a table in the mess hall. He'd finished breakfast and was contemplating, with disgust, the bitter grounds swirling at the bottom of his coffee cup. Martin Feldman, a fellow student, sat next to him. Martin was on the thin side and, at five feet, eight inches, he wasn't the shortest man in the class though he looked small next to six-foot-plus Charles. Even though Martin was anything but physically imposing, Charles knew him to be smart and studious. It was usually Martin who had the correct answer when no one else in class raised a hand.

"What are you thinking, Charles? Beer? Broads? But knowing you, it's probably some museum or an exhibit at the zoo."

"Nope. None of those."

"Please don't tell me you're going to the library again. It's a gorgeous day."

"Well, Marty, I was told that the best view in San Diego is from a lighthouse over on Point Loma. Thought I might go and check it out."

"Sounds good, but Point Loma is too far to walk. I've never seen you willing to part with your money for a taxi to town, much less all the way around the Bay."

"True, but I think I found a better way." Charles held up a sheet of paper with a map and timetable. "There's a military shuttle bus. It circles from here to the naval base, then to the ferry landing from North Island, and finally around the bay, all the way to Fort Rosecrans. It looks like only a short walk from Rosecrans up to Point Loma and the lighthouse. I'll have plenty of time to look around and still make the last shuttle back."

"If you don't mind the company, I'll tag along," Martin announced.

Charles didn't mind.

The usual San Diego morning haze lifted during the bus ride, leaving a beautiful, clear blue sky. After nearly a decade as a mothballed installation in caretaker status, Fort Rosecrans was coming back to life. The big coastal guns had been test-fired. Emplacements were under construction for a new battery of 16-inch guns. While America might be neutral in the European conflict, her shores would not be undefended.

From the fort, Charles and Martin followed a small road leading up the hill to the peak of Point Loma and the lighthouse. Departing the road for a small path on the ocean side of the summit, they marveled at the broad expanse of the Pacific Ocean merging with distant clouds on the western horizon. Cries rose from seagulls swooping along the coast below them as they climbed the hill.

"Feldman," Charles mused. "Can't say I've ever met another Feldman."

"Not surprised, Charles. There probably weren't many living where you grew up. It's a pretty common name where I come from though."

"And where's that?"

"Boston. Lots of Feldmans and other Jews there."

"You're Jewish?"

Martin laughed. "You didn't know? Of course I'm a Jew!"

"That explains why I never see you at Sunday church service." Charles wasn't aware of ever having met, much less talked to, a Jew. He had no expectations of how a Jew would look but assumed they would be somehow "different." His visualization of a Jew came from the pictures in Sunday school books. *I wonder*

15

if there were Jews in the Idaho CCC camp, and I just didn't know it.

"What are you doing in the Navy, Martin?"

"Honestly, Charles, I'm tired of answering that question."

"I'm just curious. I thought Jews were all bankers or doctors. I assume you didn't need the few dollars they pay us. Why *did* you enlist?"

"First of all, you're stereotyping me and my family, and I thought you were too smart for that." He paused for a moment, then decided to continue. "I had my reasons. My parents came from Germany, and a lot of our relatives are still there. Most of them would come to America, but now they can't leave Germany. I know you read the papers, so you must know what's going on over there. It's been slowly getting worse for a decade, but then everything completely fell apart for us. You've heard of *Kristallnacht*?"

"The night they burned the synagogues and looted the Jewish businesses last year?"

"Yes. Starting that night, anti-Semitism spread through Germany and Austria like the Spanish flu. If we don't jump in and help the British soon, there'll be no safe place for Jews anywhere in Europe. In fact, there might not be any European Jews left alive. We need to do something now."

"So, all the Jews are enlisting?"

"Hardly. I'm an exception, but there will be more after me."

"Why do this to the Jews? What does it gain Hitler?"

"Scapegoat."

"Scapegoat?" Charles asked.

"You don't really know anything about anti-Semitism, do you? That's why I wanted to come with you today. You're just about the only one in our class who hasn't told a Kike joke at some point during the last four weeks."

"I haven't told any jokes at all."

"True—but you also didn't laugh at the ones the others told."

"Probably because I didn't get them. What's a Kike anyway?"

Martin laughed so hard his eyes watered. He took Charles by his shoulders and shook him. "You're so ignorant, Charles, but I love you! By the way, my actual name was Menachem Feldman, but I signed up as Martin, and I've gotten used to it."

He looked up the hill and pointed. "We're here. That's the Point Loma Lighthouse."

ﹳﹳ ﹳﹳ ﹳﹳ

The promontory at the entrance to San Diego Bay revealed from its heights one of the most magnificent panoramas in the entire world. A serene, curving bay fronted the city and its seafront. The growing tuna fleet bobbed at the cannery dock. Piers and dry docks of the Navy Yard extended to the white beaches and resorts of the south bay.

Across the entrance channel from Point Loma, North Island provided the Navy with deep-water docks and a sizeable airfield. On the south end of the island stood the famous Hotel Del Coronado with its stately red, turreted towers. Mountains of the southern Pacific Range backdropped the rising terraces of San Diego city, giving the final touch to a perfect postcard picture.

Looking from the heights of Point Loma Charles was mesmerized by this beauty and splendor. *I read all about this place in the library. It's really where the West begins, not in St Louis. Here's where Juan Cabrillo first walked in 1542. It's where Sebastian Vizcaino built his small wood chapel in 1602. This is where the Yankee ships sailing from Boston and New York saw the first American flag welcoming them to California.*

Charles quietly announced to Martin, "I love this place."

"Yes. It's been a good couple of months."

"No, I mean I want to live right here for the rest of my life."

A short distance past the lighthouse, Charles and Martin joined a gathering of people, some in uniform, watching large airplanes climb up from the harbor. Martin walked to one of the officers, saluted, and asked "Pardon me, sir. Do you know what kind of airplanes those are?"

The surprised Lieutenant returned an abbreviated salute. "That's a squadron of PBYs heading to Hawaii. We don't usually get to see all those planes up in formation at once. That's why there's a camera crew over there filming the takeoff."

"They can fly to Hawaii without stopping?"

"Nowhere to stop. Twenty-five hundred miles is a routine flight for these planes, but I guess it's still newsworthy."

Charles watched a plane take off, not from the North Island runway, but from the waters of the bay itself. The plane's appearance was strange, if not awkward. It looked as if someone had mounted a large wing with two engines on top of a boat. It was a long takeoff.

As its speed increased, the plane rose partially from the water, hydroplaning across the bay and gaining speed for another two hundred yards. It finally lifted from the water to join its mates circling over the bay.

"That's the strangest airplane I've ever seen," Martin commented to the officer.

"It's a seaplane, a PBY. They rolled it down a ramp from their base on North Island and detached the wheels once it was in the water."

"You called it a PBY?" Charles asked.

"It's actually a PBY-4. The PB stands for 'Patrol Bomber,' and the 'Y' means the Consolidated Aircraft Corporation built it."

"'Y'? Why not 'C'?"

"Curtiss-Wright Corporation already had the 'C' designation. They're technically bombers, but because they can fly almost forever, they spend most of their time on long-distance patrolling and air-sea rescue."

"And the '4'?" Charles asked.

"The '4' indicates it's the fourth version of the airplane to be manufactured. In fact, it was built right over there." The officer pointed to some buildings along the bay to the north of the city docks. "There's scuttlebutt that Consolidated has a new Navy contract for dozens more."

Charles and Martin watched the airplanes form up over the ocean west of Point Loma before disappearing across the Pacific into the late afternoon sun.

"Nice part of the world," Martin said, "but if we don't start back soon, we'll miss the last shuttle back to Balboa."

At the top of the hill they paused once more by the old lighthouse for a last, long view of San Diego Bay.

Charles nodded to himself. *Yes. This is how I might imagine Heaven.*

７

The Hospital

Hospital Corps School, San Diego, California

November 1939

The chief of the school and an assistant stood at the front of the classroom at the end of their final exam. "You have completed two months of classroom education, and will now proceed to the clinical phase of your education. These orders assign you to one of five Navy hospitals for that training." With anxiety, excitement, or both, the students ripped open the envelopes bearing their name.

Martin beamed, "Philadelphia Naval Hospital. Not a bad assignment—I have relatives in Philly. And you, Charles? Where are you going?"

"Mare Island Naval Hospital."

"That's on San Francisco Bay, Charles. You have to be happy with that."

"It's not San Diego, but it's West Coast. Wouldn't do any good for me to complain, anyway."

Charles extended his hand, "Marty, thanks for your friendship. It meant a lot to me these few weeks."

Martin gripped Charles's hand firmly and pulled him close in a prolonged hug.

Before letting go, he whispered to Charles, "Shalom, my friend."

Reviewing his orders closely that evening, Charles had another surprise. He would not travel to San Francisco by train or bus, but on Navy ships.

Navy stores ships routinely sailed the length of the western United States coast. These armed ships displacing 4,000 tons or more performed unglamorous yet logistically vital duty, moving men and materiel between Naval bases scattered from San Diego to Alaska. Charles had TAD, or Temporary Additional Duty, orders to the USS *Rigel* from San Diego to Long Beach Naval Base. From there, he would transfer to the USS *Vega* and continue to Mare Island.

The trip on the *Rigel* to Long Beach was a pleasant excursion. Leaving San Diego on 13 December, the sky was clear and the sun warm. Charles spent almost the entire day topside, watching the California coastal towns and military camps pass by. *Not a bad way to spend my 19th birthday.*

The next journey, on the *Vega,* was less pleasant. A light rain appeared from the horizon the first evening, and it followed them for the next two days. He shared a comfortable but crowded enlisted bunkroom with two other sailors. The small room was illuminated from a single porthole during the day and from a single dim light fixture at night.

This room is too small. I feel trapped in here.

Looking for any opportunity to leave the bunkroom's confinement, he asked for and received permission to enter the bridge. Two hours later the helmsman, tiring of his incessant questions, told Charles it was time for him to go below.

After the watch changed, Charles managed another two hours on the darkened bridge before again being gently kicked out.

ᔑ ᔑ ᔑ

The *Vega* reached Mare Island on Sunday evening, Christmas Eve, 24 December 1939. As the ship steamed into San Francisco Bay, misty clouds brushed across the towers and cables of the Golden Gate Bridge. The *Vega's* topmast was dragging through low clouds by the time they passed Point San Pablo. They barely reached the Mare Island dock before a dense fog enveloped the *Vega,* the base, and, seemingly, the entire world. Navy Yard operations had shut down for the holidays. The only sound other than slapping water against the boat hull was the dampened voice of an invisible sailor securing the *Vega* for the night.

Charles hefted his heavy sea bag over one shoulder. Other than the clothes he wore and what he carried in his pockets, all his worldly possessions were in that bag. After receiving permission from the officer of the watch to disembark, he asked a local crewman at the foot of the gangway, "I'm assigned to the hospital, but I can't see a damned thing. Can you point me in the right direction? All I need is a bunk for the night."

"There should be someone on duty at the billeting office, even on Christmas Eve. It's not far. Start over there at the sign with arrows to the hospital." The sailor pointed to an abstract location in the fog. "Eventually the signs will also have arrows for the billeting office."

Leaning against the weight of his bag, Charles made his way from the glow under one lamppost to the next. *Those "pea soup" fogs of London couldn't have been much worse than this.*

He followed direction signs with arrows and eventually found the Base Housing Office. Thankfully, a light glowed through the window and the door was unlocked. Behind the receiving counter sat a heavyset petty officer 2nd class with his back to Charles. He read a paperback that was apparently quite engaging as he made no acknowledgement of Charles's arrival. After a few seconds with no response from him, Charles loudly dropped his sea bag onto the floor.

The clerk slowly turned and inquired indifferently, "Yes?"

"I'm reporting to the hospital for duty. Need a bunk." Charles handed him a copy of his orders.

"Well, a damned merry Christmas to us both," the billeting clerk said with undisguised sarcasm while inspecting the papers. "Where from? Couldn't they give you Christmas at home?"

"Just arrived by ship, from San Diego. Indiana's too far to visit with the travel time they gave me."

"Well, there's worse places to spend Christmas than here. Maybe."

He typed a short form with Charles's name and a room number. Handing the carbon copy to Charles, he said, "Building Number 3. It's right behind the main hospital building. Go back out, go left about 200 yards, and you'll come to the main hospital. Can't miss it, even in this crap. It's got four bunks, but only one roommate now, and I think he's gone this week."

"Where's a place to get something to eat?" Charles inquired. "I've had nothing since breakfast."

"You're kidding me? On Christmas Eve? Everything's closed. The big Christmas meal for most of the base was earlier today. I don't think you'll find anything until early mess."

"But it's a hospital—don't they have to feed the patients and staff?"

"Not 'til breakfast."

The housing clerk rotated his chair back to the light and returned to his paperback. Charles said, "Thank you," but received no response. He had a sarcastic impulse to salute but just turned and left to find his bunk for the night. *Too bad Mary's not here. She'd have returned that petty officer's sarcasm twofold over. It's never boring when she's around.*

The silent barracks room with its unadorned walls was depressing. He chose one of the free bunks, unpacked his bag, brushed his teeth, and crawled into the bed in his new home. It was not the first time he had gone to bed hungry, but it was the first time he had tried to go to sleep feeling this lonely. *I wonder if it's snowing in Princeton. Doesn't really seem like Christmas with this insipid, foggy weather.*

For the first time, I really miss my family.

Early on Christmas morning Charles dressed and went in search of the hospital mess. A large Christmas tree dominated one corner of the hall. Miniature green wreaths graced the tables. The center of each wreath cradled a shiny Christmas tree ball. Diffused morning sunlight broke through the dissipating fog. Sunlight, a good meal, and the festive décor vanquished Charles's down mood of the previous night. *I should probably report for duty. Even on Christmas Day, there must be a duty officer available somewhere.*

He tried the hospital administrative offices, finding them dark and locked. Eventually he located the AOD, the Administrative Officer of the Day, on the medical ward. The doctor, a lieutenant commander, leaned on the nurses' station counter chatting to a nurse. Both looked up when Charles arrived.

"Sir, I'm Hospital Assistant Beckner. I arrived last night, and I'm reporting for duty."

The AOD grimaced, not sure what to do. "I'm a surgeon. I'm not very good at this administrative stuff. What the hell, though, it's Christmas Day. Why don't you come back tomorrow when offices are open? If anyone asks, tell them you checked in with me. Merry Christmas." He returned his attentions to the nurse, effectively dismissing the young sailor.

Mare Island, actually a small peninsula, sat at the edge of northern San Francisco Bay across the Napa River from the city of Vallejo. Initially serving as a small US Navy shipyard in 1852, it soon grew into a sprawling complex of dry docks, shops, and warehouses. Over the years numerous US Navy

Mare Island Naval Hospital, California. Clinical training January-October 1940.

vessels were built or refitted at its facilities. The original 1864 hospital was replaced with a large brick masonry structure, only to have its walls shattered like a broken mirror by the 1898 earthquake. The replacement, constructed of wood, survived every subsequent tremor, including the great San Francisco earthquake of 1906.

Charles walked a hundred yards from the building, then turned back to view his new assignment. It was indeed a grand, historic structure, announcing to those who passed by that only the finest Navy medical care was administered within. His chest expanded a bit with pride, knowing he would become part of that heritage.

Then his chest tightened as he realized he was passing beyond books and theory. *I am going to have hands-on responsibility for caring for sick and injured men. This is where my real journey begins.*

Walking about the Navy complex, Charles located the Base Library, the Base Exchange (BX), the barber shop, and a movie theater—all closed on Christmas Day. At noon, gathering clouds began spitting rain. Winters in Northern California might not be severe, but they were cold and wet.

At the only open shop, a small base canteen, he bought a hot dog, smothering it with onions, pickles, and mustard. Stretching out his long frame at a bench he ate while watching rivulets of rainwater run down the windowpanes. Despite the gloomy weather, the loneliness of the prior night was gone. *It's neither freezing nor sweltering. My stomach is full, paychecks are arriving like clockwork, and I don't have to milk a single cow. Now that I stop to think about it, I'm in a Garden of Eden.*

The steady rainfall showed no evidence of slackening, so Charles pulled *Meditations* from his pocket.

Susan was exceedingly kind to give me these books. I thanked her at the time, but probably not properly enough. When I get back to San Diego, I'll make a point to do that, if she's still working there.

He opened the book. "If you are distressed by anything external, the pain is not due to the thing itself, but to your estimate of it, and this you have the power to revoke at any moment." *Hmm, this is no dime novel. There's no storyline.*

Charles turned to the introduction of the book. "*Meditations* is a canon of stoic philosophy, extending the thought of the philosopher Seneca. Its author, Marcus Aurelius, wore the robes of a Greek philosopher and slept on the floor at age eleven. Thirty years later, as Emperor of Rome, he recorded his philosophical reflections on living as a series of journal entries."

He flipped back and read another entry at random. "Do not act as if you were going to live ten thousand years. Death hangs over you. While you live, while it is in your power, be good."

Charles marked the page and closed the book.

That's more or less what the lady outside Union Station in Indianapolis told me to do.

ʕ•ᴥ•ʔ ʕ•ᴥ•ʔ ʕ•ᴥ•ʔ

Tuesday morning, the day after Christmas, Charles dressed for duty and arrived at the hospital at 0630. He was waiting at the door when Senior Chief Petty Officer, CPO, Fahey arrived at his office in the administrative wing at 0700.

"Beckner? Sounds German. I see from your records you're a Hoosier. Welcome to Mare Island. Was it a good trip from San Diego?"

"Yes, sir. No problems other than the rain and fog." *He's friendly! Nice change—I was worried everyone here would be like that housing officer last night.*

"Your purpose here is to extend your classroom training while working as a Hospital Assistant. We have you starting on the medical ward for the first month. After getting your feet on the ground there, we'll move you around until you've had experience on surgery, post-op, emergency, and the other hospital sections."

"Sounds good," Charles responded, then added, "—and challenging, sir."

"You'll start on day shifts and eventually rotate on evening and night shifts as needed. You won't have to take any written tests, but I'll get informal feedback from the doctors and nurses. I'll use that and my own observations to write performance reports for your official record. Keep your nose clean, and I'll stand by you. Otherwise—well, let's just assume there won't be an otherwise."

ᔕᕈ ᔕᕈ ᔕᕈ

The weeks passed quickly. His primary instruction came from the ward nurses and senior corpsmen. Some were wonderful teachers. Others, less so. Still, on each rotation he gained new skills and knowledge. At every opportunity, he re-read applicable sections of his *Handbook of the Hospital Corps*.

Most of the patients were young, healthy men. In addition to injuries, the hospital also received a steady stream of officers and sailors with acute appendicitis, bad tonsils, or hernias. Pneumonia and other major infections were less frequent, but often more consequential causes for hospitalization.

Charles found some of the problems he encountered were addressed nowhere in the handbook. Responding to a lonely, homesick young sailor asking to go home, or consoling another who, over and over, read the wrinkled "Dear John" letter in his hand were challenges not addressed at the corps school. His training and background were woefully short on psychiatric care and counseling. He once asked a senior NCO for advice, but the answer was unhelpful: "Tell him he's just going to have to deal with it."

Charles did not really disagree with that suggestion. *I'm younger than some of them, and I'm away from my family, just like them.* In the end, he offered nods of silent sympathy, and when time allowed brought out a cribbage board, even letting them occasionally win a game.

A month after arriving, Charles sat in the hospital mess with an empty tray and a wandering mind. *Why is it called a "mess"?* He pulled the small dictionary, now permanently curved to the shape of his backside, from his back pocket.

Mess /mes/
n. 1. A dirty or untidy state of things or of a place. 2. A situation or state of affairs that is confused or full of difficulties.

v. 1. Make untidy or dirty. 2. Take one's meals in a particular place or with a particular person, so called for the old English word for a portion of food.

So, when I eat in a Navy chow hall, I'm supposed to use "mess" as a verb, not a noun or adjective? OK.

He continued studying the small dictionary, silently mouthing new words. From his peripheral vision, he noted someone join him at the table. Looking up, he saw Chief Fahey looking quizzically back at him.

"Got a good story going?"

"It's a dictionary, sir. I just looked something up. It's only a small pocket version, so I'm memorizing the whole thing."

"I can't help but think that would be ever so boring?"

"No, and it's not the only thing I read." Charles responded defensively. "I read novels, and I read the newspapers in the library."

"What do you read for fun?"

For some reason, Charles hesitated to describe the books Susan, the librarian, had given him. "There's always a stack of Zane Grey and other western adventure books lying around the wards."

"Really?" The Chief looked dubious. "Where are you from again?"

"Princeton, Indiana. We farmed."

"Midwest. Good people there."

"Yes sir, there are."

The Chief paused, and looking at Charles, seemed to arrive at a decision. "Emily, my wife, likes for me to bring home a young sailor for a nice dinner now and then. She assumes all of you boys are suffering from malnutrition and might pass away if she doesn't feed you some of her home cooking. Are you available tomorrow night?"

"Yes sir!" Charles answered, overly quick and too loudly. He had eaten nothing but institutional food for months.

That evening, both men helped Emily prepare the meal of three distinct courses. The food was different from Indiana farm fare, but different in a good way. After dinner, Chief Fahey grabbed two beers, and he and Charles gravitated to the porch to talk before Charles returned to his barrack.

During the next couple of months, the Chief invited Charles to dinner three more times. Sitting on the porch after the second dinner, Fahey brought up his experience in the Great War. He had been a freshly minted corpsman, only nineteen years old, when he shipped out with the 5th Marine Regiment for France.

Fahey recounted the regiment's attack at Belleau Wood. "Hell, Charles, America hadn't been in the war all that long. We didn't know much about trying to take care of injuries from heavy artillery and machine guns, much less mustard gas. The Brits shared some of what they had learned, not that it helped a lot when there were more men dead or wounded from bullets and shrapnel than still fighting. The casualties didn't have just a single injury. Every one of them had two, three, or ten wounds. You didn't know where to start patching. Add our inadequate training to inexperience, and we lost more than we saved. I hope if it happens again, you guys will be a lot better prepared."

"It doesn't look like the war in Europe is going to end soon. Any advice if we end up in that fight?"

"Not *if*, but *when*, Charles. We can't sit by much longer while Britain starves to death. Other side of the world, Japan's advancing their imperial expansion. We may even go to war with Japan at the same time we do with Germany. In either case, do what we've trained you to do. With a little luck, you'll come out the other side, like I did." Fahey silently stared into the distance for a while without saying anything else. He then went into the house for a moment and returned with a thick book. "Do you have this?" He showed the book to Charles.

It was *The Merck Manual of Therapeutics and Materia Medica, Sixth Edition*, published in 1934. The book was small but thick. "No, sir," Charles replied. "I have the *Handbook for the Hospital Corps*, but not this."

"If it's not in either the *Merck Manual* or the *Corps Handbook*, then you probably don't need to know it." Fahey flipped through the book. "*Merck* covers everything from abortion, here on page one, to zinc sulphate, back here on page 1367, and everything in between. Here, take it. You like to read. That'll keep you occupied for a while. It's going to be more useful than that dictionary when the day comes."

ᔓ ᔓ ᔓ

Just as he had in San Diego, Charles spent much of his free time at the Mare Island Library. Unlike Susan, the base librarian here thought her most important task was to keep books shelved in proper sequence. Sailors with questions only wasted her valuable sorting and shelving time. The first time Charles attempted to check out a book, she explained to him, or more accurately threatened him with, the dire consequences of leaving for a new assignment with unreturned library property. "I will report you, and the Navy will find and punish you!"

Charles only nodded to the threat. *The only good thing is, this evil woman has chased away so many people, I have the place almost to myself.*

The library's subscription to the *San Francisco Chronicle* became Charles's gateway to current events. Having consolidated control of Poland, Hitler's German forces began forming new fronts. Before he could challenge Britain's Navy, still the most powerful in the world, Hitler needed better access to the Atlantic Ocean. Norway, with its deep fjords, and France, with its multiple seaports, offered that access. In April, with invented provocation as in Poland, Germany invaded Norway and Denmark. Holland and Belgium were overrun by late May. Conquest of the Low Countries took longer than anticipated, but the Germans ultimately overcame the unexpectedly strong Dutch resistance.

Damn, things are not good. Charles stood, stretched, and returned to reading.

After occupying Belgium, the Wehrmacht moved quickly to the Normandy coast, easily dismantling the French resistance. The Germans' easy and quick overrun of Normandy trapped some 340,000 British and Allied forces on the coast near Dunkirk. A chaotic evacuation, using everything from channel ferries to small fishing boats, brought almost all the men safely to England, while leaving their heavy arms and equipment on the Dunkirk beach. On 22 June, France signed an armistice. Hitler rode through the streets of Paris the next day.

Only the English Channel stood between the defiant British and complete Nazi domination of western Europe. Hitler authorized unrestricted warfare in the Atlantic and removed all restrictions on German U-boats, unleashing them to hunt down and mercilessly torpedo Allied merchant ships.

Is it possible for Germany to sink so many Allied merchant ships that it will starve Britain to the point of surrender? Charles tried to imagine the terror of sailors on a torpedoed ship slipping under the ocean's surface. *Drowning must be awful. I think I'd rather be killed outright.* Then he remembered. *I hope Susan's brother makes it through this.*

The United States, with its metaphorical drawbridge up and sitting securely behind her Atlantic Ocean moat, remained, for the time, isolationist.

Charles read a long editorial about the situation in China. "... in Asia, the Japanese Army continues its occupation and expansion along the China coast. Though limited in raw materials and modern manufacturing technology, the Japanese culture has produced soldiers of unparalleled courage and endurance. However, these same soldiers are also known to engage in acts of unequaled brutality, unchained by Western morality and respect for subjugated peoples. Should America ever engage in a war with Japan, it will be unlike anything previously known to an American Army."

8

The Nurse

Mare Island Naval Hospital

January 1940

By the end of his first month, Charles was comfortably adapted to hospital routine. Doctors performed surgery and wrote orders in the patient's chart. Nurses, hospital corpsmen, and apprentices carried out those orders and took care of the patient until discharge. On each ward, a senior nurse directed patient care, established work schedules, and managed supplies. The ward nurses monitored patients' status and progress, administered medications, made rounds with the physicians, and oversaw the hospital assistants.

The senior nurse also assumed responsibility for the continuing education of corpsmen as they took vital signs, assisted with personal hygiene, changed bandages, and performed minor procedures according to their training and competence. Specially trained nurses and corpsmen assisted with surgery and post-operative care.

In his second month Charles rotated to the night shift on the surgery ward. Shortly before 2300 on his first night he reported to the nurse in charge. She was taller than most women and moved with deliberation and self-assurance. She wore the rank of Lieutenant (Junior Grade) and a name tag, *Finian, RN*.

"Good evening, Miss Finian, I'm Hospital Apprentice Charles Beckner. I'll be working this shift for the next few weeks."

Despite having official Navy rank, within the hospital nurses were always addressed as "Miss." "Mrs." was not an option in the US Navy. A nurse had to resign and leave the service if she married, much less started a family.

"Hi, Charles." She flashed a reserved smile. "I'm Lieutenant Mary Finian."

Charles judged her to be Susan's age, perhaps twenty-five or so. A slightly oval face was complemented by light jade-green eyes and a small nose. Red hair, gathered in a loose bun, seemed ready to cascade to her shoulders if unchained. The standard Navy nurse uniform performed as designed, camouflaging her figure and leaving only clues here and there for Charles's imagination.

"I'm looking forward to working with you, ma'am." Charles gave her his best smile.

Instead of returning this overture, the lieutenant launched into her standard introduction for new sailors fresh from hospital corpsman's school. "I should let you know that I've seen dozens of new corpsmen come and go, rotating through here before going on to their permanent duty stations."

She's warning me.

"The military non-fraternization rules simplify our relationship. It is OK if you are friendly to me and my nurses, but that's where it stops." She paused for Charles to acknowledge his understanding.

"Understood, Miss Finian. Loud and clear. Let me add that I will give 100-percent effort on the job. Every day. I do hope for something in return though?"

"And that is?" she raised one eyebrow.

"I want to learn—I want to know everything about the patients, their problems, and the procedures we do on them. When you think I'm ready, I'd like to perform those procedures on my own. You'll find me capable and dependable, ma'am."

Charles paused, watching her reaction, before adding. "I know I'll eventually leave Mare Island, and the only thing I want to take with me is the knowledge and experience I gained here."

Despite her hard line, Nurse Finian did enjoy training most of the new corpsmen. Only occasionally did she encounter an enlisted man who, though baptized in the sacred respect for rank, found it difficult to submit to a woman's authority. She could ignore that attitude if her orders were followed and his opinions remained unvoiced.

She appraised this confident young sailor, thinking he could be among the better ones.

"Mary Finian," Charles repeated her name. "My sister's named Mary, and she's not only my sister but my best friend. I miss her, and you remind me of her. You even talk so like her that you could be from the same town."

"Where do you think I'm from?" she challenged him.

"Indiana? Kentucky?" Charles answered.

"Close! I'm from western Ohio. And you?"

"Southern Indiana," Charles replied. "It's an OK place to come from, but I probably won't go back there when I leave the Navy."

"Understandable." She needed to return the conversation to business. "Now for work. For tonight we have only a few patients. They'll need temperatures and pulses recorded. A couple will need incisions checked and bandages changed. Let me show you where we keep things, and you can get started. Any questions—just ask. OK?"

"I do have a question."

"Sure. What is it?"

"What color do you call your hair?"

"Careful, Charles. You're getting personal," and she gave him what was know in the hospital as the "famous Finian frown."

"Sorry, ma'am. No offense intended." Charles inspected his left shoe.

Dropping the frown, she unconsciously curled a stray strand around one finger and broke her rule against straying into personal conversations with the enlisted men. "What color would you call it?"

Charles thought of one or two different shades of red, but those were used for barns, not women's hair. He resisted the urge to pull out his pocket dictionary for synonyms. "Strawberry?" He knew he was wrong even as he uttered the word.

"God! I hope not!"

Charles tried again, "Auburn?"

"That's better, but not what I call it."

"I give up. What do you call it?"

"Red. Plain and simple red," she smiled. "Let's get to work. By the way, my full name is Mary Tallulah Finian. Mary is the Catholic part. Tallulah is the Irish part. If you hear one of the nurses asking for Tillie, that's me."

ઽෳ ઽෳ ઽෳ

As with any hospital, night shifts allowed more down time to talk than the day or evening shifts. Over the next month, Tillie and Charles developed a comfortable workplace friendship, mostly discussing Ohio, Indiana, and family. On the occasional slow nights, when only a few beds were occupied, their discussions were longer and ranged further afield.

"Why did you join the Navy?" Charles asked one night. "I mean, you're a terrific nurse, and the Navy needs you, but do you think about what happens after the Navy?"

"You know, Charles, I'm still not certain. When I was near graduation from nursing school several years ago, the few jobs available weren't all that great. More than that though, I had an urge to leave home, I mean really leave. Get hundreds of miles away. When I put on my uniform and waved goodbye from the train window, I felt completely free for the first time in my life. After that taste of freedom, I could never go back home and give that up. Joining the Navy was partly a patriotic decision, but mainly a way for me to sever all the ties keeping me home. My only regret was that I know how hard it was for my parents to let me go."

"I suppose it's harder for parents to let go of a daughter than a son."

"Maybe. I think it was hardest on my dad. My mom surprised me, though. She understood, and in her own way I think encouraged me. But in her last letter, I can see she's worried about all this talk of war."

"Does it worry you?"

"If the war comes, I'm ready, even proud, to wear the uniform and do my part for the country, no different than you." She paused before continuing, "One more thing, Charles."

"Yes, ma'am?"

"When we're alone, not working, you don't have to call me 'Miss Finian.' It makes me feel like an old spinster. 'Tillie' is fine, just not in the hospital, in front of others."

When March arrived, Charles continued his rotation to other wards and different shifts. He manufactured excuses to visit the surgical ward, hoping for an opportunity to chat with Tillie—or "Miss Finian" if anyone else was in earshot.

On a night he otherwise would have normally been sleeping, he decided instead to visit Tillie at the hospital.

"Hi, Miss Finian."

"Hello, Charles. What can I help you with?" she replied flatly, grabbing a patient's chart to inspect.

Charles was taken aback for a moment before the realization hit him. Visiting Tillie outside the constraints of the normal workplace and worktime signified a change in the relationship she could not accept. If the staff noticed his unusual visit, they would see it as obviously social, and that could lead to trouble for both. *I've just been warned off. She is not about to compromise herself by letting a casual workplace friendship evolve any further. Not even in appearance.*

"Nothing, Miss Finian. I was looking for someone, but I see they're not working now. Have a quiet shift."

Tillie remained happy to chat with Charles within her defined boundaries. "How long do you think Britain can hold out?" she asked him one night.

"I don't know. Europe has been turned into a giant fortress. With his U-boats and air power, Hitler doesn't need to invade England across the channel. In a year, maybe less, the English will be starving and out of ammunition. Then the Nazis can waltz in and take over."

"When I was little, my father often spoke of how the Great War was horrific and no one would ever want to have another one. He was so wrong."

"I think a lot of people were wrong, Tillie."

Working with patients was uncomparable to sitting in a San Diego classroom. Charles felt the real-life responsibility for another human being like a weight. With concern and gentleness, he gave treatments and guided the patients' recovery, accepting their profuse gratitude in return. Gaining knowledge and experience on each new service, he assumed tasks of increasing complexity and responsibility. The *Corps Handbook* and *Merck Manual* were his constant companions.

Charles developed a knack for drawing blood and starting intravenous lines, a skill putting him in high demand for managing patients with damaged or difficult veins. *It's simple. I just feel the vein, visualize it below the skin, and put the needle inside it.* Every new patient brought one of his San Diego classroom lectures to life.

Charles's two weeks in the Mare Island emergency room was mostly boredom, interrupted by bursts of panic and chaos.

Midway through a morning shift, a clerk on the front desk yelled back to the treatment area, "Corpsman! Up front!" Charles ran to the check-in desk. A cook from the hospital kitchen sat in a chair while another sailor held a towel tightly around the man's hand.

"What happened?"

"Knife slipped, sir," grimaced the cook. "I was trying to cut up a pineapple."

Charles grabbed a nearby gurney and rolled it over. "Lie down. I'll take you back to a treatment room and take a look."

Charles and a nurse carefully unwrapped the bloody towel. A gaping slash extended from the base of the sailor's little finger to the web between his thumb and index finger. With the towel removed, blood flowed from the wound, then splattering on the floor. The nurse slapped a compression bandage back over the hand to temporarily staunch the bleeding. Looking at the flowing blood, Charles felt clammy and a bit woozy. *Oh, crap! I can't let myself faint!*

"Are you OK?"

He realized the nurse was talking to him, not the patient. *I'm not about to admit I'm feeling queasy.* "Yeah, I'm fine."

"Good. You looked a little pale and sweaty for a moment."

"Did I? I'm fine now." *What happened? I saw bloody messes when we slaughtered hogs every fall. This is different, though—this is a person, just like me, that's hurting and bleeding. I better get used to it.*

"And what happened here?" Lieutenant Smith, the emergency surgeon on duty, strode into the room.

While the doctor examined his hand, the cook repeated his story, "Knife slipped, sir, trying to cut up a pineapple."

Ignoring the growing pool of blood at his feet, Lieutenant Smith examined the injury fully. "Wiggle your fingers. Make a tight fist. Straighten your fingers out. All the way." He replaced the compression bandage and patted the cook on the shoulder. "You'll be fine."

He turned to Charles. "I don't think we've worked together yet. Beckner, is it?"

"Yes, sir. Charles Beckner."

"OK, Charles, have you sewn up cuts yet?"

"I've had classes and practiced sewing on rubber and leather."

The doctor turned back to their patient. "Charles here is recently out of school. He's been taught how to sew up cuts, but, as you just heard, he's never done it for real. Is it OK if he and I do this together?"

"I suppose so," the cook mumbled reluctantly.

Dr. Smith wanted no doubts. "Someday you might be hurt again, and a corpsman like Charles here will be the only medical care available. You'll want him ready to go."

The cook considered this for a moment. "Then go to it, sir. You and the corpsman fix me up. I'm valuable Navy property, so I know you'll do it right," and he grinned.

"OK, Charles," Lieutenant Smith moved so he and Charles were on opposite sides of the injured hand. "Let's talk about what we're doing as we go along."

Charles talked to the patient and Dr. Smith simultaneously, recalling his school lectures and practice suturing. "First, I'm thoroughly cleaning the wound and making sure there's no contamination left before I start. Preventing infection is a hundred times better that treating one later. I'm injecting some medicine to numb your hand," then glancing at Dr. Smith, "with 1 percent procaine. After that, you won't feel a thing."

"Thanks, Doc." The cook relaxed and closed his eyes.

"Adding epinephrine to the procaine would constrict the blood vessels and slow the bleeding," Smith commented.

"Yes, sir. But the cut is across the base of his fingers, and too much epinephrine might stop the blood flow. He could lose part of a finger."

"Correct," Smith said, approvingly. "Keep going."

Following two weeks in the emergency room, Charles rotated to the operating room where surgical teams, functioning much like synchronized marching units, efficiently and safely removed inflamed appendices, excised tumors, and repaired various body parts. The corpsmen permanently assigned to these teams were specialized, experienced surgical assistants. Charles was only there to observe and learn the basic skills of a surgical assistant.

On his second day Charles watched an older surgeon, a Navy Captain, perform a simple hernia repair. Charles was not expecting to take part in the procedure, but, as required of everyone before entry into the OR, he scrubbed his skin from elbows to fingernails for five minutes. Donning a gown, mask, cap and gloves using sterile technique, he joined the team in the operating room. Charles was tall enough to peer over a surgical nurse's shoulder. Fascinated by the procedure, he leaned in for a better look.

"Sailor, your head's in my light," the surgeon said calmly, with an accent suggesting New England.

"Sorry!" Charles jerked back.

"No, no—you don't have to stop watching, just move your head slightly back. There, that's good. Thank you."

After separating some tissue, the surgeon again glanced at Charles. "What's your name?"

"Charles Beckner, Hospital Apprentice 2nd, sir."

"What will I find when I cut deeper, under here?" The surgeon pointed a surgical instrument at the patient's groin, bathed in bright light in the middle of the sterile field.

Charles looked at the area, recalling his anatomy class and the images from his book. "I believe the femoral artery, the femoral vein, and the femoral nerve are all there."

"What if this sailor had been wounded in this leg and was hemorrhaging badly—what would you do?"

"Put on a tourniquet, sir."

"And if that doesn't work, or you don't have a tourniquet?" asked the surgeon.

"I could try compressing the femoral artery until he gets to an aid station or hospital."

"And is the femoral artery here," the surgeon pointed to the outer area, "or here?" pointing to the inner part of the site.

Charles hesitated briefly and then answered, "You have to compress the artery to stop the major hemorrhage, and it runs in the middle of the femoral triangle, with the nerve on the outside and the vein on the inside, sir."

"That's exactly right: *Nerve, Artery, and Vein.* Just remember you've come from the *outside* to join the *NAVy.*"

"I suppose those Army docs have a hard time remembering," joked one of the assistants.

The surgeon interrupted, returning the conversation to a serious level, "Knowing where to apply that pressure might mean that man gets to a field hospital alive and keeps his leg instead of having it amputated." He looked at Charles and added, "Good answer."

Charles found the operating room staff more than willing to answer questions if they were addressed at the proper time and pertinent to the procedure in progress. Outside the OR, he continued questioning staff. With rare exception, hospital nurses and doctors would usually stop and discuss a reasonable question from the affable young man.

Evenings spent reading from the *Handbook* and *Merck Manual* deepened his knowledge of human anatomy, disease, and treatment. *So much to learn— good thing I'm enjoying it.*

9

Transitions

Mare Island Naval Hospital, California

March 1940

Unhappy with long, uninterrupted gray hallways, a previous chief of hospital operations convinced the Navy Yard to mount pictures of Navy ships as decoration. Soon, framed pictures of ships along with descriptive captions lined the hospital walls. Charles occasionally glanced at the pictures, but one, a composite of three pictures of the same ship, drew greater attention. Charles read the description beneath the images.

> *The first turbo-electric ship in the US Navy, a coal delivery ship named* Jupiter, *was built at Mare Island. Later, by adding what amounted to a wooden football field on top of the coal transporter's superstructure,* Jupiter *became CV-1, the Navy's very first operational aircraft carrier. She was officially named the USS* Langley, *but affectionately called the 'Covered Wagon' by her crew. In 1937 the front third of the landing deck was removed and the* Langley *converted into a seaplane tender. She retains the name* Langley *but with a new hull designation of AV-3.*

Charles stared at the pictures and chuckled. *That's one strange-looking ship. I would recognize her from a mile away.*

Charles did not find a close friend, at least not as close as Martin, among the sailors at Mare Island. Yes, he and Tillie were friends, but he could only fantasize what it would be like if Navy rules did not strictly forbid fraternization between female officers and enlisted men. He was inwardly envious, if not outright jealous, when she told him of going to see the new movie *The Wizard of Oz* on a double date the previous weekend. The US Navy had no need, obligation, or desire to enlist female sailors, so Charles's own dating opportunities were non-existent, once he eliminated the bars and cat houses in Vallejo.

I miss Martin, with his brains and sarcastic humor. He would have been a great companion to explore the Bay area with. I haven't received a single card or note from him since we went different ways after San Diego. On the other hand, I never sent a letter to him. I guess neither one of us is all that good at corresponding. Is this the way it is in the Navy? Will all my Navy friendships be like this?

Surreptitiously arranging to be around at a time he knew Tillie would take her break, Charles offered, and she accepted, to share a table and cup of coffee. "Let me ask you, Tillie, if you were a civilian nurse, how would your life be different?"

"Charles, my life as a Navy nurse is complex. There're good things and not-so-good things. In the Navy hierarchy, we are neither fish nor fowl—not real officers, but definitely not enlisted. We're something in between. We possess no official power in the general line of command, and we're paid only half as much as male officers of the same rank."

"Really? How can you accept that?"

Tillie held up her hand and continued, "On the positive side, we have clean and spacious free housing. Here at Mare Island we even have our own free mess with generally well-prepared food. All in all, it's not a terrible life for a single woman. Besides, there're enough unattached commissioned officers that the odds of my having a Saturday night date are pretty good."

Weeks later, late one March night, Charles worked on the medical ward. He manufactured an excuse to visit the surgical ward after midnight and found Tillie writing notes in a patient's chart.

"Hi Miss Finian. I came to borrow some vital signs forms for the medical ward, but I see you're busy there."

"Hi, Charles. Go ahead, you know where the forms are kept. I'm just finishing a note on Lieutenant Chapman. He was running a low-grade temperature after an appendectomy yesterday. His temperature is down, but his incision looks a little angry. I'm keeping an eye on it." Not waiting for Charles to comment she asked, "Are you making the Navy a career? I mean staying until you retire?"

The question caught him off guard. "I don't think it was on my mind when I enlisted. I had three short-term goals, earn some money, get some training, and see somewhere besides Indiana." He paused to think. "Do I want to have a career in the Navy? I don't know. Maybe. Why are you asking?"

"My enlistment is up in May, and I have to either reenlist or find a civilian job. There are a lot more opportunities out there now that the economy is returning, and I'm thinking about applying for a job in Chicago. It's closer to home, but still far enough away. What do you think?"

What do I think? I think I'm about to see another friend disappear. "Chicago has cold winters. It's windy. It's big. Otherwise, I guess it's as good a place as any." Then he added, "There're probably a lot of young doctors there if you want to get married and have kids."

Tillie frowned at Charles. "I'm not sure I'm ready for that, at least not yet. It wasn't easy to get where I am. I'll be promoted to full lieutenant if I re-enlist. I told you my dad was totally against my joining the Navy. His opinion—and a lot of his friends agreed—was that women in the military mainly serve as consorts for male officers. If not that, they assume you 'like' other women." Tillie rolled her eyes upward. "Not that I haven't seen both of those things, but I have so much personal freedom right now, I don't know if I'm ready to give it up." She stood up from the desk, "Sorry, I have another post-op running a fever I need to check on. Help yourself to those forms, we have plenty. I'll see you later, Charles."

In early May Charles stopped by the general surgery ward two days in a row, but Tillie wasn't on duty either time. When she still wasn't there the third time, he asked one of the other nurses, "When's Miss Finian coming back to work? I haven't seen her around recently."

"You won't see her anymore, Charles. She's gone."

Air left the room. He could barely speak. "Gone? Gone where?"

"She left suddenly. Must have been some sort of emergency. I don't know where she went, but apparently it's permanent. She's not returning. Sorry, Charles. I know you two were friends."

"We were."

I thought we were good friends, but she left and didn't even say goodbye. I know it's the Navy, and I'm learning that people come and go. At least Martin and I had a chance to say goodbye. But, Tillie? Just disappearing? Is it even worth the effort—making a friend in the Navy?

Most Vallejo bars enforced California's MLDA, minimum legal drinking age, of 21. The brothels, on the other hand, enforced this law no better than the other laws they ignored. Contrary to public perception, most young sailors avoided the cathouses, whether for reasons of personal morality, religion, or simply old-fashioned guilt. The corpsmen had an additional deterrent. At some point in their training, they'd all worked in the "Urological Infections Clinic," more commonly known as the Clap Clinic. The required classes with "personal hygiene" films and lectures paled in comparison to witnessing first-hand the oozing inflammation of advanced gonorrhea or drug-resistant syphilitic chancres in the flesh.

The sailors who did venture out for those weekend carnal pleasures uniformly returned broke and fervently hoping they'd be spared a trip to the Clap Clinic.

The inhibitions of fear and morality were strong in the Indiana farm boy, but a simple miserliness helped keep him on base. Among his fellow corpsmen, Charles was notorious for his ingrained frugality. By his own arrangement, three-fourths of his paycheck automatically went to his father, knowing the money would make life easier for the family.

On Saturday afternoon, sensing Charles's indecision, a group of friends pushed him to join them for a night in town. "Come on, Charles. You don't know how to have fun. Come with us tonight—what's stopping you?"

"Money, to start with, and guilt. You guys always come back with none of the first and a lot of the other." Finally giving in to their cajoling, Charles shook his head. "I'll probably regret this. I'm tired of arguing with you, so I guess it's time I see what you guys really do on a free Saturday night."

A few hours later, he was sitting with four other sailors at a table in a crowded, loud bar. He looked around. *Everything seems gaudy and cheap, including the people.* The effect left him more uncomfortable than excited.

The evening started easily enough with a waitress in a low-cut blouse and thigh-high skirt taking their order. Once she departed, an Asian girl wearing an even shorter skirt appeared at Charles's side.

"You are a tall one, sailor!" she exclaimed. "Buy me a drink?"

In unfamiliar circumstances, Indiana politeness took over. "Sure," he said, pulling over a chair.

Ignoring the chair, she wiggled into his lap. "I'm Dolly." Almost immediately his beer arrived, along with something bubbly in a tulip-shaped glass. "I love champagne," she said, downing most of her drink at once, waving the glass at the bar, signaling for another one.

Charles sipped a beer he thought flat and flavorless. He turned to complain, but the two chairs next to him were empty. "Where'd the others go?" he asked Walter, his only companion still at the table.

"No idea," Walter answered, before returning his attention to the girl sitting in his own lap.

Dolly's conversation was less sparkling than her drinks. In five minutes, she'd finished her second drink, while half of Charles's beer remained. "You need to slow down," he advised her. "I'm still on my first beer."

"No, no! This is very good champagne."

"I'm not sure why I'm feeling woozy on one beer—"

"If you not feeling good, I take you to lie down." Dolly stood and pulled at Charles's hand.

He was having trouble thinking straight but was startled to see the table empty. All his companions had disappeared. A klaxon shrieked in his head. Working hard at speaking through the slur in his voice, he stood and started for the door. "No, thank you."

"Oh please, we go find your friends." She continued pulling at his hand. He shook her off and tried to walk away.

A huge man, one of the bouncers, blocked his way. "Can't leave without paying your bill, sailor."

"Sorry." Charles was working hard to think straight. "How much?"

"Three dollars."

"Three dollars! Can't be—I didn't even finish my first beer."

"A dollar for the beer, and two dollars for the lady's drinks."

Charles shook his head to clear it. *Somebody put something in my beer, and "Dolly" was probably drinking soda water, not champagne.* With rising anger and clenched fist, he readied to swing at the bouncer, but he retained a modicum of self-control. *Starting a fight would be a bad idea. I'm not feeling so good. It's all I can do to stand and walk out of here.* He pulled a five-dollar bill from his pocket and handed them over. "I need two dollars change."

"That's your girl's tip. I'll make sure she gets it. Now get out before I throw you out."

He looked around for Walter and the others, but they'd all disappeared from the room. He managed to walk from the bar and make it back to base.

A few days later, word spread through the hospital that Walter's Saturday night had ended in the city morgue, reportedly the victim of a mugging gone wrong.

꙳ ꙳ ꙳

Sailors love gambling. With every payday, games of craps and poker sprang up like summer weeds. The men played in back corners of the barracks or any other place out of sight of senior non-coms and officers. Mostly organized and perpetuated by men who raised the practice of cheating to an art form, it was essentially robbery disguised as gambling. In poker, they used false dealing and marked cards. In craps, a skilled player could deftly swap loaded or shaved dice in and out of a game at will.

Charles watched a few of the poker games without participating. He found a book in the library, *How to Win at Poker*. Armed with what he thought was an understanding of the principles and psychology of betting, he joined his first game. In the first five hands he lost three dollars. He stood and walked away. *No more of this until I understand what just happened. Either I'm not as good at this as I thought, or I can't see the cheating.*

Mare Island was only one of many Navy bases with a gambling problem. Complaints eventually reached levels that headquarters could not ignore. Regulations against gambling were reinforced but, unsurprisingly, failed. Unable to eliminate the games by directive, the Mare Island commander changed tactics. Once his arrangements were in place, he called a general assembly of the hospital's enlisted personnel.

"I have arranged for a professional gambler to come and talk," the commander announced at a general staff assembly. "He will describe and give demonstrations showing the ease with which you can be unscrupulously relieved of your entire paycheck. I hope he'll convince you that most poker, craps, and other games are not really games of chance. No amount of skill, or even luck, will prevent you from losing your money. Sign the roster when you arrive. Attendance is mandatory."

Though Charles had sworn off poker and the other games after losing his three dollars, he had no option but to attend the demonstrations. After watching the initial examples of underhanded card dealing, Charles's interest was aroused. The card shark shuffled the deck, let one of the attendees cut the cards, and dealt five hands. Turning the cards face up, he revealed four losing hands. The dealer held the winning hand, four aces.

"Bull shit!" Someone exclaimed. "That's impossible. You cheated."

"Of course I cheated. I'll show you once more." He shuffled and dealt again. This time, the hand to his right had a full house, but the dealer again held the winning hand, a straight flush. "That full house will sucker most players into betting hard. They'll bet their paycheck and anything else they have on that hand, but they'll lose it all. It won't have been just bad luck."

From the front row a sailor asked, "How did you do that?"

"I tell the people I'm entertaining it's magic. In a poker game, though, it's not entertainment. It's cheating. It's robbery. In a high-stakes game, it's grand larceny."

"How can we level the playing field against someone like you?"

"You can't, and there're many players out there with card skills as good as or better than mine. They're just waiting for the next sucker. If you insist on gambling and want a fair game, I suggest that you go to a reputable casino where the dealer is not in the game. The casino takes a cut, but the dealer himself has no interest in who wins. It's only a matter of your own skill and, of course, luck."

"That's right," a sailor piped up. "I know a guy that took a train from Oakland to Reno last month. It was only a five-hour ride. He spent the whole night playing poker and sitting at the slot machines in the two casinos. He came back on the train the next day."

"Did he win?" a couple of others asked.

"No, but he still had half his money when he came back. That's better than I do around here."

Charles had no plans to return to poker or craps, but that last recommendation about the dealer not actually participating in the game certainly made sense. *I think there's a solution without having to go to Reno, but I need to think this through a bit before talking to anyone about it.*

That night he penned a letter to his sister, brief as always.

> *Mary,*
> *I'm content and healthy. Mare Island is a large hospital and the staff is excellent. Some of them are friendly. San Francisco has good museums.*
> *Miss you all,*
> *Charles*
> *PS: I became friends with a nurse. Her name is also Mary, but she goes by Tillie. She is a redheaded Irish girl, but still reminds*

me of you. We were only friends, of course. Not only is she older than me, she's an officer. Anyway, she suddenly left without saying goodbye. I don't know where she went. It would have been nice if you two had met. You would like each other.

10

New Horizons

Mare Island, California

October 1940

Ten months after arriving at Mare Island, Charles received a message to report to Chief Fahey.

"Beckner, you've taken to your clinical duties like a duck to water. I'm happy to inform you of your promotion to Hospital Assistant 1st Class. You've more than earned it."

"Thank you, sir," Charles paused, "and thank you for the encouragement, the good advice, the *Merck Manual*, home-cooked dinners, and—well, for everything."

"It's part of the package. The next thing I need to talk to you about is your upcoming assignment, your first real working assignment."

"I do have some preferences, sir."

"I'm sure you do, but I don't need to tell you that the Navy assignment gods can be fickle."

"So, I have no choice?"

"Yes and no. Go to the personnel office and make sure your records are updated for your BOP, Base of Preference."

"Will it make any difference?"

"Only as a tiebreaker—the Navy always assigns you to where it most needs you. If the Navy needs your skill equally at bases A, B, and C, and they see you want assignment at base A, then you're more likely to get it. Your performance

75

reports have all been exceptional, and I'll summarize them on my final report. Maybe that'll help you get one of your top choices." He chuckled. "Perversely though, it might have the opposite effect. The more qualified you appear on paper, the more attention they pay to the Navy's needs rather than your own wants. Good luck, Charles."

Filling out the "dream sheet" was easy. Charles had already identified three Navy medical facilities in San Diego, including the large Balboa Naval Hospital, as attractive assignments. *Who knows? Maybe this time I'll get exactly what I ask for.*

At breakfast the next morning, Charles told another corpsman in his training group about the discussion with Chief Fahey. "I listed three preferences, all in San Diego. What's on your list?"

"My list is all Florida. I'm from there, but the good assignments are hard to get fresh out of training. The guys returning from overseas or coming off ship assignments get priority. Encouragingly, I heard Navy Headquarters is positioning men and materiel at East Coast bases. When Washington finally decides it's time to go and kick the Germans back to Berlin, our troops will already be staged and ready to move out."

"Makes sense," Charles agreed, "But won't that mean they'll be overstaffed on the East Coast?"

"Maybe at first, but more slots are opening up. Even though we're neutral, we will defend our coasts. The government is bringing ships out of mothballs, and those ships need crews. They are *doubling* the size of new classes at every Navy basic training base."

"That doesn't surprise me. If we're not over there sooner rather than later, there'll be no England left. London is being bombed every day. Families are sleeping in underground rail stations every night. U-boats are sinking supply ships before they reach port. Food is tightly rationed. Britain is desperate—for everything."

"Charles, you're acting like it's all over. England's holding out OK, so far."

"Not for much longer. In the *Chronicle* yesterday I read that if it weren't for the fighter pilots still going up every day against the German bombers, Britain might have already fallen."

"You and I can't fix the world, Charles. Florida's nice this time of year. Put it on your list and come with me."

"No, thanks. You've thrown cold water on my plans for San Diego, but I can hope."

ᔓ ᔓ ᔓ

Every few days, orders arrived for finishing students. Occasionally, they were sent to one of their top choices. More often they were disappointed.

Finally, a thick manila envelope arrived for Charles. He turned the routing envelope over twice without opening it.

A clerk at the desk watched him. "You can't change those orders by staring at them."

"I know. I have a lot riding on this, though." Charles extracted the thick stack of papers. Half of it was the multiple carbon copies that came with all military change of station orders. He scanned the document and found the "Proceed To" section of his orders.

"So, where're you heading?" the clerk asked.

Charles did not answer. He just stared at the top page.

Proceed to: Canacao US Naval Hospital, Cavite, Philippine Islands. He read the typed destination twice more, trying to comprehend the words. *OK—I know Philippine Islands are somewhere in southeast Asia. But Cañacao? Cavite? Where the hell is that?*

"Yes?" The clerk still waited for Charles to reply.

"Sorry. It seems I'm going to a place called 'Cavite,' in the Philippine Islands."

The clerk's face lit up. "Great assignment, Doc. I had a buddy who spent time at the Cavite Navy Yard. He said he had a fucking great time. Literally."

"Right. Thanks." Charles was still frowning when he returned to his barracks. A brief consult with his pocket atlas showed Cavite to be a small bump along the contour of Manila Bay, about ten miles south of the city of Manila.

Jesus Christ! They're sending me to the jungle. Charles tried, unsuccessfully, to imagine the Philippine landscape. He could not picture anything beyond the terrain map in his atlas.

He read the next page of his orders, "Report San Francisco POE," *Damn Navy acronyms. I think that must be Port of Embarkation*, "on 12 October for transport to Manila, Philippine Islands, on the USS *Chaumont*."

Not San Diego. Damn it!

Charles slumped on his bed, beyond disappointed.

He knew that at this point the assignment could not be altered. A passage from *Meditations* came to mind. It was something to the effect that *If you are distressed by anything external, the pain is not due to the thing itself, but to your estimate of it; and this you have the power to revoke at any moment.*

Marcus is right, of course. Fretting over an assignment I can't change does me no good. San Diego will just have to move to the back burner. After all, for my next assignment I'll be returning from this overseas assignment, and I'll most likely to get my first choice. San Diego will still be there when I come back from—where was it?

He looked again at his orders. *Yes, Cavite.*

He put away his pocket atlas and headed to the library. *Time for a more detailed map and some deeper research on the Philippine Islands.*

By the time he'd pulled the *Encyclopedia Britannica* from its shelf, he had forgotten about San Diego, imagining himself for the next year or two in what might prove an even more exotic and exciting location.

11

The *Chaumont*

San Francisco Port of Embarkation

12 October 1940

The USS *Chaumont* waited at the middle pier. Fuel oil smoke rose from her single stack, signaling to crew and passengers that departure was not far off. An aesthetically challenged ship, she was functionally modern and an experienced traveler. Stretching 448 feet and displacing 13,400 tons, she shuttled military personnel and dependents, government workers, diplomats, and members of Congress, all in support of America's Far Eastern diplomacy. She regularly called at the ports of Honolulu, Guam, Manila, Chinwangtao, Tsingtao, Shanghai, and Hong Kong.

The *Chaumont* broke this routine twice, first in 1932 and again in 1937, when she was drafted to rush US Marine reinforcements to Shanghai.

The passenger manifest for this trip listed the usual mixture of military officers, sailors, soldiers, Marines, and civilians. About a third of the passengers were either government contractors or military dependents. Charles recognized no one among the waiting passengers. He spotted a Navy petty officer wearing the insignia of a Pharmacist's Mate 1st Class, sitting on his sea bag reading a newspaper. Navy corpsmen were a fraternity, considering themselves better trained and qualified than Army medics—with some justification.

"Morning. I'm Charles Beckner."

"Hi. Colin Pope." The blond sailor stood and extended his hand. Unfolding his long frame, he proved to be one of the few men standing taller than Charles.

His angular face bore the scars of chicken pox. He was probably no more than thirty years old, but exposure to sun and ocean had prematurely aged his skin with wrinkles and pigmentation.

Recognizing the red cross on Charles's sleeve, he gave a broad smile and strong handshake.

"I'm heading to Manila. How about you?" Charles asked.

"Fortunately, I get to jump ship in Hawaii for duty at the Pearl Harbor Submarine Base. At least for now it's shore duty, and I hope it stays that way."

"Sorry to disturb your reading."

"That's OK. Most of the stories are about movies and actors and rich people—except for a couple of items you and I might find more personally noteworthy."

"Such as?" Charles asked.

"Well," Colin responded as he turned back to the front page. "The Brits managed a bombing run on the German Port at Hamburg, but it doesn't seem they had much effect. The Luftwaffe then bombed St. Paul's Cathedral in London, but they didn't do much damage either. Churchill is still begging for more help from the United States."

"Even if America joins the Brits, you and I are out of it. We'll be on the other side of the world."

"That doesn't necessarily leave us above the fray." Colin furrowed his brow and pointed to another front page story. "Japan closed its banks in London. Probably related to that is another story about an Anti-Aircraft Regiment of the California Guard that's heading to Hawaii to strengthen our defenses. It sounds to me like someone's at least a little concerned about Japan's intentions."

Colin turned to the third page. "And here's the story that's keeping me up at night. Washington is recommissioning thirty-six old mothballed submarines. I don't know if they're going to try to put a corpsman on each one, but I don't think my nerves would survive going underwater in one of those ancient leaky excuses for a boat." Colin looked back at Charles, "What's up in Manila?"

"I've been assigned to Cañacao Naval Hospital. I don't know a whole lot about it except that it's at Cavite, just south of Manila."

"You'll probably like being there," Colin grinned. "A buddy of mine came back from the P.I. last year. He said it was a great duty station. Hot and humid, but his work was easy, and everything's cheap. You won't even have to do your own laundry."

"Doesn't sound all that bad."

"If you find yourself on Mindanao or some of the other southern islands, don't wander away from the cities alone. The countryside is Moro land. They're

Mohammedans. They resisted the Spanish Christians for a couple of hundred years, and now they like Americans even less."

"Why the antagonism?"

"Go read about the Moro rebellion. We weren't all that kind to each other."

"Great—want to trade assignments?" Charles smiled.

"Nope! If we go to war with the Japanese, it'll be you guys in the Philippines. Hawaii's too far from Japan."

❧ ❧ ❧

The *Chaumont* was designed to carry 1,200 men in wartime. On these peacetime runs, the manifest was rarely more than 500 passengers, and fewer than 400 were boarding for this departure. She was no pleasure liner, but the small manifest allowed elbow room for most. Civilians and commissioned officers enjoyed the luxury of individual cabins on the mid- and upper-deck levels. Junior-rank soldiers and sailors bunked in lower-deck group quarters.

Charles and Colin carried their bags down to a waterline berthing compartment. Triple-stacked bunks, bolted and welded in place, lined the walls. Charles looked around. "Sort of a closed-in arrangement."

"Your first time on a ship?" Colin asked.

"I was on a supply ship going up the West Coast, but it was small compared to this one."

"I see barracks-style bathrooms and showers down at the end of the room," Colin pointed. "Convenient, at least."

Charles looked around. "Dim lights, complemented by an eau de fuel oil. This could get old quickly."

"We'll probably feel the engine vibrations when we're at sea. Some complain about it, but it lulls me right to sleep."

Colin and Charles claimed adjacent lower berths for their "home," and returned to the open deck for departure. Steaming under the recently completed Golden Gate Bridge drew emotions from most of the passengers, accentuated by a single cannon salute from Fort Baker. They spent the afternoon trading lies with other sailors and soldiers, had their supper in the ship's enlisted mess, and then went to sleep, rocked by the *Chaumont's* roll in the Pacific Ocean's low swells.

The next morning, Colin warned Charles, "We're probably going to be assigned to some maintenance crew. Constant saltwater spray causes rust that needs to be scraped and repainted. On my last voyage I asked why Army soldiers were never assigned to these work crews. They just told me, 'Those Army grunts don't know bow from stern. You, on the other hand, are a trained Navy sailor. Enjoy the adventure.'"

Indeed, the second day at sea, both Charles and Colin drew duty assignments that included mopping the mess floor after each meal. The next day, Colin disappeared during breakfast. When he returned almost a half hour later, he was grinning widely.

"Guess what, Charles. We are relieved of all maintenance work details for the rest of the cruise."

"You make me happy, Colin. Now tell me how the hell you managed that."

"I talked to the corpsman and doctor in the ship's hospital. Colin Pope and Charles Beckner are now officially assigned to assist with daily sick call. We'll alternate. In return, we are off the general duty roster—how's that?" He still couldn't get the grin off his face.

"You're my hero, Colin. I'm sticking with you." *Experienced NCOs, like Colin, really know how the system works. I expect they can teach me things about the Navy that I'll never find in the books.*

"This is plush duty, Charles," It was the third night at sea, and Colin and Charles sat on their bunks. "On my last long cruise, it took me an hour every evening to clean grease and paint from my hands. Doing sick call is a piece of cake. Today, it was almost over before it started—just one seasick civilian and a seasick soldier. That was it."

"What'd you do for them?"

"The usual. I told them to stare at the horizon. If that doesn't work, go below and stare at something across the room that doesn't move. I suggested they lay off all food except for bread and water. In all honesty, I'm not sure any of that works, but it gave them something to do."

"I do appreciate your getting us off the maintenance details, Colin. Thanks." Charles paused a moment, then cautiously continued. "I have a problem. I've never experienced it before, and it's caught me off guard."

"What's that?" Colin asked.

"I'm not sleeping."

"OK. Tell the doctor about it," Colin swung his legs off the bunk, squared his feet, and stared at Charles.

"I tried to go to sleep the first night in this dark smelly room, but I felt unsettled. Shaky. I found myself sitting here, staring at the hull, thinking about the mass of ocean water on the other side of that steel plate. My stomach was churning, and I felt a sensation of impending doom. I was cold, but my shirt was soaked in sweat. My heart pounded, but when I took my pulse it was only fifty. I knew I couldn't go back to sleep, and I knew I couldn't stay here."

"So, what'd you do?"

"I was going to ask you about it, but you were sleeping like a baby. The seas were calm, so I went topside to the open deck for enlisted and non-coms. It was nearly deserted. Only two other men were there, leaning against the rail. I took a deep breath of fresh air, joined the other two at the rail, and looked at the moonlight reflecting to a distant horizon on that empty, vast ocean. A sailor at the rail asked me 'How're things?'"

"What'd you tell him?" Colin kept the story going.

"Without thinking, I said, 'Just great!' And it was true. The feeling of doom and my pounding pulse had disappeared. I looked at my hands, and they weren't sweaty or trembling."

Charles paused before asking, "How could I have gone from feeling so miserable to feeling so good in such a brief time?"

"Are you claustrophobic?" Colin suggested.

"No. At least I don't think so."

"Have you ever felt trapped in a small or dark room?"

"Not unless I was too young to remember it. I just felt the ocean might push the hull in on us."

"Pal, you're gonna have to stay far away from submarines."

"This is crazy. I'll just have to deal with it."

"Did you deal with it last night?"

"Yes."

"How?"

"I went topside again. I'll probably have to do that again tonight."

"Yep, you definitely should stay away from submarines."

Before lights-out, Charles looked in his dictionary, the *Hospital Corps Handbook*, and the *Merck Manual* for "claustrophobia" and then cross-referenced "agoraphobia." *Crowds never bother me. But confined spaces? Maybe. Like I told Colin, I can deal with it. No other option.*

Charles eventually forced himself asleep that night but woke two hours later with the same disturbing symptoms. He quietly pulled on his uniform, grabbed his coat, and climbed topside. Again, the symptoms disappeared. The weather continued fair all the way to Hawaii, so spending his nights on the deck became routine, talking with other insomniacs, stargazing, watching the moon's reflection dancing across the waves, and nodding in and out of sleep while waiting for dawn.

❧ ❧ ❧

After a few days at sea, boredom set in. Soldiers and sailors responded in time-honored fashion. Cards and dice magically appeared, and money changed hands. The losers mostly bemoaned their bad luck, but on occasion, they suspected they had been cheated—likely with some justification.

A late evening, halfway to Hawaii, Charles was topside contemplating a mattress and sleep, but knew if he tried sleeping below his symptoms would send him back to the open deck.

Colin came up the ladder and joined him. "Damn, Charles, it's getting hot down there."

"Vent shaft closed?"

"No, I mean tempers. One of the soldiers lost a big pot. He had a King-high straight and was reaching for the cash when the dealer, that short sailor, Samuel, I think that's his name, laid down a flush. The soldier took a swing at Samuel and yelled at him, calling him a cheat. He probably would have killed the guy if the others hadn't held him back. Things are still simmering. He's sure

USS Chaumont. *This ship took Charles to Manila in October 1940.*

he was cheated and isn't going to let it go. Everyone's retreated to their corner, at least for the time being. A couple of us think there might in fact have been some cheating."

Charles was silent for a minute, mentally going back to the card shark lectures at Mare Island. He tilted his head at Colin. "Let's go down. I have an idea."

In the deep hold of the ship the players had formed sides, stewing at opposite ends of the compartment. They wanted to continue playing—but not in what they suspected to be a dishonest game. Asking the six men to gather in the back corner, Charles made his pitch. "You're obviously a pretty hot group right now. Some think there's been cheating, others disagree. If anyone is interested, I think I might have a solution. You can have a poker game, and no one has to worry about cheating, just like you were in a proper casino."

"Yeah, and how you going to do that, son?" an older NCO challenged Charles, the lowest-ranking and youngest man in the room.

"Here's my proposal. I'm the dealer the whole game, but I don't deal to myself. I don't bet or have any other stake in winning or losing. We use my cards, and I guarantee they won't be marked. Anyone in the game can call for a cut anytime."

"And you're doing this because you like to deal cards?"

"No. I'm taking a five percent cut of every pot up to ten dollars. If it's a five-dollar pot, I get a quarter. I'll never take out more than fifty cents, so any pot over $10, no matter how large, my take will be just fifty cents. That's a fair share in return for a fair game." He paused, but everyone waited to see what else he would say.

"Everyone in the game knows that when it's over, win or lose, your chances were equal to everyone else. It'll be an honest game, with no cheating."

"That doesn't seem fair to the rest of us. You can't lose."

"Nor can I ever win a pot," Charles pointed out. "I'm not here to talk you guys into this. I was told you have a problem down here, and I'm trying to help, but only if you want me to. I really don't care. I'm going back topside now."

Fifteen minutes later Colin came up and found Charles. "They decided to take up your offer. In fact, there's five guys down there waiting for us. We all agree that this needs to be kept in the dark. Some officer might misunderstand the whole arrangement and feel a need to exercise his authority. He might even decide you're the ringleader, so be careful."

Charles stood up. "I hope I don't have a tiger by the tail."

The *Chaumont* being a passenger ship and not a battleship, they descended stairways instead of sliding down steep ladders.

Colin looked forward to this experiment. Charles was nervous.

With everyone ready to play, Charles unwrapped one of two new decks of cards he'd brought from Mare Island, thinking he might practice some card tricks. The game started with the usual tension and excitement, accompanied by rapid betting. After the fourth hand, Charles gathered the cards and was about to shuffle them when he noticed something. The otherwise smooth edge of the stacked deck was interrupted by two cards with slight crimps. He separated those cards; the Ace of hearts and Jack of hearts. A deep fingernail impression marked a different place on the edge of each card.

He placed the deck aside and pulled his spare deck from his pocket. He looked for a moment at each player. "Someone is trying to mark my cards. If it happens again, I'll go back topside, and you can kill each other for all I care."

Ultimately there were losers and winners, but in the end, everyone seemed satisfied that the game was fair. An older NCO even thanked him for dealing. After each hand, Charles had quietly put his small share of the pot in his pocket. At the end of the game, no one thought to ask how much Charles had collected.

Colin was curious. "When did you start running poker games, and why wait until there was a fight before making the offer to deal?"

"Never did it before—tonight was the first. I'd thought about it before. It's how they do it in a casino. These men knew I'm never in their poker games and accepted me as a disinterested dealer. It's mostly about trust. I thought five percent with a fifty cents limit was a fair take for guaranteeing a clean game."

"It worked out tonight. I'm sure they'll ask you to do it again."

"I have a nagging sensation there's a downside for me, somewhere, but right now I can't quite put my finger on it."

After six days of smooth sailing, on 18 October 1940, the *Chaumont* reached Hawaii. Charles and Colin stood at the rail, unabashedly gawking, as they passed the USS *Arizona*, steaming from Pearl Harbor for her scheduled overhaul at the Bremerton Naval Yard. The *Chaumont* docked for two nights at Pier 9, next to the 1926 lighthouse named Aloha Tower. A third of the passengers disembarked, Hawaii being their final destination. Stevedores began offloading cargo and replenishing the ship with fresh food and water.

Colin and Charles shook hands at the top of the gangplank. Charles joked, "Stay clear of those submarines," before adding, "We'll have to get together someday."

Colin, older and more experienced, responded truthfully. "In all honesty, maybe we will, but probably we won't. Sailors like us take one day at a time, Charles. We meet and become friends. Then one of us moves on. It's the Navy way."

He paused then smiled. "But I can tell you this. If I ever run into you again, I'll remember you, and we'll pick up from this point and go forward as if we were never apart. If ever the chance occurs for me to help you, I will. You and I are, and always will be, friends."

"Thanks, Colin. I'm OK as a loner most of the time, but now I'm having to say goodbye to every good friend I've made since starting basic training."

"Charles, in the Navy you're going to make a lot of good friends. Having to say 'goodbye' to someone is not losing them. You'll always have those friends, and you'll accumulate more. Fact is, I have so damn many good friends I've lost count, and I treasure every single one of them. Whether we meet again or not, it doesn't matter. Our friendship will always be there." He squeezed Charles's shoulder, "Good luck at Cavite."

He then turned and trotted down the gangplank without looking back.

Charles watched him disappear into the crowds. *Did Colin just give me one of the most important lessons about life in the Navy?*

The *Chaumont* continued its journey with a short stop at the tiny island of Guam. On the last night before reaching Manila, Charles, as usual, spent most of the night on deck. The sea was unusually calm, almost a mirror. A shimmering phosphorescence followed in the ship's wake.

He was standing at the deck railing when a thin red-orange line announced the coming dawn. A few minutes later, the sun breached the horizon, revealing land off both the port and starboard bows. *This must be the entrance to Manila Bay. I'm finally here.*

An older sailor, a chief petty officer, joined him at the rail. "Getting off here?" he asked.

"Yes, sir. Cañacao Hospital, at Cavite."

"You can't see Cavite from here. It's over there to starboard, on the south side of the bay. When we get a little farther in, you may be able to see some smoke or steam from the Cavite Navy Yard. If you have sharp eyes, you'll probably be able to see the top of the cranes."

"I take it you've been here before?"

"When I was about your age, my ship spent six weeks being serviced at the Navy Yard. I always wanted to come back, and finally I'm here. I'm going to be managing Navy supplies on Corregidor, right over there," he pointed to a double-humped mountain island on the port side. "Those higher mountains rising behind Corregidor are on Bataan. A deep-water passage, called the North Channel, runs on the other side of Corregidor Island, between it and the tip of the Bataan Peninsula. This wider passage we're in is the main channel. South, directly to starboard," he pointed, "Mount Palay-Palay marks the southern entrance to Manila Bay."

The older sailor continued talking as if he were describing his hometown to a stranger. "Manila Bay is one of the best harbors in the world. As I recall, it stretches twenty to thirty miles across, depending on where you measure. The average depth of the bay is well over fifty feet, so large ships are comfortable here. It's only the north side of the bay that's too swampy for any serious development." He pointed straight ahead. "In a few minutes you'll have your first glimpse of Manila itself."

The older sailor fell quiet as they both squinted into the morning sun.

For the next hour the *Chaumont* slowly steamed eastward through the bay.

Manila came into full view as the ship maneuvered towards City Dock No. 7. The city was much larger than Charles had imagined. Multistoried, modern buildings punctuated a broad expanse of one- and two-story structures. Looking directly south, he could indeed just make out Navy Yard cranes on Cavite piercing the horizon.

Charles sniffed the air. *That's something strange. It's not the usual fishy smell of seaports. It's something different.*

Anticipatory excitement passed through his body.

Part II

12

Arrival

Manila, Luzon Island, Philippine Islands

5 November 1940

Charles retrieved his sea bag and returned to watch crewmen maneuver the gangway into place. A man in civilian dress carrying a satchel and suitcase joined him at the rail. In his fifties, he wore steel-rimmed glasses on a long nose. "Are you disembarking too?" he asked Charles.

"Yes, sir. My first time in the Philippines. And you?"

"It's my third time to arrive at this dock. Even though it's 7,000 miles and three weeks from San Francisco, I look forward to the cruise every time. Unfortunately, I never get to stay in Manila for as long as I'd like. Most of my business is on the southern islands."

"Why are you on a government ship, if you don't mind my asking?"

"I work for a company setting up rubber processing plants. Rubber is a strategically critical product, so the government provides free passage if I'm traveling for that business. We have a plant on Basilan. I'm here for a few months to investigate sites for more plantations and processing plants. I'll primarily be looking for a site on Mindanao."

"I know about Mindanao—it's a big southern island. I haven't heard of Basilan, though."

"I'm not surprised, it's a small island but perfect for our rubber trees. The Philippines have a commonwealth government for now, and full independence is scheduled for 1946. My company wants to have established plants and

91

financial ties in place by then. By the way, my name is John."

"I'm Charles. You said you like Manila?"

"Love it dearly. Most Americans think that the Philippine Islands are undeveloped, and the Filipinos are nothing but half-naked brown-skinned people living in thatch huts. Look at that city though. It's a wonderfully diverse metropolis of almost 700,000 people. Besides the Filipinos, who are quite gregarious and a beautiful people, you'll encounter residents from every Asian and most European countries. I think close to 10,000 of us Yanks live here, and that doesn't count you military people."

"Do these different cultures get along with each other?"

"Well," John considered his answer, "the different nationalities tend to self-segregate, mostly socializing at their own clubs and restaurants. A terrific side benefit for me is that within those enclaves I've been able to find some of the best food in the world."

"What about the Japanese? Considering what they're doing in China, how do they fit in?"

"It's a complicated story."

"I'm not going anywhere."

"In a nutshell, then. After the Great War, Japan was ceded several regions and islands previously claimed by Germany, including territory on the Shandong Peninsula. The Shandong occupation was an insult to the Chinese for many reasons, not the least because Confucius was born there. Japan was forced to officially return that territory to China in 1922, but they kept their economic interest in place. They're now again claiming it to be Japanese territory."

"Why hasn't the rest of the world come to China's aid?"

"Like I said, it's complicated. In school, they probably didn't teach you that we, the U.S., overthrew the Hawaiian Kingdom in 1893 with a coup d'etat against Queen Lili'uokalani. That's how Hawaii became an American territory."

"They never talked about that, but I do know we have the Philippines as a result of the Spanish-American war."

"Yes, that tidy little war. The Filipinos were struggling with Spain for independence when we waltzed in and declared ourselves the new sheriff in town. We crushed their fight for independence in short order. Only 50 years later are we finally allowing the Filipinos their independence and self-determination. The world today might look down on imperialism, but it's actually a quite recent change in thinking. In their mind, the Japanese only followed the example of many other countries, including the United States."

"The encyclopedia said Japanese are living right here."

"Indeed, there are almost 10,000 Japanese living in Manila and perhaps twice that down south around Davo City on Mindanao. In their communities they speak only Japanese. Most of those I've met in business know at least a little English." He looked directly at Charles. "Let me give you some advice. You will find the Japanese unusually polite. Remember though, never, ever confuse 'polite' with 'friendly.'"

This place is more diverse than I realized. It brings to mind the Tower of Babel with people all speaking different tongues. "Is there a common language, one that Filipinos use in general?"

"It depends on where you are. Because of the American bases around Manila, almost everyone speaks at least a little English here. Outside Manila, you might hear some Spanish, but almost no English at all. It'll mostly be one of the hundred or more variants of Tagalog. Down south in the Visayas, they speak Cebuano, also called Bisaya. It's like Tagalog, but different," John shrugged.

Charles picked from the hundreds of questions running through his head, "I didn't expect so many large buildings."

"You're not the first," John chuckled. "It surprises most Americans when they first arrive here. It's really a quite modern city. Do you see that large six-story building down there on the waterfront?" He pointed.

"The huge one?"

"Yes. That's the Manila Hotel. It's fully air conditioned, and Douglas MacArthur lives with his family on the top floor. President Quezon treats his field marshal quite well."

Charles nodded as he took in the view from the railing. Surrounding the docks were staging areas, warehouses, and low-rise offices. Beyond the dockyards, color and texture were added by trees and bushes scattered among multi-story buildings. Smoke from cooking fires drifted among the buildings and down the streets.

This is a new, very different world. I'm a little anxious—but not scared.

The *Chaumont* secured at Pier 7, claimed by some to be the longest dock in the world. People packed the arrival area between the ships and terminal buildings, waiting expectantly for the new arrivals. Officers on the dock shouted and excitedly waved when they identified their arriving family at the ship's railing.

Charles slung his sea bag over one shoulder and offered to carry John's suitcase to the dock.

"Might as well take your pack off, Charles. My experience is that they are more formal with arrivals here than in Hawaii. I expect they'll announce instructions for disembarkation in pre-arranged groups. The diplomatic corps will be first, military officers second, nurses next, and then you enlisted troops. Civilians like me are the bottom of the pecking order. It's a good show though," John nodded towards the gangway.

The first to depart, an elegantly dressed diplomat, stepped onto the gangway, and a small band in white dress uniform began to play.

The concert continued as military officers descended to the dock, followed by a dozen nurses. Charles watched the nurses make their way down the gangway like debutantes, dressed in their finest, including hats and heels. *That was amusing.*

Officer-husbands greeted arriving family and led them from the dock. The Army nurses assembled for their official welcome by an Army major before being ushered through the terminal to waiting cars. These nurses were whisked to one of four Army hospitals around Manila. Two Navy nurses were greeted

Cavite Peninsula, aerial view, October 1941. Cavite City and Navy Yard in foreground. Sangley Point in background, with USS Langley *(AV3) at dock.*

with a warm handshake and escorted to a Navy sedan.

When the last nurse stepped to the dock, the small band stopped playing and disappeared with their instruments through the crowd. Loudspeakers finally announced, "Non-commissioned and enlisted U.S. military with orders can now leave the ship." Charles shook John's hand and joined the other sailors and soldiers walking down the gangway. None expected a special reception. They were not disappointed.

A few feet after leaving the gangway, Charles stopped to absorb a fresh sensation. *There's no ship's roll! I'm standing on solid ground. I haven't been off the* Chaumont *since departing San Francisco twenty-three days ago and it's a little disconcerting. I wonder how long it'll take to get my 'land legs' back?*

At the end of the dock, outside the terminal building, a blue Navy bus waited. A printed sign, reading "Cavite," leaned against its front windshield.

"Does this bus go near the Cañacao Navy Hospital?" Charles inquired.

"Near enough to leave tire tracks on the grass," the seaman in the driver's seat confirmed. "I'll stop there first and then turn around for the Navy Yard. Throw your bag on the rack and grab a seat."

With a dozen passengers hanging on, the bus picked its way through the rather seedy dockside part of the city. A half-mile later they passed through streets lined with businesses of every type. The commercial street gave way to attractive city boulevards and finally narrowed to a small road through the rural countryside south of the city.

Sitting in the front bench seat, Charles asked the driver, "What's that unusual odor I've been smelling since the ship docked?"

The driver laughed. "You mean that pungent smell like nothing you've ever smelled before?"

"Yes, that."

"It's copra, drying coconut meat. The locals spread it out to dry and then extract the coconut oil. Get used to it. That smell is everywhere in the Philippines."

Outside the city, the copra odor mixed with wafting fumes from charcoal hibachi cooking fires. Underlying the copra and charcoal smell was the powerful fecundity of equatorial forest. The bus passed into scenery that reflected most Americans' image of the islands: Steep-roofed thatch huts on stilts lined the road, with naked children playing underneath the thatch. The bus competed with trucks, bicycles, two-wheeled horse-drawn cabs, and wagons pulled by *carabao*, the ubiquitous Philippine water buffalo.

Charles found some familiarity in the experience. *Even though the smells are strange, and the houses look different, beneath that there's similarity to my family back in southern Indiana. Good people, scratching a living from the land.*

It was near noon, and Charles found the heat and humidity palpable. "Is it always this hot and sticky?" he asked the driver.

"Yep. You'll just have to get used to it. We're only a few degrees north of the equator. Temperatures will reach 90 most days and drop only to the mid-70s at night. The humidity is usually above 80 percent, even if it's not raining."

"When's the dry season?"

"The rains are less frequent between Christmas and Easter, but it's still hot and humid."

"I can see why people live in those grass houses. It's probably cooler up on those stilts."

"Those are called *nipa* huts." The driver was used to new arrivals and accustomed to their questions. "*Nipa* is the local fiber they're made from. They build them on stilts to get above the water and mud in wet season. It also keeps wild animals from wandering through the houses at night."

"I don't see any electric wires or plumbing."

"Because most of them don't have either one—a hole in the floor serves for a toilet. Everything drops into a pit dug in the ground underneath. All their water is carried up in five-gallon cans. It's not as romantic as it might look from a distance."

"I suppose not." Charles tried to gain some relief by holding the sweat-soaked shirt away from his chest and letting air blow through the window. It didn't help.

"You can see the Cavite Navy Yard now." Keeping one hand on the steering wheel, the bus driver pointed across the bay to a strip of land with ships, dry docks, cranes, and warehouses.

Charles remembered looking at Cavite on the map; the peninsula jutted into Manila Bay like a claw. He had pictured it by making a letter "C" with his left hand in front of his face. His wrist was the main peninsula, his thumb the lower pincer of the claw, and his fingers the upper pincer.

That must be the old towns of San Roque and Cavite at the base of the peninsula. The rest is obviously the Navy Yard, with all those docks, cranes, and warehouses. That point of land has been a shipyard for centuries. I read that the Spanish Empire reached its greatest extent when it colonized these islands, and what's now our Navy Yard was where the Spanish built their famous Spanish Galleons, the sailing ships that took all the wealth back to Spain.

I can't see it from here, but I know the upper pincer of Cavite Peninsula is Sangley Point, originally a Spanish coaling station and arsenal.

On a strip joining the upper and lower pincers, three giant, 600-foot-high

Cañacao Naval Hospital, Cavite, Philippine Islands, 1941. The Hospital Reservation is in the trees in front of the three 600' radio towers. Sangley Point is off the picture to the right, and the Navy Yard is off the picture to the left.

towers stretched skyward. Pointing to the soaring towers, Charles said to the driver, "I've never seen anything that tall—what are they for?"

"Radio towers," the driver answered, "for military communications. The Navy uses them to keep in contact with ships and submarines around the Philippines and out into the South China Sea. Here's the hospital reservation, Doc, right next to those towers. Have a good tour."

Wow! In front of Charles stood what was perhaps the finest hospital facility in Asia. The attractive three-story structure stood among shade trees. Sun awnings shielded the windows of the first two floors, while oversized eaves protected those of the top floor.

Nurses' apartments stood next to the hospital, shaded by a huge, multi-rooted banyan tree. Landscaped walkways crisscrossed the hospital grounds. A shaded arcade of mahogany trees led to the small hospital ferry dock. Miniature lighthouses illuminated the adjacent seawall.

Charles surveyed his new home for a moment. *So far, very impressive.* He entered the main door to stand on two-inch solid mahogany plank flooring, polished to a high sheen with coconut oil. *I'm still impressed. Now to find the administrative offices.*

"Hospital Apprentice 1st Class Beckner reporting for duty, sir." He handed a copy of his orders to Senior Chief Petty Officer Toole. The chief sat behind a dark mahogany desk that seemed itself to grow from the mahogany floor.

"Welcome aboard, Charles. Have a seat. You'll learn your way around soon enough, but let me give you the quick overview. We may be a small hospital, but we provide first-rate medical and surgical care for all Navy personnel in the region. That includes close to a thousand men and a hundred or so dependents here on Cavite. There're also several thousand civilian workers here, but for the most part they're not our responsibility. Occasionally we send one of our patients up to Sternberg Army hospital if they need specialty care we don't provide here. The Shipyard has its own dispensary, staffed with general medical officers and corpsmen for routine checks and physical exams, in addition to minor illnesses and injuries that don't need a hospital."

"What's our staffing?" Charles asked, already using the possessive term for his new assignment.

"We have about 125 sailors and officers—fourteen are commissioned officers, including the commander and ten doctors."

"What about nurses?" Charles asked.

"OK, that's another thirteen officers. I think you'll find them good at their jobs and happy to be here. In the Philippines, a single American woman is a rare commodity. I doubt they ever pay for a drink. We're a big family here and a bit less formal than stateside, but remember that for you, the nurses are untouchable."

"Understood, sir."

"Now, just a few more points. Corpsmen work 'tropical hours' in the hospital. That's 0700 to 1300 hours one day and 0700 to 2100 hours the next day. It's the same as 'head-and-toe' shifts back in the States, or 'port and starboard' as we call it in the Navy. The night shift is long, 2100-0700 hours. Most people find it near-impossible to sleep in the daytime heat, so everyone shares the night shifts equally."

The chief continued with what Charles now realized was his standard talk for new enlisted men. "Depending on your interest, Manila is where most of the action happens. You can catch the ferry right out there at the hospital dock. It runs the eight-mile route from here to Manila on a regular schedule. Be careful in Manila, especially on the first day or two after a big Navy ship arrives and gives the men shore liberty to blow off steam. Drinking and cat-housing often leads to fights. Most often it's just a couple of sailors, but occasionally swabbies square off against ground pounders. Stay away from drunk Marines. They stick together like glue and fight in packs."

He paused. "And trust me, neither sailor nor Marine wants a faceoff with the Army MPs—they don't like you and it shows. If you're in a tight spot, try to find the Shore Patrol and turn yourself in."

Looking at the calendar on the wall and then at Charles, he went on. "Today is Tuesday. I'm giving you tomorrow and Thursday to find your way around and get settled. I'm putting you on the surgical ward for now. Report there at 0700 hours Friday. Check with the nurse in charge, and she'll orient you. Any questions?"

"Just one, Chief Toole. Is there a good library around here?"

13

Surprise!

Cavite, Philippine Islands

6 November 1940

Refreshed from his first full night's sleep in a bed since Mare Island, Charles began Wednesday signing paperwork in the personnel office and arranging for the paymaster's office to continue sending most of his salary home. After lunch, he walked the hospital reservation and sat at the hospital dock, watching ships and barges cross the bay. He took note when the shuttle ferry arrived and exchanged passengers. *I think I'll take the early ferry to Manila tomorrow.*

It was still dark when he got out of bed on Thursday. While showering and shaving, he made new plans. *Manila can wait. I need to explore closer to home first. The Cavite peninsula's not that large. I think I can walk the whole place, top to bottom, today.*

Full of coffee, bacon, eggs, and toast, he walked north towards Sangley Point. In only a few minutes he arrived at a long floating dock, recently built for Pan American Airways. A China Clipper seaplane floated at the end of the dock with engines idling, while three men removed tie-down lines in preparation for departure. The four-engine plane was huge, larger than any Charles had ever seen.

He walked down the dock for a closer view, encountering a fourth crewman blocking his way, who said, "I'm sorry, you can't go out there right now."

"Sorry—I've just never seen a plane like this before."

"It's something, isn't it! That's a Martin M-130. It needs only six days to

100

bring mail and packages from San Francisco to Manila."

"What about passengers?" Charles thought he could see people inside the short row of windows.

"Yep, people too, if weight permits. She brought a dozen people from San Francisco on this last trip. The passenger cabin is small, but it's pure luxury."

"Surely they are not flying the whole six days?"

"Of course not," the crewman laughed. "Actual flying time is only sixty hours. It stops for fuel and supplies at Pearl Harbor, Midway, Wake, and Guam."

"That's pretty much where my ship stopped on the way here. How often do they make that trip?"

"Lately, it's been only three times a month. The *Hawaii Clipper* disappeared during a flight earlier this year, so every fourth or fifth flight had to be cancelled. A new Boeing 314 was just added to the fleet, so we'll be returning to a weekly schedule next month."

"I'll look for it then."

Charles watched the men cast off the last line and push the plane from the dock. *Should they be called a water crew instead of a ground crew?*

The plane taxied a short distance into the bay and the four engines roared to full power. After trailing a spray of water for two hundred yards, it gracefully lifted from the bay's surface and banked to the east.

Cañacao Naval Hospital, 1927.

Watching the seaplane shrink to a dot and disappear, Charles squinted into the morning sun. *They were right about the heat. It's only mid-morning, and I'm sweating like a sinner in church.*

He returned to the road and continued to Sangley Point, passing two long boat repair slips. Beyond tall stacks of oil barrels and large tanks of fuel, a concrete seaplane ramp sloped into the water next to a small dock. Several Navy seaplanes floated offshore, attached to buoys. *I think those are the same PBYs Martin and I watched take off from San Diego Bay last year.* Three more PBYs, fitted with wheels, sat on the tarmac near a hangar still under construction. Shirtless, sweating sailors worked on one of the plane's engines.

"Hi there," Charles approached the men at the plane. "Charles Beckner. Fresh from the States and starting at the Cañacao Hospital tomorrow. I'm just exploring."

"Too bad," one of the sailors replied. "This place is a real shit-hole."

"Yep," said another, "you're going to hate it. Hopefully your mother will get a deadly disease, and the Navy will send you back home early to take care of her."

Charles was too stunned to reply. Then the men all erupted into laughter.

The mechanics moved Charles to the shade of the PBY's broad wing.

"Welcome to Cavite, Doc," said one, noting the red cross insignia on Charles's sleeve. "You're going to love this place. Once you get past the heat, it's more than OK. Price of living is cheap, and quality of life is good! The officers out here are mostly good guys and more concerned with their golf score than riding our asses. Frank, our corpsman, isn't here right now, but since you're at the hospital, you'll probably run into him before long."

The banter continued until someone mentioned that it would be a good idea to finish their work on the engine before the real heat descended after noon. They all shook hands again, and Charles took his leave.

Using the giant radio towers for orientation, he backtracked along Cañacao Bay, passing the Pan American dock and the hospital reservation. Following signs to the US Navy Yard, he crossed a narrow causeway to the southern arm of the peninsula. Cañacao Bay, where the seaplanes floated at their moorings, was to the north, on his left. South, on his right, was Bacoor Bay. The Navy Yard's docks and piers faced the larger, deeper Bacoor Bay.

Decayed remnants of old stone fortifications and the historic San Roque gate were reminders that Cavite had once been Spain's center of commerce in the Far East. Inside the gate, church towers rose above the town's lower buildings. *I remember a long Britannica paragraph on religion in the Philippines. It described it as mostly Islam and Christian today, but older native beliefs like animism still mix with both of those religions.* Peering through a church door out of curiosity, he removed his hat.

"Welcome to Santa Monica."

Charles turned toward the voice, seeing a diminutive figure. As his eyes adjusted to the dim light, he saw it was a Filipino priest arranging candles before a statue of the Madonna. "Good afternoon. I didn't mean to disturb you—uh, Father?"

The priest finished with the candles and turned to Charles, smiling. "Questioning how to address me suggests you are not Catholic. I assume you are Christian, so you are welcome here whatever your denomination."

"If you are Filipino, your English is remarkably perfect. Is that the case with all priests here?"

"Not all. I am from the islands, but I spent four years in California as a young man. It was an excellent opportunity to acquire fluency in American English. With all of you Americans here at Cavite, I stay in practice. Are you new to our community?"

"Arrived day before yesterday. I'm starting at the Cañacao Hospital tomorrow, and I'm walking around Cavite today, just exploring. This looks like a very old town."

The priest smiled. "You can call me 'Father Francis,' or just 'Father.' And your name is?"

"Charles, Father Francis."

"Yes, Charles, my town is very old. Did you know that Ferdinand Magellan arrived in the Philippines 400 years ago?"

"He was the Spanish explorer who first circled the world?"

"Well, he was Portuguese, but you are correct, that voyage was funded by the Spanish King, and he didn't quite make the full circumnavigation. At any rate, Magellan never reached this bay. He was killed south of here, on the small island of Mactan, across from Cebu City. Cavite, here where we stand, was permanently settled by the Spanish almost 300 years ago. Those early Spanish ships always carried priests to bring the light of Christianity. At one time Cavite City boasted eight churches and a Jesuit College within these fortifications."

"Are there any American churches? I mean, Baptist or Presbyterian maybe?"

The priest shook his head. "Need I remind you that the Philippine Islands are only recently and quite temporarily 'American'? To end their war with the United States, Spain 'gave' my country to your country. We are for now an American Commonwealth, but in six years will finally gain our complete independence. As for your question about other churches, look on your own bases. Otherwise you'll be hard pressed to find anything other than a Catholic church on Luzon. Elsewhere, especially on the southern islands, you will also find Islamic mosques."

"Will America close these bases and leave when you, the Philippine Islands, become independent?"

"Not at all—the independence is accompanied by treaties and agreements, besides which we are economically dependent on each other. The old shipyards and stone walls of Fort San Felipe were torn down or built over by the US Navy, and now my town and your Navy base are inseparable, geographically and culturally as well as economically."

"Is that, for you, a good or a bad thing?"

"Maybe more good than bad," Father Francis mused. "Almost everyone here depends on the US Navy. Even if we don't work on the base, we depend on the sailors to spend money in our stores or businesses. Still, I think we could do fine on our own, without you." The priest sat down, inviting Charles to join him on the pew, ready to extend their discussion.

"I have a lot to learn about this country. Thank you for the information, but maybe I could come back another time?"

"Of course. You are welcome to come here anytime, to talk or to pray. *Vaya con Dios.*"

Leaving the church and continuing his eastward walk through the town towards the Navy Yard, Charles shared the street with pedestrians, cars, *carabao*-pulled wagons, and two-wheeled horse-drawn carts the bus driver called *kalesas*. Somehow this mixed traffic moved with reasonable efficiency.

At the eastern edge of Cavite City, Charles crossed to the gate of the US Navy Yard Reservation. Civilians, sailors, and soldiers passed in and out of the entrance. Charles approached a gate sentry. "I'm a new arrival at Cañacao Hospital. Can you tell me about this place?"

The guard checked a truck onto the base, turned back to Charles, and furrowed his brow. "I'll try, but I've been here less than a year myself. The Yard is our base for the entire Asiatic Fleet. Barracks. Deepwater docks. Refitting and resupply. Machine shops. Some dry docks. Warehouses. *Lots* of warehouses. Some gasoline and fuel oil are stored here, but there's more fuel storage over on Sangley Point."

"Looks like a busy place."

"I think there's around 500 US Navy assigned here, and about the same number of Filipino Navy reservists. Most of the people working here are civilians, several thousand of them. All this is stuffed onto only fifty acres, so it's crowded. Go ahead and explore if you want to. The restricted areas have warning signs."

Past the gate, Charles entered a different world, full of activity and noise. Marines and sailors worked alongside civilians. Cranes unloaded barges while forklifts and tractors moved goods to warehouses and storage pads around the base. The sounds of truck engines, cranes, and machine tools came and went as he walked about the yard. Clicking from typewriters spilled through the window of an office building. At a short dock, passengers waited for the Manila ferry. A seaplane flew low over the adjacent bay.

He struck up a conversation with two sailors on smoking break. They took time to give Charles unsolicited advice. "Cavite is OK, but the action is all up north in the city. There's an E-5 and below club here, but the Army and Navy Enlisted Club on the Manila docks near the ferry landing is much larger and, for my money, much better."

The other sailor added, "I think you'll find better-looking girls in Manila than here. If the fleet is out, their business will be slow, and for ten bucks you can spend the night."

"If you do that, you better sleep holding your wallet instead of the girl," laughed the first one.

Returning to the hospital reservation and his barrack, Charles showered off the sweat and put on a dryer uniform before going to mess. Afterward, he continued what was now a daily routine of memorizing at least one new word from his dictionary.

Machination /*ma-kə-ˈnā-shən*/
n. 1. an act of machinating. 2. a scheming or crafty action or artful design intended to accomplish some usually evil end.

Hmm. I'll look for an opportunity to use that tomorrow. He lay back on the bunk and considered the day. *Once I get used to the muggy weather, this should be an OK place to spend a couple of years. After that, it'll be back to the States, hopefully San Diego.*

ʕ ʕ ʕ

The next morning Charles had coffee, powdered eggs, and sausage at 0600 and walked into the hospital a few minutes before 0700 for his first day of work. Smartly dressed in lightweight hospital duty whites, he approached the surgical ward nurses' station. The nurse at the main desk was writing notes with her back to Charles, and all he could see was her hair. He coughed to announce his presence; and she raised her hand, signaling for him to wait.

When she finally turned, he was momentarily overwhelmed, too shocked to move or speak. *I should have recognized that hair!*

"Tillie! I mean Miss—"

"Charles!"

Tillie rushed to his arms and held him in a long, tight hug. When they realized other staff were staring, both stepped back, but momentarily held hands before recovering some decorum.

Tillie stared at Charles. It was only six months since she last saw him on Mare Island, but in that time he had grown taller. He still looked, and felt, lean and sinewy, but not skinny. The thick dark hair and blue eyes remained, and his smile was as engaging as ever. Despite the boyish good looks, he was unmistakably more man than boy.

Charles spoke first. "You disappeared from Mare Island without a word. I was told you'd had some type of emergency, and I thought you might have gone home."

"No, Charles. After you and I talked about it that one night, I realized that

Cañacao Hospital Staff, 1941. Charles is in 5th row, middle (See insert).

my life was pretty good as a Navy nurse. Independence, steady income, all that. I'd already decided to extend when I got a call asking if I wanted to fill an open assignment here in the Philippines. Two positions opened when one of the nurses decided to get married and another developed a serious medical issue. They offered me one of the positions but needed a decision on the spot. I had to drop everything because the *Chaumont* was already in San Francisco and leaving the next morning. I packed, picked up my orders, and jumped on the first ferry to the Embarcadero. So, here I am!"

"It would have been nice if you'd said goodbye." Charles knew he sounded petulant.

"I assumed administration would tell everyone what happened to me, but I guess the word didn't get around the hospital. I'm sorry. If it makes you feel any better, I didn't get to say goodbye to most of my other friends either. Please forgive me?"

"Of course. You look happy. This place must be treating you well?"

"It's OK here. We have our own two-story nurses' quarters with screened-in verandas. Help is cheap. We pool money to pay a group of Filipinos to keep everything from the floors to the windows spotless. A woman comes by every other day for our laundry. Most of us get our uniforms and civilian clothes custom-made in Manila or Cavite City. Drinks in the officers' clubs are five and ten cents, and the food's almost that cheap. One of the few downsides is the muggy weather, but one learns to live with it. All in all, it's hard to complain."

He was amused by her exuberance. "And I expect the ratio of handsome officers to young nurses is to your advantage?" Charles raised his eyebrows.

Tillie gave him a "Do you really want to ask that" look before responding, "Well, you know I won't have anything to do with those I know are married, but there are still enough single officers to keep my dancing shoes limber."

Agreeing they'd make time for more catching up later, Tillie gave Charles a quick tour of the ward and introduced him to two other corpsmen. "These guys will bring you up to speed."

Four large bays held ten beds each. The first bay was for eye, ear, nose, and throat surgery patients. The second bay was for patients having "clean" surgery, procedures with low risk of infection such as hernia repair. The third bay was for patients undergoing "dirty" surgery—appendectomies, intestinal operations, or repair of contaminated injuries. By segregating these patients in a separate bay, it was hoped to prevent contamination and infection of the recovering "clean" patients.

It took Charles only a few days to adapt to hospital routine. He and the other corpsmen performed most of the basic nursing functions. They changed bandages, drew blood for tests, emptied bed pans, and recorded vital signs. Filipino employees changed bed linen and did other housekeeping chores.

At the end of the first week, Charles exchanged smiles with Tillie as she left the hospital. He recalled her hug and the feel of her body against his when she saw him the first day here at Cañacao. *Tillie still reminds me of my sister Mary, but I sure don't think of her as a sister right now. This could be difficult.*

ᔕ ᔕ ᔕ

The small hospital library maintained a reasonable mixture of newspapers. Though days or even weeks old, the English-language British, Australian, and American newspapers provided news from the European front.

More current, though less detailed, broadcasts from the U.S. reached the Philippines by shortwave radio. Some stories were re-transmitted, most consistently by radio station KZRH in Manila, as part of their normal programming.

Official military communications flowed continuously between the American high command and Washington, D.C. Some of that information was passed down from headquarters, through the official chain of command, to the general troops. More often, military news moved by the unofficial, unsanctioned information network that exists in any military organization, the 'jungle telegraph.' In the old sailing ships, sailors exchanged news and rumors while gathered around the 'scuttled butt' that held fresh drinking water. 'Scuttlebutt' became Navy slang for this unofficial mixture of rumor, fantasy, and occasionally accurate information.

At present, all civilian and military sources agreed that the war was not going well for Britain. The German bombing blitz on London began in September with conventional explosives. The Luftwaffe soon discovered that incendiary bombs were far more destructive. The resulting firestorms raged throughout the city, and London was gradually losing its architectural treasures. Anti-aircraft batteries had some success against the German bombers, but more effective were the RAF Spitfire fighter planes that flew from scattered farmland runways and engaged the German bombers daily. The Battle of Britain was underway.

Hitler pressed Churchill to surrender. Roosevelt urgently called for America to increase aid to Britain as the "best way to halt dictators and avoid war." Even American isolationists, finally alarmed by the Führer's occupation of Norway and France, began questioning the wisdom of continued neutrality.

In the distant Philippine Islands, many Americans chose willful ignorance. Dining and dancing in the Army and Navy club, golfing, game hunting, and the pleasures of Manila nightlife were effective diversions. On base, food and liquor were heavily subsidized. Filipino houseboys, cooks, seamstresses, and washer women provided cheap services. All of this allowed a life of luxury, suppressing thoughts of the conflict consuming Europe to the point of complete denial. Most married Army officers on Luzon were accompanied by their families and continued their country club lifestyles, seemingly oblivious to any threat of war.

The Navy command was more circumspect. In the summer of 1940, with little fanfare, the Navy halted approval for dependents to accompany men newly assigned to the southwest Pacific. Shortly thereafter, Navy dependents still in the Philippines received instructions and passage to return to Hawaii or the American mainland no later than December 1940.

The Navy, if not the Army, believed war with Japan was inevitable.

14

Guns and Medicine

Cañacao Naval Hospital, Cavite Peninsula, Philippine Islands

December 1940

Charles left the hospital after a double-back shift, having worked twenty-four hours straight. He was exhausted but the afternoon was too hot for good sleeping. He had just dozed off when unusual noises from multiple aircraft woke him. The engine sounds were not the distinctive and familiar harmonics of the B-17s from nearby Clark Field. Curiosity overcoming fatigue, he threw on some clothes, left the barrack, and looked skyward where fourteen twin-engine aircraft circled. One by one, each broke from the formation and descended to land in Cañacao Bay south of Sangley Point. When they were closer, Charles recognized the planes as PBYs, but their hull numbers were from a Squadron 26, not the Squadron 21 based at Sangley Point.

I can't sleep. Might as well go to the seaplane base to see what's up.

Twenty minutes later he arrived at Sangley Point, sweating from the fast walk. He found the squadron corpsman sorting files. "Hi, Frank. Are these new PBYs reinforcements, or are they just stopping on their way to somewhere else?"

"Hi to you too, Charles. I was just getting medical record folders ready for our new aircrews. Let's go watch them come in." Frank talked while they watched the last plane land and the PBY crewmen brought to shore in small launches. "This new group is Squadron VP-26 from Hawaii. Their fourteen PBYs are permanently joining us here at Sangley Point. Squadrons VP-21 and

110

VP-26 are being renamed VP-101 and VP-102. The two squadrons, along with our utility squadron of five single-engine seaplanes, are creating a new unit, Patrol Wing 10."

Charles thought a moment. "You've more than doubled in size. Will your operations change?"

"It's already changed. A year ago, we were mostly moving people and supplies around the islands, with an occasional search and rescue. For the past month though, ninety percent of our flight time is on extended patrol. We're observing Japanese ships and tracking their movements along the coast from Shanghai all the way to Saigon. I'll be honest, the Japanese military incursions and occupations are impressive, both in size and speed."

"Is that general knowledge?"

"To be honest, Charles, there aren't any secrets around here. The flight crews all talk after returning from patrol. I can tell you that the Japanese army and navy have been moving in parallel down the coast of China, occupying the coastal cities and harbors with virtually no resistance. So far, we do nothing more than watch it happen." Frank looked at the new planes bobbing in the bay. "I guess we can do a lot more watching now. Meanwhile, I've got to get medical records set up on all these new men. Always good to see you, Charles."

Many of the Filipinos living close to Navy bases were official U.S. government employees. An almost equal number were paid directly by the sailors for personal services. Laundry, shoe shining, and a myriad of other chores could be cheaply hired out by the relatively wealthy Americans, even junior enlisted sailors. Since these Filipinos understood at least elementary English, few Americans made any effort to learn Filipino languages.

Charles worked alongside native employees in the hospital and considered them a generally happy people. Speaking Tagalog, they often laughed among themselves. In fact, they laughed a lot. Sometimes they even laughed when working alone. For some reason, this bothered Charles. *Am I paranoid, or are they making fun of me?*

He decided to force the issue when he heard two Filipinos laughing behind him.

Turning, he asked, "What's so funny?"

"What you mean?" the older man was smiling.

"I mean, are you laughing at me? Am I funny?"

Charles was not wearing his friendly face.

"Oh no, sir!" The man smiled even wider. "This is my nephew Arthur. He does not speak very much English. He was only telling me that his wife was mad at him yesterday and made him sleep outside because he complained about her food. I told him he was lucky she didn't hit him with her iron pot. I think you are new here?" He pointed to his name tag, "My name is Armando."

Oh. They weren't making fun of me. "Sorry, I didn't know why you were laughing. You were speaking Tagalog?"

"Sort of—it was mostly Tagalog with some Spanish mixed in. I think I threw in some English words here and there too. Sometimes I'm not sure myself what language I'm saying!" Arthur and Armando laughed together.

"Arthur is an English name, and Armando sounds Spanish. I expected, well, I thought—you'd have more traditional Filipino names."

"No, sir. Here around Manila, people think Tagalog names are old-fashioned. Our parents have Spanish names mostly, but a lot of younger people, like Arthur, have American names."

"Armando, if I wanted to be able to speak to Filipinos who don't understand English, should I learn Spanish or Tagalog?"

"Well, sir, here in Manila, or even around Luzon, it doesn't make much difference. If you want to travel anywhere else, you should learn at least a little Tagalog, even if it is a little different on every island. Down south you will hear Bisaya, same as Cebuano. It's like Tagalog, but not really."

"So I've been told." Charles acknowledged, then asked, "Can you teach me a little Tagalog?"

Armando grinned. "I will teach you the Tagalog of Manila, and if you can be very patient, we can both try to teach my nephew some American English." They laughed, with even Arthur joining in.

Charles studied the words and phrases from Armando with the same intensity he gave to his dictionary. Eventually he tried his halting Tagalog with other Filipinos in the hospital. It would have been a stretch to call it conversational, but gradually he gathered enough courage to try using Filipino words at local shops and food stalls.

By the end of February, he was ready to attempt a test run in a Cavite City restaurant with two friends. Charles waited until last to order and said haltingly, "*Magkakaroon ako ng isang malaking San Miguel at ang pritong isda.*"

Charles was relieved when the man taking his order smiled broadly. Not only were his friends surprised and impressed, Charles was himself a bit surprised when the waiter brought the San Miguel beer and fried fish he was hoping he'd asked for. From that night, in Filipino bars, food stalls, and restaurants, he made his request in Tagalog. It wasn't only his pleasure at the look of surprise in his companions' faces—it often seemed his beer was colder and his serving larger when he ordered in the proprietor's native language.

Cañacao Hospital was not simply a small version of Balboa or Mare Island hospitals. The patients, often teenagers or barely beyond, were in a strange land a long way from home for the first time. Enlisted sailors with an unexpected medical problem often viewed their corpsmen as their general practitioner—finding it easier to speak freely and frankly with a corpsman, their peer, than to a nurse or doctor.

In the barracks, mess halls, and enlisted clubs, Charles and the other corpsmen were regularly approached for informal opinions on minor medical problems or unexplained symptoms. Sometimes the corpsmen had to assume the role of chaplain. Confronting homesickness, disappointment, or guilt, a sailor could trust most corpsmen to be a discrete confessor and non-judgmental listener. More than once, a sailor pulled Charles aside and whispered "Hey, I've got this problem. Understand what I'm talking about?"

He was not entirely unprepared for that question. Back at Mare Island Charles had trained for two weeks in the Clap Clinic. Gonorrhea, or "clap" from the old French word for brothel, *clapier*, was endemic in most Asian ports. The medical officer in charge of the Mare Island clinic had been a Navy-trained tropical disease specialist, and he was considered the local expert in sexually transmitted diseases.

Charles clearly recalled the day he asked if gonorrhea and syphilis were still a major problem in the Navy. It was as if he had flipped a switch. The doctor turned to face Charles directly and launched into his standard classroom lecture, kept in reserve for that very question. "Venereal disease management in the service is not simply a moral issue, it has practical and tactical importance. If someone's not healthy, they either can't do their job, or they don't do it well." He paused to light a cigarette before continuing. "Blood test evidence of previous or current syphilis in Army enlistees is about the same as the civilian rate; 25-30 percent. The Navy's active duty rate is about twice that, and the rate for gonorrhea is even higher. If it's necessary to hospitalize a man for treatment, he could be off duty for weeks. Some cases prove incurable, and he'll eventually be discharged and sent home."

"And all that costs the Navy resources and money?" Charles suggested.

"That's right." The doctor inhaled deeply, then blew the smoke upward towards the ceiling. "End of lecture and smoking break. Back to work now."

Charles pulled his mind back to the present. *I need to find out how this is handled over here. Chief Toole should be willing to fill me in.* He began a closed-door session with the Chief by asking, "What's the Navy doing about . . well, about the gonorrhea that seems to be rampant here in the Philippines?"

Toole tilted his head and realized Charles's question was not a challenge to Navy policy, but a serious question. "The Navy, officially at least, believes that attempts to segregate and regulate prostitution don't work. In other words, the official policy is not to regulate and inspect the sex workers. We're supposed to pretend they're not there."

"But they are," Charles retorted. "That doesn't sound like a realistic policy, sir."

"Of course it's not. While it's not officially allowed on the bases here or in Manila, the Navy couldn't shut down prostitution if they tried. The houses are run like assembly lines and vary from very cheap, around $1 at the upper-class places, to incredibly cheap, as little as a quarter for a brief encounter in the places with no class." He looked at Charles, "I may not be telling you anything you don't know or haven't already heard."

Charles pressed the issue. "If a sailor is officially diagnosed with VD, is he in administrative trouble?"

"To be truthful, it's not that simple over here, and it's not limited to the enlisted. Some of the single officers and Class B bachelors, those whose wives or fiancées are back in the States, enjoy their liaisons as well. For as little as $50, they can have a *nipa* hut built and maintain a personal concubine. One benefit of that practice is that the monogamous arrangement lessens the likelihood of contracting an STD."

"So, it's unofficially sanctioned?"

"Unofficially ignored. And then there's the White Russians—"

"Wait—the whats?" Charles interrupted.

"A 'White Russian' is a term for anyone who openly supported the Czar. After the revolution, a lot of them left Russia, and some came to Manila by way of Singapore. Those tall Russian women can be very attractive to American men. Some of them provide escort services of, let's say, a higher class."

"So, how should I handle sailors who approach me unofficially and not get in trouble myself?"

"No easy answer. Here's how things have been for the past few years. We can't change the availability of cheap girls and cheap alcohol, so we do the best we can through education and prevention. Long before you arrived, we got approval to set up condom stations on Cavite and at the Manila bases. Condoms are provided free at a rate of six per man, per month. It's not a perfect solution, and we still see regular cases of gonorrhea. It's only our good fortune that syphilis is relatively uncommon around here."

"What about treatment of new cases? I heard that the new sulfonamide antibiotics work for gonorrhea."

"Supposedly. We were promised they'd be effective seventy to eighty percent of the time. I think you'll find they don't actually work that well— maybe we have a different strain of gonorrhea here in the Philippines. For the flying units, it's another problem. Sulfa drugs lower the ability to tolerate low oxygen pressures at high altitudes. That means any flying crewman taking them has to be grounded."

"That must be a delicate problem—in more ways than one."

"For them and for you. You're going to find yourself walking a narrow line. You'll be asked for favors, and you'll want the men to know you're on their side. Try to be as sympathetic as possible, but don't forget what you're dealing with. One of the doctors here has some unbelievably ugly pictures of advanced gonorrhea in men who waited until too late to get treatment. Just seeing the pictures might be more effective than anything else."

"Chief, can you get me a copy of those pictures?"

The Cavite Christmas and New Year of 1940/41 was hot and humid. Charles tried to ignore the sweltering weather and threw himself into hospital work. Despite long hours of study in Corps School and at Mare Island, he still had much to learn about injury, illness, and medical care, and spent the bulk of off-duty time with his medical manuals. He continued memorizing a new word from his dictionary every day, usually over his breakfast coffee.

No explanation accompanied the message for Charles to report to Chief Toole's office. That made him apprehensive.

Did I screw up somewhere? Has someone complained about my involvement at one of the poker games? I only deal once a week or so and keep a low profile. Still.

"Yes, sir?"

The chief did not seem upset. "Good morning, Charles. How are things going for you these days?"

"Pretty good, sir. Is there a problem?"

"I hope not. I've got something for you though." He handed Charles a paper, and his serious face broke into a grin. "You've been promoted to Petty Officer, Pharmacist's Mate Third Class. Congratulations!"

Charles couldn't keep from grinning. He knew he was eligible for the promotion, but unsure when it would happen. The elevation to PhM3c raised him from pay grade 5 ($54 monthly) to pay grade 4 ($60 monthly), and the new rating also raised his specialist monthly pay from $6 to $15.

Together it was a very nice pay raise. He did some quick mental arithmetic. *The poker games are usually enough for my expenses here, so I'll have the paymaster add $8 more to what I'm sending home to Dad.*

"Plan to celebrate?" the Chief asked.

"Any suggestions?"

"Most new NCOs get a portrait photo to send home, showing off the new rank on their uniform. Most of the them use Garduño's Photo Studio in Cavite City. The price is reasonable, and Benito does a great job."

He paused. "One more thing. Your promotion makes you the senior corpsman on the medical ward. Instead of doing general night duty as a ward corpsman, I'm putting you on the Sergeant at Arms rotation for night shifts. Also, you're moving to the top of the list of corpsmen for Special Watch, taking care of mental or physically threatening patients. The chief nurse told me her officers feel safer around the crazies when you're close by."

🙦 🙦 🙦

Charles began regular rotations, usually weekends, working sick call and emergencies. The doctors expected Charles to independently diagnose and treat minor illnesses and injuries without direct supervision. This privilege came not because the medical officers were lazy, but because corpsmen like Charles were destined at some point in their career to be assigned "Duty Independent of a Medical Officer." An independent duty corpsman, by definition, had to manage injuries and illnesses in the absence of a medical officer. Thus qualified, these corpsmen were eligible for assignment to Navy or Marine units in the field, remote from hospitals or clinics.

The medical officers at Cañacao were purposefully preparing Charles for that eventuality.

Charles, photo taken at Garduño Studios, Cavite City, on promotion to Petty Officer, Pharmacist's Mate 3rd, 1941.

In late March, Charles was once more called to the hospital chief's office without explanation. *Why do I always have a bad feeling about these summonses? Was I too rough with that patient who took a swing at a nurse last week? Is it the games?*

Hopefully, it's just some administrative matter. Hopefully.

Nervously, he adjusted his uniform before knocking at the door.

Looking up, Chief Toole motioned Charles to an empty chair. "How do you feel about a change of scenery?"

Change of scenery? "Not sure what you mean, sir."

"Any time live fire is scheduled at the gunnery range, and that's most days, regulations call for an onsite medical response. We don't have anyone scheduled past March, and I need to fill in some names for April and May. It's not like independent duty in the boondocks. If some stupid SOB shoots himself or anyone else, you just need to plug the bleeding and transport them straight here for treatment. Think you can manage that?"

"Yes, sir!" Charles's quick response betrayed his excitement at having a change from the hospital routine.

"OK then. April 1st—how appropriate—is next Tuesday. At 0600 check out an ambulance and drive over there. You can drive?"

"Yes, sir. I've driven a truck before. I don't have an official driving license, though."

"That's good enough for the Navy. Take a field medical kit, and be sure you're onsite by 0630. They usually shut down around noontime, so report back here to the charge nurse. As long as you're not otherwise needed here, you'll be free the rest of the day. You take that first week, and I'll find someone else for each of the next three weeks. I'll adjust the hospital schedule to cover everyone's shifts."

He glanced back down at the papers on his desk. "Oh, and, one more thing—"

"Yes, sir?" Charles was halfway out of the chair but sat back down.

"At the end of morning report with the hospital CO today, he said he overheard one of our corpsmen was organizing poker games, and he wanted to know if that was the case."

Uh-oh, here it comes. "Yes, sir?"

"I told him I didn't know anything about that, but it's been months since we had a fight or complaint over gambling. I knew better than to try to convince him the sailors had stopped gambling, but I admitted that something must have changed. I gave the CO my opinion that, for the moment, we do not have a problem, and he accepted that."

Chief Toole looked straight at Charles. "Still, whatever it is you are—not—doing, keep it low-profile."

The gunnery range was a large area cleared of trees and surrounded by a wire safety fence. The range manager and staff occupied a wood building that also housed a secured small arms locker. Parallel to the pistol and rifle range was a longer range for machine gun qualification. A masonry building, fortified with earthen sides, secured ammunition, mostly practice rounds with reduced powder charges. Metal roofs over firing positions on both ranges provided shade year-round and shelter in the rainy season. A thirty-foot-square metal roof sheltered a large table and two rows of elevated benches, creating an open air classroom for instruction and training.

At 0620 on Tuesday, 1 April, Charles reported to the range manager, a Marine gunnery sergeant. "Morning, sir. I'm your corpsman for the week. Any special instructions?"

"Only one, Doc. Stay behind the guns, not in front. That's about it. Limited live fire today. Mainly, we're holding a certification class at the table." The sergeant indicated the shelter with the table and benches. "Once that group is dismissed, you are free to leave."

Charles thought about finding some shade to read the book in his pocket. Instead, he asked, "Is that class something I can listen in on?"

"This week it's a re-certifying class on the Browning .30 and .50 caliber machine guns. I don't think anyone will mind if you watch."

The instructor, a Navy gunner's mate, stood at the mounted .50 caliber machine gun reinstalling what he called the "back plate group" on the rear of the weapon.

"Morning, sir," Charles introduced himself. "Charles Beckner. I'm your corpsman for the week. Mind if I stand around and watch?"

"No problem, Doc. We're just starting primary and re-certification class on this gun. You're welcome to join us."

By 0700 five other men arrived and signed in for the course. Most sailors had multiple qualifications, and this class would give them one more. On ships and airplanes, it was a simple matter of practicality to have a backup for anyone who fell sick or was killed or injured during a mission. Knowing how to load and fire a machine gun was a desirable secondary skill in any unit.

The instructor began, "I'm CPO Williamson. This is the M2 Browning .50 caliber machine gun. The Army uses many versions, including a water-cooled one. The Navy uses primarily two versions, both air-cooled. This M2HB, or heavy-barrel version, is what you'll most often find on ships and boats. Aircraft use the lighter, AN/M2 version. You'll often see M2s combined in a dual mount, and you might even have seen a quad mount on a cruiser or destroyer. It fires a normal round with a muzzle velocity of 2900 feet per second. You can switch between right and left feed in a matter of minutes. The maximum range is over a mile, but the generally effective range is half that. An armor-piercing round will penetrate an inch of steel at a thousand yards or more. The various versions fire from 600 to 800 rounds a minute."

He paused to let the men absorb some of what he'd told them before going on. "An M2 is only fired in three- to four-second short bursts, allowing cooling intervals of five seconds or more, depending on ambient temperature and airflow. Continuous fire will of course result in overheating and deformation of your barrel. You find this basic gun in many Army and Navy units because maintenance is simple, it's sturdy, and it's reliable."

"Do I have to remember all those numbers for a test?" one of the men interrupted.

CPO Williamson ignored the question and continued. "We will review all procedures to maintain and operate the M2. We'll start with the basic task of changing the barrel and then totally dismantle and reassemble the firing assembly. I will review the recognition and resolution of the seven ways a jammed round can disable the gun. I will also go over quirks of the M2, including the need for precise adjusting of the head space after you change the barrel. At the end, you will have a time-limited test to pass."

"What about live fire?" a sailor interrupted.

The instructor paused momentarily, irritated by this second interruption, but addressed the question.

"We use practice rounds, even though they have barely enough kick to eject the empty shell and occasionally cause the firing mechanism to jam. We'll use those occasions as a practical exercise in managing that particular malfunction." He returned to his set lecture. "I'm giving you each a copy of the M2 maintenance manual. After we review the introduction, we'll begin by working with each assembly separately. We'll also review the Browning .30 caliber, a mechanically similar weapon. There will be a test, and I'll file papers recommending certification if you pass."

He turned to one of the men, a machinist's mate, "You said you are with the seaplane squadron. Have you had any formal aerial gunnery theory or practice?"

"No, sir."

"Unfortunately, we don't have the facilities for teaching 'leading from behind' and other skills unique to aerial gunnery. I'll include the theory in a lecture, but there's no setup here to practice it."

He turned back to the gun. "OK, I'm going to demonstrate how to check this gun and see if it's ready for loading. This is how you set the belt ready for firing . . . OK, it's ready. First man up. On my orders, fire a one-second burst at the target. No longer."

The target was a five-foot square banner between two poles near the end of the range. Each of the five sailors took their turn. Clouds of dirt kicked up on the hill behind the target, but only random hits penetrated the banner downrange. The instructor then looked at Charles. "Your turn, Doc. Let's see if you were paying attention."

The order to participate surprised Charles, but he quickly stepped up. The target, about a hundred yards away, looked small in the sights, but no smaller than a squirrel in an Indiana tree or a turkey on the far side of a field.

He took a spade handle grip in each hand, flexed his elbows, aligned the sights, and gave the trigger between the grips a brief pressure. The firing was loud and shook him to the shoulders, leaving empty shell casings and clips rattling to the ground. *That was exhilarating!*

"You did OK, Doc," said the instructor, looking down-range with binoculars. "Seriously. Several of those rounds hit the target."

At the end of class, Charles was at the ambulance door, about to return to the hospital when the instructor approached. "Doc, instead of just hanging around my class, why don't you ask your CO if you can formally join us? I don't have an authorization for you, but I can still try to get you officially qualified. I know you're a corpsman and under the Geneva Convention. On the other hand, the M2 is a ubiquitous gun, and you never know when you might be the only qualified gunner left standing."

Charles responded noncommittally, "Interesting suggestion, sir. I'll have to give that some consideration." *Damn right! I'm going to get that approval this afternoon.*

Charles returned to the hospital, found the chief in his office, and made his case. "Chief, I have a proposal. If it makes sense to you, and you think it's not only a good idea for me but a good idea for the Navy as well, then maybe you could take it to the hospital CO for approval?"

To Charles's surprise, the Chief enthusiastically agreed. "When corpsmen are with a Marine or Navy unit in the field, their job is to assure everyone that they'll crawl over glass and through bullets to care for any casualties. On the other hand, if things get desperate, they'll expect their corpsman to take up whatever arms are available and join the fight. As far as I'm concerned, your request is perfectly reasonable, considering the deteriorating situation the world's in right now."

Within an hour, Charles was verbally approved. He was to continue as the range corpsman with his primary duty medical response for any range accidents. Otherwise, assuming no one shot themselves or smashed a thumb, he could devote his time to completing the qualifying course.

He passed the final exam, and the instructor filed certification papers for Charles on the .50 and .30 caliber Browning machine guns. "I'm not sure this'll go all the way since I didn't have the normal authorization papers in hand, but I'm forwarding it up, and we'll see if it works."

After the welcomed break from hospital routine, Charles returned to hospital duty as a surgical assistant in the operating room. Finishing early on a light day, Charles stopped by the surgical ward. He found Tillie at the nurses' station, looking worried and staring at rivulets of rain running down the window.

"What's up, Lieutenant? You don't look so happy."

Tillie looked up. "Oh, hi, Charles. I'm just a bit concerned. The hospital commander has 'suggested' that we nurses send home everything that can't fit into a single sea bag. Our stuff will accompany the next nurse rotating back to the States and be forwarded to our family or someone Stateside."

"Ominous," Charles agreed. "Do they know something we don't?"

"The commander told us 'Nothing has changed,' but at the same time said we might have to move without enough time to ship stuff back. I find it hard to reconcile those two statements."

"Well, between the scuttlebutt and the few newspapers I can find, it does sound like things are heating up," Charles said. "Roosevelt and Churchill announced a halt to shipments of steel, oil, and other critical commodities to Japan. If the Japanese can't get those things from us, they might just head to where they can take it for themselves. Their most likely sources are the Dutch East Indies, or even Australia."

Tillie looked at Charles. "But to get there—"

"Yes, we're here, right in their way. The Philippines are already surrounded on three sides by Japanese forces. Japan and Taiwan to the north, China to the west, and the Marianas and Carolines to the east. Everyone in Washington knows how vulnerable we are. Another fleet of cargo ships loaded with tanks and men arrived here last week. In a radio interview MacArthur said the geography of the islands will make it easy to repel any attempted invasion."

"And yet we've been told to send our belongings home. The Japs scare me, Charles. I know you've heard about Nanking."

Charles and everyone else in the Pacific knew about Nanking.

After the Japanese won a bloody battle for Shanghai in 1937, they moved forces towards the then-capital city of Nanking. The Chinese Nationalist leader Chiang Kai-shek knew a defensive stand in Nanking at that time would decimate his remaining regular troops, so he made a strategic decision to withdraw to the vast interior of China, leaving Nanking virtually defenseless. The Japanese occupation turned into a massacre. Murder, rape, and executions went unchecked. Tens of thousands of civilians, perhaps more than a hundred thousand, were killed in the rampage. Pundits debated whether the blame should be laid on the soldiers, their officers, or the military command in Tokyo.

For the victims, it made no difference.

Tillie shook her head. "I don't understand the Japanese military mind. I try not to imagine what would happen if the Japanese invaded and occupied the Philippines."

"Not a pretty picture. Realistically though, we have soldiers, ships and aircraft to defend the islands. If Japan attacks despite that, then our entire Pacific Fleet can get here from Hawaii in only a few days. With all those battleships, carriers, cruisers, and supply ships standing by, I don't see Japan risking it."

15

Reassigned

Sangley Point, Cavite, Philippine Islands

June 1941

On Monday, 2 June 1941, Charles discussed the relative merits of various Filipino beers with his patient, an injured cook, as he gently spread ointment on second- and third-degree burns on the cook's left arm.

A nurse leaned her head into the dressing room, "I'm to tell you to go see Chief Toole before noon."

Charles looked up. "Not again! What for this time?"

"Didn't say, but he's probably going to tell you to stop flirting with the nurses," she retorted, flashing a coquettish smile.

Charles rolled his eyes. "You're letting your reveries repeatedly run richly rampant."

"Let me think on that one," and she popped out of the room as quickly as she'd appeared.

"Yes, sir?" Charles once more stood in front of Chief Toole, wondering if he had finally, if unwittingly, stepped over some line.

"Good news and bad news, Beckner." Toole's expression was neutral. "You're being reassigned. Sea duty. You're moving to a ship."

What the hell? I've been in the Philippines less than a year, and they're supposed to leave me here for at least two. Sea duty? That could be literally anywhere in the world.

Charles forced himself to speak calmly, "And what ship will that be, Chief?"

124

Toole ignored the question. "You have no travel time or allowance. You'll walk to your ship and report in the morning."

Charles frowned. *He's giving me a puzzle. This ship must be docked close by.* He stepped over to the window. There was only one sizeable ship in Cañacao Bay, and it was at the Sangley Point dock. *I recognize that silhouette. There was a picture and description of it hanging on the Mare Island Hospital wall. Never dreamed I would be assigned to her myself. It's a small world.*

"Sir? You're sending me to the *Langley*?"

"Officially you're reassigned to Patrol Wing 10. But yep, that funny-looking ship off Sangley Point is your new home. It's just returned from a refit in the floating dry dock *Dewey* up at Olongapo. During her refit, some of the crew rotated back to the States. They need a corpsman with OR experience. We'd like to keep you here, but the performance evaluations I wrote up on you were apparently too good—you'll be replacing an OR assistant on the *Langley*. I can't be selfish and stand in the way of your career advancement."

Before Charles had time to comment, he added, "Before you leave, I have something for you."

Chief Toole stood, pulled a knapsack from under his desk, and withdrew from it a huge knife with a leather scabbard. "This was given to me when I first arrived, but I was never assigned outside the hospital or sent to the bush, and I'll be returning Stateside soon. In PatWing 10 you're more likely to move around the Islands, so I'm passing it on. To you." He handed it to Charles.

"A machete? It's damned heavy—sir."

"Not a machete, Charles. It's a military knife, a Model 1904 Hospital Corps Knife. I think they stopped making them after the Great War, but there's still a few around. That weight gives it added heft for cutting saplings or small trees for splints or for constructing a litter or shelter. The rounded tip is useful if you're digging a slot latrine. And, yes, it could be used like a machete for clearing brush. Care for it and pass it on when the time comes."

"Thank you, sir."

"It's been good to have you aboard, Charles. Do your best out there."

A few minutes later, Charles interrupted Tillie on her ward. "I'm being reassigned, Tillie."

"Oh no!" Tillie was more distraught than Charles expected. "You're a good corpsman, and everyone here likes you. It seems you just got here—why are they moving you already? Where do they need you more than right here?"

"It's sea duty. For career advancement, the chief told me."

"Really? I guess that's good. Still, we are going to miss you. *I* will miss you."

Charles smiled and pointed through the windows to the north side of

Cañacao Bay, "I'm going to the *Langley*. You can see her from here. I'll wave to you from the deck and find an excuse to visit the hospital now and then. You're not getting rid of me that easy."

Goodbyes were brief, and there was no speech or party. Arrivals and departures were too frequent to make a fuss every time someone other than a senior officer departed. Charles did not feel slighted. *Moving a few hundred yards across the Bay barely counts as leaving.*

𝔰𝔴 𝔰𝔴 𝔰𝔴

Once aboard the *Langley*, Charles tracked down the senior corpsman.

"Welcome aboard, Charles. Call me Pete. I heard good stories about you."

"They're all true, but probably understated," Charles grinned.

Pete walked Charles through the *Langley*'s dispensary and small OR. "How about a cup of Navy coffee? If nothing else, it's strong and black."

"My kind of coffee. Would you bring me up to date on the organization?"

"PatWing 10 is on virtually continuous alert these days. There are no training exercises anymore—every flight is an operational mission. The Japs keep moving farther south into Indochina. In addition to the *Langley*, PatWing 10 has three other tenders, each with corpsmen. They've been moving around the islands with small groups of PBYs. The *Langley* is the largest, the only tender with doctors and an equipped operating room. For now, she's staying right here, supporting PatWing 10 headquarters."

"Where do I fit in?" Charles asked.

"You're replacing an OR assistant who returned to the States while we were in dry dock. The surgical schedule is usually light, and you'll also work in the dressing and casting room when there's no surgery scheduled. We all shift around as needs change, so be flexible. I'll take you to the wing HQ building to get your paperwork filed. If Captain Wagner, the wing commander, is there, I'll introduce you. Wagner's OK, but he runs a tight operation, so don't cross him."

"What can you tell me about the other PBY tenders? They're smaller?"

"They are, but they each have their own corpsman. The *William B. Preston* and the *Childs* are converted destroyers. They're far less spacious than the *Langley*, but they can move out at 25 knots. Compared to them, the *Langley*'s a plodder. In a calm sea she might do 13 knots—could be the reason they let us sit here."

"You said there's a fourth support ship?"

"The *Heron*, an old converted minesweeper. The *Heron* supports our utility

126

squadron of single-engine seaplanes. Right now, that's four Grumman Ducks, five Vought Kingfishers, and one Curtiss Seagull biplane."

"Where are the tenders now?"

"One's down in the southern islands, and the other two are somewhere in transit. They're constantly relocating to some small dock or anchoring in some deserted bay. We carry aviation fuel, ammunition, bombs, and torpedoes for our twenty-eight PBYs and the five utility planes. Each of us is a complete, mobile seaplane base with machine shops and parts for maintenance and repairs."

"Sounds like the Wing's fully operational."

"Yes, at least in terms of planes, tenders, and supplies. All four tenders were recently in dry dock to have their bottoms scraped and maintenance. We're fully stocked with fuel and ammunition. Unfortunately, the unit's been chronically short of support personnel. Our full complement would be around 300, counting flight, ground, and command personnel. We're below that now, and Wagner's doing everything he can to remedy it, and I assume it's how you got pulled here from the hospital."

At headquarters, Captain Wagner interrupted his reading of patrol reports to briefly welcome Charles to PatWing 10.

Charles filed copies of his orders with the wing clerk before returning to the *Langley* to stake out a berth and introduce himself to the rest of the medical staff.

ꔷ ꔷ ꔷ

The two squadrons of PatWing 10 were currently flying from separate locations. VP-101 flew missions directly from Sangley Point. VP-102 based its planes and personnel at Olongapo Naval Base, on Subic Bay some fifty miles northwest of Sangley Point. Each squadron consisted of fourteen PBYs with flight and ground crews. From each of the two squadrons, smaller groups of three or four planes continually repositioned to various bays and harbors around the Philippines as missions required. For extended deployments, one of the tenders repositioned with the planes.

A seaplane tender was not needed for VP-102 at Olongapo. Spare parts, tools, munitions, and fuel were available on the base. What Olongapo did lack was much in the way of entertainment for the men, either on the base or in the small Barrio of Olongapo. At one time the squadron commander had authorized weekend liberty flights to Manila in one of his PBYs. No longer,

No. 1605   The Langley   *Official Photo U. S. Navy.*

PBYs overflying the seaplane tender USS Langley.

though. Observing Japanese ship movements was more important than sending a junket to the city.

Charles by now knew to expect surprises from the Navy.

Nevertheless, he was stunned after only three weeks aboard the *Langley* to be handed TAD, Temporary Additional Duty, orders. Men could be assigned TAD to another location for up to six months. If the temporary duty lasted beyond that, the Navy made the assignment permanent.

While on TAD, Charles would still be assigned to the *Langley* administratively.

"I was just beginning to feel like a real member of the operating team on the *Langley*," he complained to the clerk at PatWing 10 HQ. "Is this good news or bad news?"

"Depends on your viewpoint, but in fact you're only moving onshore. The *Langley* may have to reposition herself, and Captain Wagner wants to make sure we leave adequate medical support here on Sangley Point. You're still assigned to the *Langley*, but you and a medical officer are moving onshore to augment staffing at the Sangley Point dispensary. You'll be working close to

HQ staff and operations. If you don't screw it up, it could help your career."

꒰ ꒰ ꒰

Charles took the opportunity for a weekend liberty before moving from the *Langley*. He and Frank, the VP-101 corpsman, took the ferry from the hospital dock to Manila. Frank arranged for them to meet two of his friends, both Army medics from the Sternberg Army Hospital. Walking to dinner, the four men passed the magnificent and imposing Manila hotel. It was still the symbol and center of high social affairs during these "golden years" of Manila.

Charles shared what he knew of the hotel and its famous occupant. "You all know that Douglas MacArthur and his family have the entire penthouse floor?"

"Everyone knows that, but can you tell me exactly why he's so cozy with President Quezon?"

"A businessman on the *Chaumont* told me the story behind that. MacArthur came here as a young officer after the Spanish-American war, around 1903. He met this young lawyer named Manuel Quezon and they became lifelong friends, even when Quezon was part of the rebellion for independence from America. After Quezon was swept into the presidency he asked MacArthur to be his military adviser. President Roosevelt and MacArthur had been at odds over the Army's funding, so Roosevelt was happy to endorse MacArthur's appointment to be official Military Advisor to the Commonwealth of the Philippines and see him move to the other side of the world. Quezon, separately, gave MacArthur the rank of Field Marshal."

One of the Army medics added, "It's a sore point for some of us. MacArthur's being paid by both Quezon and the Army, all the time living here in luxury. The general even has Captain Hutter, his personal physician, and Hutter's family living up there as well."

"It's a different world," Charles mused. "Hard for me to imagine."

During dinner in a tiny Japanese restaurant, the four returned to their discussion of MacArthur. "So, what exactly does MacArthur have for an army?" Charles asked.

"He's supposed to be training a Philippine Army of more than 100,000 men. I know from good authority that his actual Army is only 12,000 or so Filipino Scouts. The other 100,000-plus troops mostly exist as paper reserves. Most of those reserves have no uniforms or guns. If the Nips—" he glanced at the Japanese owner of the restaurant, "If the Japanese come with a full-scale invasion, those reservists are so badly equipped and poorly trained that they'll be overwhelmed by trained Jap troops. They're undoubtedly brave men, but that's not enough."

"What about the U.S. Army?" Charles pressed. "Don't you guys have this place pretty well garrisoned?"

"Hardly. There's only 20,000 of us. We'll have to do, though, because we sure can't expect you lubbers to keep them off the beach, can we?"

"That's *opprobrious* talk," Charles emphasized the word he had memorized only the previous evening and had been waiting in verbal ambush to use. "But then you're probably right. There're no battleships out there," Charles waved his hand towards the bay. "The biggest ship in Admiral Hart's Asian Fleet is an old heavy cruiser, the *Houston*. Command says that if the Japanese try to attack us, the Pacific Fleet's battleship and carrier groups will steam from Hawaii and put the Imperial Navy out of commission. With us controlling the sea, they can't invade. At least that's the plan."

"First question," the medic looked seriously at Charles. "What the hell is o–oppbro–whatever the hell you said?"

Charles repeated, "Opprobrious, from *opprobrium*. It means outrageously disgraceful or shameful. Especially when you're talking down the Navy!"

"Yeah, fuck you too."

Charles held both palms up. "Sorry. I couldn't resist trying out a word I just learned last night. Don't take it seriously—I was just practicing."

"In that case, here's to the Navy." The medic raised his beer in a toast, "May you keep those Nip bastards off our shores," oblivious to the bar owner's glare.

Charles, uncomfortable with the slur and embarrassed by the Japanese bar owner's presence, let it go and made his own toast, "And here's to the Army— may you never get seasick."

As they prepared to leave, a group of British sailors took over the adjacent table. "Do you have a ship here?" Charles asked.

"No secret, mate. The *Liverpool*. We've anchored off Cavite, getting fitted up before we take her to an American shipyard so she can be rebuilt. Ran into a bit of trouble. An Italian seaplane managed to slip a torpedo into our bow."

The Americans looked at each other. "Sorry, none of us heard about it."

"You must not be reading your newspapers, mates. There's a war going on—and it's not only in Europe."

Returning to Cavite, conversations among the ferry passengers stopped when they passed the *Liverpool*. Her damage was terrible, much worse than the understated Brits had suggested. The bow of the ship was nothing more than mangled steel and empty space. What was left of the big forward three-gun turret sagged over the void. A man on the ferry crossed himself.

Charles watched until the *Liverpool* disappeared from sight when the ferry rounded the shipyards to deposit the two corpsmen at the hospital dock.

I'll write to my brother tonight.

5-28-41

Dear James,

You said you wanted me to tell you about the Islands. At first they're swell, but if you've seen one, you've seen them all. Maybe it's not quite so bad on this particular one, but there's nothing like the States.

By the time you get this it will be old news, but here goes. The "Limey" ship HMS Liverpool *pulled in the Cavite yard to get provisions. She was torpedoed somewhere in the Mediterranean and her bow was a wreck. Her forward gun turret was half-blown away. Fifty-seven were killed in this one fight alone, according to the British sailors I was with. The ship was sure a wreck. The Brits are taking her to the Bremerton (Washington) Navy yard, crossing the States by train, and taking back a couple of destroyers to England while they fix up the* Liverpool. *If some enemy ship catches her going back to Bremerton she's just "cold meat." No doubt there will be a US warship in the background someplace, so it should get back OK.*

We also have three Danish merchant ships sitting out here in sight of the quarters. They were confined here in Manila Bay for the duration of the war. They have guards on all of them, but the Danish crew seem perfectly satisfied. They're drawing war pay and do no work at all. At home they might be in a concentration camp. They consider themselves lucky. They do want to go back to Frisco though, and I don't blame them. I want to, too!

I told you about the Manila fire, didn't I? It burned out the whole Tondo district. About one hundred square blocks. About two good buildings were in it too. The rest were nipa huts.

131

I made out an allotment of $35 a month starting 5 July to last for one year. I have plenty on hand now where I can get it in a real emergency. This will leave $25 per mo. for expenses & liberty, but just watch me take it easy and study. That's the thing I need so much of.

I'm writing this half asleep. It's past bed time several hours. Write a little sooner than once every two months. And don't ever think you want to see any of these islands. You're doing okay in Princeton. So, take it easy and ans. soon.

Yours, Charles

P.S. Enclosed is a photo I had taken after my promotion. I'll send you a pack of those British cigarettes for a birthday present if you'd care for them. They're somewhat like Philip Morris.

So Long

16

The PBY

Sangley Point, Philippine Islands

July 1941

The windowed rooms of the Sangley Point clinic and barracks brightened Charles's day literally and figuratively. The deeper in the bowels of ships like the *Chaumont* and the *Langley* Charles found himself, the more restless and anxious he was. *Colin, the corpsman with me on the* Chaumont, *could have been right. I probably do have a bit, maybe more than a bit, of claustrophobia. I hope to hell I'm never assigned to a submarine.*

An NCO from the squadron was detailed to show Charles around. "Hello, Doc. I'm Joseph, call me Joe. I'm one of the squadron's AMMs, aviation machinist's mates. I'm from the great state of Ohio, and I went through Great Lakes NTS in August 1938."

"You're exactly a year ahead of me. I was at Great Lakes in August '39, and I'm from your upscale neighbor, Indiana."

"Everyone can't be from Ohio, so I won't hold it against you," Joe grinned. "I'm supposed to give you the tour and introduce you to the men this morning. How much time did they give you?"

"I have the whole day to get my feet on the ground, so it's whatever you want."

"Great! In that case, we're going to take a ride. My plane is about to hop over to Olongapo and pick up a sailor with a broken leg and fly him back here to the hospital. VP-102's planes must all be staged at some outpost, out on patrol, or getting maintenance, so we're going over to pick him up. You ever flown on a PBY, Doc?"

"I've never been higher than an oak tree, and I've never seen the inside of an airplane. Is this a good one to start on?"

"You couldn't pick a better plane for your first ride, Doc. In fact, I'll see if I can get you a special seat!"

They walked past a PBY at the short pier. "This one's waiting to be refueled," Joe said, "Our ride's on the water, and the pilots and flight engineer are already on board." The two joined a radioman on a small skiff and motored to the waiting PBY.

"Think it's a funny-looking plane, Doc?" the radioman asked.

Instead of taking the bait, Charles only said, "It does look big up close."

"That's all right, Doc—you don't have to say it's pretty," Joe answered. "But if you're floating on a life raft in the ocean, you'll look up and think it's the most beautiful thing you ever saw. And you're right, Doc, it is big. It measures sixty-four feet, nose to tail. That enormous wing is over a hundred feet tip to tip, and fourteen feet wide! Not only does it give tremendous lift, but the wing tanks hold right at 1,400 gallons of aviation fuel."

"So, on a normal patrol, you just fly out, track the locations of Japanese ships, and fly back?"

"A PBY's a versatile creature, Doc. She can do convoy protection, anti-submarine patrol, night bombing, and air/sea rescue. The admirals and generals love to use us for rapid mail and transport service. But you're mostly right. Almost all our patrolling these days is to search, identify, and record Japanese ship movements."

"It's not really a fighting plane, though?" Charles interrupted.

"Yes and no. We have .50 caliber machine guns at the waist ports and a .30 caliber gun you can swing out the open nose hatch—if you're brave. The 'PB' does stand for 'Patrol Bomber,' and we have 500-pound bombs we can strap on for low-level delivery. That said, you'll never see a high-altitude formation of PBYs on a bombing run. Truth is, the PBY's slow as a turtle and doesn't have self-sealing wing tanks. If a fighter attacks us, we'll use our guns, but the odds are pretty heavy against us."

"Earlier you said 'my plane.' Does each plane have its own crew?"

"Flight crews do tend to stay together. The Navy considers each PBY aircrew as a unit assigned to a particular plane."

"How many in your crew?"

"A full crew is eight or nine men, usually three pilots, two of them officers. The third pilot is an enlisted Navy Aviation Pilot, or NAP. He's always a senior machinist's mate. The NAP sits in the tower when he's not flying the plane."

"But he's a fully qualified pilot?"

"More than qualified. Our NAP has more flying hours than either of our two officer pilots. On occasion a plane flies with one NAP in the tower and a second NAP sitting next to the officer pilot."

"The tower"? I'll ask what that is later. "And the other crewmen?"

"Besides those three, we have two radio operators and three machinist's mates. Almost every flight crewman has at least two ratings, so there's backup. One or two of the engineers can also operate the radios. At least three of us are rated on the machine guns."

"That's eight—what about the ninth man?" Charles asked.

"The ninth man is officially for the aft belly gun, but it's an imaginary position. It's far back and supposedly allows us to target a plane on our tail. But, it has such a limited field of view you'll never see anything to shoot at from there."

"No corpsmen on the flight crews?"

"Never. It wouldn't work anyway, unless he happened to be qualified as pilot, radioman, or mechanic."

"I'm none of those, but I am qualified on the M2 .50 caliber," Charles said, stretching the truth slightly.

"How about that, Doc! So am I. My battle station is the port waist gun. We'll have to get you on a flight for some practice. Maybe you can shoot a whale."

Charles asked, with a straight face, "How do you field-dress a whale?" Joe just looked puzzled, so Charles changed the subject. "What's in there?" he asked, pointing to the oval structure connecting the fuselage to the elevated wing.

"That's the *tower*, it connects the hull to the wings. The plane was purposefully designed with an elevated wing to keep the propellers well above the water. Inside the tower are the gauges and controls for fuel lines and other mechanicals. It's where the plane captain, a chief machinist's mate—usually the NAP—sits during flights. He monitors and manages fuel consumption, oil pressure, engine temperature, and other mechanics from up there."

Their small boat pulled to the side of the plane. Charles, Joe, and the other crewman crawled through the sliding hatch/gun port at the plane's waist. Joe walked Charles through the waist compartment, crew quarters, and radio/engineer room to the pilot's compartment while yelling brief introductions over the engine noise.

After talking to one of the pilots, Joe pushed Charles between the pilots into the bow compartment in the nose of the plane. Crouching between the pilots, he introduced Charles to the small space. "Here's your special seat I promised, the best one in the house. It's normally for a nose gunner or bombardier. We better strap you in—wind's kicking up small waves in the bay, so it'll be a little bouncy on takeoff. One more thing. There's a protective cover over the nose window down there. You can open it with this lever, but not until we're airborne, and it *must* be closed when we land. Got it?"

"Got it," Charles nodded.

"The new PBY 5-series has a plexiglass-enclosed machine gun mount up here, and plexiglass gun blisters replace the sliding metal hatches back at the waist. The Dutch Air Force already has some fives, and that really pisses me off."

"Why's that?"

"Because the new planes have retractable landing gear and don't need a beaching crew."

"Beaching crew?"

"You'll find out later, Doc. I'm heading back to my post. Hang on!"

The slowly turning propellers came to life with a roar, and the plane lurched ahead, picking up speed.

Joe was right. From the nose Charles had a great view, with windows forward, on both sides, and tilted downward at the nose. A hatch above his head allowed the .30 caliber machine gun to be swung out for firing. *That'd be the equivalent of trying to shoot at a darting small bird while standing in a gale.*

Charles found his first airplane takeoff disconcertingly rough. As the plane gathered speed, the hull smashed into every wave. *I'm inside a giant aluminum can, being hammered with a shovel while rolling down a potholed road.*

The bay water boiled back, lashing at the windows and soaking the underside of the wings. Rainbows danced in the turbulence of the propellers. The plane grudgingly rose from the water, riding higher and higher on the keel until she was "on the step" and hydroplaning across the waves, riding only on the four-inch step-off running transversely across the contour of the hull. Speed increased and they finally lifted smoothly from the water.

Looking to the side, Charles saw the wing tip pontoons retract upwards, extending the aerodynamic wing by two additional feet on each side. They had magically transitioned from boat to airplane.

Suddenly the plane lurched upward, leaving his stomach somewhere below. The ships and buildings of the Cavite shipyards shrank as the plane gained altitude and distance. Unlike being in dark, enclosed spaces, Charles found this experience exhilarating. *At least I'm not acrophobic.*

He scanned the entire sweep of land from Cavite and Manila to the Bataan peninsula with the "fortress island" of Corregidor at its tip. *It's like looking from Point Loma in San Diego, but from a much higher viewpoint.*

They remained over water, flying west around the Bataan highlands. In minutes they were over Subic Bay, heading for the Navy base and village of Olongapo on its eastern shore.

The water at Subic Bay was reasonably smooth. Even so, the landing was no less dramatic than takeoff. The pilot reduced throttle for his approach. Close to water, the waves started flashing by. Charles knew their speed had dropped, but it seemed they were going faster and faster. He felt a *kerrasch!* as fifteen tons, moving at sixty miles per hour, made a "stall landing" on the bay.

They taxied close to the Olongapo dock and waited for the patient to be ferried from shore.

Crawling out of the nose compartment wearing a huge grin, Charles nodded to both pilots. "Thanks. That was exhilarating."

The sliding waist gun hatches were opened for cross-ventilation and to give a view of activities on shore.

Charles patted the Browning M2 machine gun, and Joe gave Charles a thumbs-up and said, "Soon."

While they waited for their patient, the pilot, Lieutenant Thomas Pollock, came aft. "What'd you think of the flight, Doc?"

"To be honest, I never thought my first flight wouldn't involve a runway, or even a field."

"Actually, Doc, we had the biggest runway in the world—the ocean. If I had to, I could take this plane down on a reasonable-sized lake, or even a good-sized river. We may be slow, but we can patrol or rescue and return from as far out as twelve hundred miles. That's a big circle."

"So, anywhere there's a tender, you have a seaplane base?"

"We're even more versatile than that, Doc. We have hundreds of barrels of 100-octane aviation fuel cached on small islands, bays, and lakes all over the Philippines. We can use any of those places as a temporary base until either the fuel's gone or we have to return to a tender for ammunition or repairs." Pollock pointed through the hatch. "Here comes our passenger."

The boat crew carefully maneuvered the stretcher through the hatch and strapped the sailor to a bunk on the starboard wall of the crew compartment. The corpsman who rode out with the patient saw the red cross on Charles's sleeve. "Great! I didn't expect there to be a corpsman on board. I'll brief you about our patient, and you take him from here."

Charles would need to accompany the patient to Cañacao Hospital on their return, so he and Joe agreed to finish Charles's tour and introductions another day.

Back at Sangley Point, they maneuvered their patient from the PBY to a skiff and then to a waiting ambulance for the short ride to Cañacao Hospital.

ᔑ ᔑ ᔑ

Charles smiled when he saw it was Tillie waiting for them at the surgical ward.

After exchanging a status report and the medical records from Olongapo, Charles and Tillie agreed to meet briefly over coffee, once Tillie's patient was checked in and on his way for X-rays.

Charles was on his second cup of coffee by the time Tillie walked in and sat down across the table. "Charles, I'm getting more worried. Since having us send our stuff home, the command stopped releasing any further information. You're working at the Patrol Wing 10 HQ—what's the scuttlebutt over there?"

"You know of course that Germany and Russia are now fighting each other?"

"Yes."

"And you noticed the *Liverpool* in the bay?"

"Everyone did."

Tillie nodded as Charles continued listing recent events. "There was the sinking of the British *Hood* by the *Bismarck,* and the subsequent sinking of the *Bismarck* by British ships and planes. Britain still rules the sea, at least for now. As for America, I read in a week-old newspaper that we've closed all the Italian and German consulates in the U.S. and frozen their assets, things usually done only after you're at war with another country. If we do the same to Japan, it'll be on top of existing oil and steel embargos. The path we're on will almost certainly lead to a war with both Japan and Germany. The question being asked by the newspapers is, can America manage wars simultaneously on two fronts, Asia and Europe?"

"So, you do really think the Japanese are going to attack us?" Tillie asked. "There are so many Japanese families living here, they're friendly, and it's hard to see them as brutal enemies."

"First, Tillie, I was once told not to mistake polite for friendly."

She nodded again, and he continued. "Second, we've been told to trust no civilians, but especially not any Japanese. I take that as reasonable advice for the time being. And finally, yes, I think the Japanese will make a major attack somewhere on the Philippine Islands, and it will be sooner rather than later. Our planes see Japanese ground and naval activity accelerating. Our crews who've been watching with their own eyes can't explain it any other way than a preparation for an invasion."

"I might have heard something you haven't," Tillie offered. "It isn't good. Yesterday a captain was on my ward visiting one of his officers, and I overhead some of their conversation."

"And what'd you hear?"

"The Japanese have called up a million men for immediate military service."

17

Malaria

Sangley Point, Cavite, Philippine Islands

July 1941

"Lieutenant?" Charles called through the door. "Got a patient in here I need you to see."

"What do you have?" the doctor asked, following Charles into the treatment room.

"Sir, Johnny's one of our aviation mechanics. He slipped on a ladder and cut his forearm on the engine cowling. The cut is long, but not deep. I checked range of movement and sensation. Both are good, and it doesn't look deep enough to have done any tendon or muscle damage. The bleeding is slow. No major vessels seem to be involved."

"OK, what do you want to do?"

"To start with, a good sterile clean up. I think it's too deep and long to just tape up, and with the rain we're having every day, tape might not even stay on all that long. If we sew him up, there's a better chance for healing, he'll probably have less scarring, and he could get back to work faster."

"OK. Has that new vaccine for tetanus arrived?"

"Not yet."

"Too bad. It's supposed to be 100 percent effective. Go ahead, scrub it well and stitch him up." The doctor returned to his office.

"You heard that, Johnny. Any questions?" Charles asked.

"Nope. Go to it, Doc."

Charles cleaned thoroughly, then stitched the cut with precisely placed sutures. *Good job, Charles,* he said to himself, *straight stitches with the skin edges smooth and perfectly aligned. I don't think the doctor could have done any better.*

⸜ ⸜ ⸜

While PatWing 10 planes continued routine patrols, Charles held routine sick calls, did routine crew physical exams, and filled out routine records. Between these duties, he often enjoyed bull sessions arising spontaneously under a PBY's wing when men gathered for protection from sun or rain. Like sailors from time immemorial, if not talking about women, they traded stories of how awful things were, most often relating to their work, the weather, or some seemingly senseless Navy policy. When it came to PatWing 10 though, there was consensus they were members of a decent organization, with Wagner a better-than-average commander.

PatWing 10 added regular night patrols. Flying in darkness a PBY was almost invisible, but a Japanese ship could be easily spotted on a moonlit ocean. Repair and maintenance requirements increased with the greater frequency and duration of patrols. For major mechanical repairs, a PBY was fitted with wheels while still in the water, then hauled up the ramp for maintenance on the tarmac. Major overhauls were carried out in the shelter of the hangar. Charles occasionally helped the machinist's mates, giving them a third or fourth hand when needed. The bewildering arrays of tubing, wires, and mechanical devices on the air-cooled radial piston engines were as incomprehensible to Charles as a Slavic language. *These guys are no less skilled professionals than any other man in the squadron, me included.*

Charles incessantly tried to talk himself aboard patrols. He was so persistent in asking to be assigned a waist gunner position that Lieutenant Pollock took him aside one afternoon.

"Listen, Doc, everyone's happy with you as our squadron corpsman, and it's OK to have you ride along now and then, but forget about replacing one of my flight crew. A radioman, NAP, or machinist's mate who is also qualified on the guns is always going to be more useful than a corpsman when it comes to flying the mission and bringing the plane back in one piece. It's nothing personal—it's just the way things are."

Duly chastised, Charles gave up efforts, if not hope, to fly on patrol as crew.

The next Saturday, Joe came by with an alternative offer. "Doc, are you busy tomorrow morning?"

"Not really. What do you have in mind?"

"I'm going to keep a promise I made to you. We have a dawn flight to take a radio and other supplies to three planes flying from one of the small islands. Don't be late!"

At first light Sunday morning the plane, Charles aboard, cleared Manila Bay and turned south over the South China Sea.

"Doc, Pollock must feel bad about turning you down, so he's letting me keep that promise I made that first day we talked."

"What promise?"

Instead of answering Charles, Joe slid open the port waist hatch cover and swung out the Browning machine gun. "After we reach open water on a patrol, we clear the guns. Pollock said that if he sees something that can serve as a target, he'll make a pass over it. Just for you," Joe grinned. "He hasn't changed his mind, but he is going to let you prove yourself. Now, show me that you were not just bullshitting me about being a gunner."

Joe stood back and watched Charles check the gun before loading a belt of ammunition and setting the first round.

There was no whale, but Pollock did find some floating debris. He dropped the PBY down for a pass.

Charles fired several rounds at the makeshift target. They all splashed well in front of the clustered debris.

"Doc, you ever heard of 'leading from behind'?"

"Actually, yes—I need to take account of my own airspeed. Right?"

"Right, and what do you know, Pollock's actually circling to give you another pass. Try it again."

Charles fired another rapid burst, aiming thirty yards behind the target. This time bullets splashed across the debris. The last round jammed. Charles waited five seconds before pulling back and releasing the bolt. He tried to fire again, but nothing happened. The round was a dud. He quickly extracted the round manually, tossed it into the sea, and reset the belt.

"Nice job," Joe said.

"Thanks."

"Floating crates aren't much of a target. Someday you'll have something more challenging to shoot at."

Pollock sent back a message, "Good shooting."

On weekends, Charles was left to hold squadron sick call alone with the standing instruction, "If something bad comes in, send them straight to the hospital."

This Saturday morning was tediously slow. Only one sailor reported, limping to the closest chair. "Look there, Doc. My foot's red around the toes, and the skin's got some cracks that are starting to hurt. I thought it might go away, but I think it's getting worse."

"Bill, see that red skin and fissures between your toes? That's only part of your problem. I can also see a cluster of tiny blisters underneath your toes."

"Is it something bad, Doc?"

"You've got foot fungus. If we don't stop it now, you might develop full-blown 'jungle rot.'"

"That sounds bad."

"Very bad. You might be laid up for weeks, or even months."

"Can't let that happen—I've got big plans for my next liberty."

"Have you been keeping your feet dry?" Charles asked.

"Well, no," Bill said sarcastically. "I've been on beaching duty. We've been taking planes in and out every day this week. Plus, you know, all this rain. On top of that, my spare pair of socks fell apart and I threw them away. I should probably get another pair."

"Let's talk about that while I cauterize the worst fissures with some silver nitrate. Then I'm going to paint both feet with boric acid. It's not a treatment in the books, but another corpsman told me about it, and it seems to work quite well. I'm also giving you some powder to put on your feet twice every day. What you really must do, though, is keep your feet dry. Not just this week, but for the rest of your tour."

"Hard to do on the beaching crew, Doc."

"I'll get you off that for a while, but in the meantime air out and dry your feet twice every day. Find yourself three more pairs of socks, and put on a clean, dry pair every morning and afternoon, otherwise it'll never get better. Come back in during Monday sick call for me to see how it's doing."

Charles finished walking Bill through the rest of his standard foot fungus instructions, wrote a note in Bill's medical folder, and sent the sailor off to find some dry socks.

With no warning, the door burst open. Two men supporting an obviously ill third man between them stumbled into the room. It was Johnny, the aviation machinist's mate with the long cut on his arm from the previous week. "What's his problem?" Charles quickly checked the scar on his forearm as they rolled him onto a gurney. *His arm's healing nicely. No infection there.*

143

"Don't know what happened, Doc. Johnny was supposed to have a flight this morning, and when he didn't show, we went by the barracks and found him this way."

Charles did a quick exam. Simultaneously sweating profusely and shaking with chills, Johnny did not respond to Charles's questioning. "He's burning up, guys, and there's scleral icterus and his pulse is high, over 100."

"What's icterus?"

"The whites of his eyes are yellow." Charles had seen patients like this brought to Cañacao Hospital from other regions or islands with severe bouts of malaria, but it was rare to acquire malaria without leaving Cavite.

"Has he traveled anywhere lately? Is he taking quinine tablets?"

The sailors looked at one another. "I don't know about the quinine, but he's been to Olongapo," said one.

"When?" asked Charles.

"Not long ago. He flew up a couple of weeks ago. Coming back, he rode a truck to Mariveles and took a supply tug from there. That was a few days ago."

That explains it. "This is malaria. That truck ride took him through the Bataan Peninsula. It's full of mosquitoes."

"He looks like he might die. Are you sure it's malaria?"

"Almost certain, but I suppose it could be dengue fever. That's another mosquito-borne disease that's common here, but their eyes usually don't get this yellow with dengue. It causes headaches and severe muscle and joint pains so severe the disease is also called *break-bone fever*. It might not kill you, but you might wish it would. Help me get him into the ambulance and we'll get him over to Cañacao Hospital. I'll drive."

The Medical Officer of the Day, Dr. Simmons, had them take Johnny straight to an isolation room. "He's from our unit at Sangley Point," Charles explained, "but two weeks ago he rode a truck from Olongapo down to Mariveles. I think it's malaria."

"Find the lab tech and tell him we need blood smears."

"Yes, sir. Thick and thin preps."

"Right. Meanwhile, I'm going ahead and starting him on quinine, assuming it's malaria. Let's get some aspirin into him as well." He turned to the nurse, giving more instructions. A half hour later, Dr. Simmons walked into the lab. Charles and the tech were each looking at the slides on separate microscopes. "Has he got it?"

"I think so, sir," Charles responded before the laboratory technologist could speak. Lately, he found himself less inclined to remain quiet or to back down when he was certain he had the correct answer, which in his mind was always the case. "In fact, I think he's full of it—looks like he's got more infected red cells than not." Charles moved away from his microscope, letting the doctor take his place.

After examining for himself both the thick and thin smears, the doctor looked at the other two. "Yep, an infestation of malaria. Do we all agree on the type?"

Charles was again first to answer, "It looked like rings in the red cells on the thin smear. Considering he was on Bataan a couple of weeks ago, I think it's *Plasmodium falciparum*."

"Yes, I agree. A heavy dose of the nasty type—we need to treat this aggressively. I'll switch him from quinine to Plasmochin." He looked at Charles. "That's a combination of an aminoquinoline and quinine. If the pharmacy doesn't have any on their shelf, we'll send a driver to Sternberg to pick it up. We'll replace his fluids and try to bring down his fever."

"You think the Plasmochin will work?" Charles asked.

"There's no guarantee, but, yes, he'll probably survive this." Dr. Simmons then shook his head, "The Philippines would be a great place, if it weren't for the goddamn mosquitoes."

Before returning to Sangley Point, Charles stopped at the hospital pharmacy. "We just had to hospitalize one of our men from Patrol Wing 10 with a bad case of malaria. Sangley Point's not an infested area, but our crew fly all around the islands and might find themselves in an endemic area at any time. I need to make sure our malaria prophylaxis SOP is ready for that. We only have a small supply of quinine over at our place. What can you spare us?"

"I think we have plenty." The pharmacist disappeared for a minute and returned with two bottles. "Here's a thousand tablets of quinine. I'm also letting you take a bottle of quinacrine. It's a new synthetic antimalarial drug, brand name Atabrine. I'm not sure how much more we'll be getting, so you might want to hang onto it—in case someone comes down with a resistant case out there in the jungle."

At Sangley Point, Charles bypassed the pharmaceutical closet and stashed both bottles, the quinine and the quinacrine, out of sight in the bottom of his sea bag. *Just in case ...*

Johnny was eventually allowed to return to light duty. He found Charles in the Sangley Point dispensary. "Here, Doc. I understand you took good care of me back when I got sick, and at the time I was in no condition to say thanks." He handed Charles a bottle of quality whiskey. "The doctors told me I was within hailing distance of death, and I want to thank you for bringing me back."

❧ ❧ ❧

Two weeks later, Charles stood with other squadron members sharing coffee in the shade under a beached PBY's wing. Among the coffee drinkers was the new VP-101 squadron commander, Lieutenant Commander J. V. Peterson. He took charge of the squadron in June, only days after Charles arrived. Peterson was a charismatic and respected leader who knew the name, rank, and qualifications of every man in the squadron.

"Sick Call calls," Charles said as he finished his cup, starting for the dispensary.

Commander Peterson also left the group and walked a short distance with Charles.

"Doc, fortunately I've been healthy, and you haven't seen much of me. How are things going for you here?"

"Just fine, sir," Charles responded, curious as to why the squadron commander had taken the opportunity for a private conversation.

"Corpsmen are important to us, and a good one helps morale. Most of you are OK. Some of you are better than that. For what it's worth, the squadron thinks highly of you, if you didn't know that already."

Charles just nodded his head with appreciation.

Peterson stopped walking. "Captain Wagner says the consensus in headquarters is it's only a matter of days until the Japs make their move to take the islands. When they do, we'll need every good man on deck, and we need you to be ready for it."

"Yes, sir. I'll review our protocols and supplies. And, for what it's worth, I can't think of any other unit I'd rather be in right now."

"Good! That's what I wanted to hear. If you have any problems here, Doc, let me know." Peterson turned and walked to the Squadron office.

Charles tried to sort out his emotions. *I appreciate that compliment, but did he just say the Japanese were about to attack us? In a matter of days?* He imagined the panic and carnage following the torpedo hit on the *Liverpool*. *All those dead and dying. Dismembered. Terrible burns. Am I really ready for a war?*

18

The Lesson Revisited

Sangley Point, Philippine Islands

September 1941

From the launching ramp, Charles, three other sailors and one of the pilots, Lieutenant Deede, gazed at the bank of dark clouds, first evidence of the oncoming typhoon—*bagyo* to natives.

Charles pointed to three small boats speeding around Cañacao Bay between Sangley Point and the Cavite Navy Yard. "I don't think I've seen those boats before."

"Aren't those the Q-Boats, the small torpedo boats we sent to the Philippine Army for patrolling the bay?

"I don't think so," Charles replied. "These boats look larger, and I see twin fifties both starboard and port. The Q-Boats don't have the twin machine gun turrets that these have, and the Q-boats only have one torpedo tube on each side. These have two on each side."

Lieutenant Deede spoke up. "I think those are the Navy boats that arrived a couple of weeks ago on the deck of the *Guadalupe*. I met one of the boat XOs at the Officers' Club. It's a squadron of six PT boats with their own dock, over there on the north side of the Navy Yard."

"PT boats?"

"Don't see them having much effect against a destroyer or cruiser."

"They're well-armed—four torpedoes and four .50 caliber machine guns— and a destroyer would have to catch one first. That ensign said they can do better than forty knots in a normal sea. According to him, each of those boats has three engines and more total horsepower than a PBY."

"No wonder they're so loud."

"Yep. Close your eyes and tell me you don't think they sound like one of MacArthur's P-40 Pursuit squadrons."

While they talked about the PT boats, the sky darkened and wind intensified, bringing with it the first heavy drops of rain. "Meteorologists say that typhoon's going to hit us square on," Deede said to the group. "Those planes that took off earlier today flew south, to get out of the storm. Only these two are staying here, anchored to the tarmac until the storm blows over. Get yourselves ready and stay dry, guys," Deede pulled up his collar and ran for shelter.

Joe pulled Charles to the leeward protection of a PBY hull. "I almost forgot to ask you, Doc. Since the weather's looking lousy for the weekend, some of us think it's a good time to hunker down for a game. Can you deal?"

"Sure. When and where?"

"Back of the hangar. Fifth watch, Saturday evening. Eight bells." Joe replied, using traditional Navy terms for time.

Running with Joe for the hangar, Charles complained, "Is it ever going to stop raining?"

Joe laughed. "By Christmas, Doc!"

ॐ ॐ ॐ

By Saturday evening the eye of the typhoon was crossing southern Luzon, raking Cavite with damaging winds and buckets of rain. In the shelter of PatWing 10's hangar on Sangley Point players gathered around the improvised poker table.

"Ready to go?" Charles shuffled the cards and pushed the deck for someone to cut.

Normally, the players were all PatWing 10 men. Occasionally sailors from the hospital or the Navy Yard were invited. Soldiers were never included in the games at Sangley Point. This night, one of the sailors, Jimmy, brought along a friend from his hometown, a Lance Corporal Marine. "Everyone, this is Jack. He's here at Cavite for a few weeks."

Jack shook hands, but as the evening progressed didn't engage in the ongoing banter. He did periodically sip from a hip flask between games. Charles shuffled and dealt hand after hand. Jack stayed mostly sober but steadily lost his stake.

They stayed dry inside the hangar while outside the typhoon lashed the roof and walls with heavy rain. At midnight Charles paused the game for a moment by removing and cleaning his glasses. "We have some winners and losers. The weather's not improving. Should we keep going or call it a night?" No one wanted to drop out, so he continued the game.

An hour later, through a combination of bad bets and bad luck, Jack was out of money. He quietly got up and without a word walked out the door. Jimmy followed him out, and in a few minutes came back wiping the rain from his forehead. He looked worried.

"Jack thinks he was cheated tonight," Jimmy said, looking at Charles.

"How?"

"He blames you, Doc. He doesn't know how but assumes that you were dealing him bad cards so your friends could win."

Charles shook his head. "It was a fair game. He can think what he wants, but he won't be in any more games I deal."

"I have a feeling he didn't go back to his barracks yet. Understand what I'm saying? Watch your six o'clock tonight."

"Always do." Charles was not overly muscled, but he was reasonably fit and an inch or two taller than most other men. His physicality and reputation for no-nonsense dealing usually dissuaded players from challenging his dealing. Rather than arguing with players, Charles had taken to using a quiet, menacing stare to deflect accusations.

They played for another hour before breaking up the game. Clutching their ponchos, Charles, Joe, and a third crewmate stood at the hangar door preparing to make a run for the barracks. "Go ahead. I have to stop by the clinic," Charles told the other two.

Joe was suspicious, "Are you sure? We can wait for you."

"Nope. I'll be fine."

"Then be careful," Joe warned, and the two sailors ran into the dark night, ponchos flapping in the wind and rain.

That Marine didn't confront me before leaving, so I think I have to take his silence itself as a threat. Best to resolve this here and now. I don't want to be looking over my shoulder for the rest of my time here.

Inside the dispensary Charles opened a locked cabinet and withdrew his field medical kit. The bag contained supplies he'd need in a field deployment: bandages, instruments, and medications, including morphine in syrettes, and single-use collapsible tubes with an attached hypodermic needle for administering fluids. Reaching deeper, to the bottom of the bag, he withdrew the Model 1904 Hospital Corps Knife Chief Toole had bestowed on him on his assignment to the *Langley*. He closed the bag and locked it back in the cabinet.

Charles pulled the knife from its sheath and rocked it back and forth. It was seventeen inches long, nearly three inches broad, and heavy—almost three pounds. A slight curve through its length exuded menace. Charles ran his finger along the finely sharpened edge that extended through the rounded tip and slipped the knife back inside the leather and brass scabbard. *I've stored this out of sight until I needed it—that could be tonight.* He looped the scabbard through the back of his belt, covering the knife with his poncho. After locking up, he paused outside the door and looked around. Seeing no one, he took a deep breath and dove into the rain.

It happened as he'd expected, at a dark and isolated spot. Jack suddenly stepped into his path, wielding the standard-issue Marine fighting knife with its enclosed grip and stiletto blade. The darkness and pelting rain limited their world to a ten-foot radius. Charles assessed the Marine's condition. *Even with the rain, I can see he's flushed and sweaty. He probably finished off his hip flask. Even so, his eyes are steady, and he's not staggering. I think he's had just enough booze to be dangerous.*

"OK, asshole," Jack demanded, "I'm not sure how you did it, but I know you threw cards to your buddies. I'm not robbing you—I just want back the thirty dollars I lost. Hand it over, and this goes no further."

Charles stood still while the blinding rain blew horizontally past them. A palm frond flew from a tree, striking Charles in the chest. Had there been less adrenaline flowing through his veins he'd have winced with pain, but at this moment he was barely aware of it.

Forcing himself to stare at the Marine's eyes rather than his knife, Charles spoke slowly, firmly, and just loud enough to be heard over the wind. "Jack, it seems to me you brought closer to twenty dollars, and maybe not that much. In any case, I don't have your money. You lost it to those other guys, including to your friend Jimmy. It was a fair game. There was no cheating. You were unlucky. On top of that, your betting was abysmal, atrocious." He paused for a beat before adding, "That means really bad."

"Just stop talking," Jack raised both his voice and knife, "and give me my money, now!"

Charles was left-handed but held up his right palm to the Marine, "Hold on a second." Reaching back with his left hand as if he were reaching for his pocket, he instead gripped the wood handle of the Hospital Corps Knife, smoothly extracting it from the scabbard. "Are you sure you want to do this?" he asked the surprised Marine. He let the Corps Knife hang at his side, ready but not threatening.

"Huh. I've never heard of a corpsman trained in hand to hand," the Marine gave a short laugh.

Charles knew that he had caught the Marine off guard. Jack had chosen to confront Charles when they were alone in the darkness and storm, and he had obviously assumed Charles would be unarmed. Now he faced this machete-wielding, confident-sounding corpsman standing an inch or two taller and looking at least as fit as Jack himself.

Charles responded with an unintimidated, matter-of-fact voice, "You've got barely seven inches of blade there. You'll need some luck to drop me with a single cut or poke. At some point before I go down, I'll get a swing at you."

He held the knife up for the Marine to see. "Do you know we can do emergency, single-stroke amputations with these knives?" *Good—he leaned back. He thinks that bit about amputations might be true.* "When we're finished here, I could be bleeding, but you'll be dead."

The Marine stared at Charles for what seemed a long time. He backed up a few steps, turned, and walked into the darkness. The wind carried Jack's parting words, "This is not over."

Charles willed his muscles to relax and his pulse to slow. It took three tries to put the knife back in the scabbard. *My hands are shaking. I never thought of Dad being scared when he stood up to Frank with the pitchforks in the stable. Maybe he was. I was damn sure scared tonight.*

19

Independent Duty

Sangley Point and Olongapo, Philippine Islands

October 1941

In June, despite a non-aggression pact, Germany invaded Russia. In August, aboard the *Prince of Wales* in Placentia Bay, Newfoundland, Churchill and Roosevelt signed the Atlantic Charter to "ensure life, liberty, independence and religious freedom, and to preserve the rights of man and justice." A few days later, the Reich ordered all Jews to wear a yellow star.

In October 1941, U.S. military intelligence considered all available information and reached consensus that Japan would probably attack and invade the American stronghold on Luzon, focusing on the forces surrounding Manila Bay. They also decided with reasonable certainty that the invasion would come in the spring or summer of 1942, but certainly not before April.

In preparation for an invasion, the US Army and Navy laid mines across the North and Main Channels at the entrance to Manila Bay. These included electrically controlled mines that could be remotely turned off long enough for Allied ships to enter or depart the bay.

༄ ༄ ༄

Charles walked to Cañacao Hospital using the excuse that he needed to obtain some fresh medications. That accomplished, he went to Tillie's ward and waited for her to have a free moment.

"Charles, I'm going to have to live in my uniforms from now on. All my dresses, shoes, and accessories are gone, back to the States."

"That's OK. You look good in uniform. Actually, you look good in anything."

Tillie responded sarcastically, "They keep telling us to be prepared for 'rapid movement,' but exactly where are they going to send us? Should I dress for the ocean or the jungle? It's one or the other because the only other option I see down the road is a Japanese prison."

"Sorry. I was only trying to keep your spirits up, but I wasn't lying, and I don't blame you for being concerned."

"We all are concerned. We watched the Navy send families home last year. Now the Army is scrambling to book passage to the States for all their wives and children. Why aren't they worried just as much about you and me! Why in hell don't they reinforce the islands with more men and weapons if they're really expecting an invasion?"

"Well, they did recall MacArthur to active duty. He's in charge of the U.S. Army in the Far East now. Don't you think that signals they're preparing a defense of the islands?"

"Maybe so," Tillie admitted, "But in my opinion it's going to take more than one general, no matter how famous, to push back a Japanese invasion."

PatWing 10 accelerated preparations for conflict. Seaplane tenders *Langley, Preston, Childs,* and *Heron,* packed with fuel, oil, munitions, and one spare PBY engine each, steamed to separate anchorages. Fuel barges and a floating bladder of aviation gasoline were towed to Olongapo, fifty miles north of Manila Bay. Patrols were flown by single PBYs rather than pairs, allowing wider regions of search.

Preparing for a Japanese attack without knowing when or exactly where it would arrive increased stress on the men, both mentally and physically. The Wing added to the thousands of fifty-five-gallon drums of gasoline and oil already hidden in small bays and coves throughout the Philippines. Each cache could allow two or three planes to patrol in the area for a week or more. Doing so was demanding duty on the flight crews. To refuel an empty PBY, thirty barrels of aviation gas had to be muscled to the plane and hand-pumped into the wing tanks.

The machinist's mates and radiomen had to keep their craft serviceable using only the tools and parts carried on their plane. The sailors worked with

Olongapo Naval Yard and PBY Base, 1941. Note the mothballed USS Rochester *tied to the dock. The arrow-shaped structure in the bay is a fish trap.*

an ear to the sky and an eye to the horizon should the appearance of Japanese warships or heavy bombers be the first sign of the invasion.

ॐ ॐ ॐ

"Pass me that 5/8-inch socket," Joe asked from a stand next to the engine of a PBY in the Sangley Point hangar.

"Here you go." Charles handed him the socket before asking, "Are we ready?"

"You mean the squadrons? I think so. Our planes are in fair condition. They were designed and built for long-distance patrols."

"Patrolling, OK. But what about actual war? Confronting Japanese fighters?"

"Combat's a different matter. Are you aware there's no protective armor on this plane?"

"Honestly, I haven't thought about that."

"Yeah, well, I'm thinking about it a lot. We're big and slow. Sitting ducks really. Supposedly, MacArthur's P-40 fighters are providing us with escort and cover—but so far, I've yet to see a single escort. When it starts for real, I expect they'll all be flying cover for his precious B-17 bombers, not us."

"You have the machine guns."

"For what little good they'll do against a fast-moving Zero coming from above or below you. We don't even have any reliable ammunition."

"What do you mean?"

"Almost all of our ammunition belts are practice rounds. Supply either doesn't have any belts of the armor-piercing .50 caliber rounds, or they're hoarding them for later."

"You're thinking later will already be too late, and I have to agree with you. Personally, I hate this waiting, not knowing when or where it'll happen. Need anything else before I go?"

"Nah, I've got it. Thanks for the help though."

Charles walked to the small Sangley Point dock. In the distance he could see the USS *Arizona* refueling and resupplying at the Navy Yard. *She must have just escorted another convoy of transport ships loaded with tanks and supplies for MacArthur's army. They'll probably unload in record time so the* Arizona *can herd them back to Pearl Harbor.*

"Hey, Doc!" a crewman called across the tarmac.

"Yes?"

"Wagner wants to see you."

Why does he want to see me?

Wagner was straight to the point. "Doc, we're making some changes."

Oh crap! Here we go again. Good thing I've learned to 'go with the punches' by now.

"Yes, sir?"

"The corpsman with VP-102 is moving. Medical HQ says you're qualified for independent duty, so we're sending you to Olongapo to replace him."

"Yes, sir." Charles's pulse quickened. *This is it! I'll be on my own.* Excitement wrangled with anxiety in the pit of his stomach.

"You'll have backup. All 4th Marines replacements originally ordered to China are now diverting to the 1st Separate Marine Detachment at Cavite. The 800 4th Marines still at Shanghai are in the process of moving to Olongapo. When their field hospital is set up, that'll be your immediate support. One of the utility squadron planes can fly you to Olongapo tomorrow morning."

"It won't take me long to throw my things together. Is there anything special you think I should take?"

"Actually, yes." Wagner paused for a moment. "Japan signed on to the

Geneva conventions, but they didn't ratify them. From what we know has happened in China, a red cross on your sleeve means nothing more to the Japanese than a good target. Subic Bay is isolated. If you feel comfortable with a sidearm, sign one out this afternoon. Nobody should question you. If they do, refer them to me."

If I feel comfortable? The Navy trained me. Besides, I hunted Indiana fields and woods with a gun, alone, when I was ten years old. "Yes, sir. I'll do that as soon as I leave here."

Early that evening Charles walked to the hospital to share his news. Tillie wasn't working, but he sent a message into the nurses' quarters. Only a few seconds later, she joined him under the banyan tree.

Her response to his news was neutral. "That's good, both for you and for the squadron you're going to. I guess you're at no greater risk out there than you would be at Sangley Point."

"Probably not."

"Charles, this waiting for the Japanese to do something, it's stressful on all of us. Is it really going to happen?"

"Everyone in PatWing 10 is convinced it is—and soon. Wagner hasn't said it explicitly, but it's clear he expects the Japanese to attack any day now, even if command still insists it won't come before April. Any news here at the hospital?"

"Nothing. Everyone's just waiting for the other shoe to drop."

"Will they be sending the nurses to Hawaii or Stateside?"

Tillie's temper flared. "Neither one, Charles! Who do you think will take care of the wounded when the fighting starts? I'm a woman, but I'm in the Navy, just like you. I will perform my duty, just like every other Navy officer. Every other nurse here feels exactly the same way. We are as brave as any man. Don't patronize us!"

"Sorry," Charles tried to recover, "It's just that most of the civilian women are being sent home, and—"

"I know, I know," Tillie softened her tone. "But if you think about it, we nurses become even more important when combat starts. Just like you, we've trained for this, and when it comes we're not about to run away."

Happy to have avoided the hours of travel to Olongapo over bad roads, Charles enjoyed his view from the passenger seat in the utility squadron's single-engine Grumman Duck seaplane. On his first and only previous visit to Olongapo, he'd not even stepped ashore. Now he stood on the dock and surveyed his new home. Several PBYs rocked gently at buoys strung in the bay opposite a disused coaling facility. A fuel barge loaded with hundreds of barrels of aviation gas floated at an otherwise abandoned dock. Next to that barge, a large bladder full of avgas floated low in the water. An old but well-constructed rock wall bordered the bay.

"Hello!"

A corpsman walked towards Charles. "I remember you. You were the corpsman in the PBY that picked up our man with the broken leg." He grabbed Charles's bag. "I'll take you by HQ to meet the boss, then we can walk to my place."

"If my recall is correct, your name was Robert?"

"Robert, Bob, hey you, or anything else. As of today, just call me 'gone.'"

At the Squadron headquarters hut Charles received a brief introduction and welcome from Commander Perkins and several other officers and sailors before Bob guided him outside. "Let's go grab my sea bag. I'm ready to get out of here."

"Is it that bad?"

"Not really. Mostly boring, in fact. Twenty years ago, this was *the* naval base in the Philippines. But after the war, a treaty with Japan had us dismantle most everything at Subic Bay, leaving it a pretty small operation."

"What happened to that giant floating dry dock I saw when I flew up here a few months ago?" Charles asked.

"That was the USS *Dewey*. It'd been here since 1907, I think. They towed it down to Mariveles last summer—supposed to be safer from the Japs down there."

"This is a fine-looking place though," Charles commented, looking around. "I'm surprised at the extensive landscaping."

"I guess it's nice," the corpsman answered without enthusiasm. "Back when we weren't worried about fighting a war, someone started a beautification program. They lined the streets with coconut palms, hibiscus, and gardenias, and even built a golf course. Now everyone's wishing they'd spent a little more effort and money on anti-aircraft batteries. At least our air defenses will get upgraded when the 4th Marines arrive."

"I know the Marines are leaving China and moving here, but I never heard why."

157

"It was unexpected. The Marines have been in China for more than a hundred years. But when the British needed their China troops elsewhere, and the Vichy government ordered all French troops to cooperate with Japan, it left our Marines vulnerable. They're moving here before they wind up in a Jap prison."

"I've seen a couple of Marines while we've walked around."

"Those are part of a small advance contingent. They're converting some warehouses into quarters before the others arrive. Two American President Line ships, the *Harrison* and *Madison,* I think, will arrive this week from Shanghai bringing us around 800 Marines." Bob walked them back to the squadron's combination headquarters, officers' rooms, and parts storage. "Here's my desk for sick call and keeping paperwork. Pretty thin records. Everyone's healthy, and I haven't had any major injuries to deal with."

"What's Olongapo like?"

"About a mile down the road, past the Navy Yard and rifle range, that little fishing village on the bay is Barrio Olongapo. It's got maybe a half-dozen flea-bitten bars, most of them little open-air affairs with a dance partition next door. The taxi girls know the Marines are on their way and are looking forward to a lot of business."

"Is their beer cold?"

"Not really, but be careful about drinking anything else. A bottle of San Miguel might be all right, but they dilute their whisky and gin with some unknown, locally distilled spirit. I can whiff an overtone of kerosene in the drinks, and it leaves the sailors who drink it with a horrible hangover. I would stay far away from that stuff if I were you."

"Good to know." Charles nodded. "What's the option?"

"The senior NCOs and officers tend to pass up that first set of bars and travel further down the road to Barrio Santa Rosa. There's a quiet bar there overlooking the river. The booze is OK, and it's a little safer."

The corpsman then dropped a surprise. "The squadron command is changing this week. Lieutenant Commander Perkins has been in command of VP-102 for more than a year. We call him the 'Southern Gentleman'—he's pleasant and undemanding—some say easygoing." They reached the enlisted quarters. "Here's my little corner of Olongapo."

"This'll do." Charles looked the space over. "A new squadron commander you said. Who are we getting?"

"Perkins's replacement is a Lieutenant Commander Edgar Neale, and things might not be so laid-back in the future. The scuttlebutt is that Neale's all business and has a sharp temper. He's supposed to be fair and know his stuff, but everyone's holding their breath until they find out if the rumors about his temper are true—here's my ride." He hoisted his bag to leave. "Sorry to run, but this truck's leaving for Manila, and I'm outta here. Good luck!"

Charles dropped his bags in the newly vacated space. *I can unpack later.* He set out to meet other sailors in the squadron and explore the small seaplane base. He immediately encountered a crewman next to the launching ramp, busy on a wood construction project. "Hi. I'm Charles Beckner, your new corpsman. That's interesting cabinetry you're working on there."

"Heard you were coming. Welcome aboard, Doc. I'm Carpenter's Mate George Gaboury."

"What are you building here?"

"Can't you tell, Doc? It's a PBY. We already have one built and floating out there." George pointed to an aircraft-shaped structure in the bay.

"Decoys?" Charles guessed at the purpose of his creations.

"Right," George smiled with pride. "The pilots tell me that from 5,000 feet it looks like a real PBY. This is the second one, and if we have time, I'll make a third."

Moving along to a wide dock on the north side of the base, Charles inspected an old, decommissioned armored cruiser, the USS *Rochester.* It looked to have been tied to the dock for years. Most of her operational fixtures were absent, and rusty streaks ran down the superstructure and hull. But even old and rusted, the *Rochester* was impressive. Charles climbed up the gangway and explored the old ship for over an hour. Absent her small armaments, the remaining 8-inch guns still recalled a time when she could project overseas power for the United States. Later, at evening mess, Charles asked about the old cruiser and was told, "It's been there forever, Doc. It was commissioned before the Spanish-American War. They decommissioned her seven or eight years ago, and she's floated at that dock ever since."

Charles soon learned the rumors about Edgar Neale were at least partially true. He was demanding and exhibited little patience. A day after assuming command, Neale met with his senior officers before addressing the entire squadron. "Our readiness has to be bumped up a couple of notches. I'm certain an attack is coming any day. You've watched the Japanese positioning warships and troop transports down the coast of Indochina. Now, there're reports of Jap fighters making threatening passes on patrolling PBYs. We can only assume they're practicing for the real thing. None of us can stop a war from happening, but this squadron can be ready when it does."

"Does that mean our routine's changing?" an NCO asked.

"For right now, we'll continue searching and tracking. Admiral Hart and General MacArthur need us to see the Japs coming from a distance. If we give them enough advance warning, our ships and subs can intercept them while MacArthur's troops and air forces prepare a welcome ceremony at the beach. No more liberty. Let's get ready."

After the briefing, Neale asked Charles for a medical status update on the squadron. "Any major problems, Doc? Everyone's gotta be healthy. Anyone who's not one-hundred percent I'll send back to Cavite."

"Everyone's good to go, sir. Our medical supplies are adequate, at least for now."

"Let me know if that changes."

"Will do, sir."

Similar preparations were underway back at Sangley Point. Aircrews received their wartime codes. Patrols searched to the limits of their fuel range. PatWing 10 tenders and planes dispersed, lessening the possibility of losing them all in a single attack. The *Heron* and four light planes of the Utility Squadron moved to the southern tip of Palawan Island. The *Preston* and three PBYs moved far south to the Gulf of Davao. Several PBYs shifted to a temporary base at Los Baños on Laguna de Bay, southeast of Manila. Anchored near the docks at Manila, the crew of the *Childs* attempted to camouflage their ship by rigging a canvas tarp between the bridge and the forward funnel. The *Langley*, for the moment, remained at Sangley Point.

On November 30th, the SS *President Madison* arrived at Olongapo with 400 men of the 4th Marine Regiment, the "Shanghai" Marines. The next day the SS *President Harrison* arrived with 300 more of the 4th. The *Harrison* quickly replenished with food and fresh water and steamed back towards Shanghai to pick up the last few Marines.

Curious, Charles mingled with the Marines moving into the old warehouses, now their new quarters. "How was the trip from China?" he asked one of the men still stretching from confinement on the crowded transport.

"Not bad."

"Really?"

"Really? OK, it *was* bad. We were stuffed in the hold with three-high bunks. It was so hot, the hatches were left open. We pitched and rolled to the point that water poured through the open hatches into our compartments. Every time there was a big roll, the bottom bunks at the walls were submerged. It was fucking miserable!"

Surprised, Charles weakly offered, "Should be better here, don't you think?"

The Marine looked around, smiling. "Yeah, and that trip's over. A Marine looks forward, never back. This is a goddamn palace—I could stay here forever!"

Marcus Aurelius would have loved to have this guy in his army.

It didn't take long for the 717 men of the 4th Marines to adapt the Navy Yard to their needs. Cooks set up kitchens and immediately began serving hot meals. Finding the existing sanitation facilities beyond capacity, the Marines constructed temporary latrines by fastening long boards with regularly spaced holes over bay waters. They were open-air, but functional in the short run.

Charles admired the Marines' speed and efficiency setting up the regimental Marine hospital. "How many beds are you going to have?"

"For now, we're setting up our basic configuration, only a dozen beds. If needed, we can quickly expand to a hundred."

The Marines immediately established a defensive perimeter and began adding strategically placed sandbag machine gun emplacements. *These guys mean business. That Marine who came after me with the knife notwithstanding, I truly admire them.*

Squadron 102 flew their patrols, returned, refueled, and after a few hours' rest flew back out again and again. They were the eyes of the Army and Navy in the South China Sea and along the Chinese coast. Daily they reported Japanese ship sightings and movements to Admiral Hart's and General MacArthur's commands. Japanese air, sea, and ground forces were undoubtedly positioning for their invasion of the Philippine Islands.

Part III

20

Govern Yourselves Accordingly

Olongapo, Philippine Islands

2-8 December 1941

The patrol reports PatWing 10 Commander Wagner forwarded up the chain of command were officially confidential. Within the close-knit community of VP-102, though, there were few secrets. The combined stories from returning crews painted a clear picture of dozens of Japanese ships positioning for a direct assault on Luzon. On Taiwan, only a few flying hours north of Manila, A PBY observer counted hundreds of Japanese heavy bombers and fighters waiting expectantly along the runways.

On 2 December, a VP-102 PBY flown by Bill Robinson and Andrew Burgess found more than twenty Japanese merchant ships in Cam Ranh Bay.

On 3 December another patrol was shocked to find a fifty-ship flotilla, including destroyers and cruisers, steaming off the Indochina coast. Follow-up patrols the next day failed to locate those ships.

On 4, 5, and 6 December, multiple PBY patrols encountered Japanese bombers flying off the coast of Luzon.

Despite Washington's persistent predictions of an April or later assault, commanders in the Philippines knew the Japanese would not position their forces for attack, only to hold them there another four months.

At Olongapo the men of VP-102 talked of little else. One sailor offered his own contrarian prediction, "I think it's all for show. Attacking us would be poking the hornet's nest. Roosevelt would throw everything we've got and send

165

them back to Tokyo with their tails between their legs. Right, Doc?"

Charles only shrugged. *I'm not so sure. Pearl's a long way from here, even if they were ready to sail immediately.*

Sunday morning, 7 December, Edgar Neale assembled the squadron for a sobering all-hands meeting. "I suggest you all make sure your affairs are in order. You don't need a legal document. Use a clean sheet of paper. Write simply, in your own words, where you want your stuff to go. Sign and date it."

"I don't have anything but dirty clothes," a voice called out. "Do I write a letter for them?"

Neale didn't laugh. "You may not think you have anything valuable, but most all of you have something. What do you have back home? A stamp or card collection? A car or motorcycle? Do you want your mother or your wife or a brother to have something special? Just use simple language, and let someone back home know what to do if you don't make it back."

Neale paused for questions, but the men understood exactly what was happening and wrote their letters in silence. Along with instructions to survivors, some envelopes contained checks. The letters would be posted for delivery on the next transport, though it was anyone's guess when that might be.

Charles thought for a few minutes. He really didn't own anything except for a few books, and the Navy was already sending most of his paycheck home with instructions to "use what you need and hold the rest for when I come home." He finally put pencil to paper:

To Mary Beckner,

My body and mind are in fine shape, and I expect to stay that way until I return to Princeton. However, we have all been ordered to send instructions to our families. If the Navy loses track of me this year, my money and any personal property should be given equally to you, my sister, and James, my brother, to hold until I am located. This includes any money held or owed to me by the US Navy. I know you will do the right thing with it.

Charles Conrad Beckner PhM3
Navy Base, Olongapo, Philippine Islands

7 December 1941

꿩 꿩 꿩

Because of the international date line between Hawaii and Luzon, Olongapo was a day ahead of Hawaii on the calendar. It was 1200 hours Saturday, 6 December, in Honolulu, but it was 0900 Sunday, 7 December, for VP-102 in Olongapo. Local Filipinos busily prepared for the feast and festival of the Immaculate Conception, held every December 8th. Though small, Barrio Olongapo possessed its own richly ornate statue of the Blessed Virgin for parading down the avenue after an early Mass. With less public fanfare, cockfighting arenas and gambling dens prepared for a busy day, and the dance bars scheduled extra staff.

Rather than writing more letters that might never leave Olongapo, Charles decided to stuff his field medical kit with as many bandages and other supplies as it would hold. He had no experience of combat, but he recalled war stories shared by the senior petty officers and chiefs during his time at the Mare Island Hospital. *Most of what I've seen in sick call is sunburns, VD, and sprained ankles. Am I ready to treat men with severe burns and machine gun and shrapnel injuries?*

He sat on a bench, pulled a book from his kit, and adjusted his glasses.

"What are you reading?" a passing sailor asked.

Charles held up his *Hospital Corps Handbook*. "I'm just reviewing some things I haven't read since I was in the Corps School. Look here, on page 100, *Gunshot wounds caused by bullets*. Redundant, don't you think?"

The sailor either didn't grasp the sarcasm in Charles's comment or ignored it. "It's really about to happen, isn't it?"

Charles thought a moment. "I guess so," he finally answered.

Fading reds and oranges in the western sky gave way to darkness. Under blackout, the base seemed unusually quiet. Sailors and Marines, alone with their thoughts, tossed and turned in their bunks. The Stoics and fatalists, though, slept soundly.

꿩 꿩 꿩

On Monday, 8 December, at 0315 hours, the communications duty officer at Cavite, Ensign Arthur Jacobson, received a decoded message from Admiral Hart's headquarters. He quickly forwarded that message to several naval commands, including PatWing 10 at Sangley Point. Russell Enterline, an aviation radioman on mid-watch, yanked off his earphones and ran to the other side of the building to wake the sleeping wing commander.

Captain Frank Wagner read the message and jumped up. "This is it!" Still in his polka-dot pajamas, Wagner sprinted downstairs and rang the warning bell for all hands to fall in.

At Olongapo the night duty officer, Ensign Frank Ralston, received the message.

"Commander Neale! Commander Neale!"

"What time is it, Ralston?" demanded a groggy Edgar Neale, struggling to fully wake up.

"Oh-three-thirty. There's a message from wing HQ you need to see."

Edgar Neale took the message from Ralston and read it fast. He then reread it slowly.

From: Admiral Hart, Commander in Chief Asiatic Fleet.
JAPAN STARTED HOSTILITIES
GOVERN YOURSELVES ACCORDINGLY.

Neale read the message a third time with a furrowed brow, then said quietly. "Roust the squadron."

Lights blazed throughout the quarters. "On your feet! The war's started!"

"With Germany or Japan?" a sleepy voice asked amid the confusion.

"Where?" asked another. "I don't hear anything."

"Don't know, but get your ass to the hangar in ten minutes. Commander Neale's going to tell us what's going on."

In the officers' hut, Tom McCabe was already up and shaving in preparation for an early patrol when a friend rushed in.

"They're waking us all up, Tom. We have to report to the hangar."

"But I have a flight now—"

"Plans may have changed. I think the Japs have attacked."

"When? Where?"

"No one's told us that yet."

꙲ ꙲ ꙲

At 0400 Commander Neale joined the assembled squadron in the hangar and called for everyone's attention, "We received this a few minutes ago from Admiral Hart." He paused, then read out loud, "'Japan started hostilities. Govern yourselves accordingly.'"

Murmurs went through the assembled men. Charles thought the message more cryptic than informative. *Obviously, there's been no attack here at Olongapo. Did they bomb Manila or Cavite? Maybe they're landing troops on one of the island beaches?*

"Where'd they attack?" someone shouted out.

"I don't know that—I don't even know if it's a landing or just an air raid. When I have that information, I'll pass it on. In any case, we are now at war. I haven't received any specific new orders, but we should assume they'll attack Sangley Point and here. When I know more, I'll pass on updates. Meanwhile, hang 500-pounders on your planes, and get them in the air."

As the men dispersed, Charles asked a pilot next to him, "What does 'Govern yourselves accordingly' mean?"

The ensign shrugged. "I have no idea what in hell Admiral Hart meant by that, but I'm going to assume it means 'try and stay alive.'"

"Started hostilities" was indeed a vague characterization for an attack. The uncertainty over where the attack had taken place and how much damage had been inflicted was unsettling to say the least. Bravado, false or not, was a common response to the news. As one sailor voiced it, "They just poked us with a stick. Let's go kick their ass."

Charles sat with a furrowed brow. *The German army rolled right over Europe. The Japanese might try to do the same out here, throwing everything they've got, hoping to overrun these islands quickly.*

Then his thoughts refocused. *What about Tillie? Did they attack Cavite?*

ʃ∾ ʃ∾ ʃ∾

While crews winched up bombs and secured them to the wings, Charles helped load boxes of .30 and .50 caliber ammunition, pausing to examine a box label. "Hey!" he exclaimed. "These belts are practice rounds—" and tried to push the ammunition box back out.

The sailor pushed it back glumly, stating, "No mistake, Doc. This is all we got left. There's supposed to be more ammunition somewhere on a barge between here and Sangley Point. Maybe until then the noise'll just scare them off."

He saw the radioman go forward to the pilot's compartment to relay a message he'd just received. Charles heard some unintelligible conversation, and then a loud "Nonsense!" from Tom McCabe, the pilot.

Charles stuck his head into the radio compartment. "What was that all about?"

"We got a message that the Japanese attacked Pearl Harbor a few hours ago, and I just passed the word to the pilots. The lieutenant says it's not possible."

"Seems unlikely, if they're busy attacking us here," Charles agreed with McCabe.

"Then you tell me why they sent the goddamn message."

With all those ships and bombers circling Luzon, how could they have also attacked Pearl? Hawaii's in the middle of nowhere, halfway to San Francisco. Why attack there? The Pacific Fleet's so large that even if they did sink a couple of our ships, we'd still be the strongest navy in the Pacific by far. It doesn't make sense.

"Pearl Harbor? I'm confused. You mean they've attacked here in the Philippines *and* at Pearl?"

The radioman turned back to his console. "That was the message, Doc. I don't think it was a joke."

Charles felt the plane start its roll to the launching ramp, crawled out the hatch, and jumped to the tarmac. PatWing 10 was executing plans they'd been practicing for months. Seven of VP-102's planes flew from Olongapo to advance temporary bases. The seven remaining planes, heavy with 500-pound bombs, flew out in search of Japanese warships.

Whether or not they found any ships to bomb, it was best for the PBYs to be somewhere else if Olongapo itself was attacked.

With all of our planes out, it's eerily quiet here. Fortunately, there wasn't even a mashed finger in the rush to hang the bombs and get the planes airborne. It seems I should be doing something, though.

Charles heard a faint sound and tilted his ear in that direction. *Are those aircraft engines? Yes, and a lot of them. Maybe the B-17s from Clark Field or P-40s from Nichols Field are heading to bomb the Japanese airfields up at Formosa? No, those are unsynchronized engines, a different sound from the B-17s—I hear explosions in the distance. Bombs? Maybe I can find out what's happening at the commander's office.*

Neale's usually open office door was closed. Charles raised his eyebrows and tilted his head questioningly at the clerk, who frowned and gave a quick shake of his head—obviously not the time for a casual chat.

Charles left the office but stayed nearby until he saw the clerk leave. He caught up with him at the latrine. "Hi, headed my way?"

"Only if you need to piss."

"As a matter of fact, I think I do."

Charles opened the door, and they entered the unoccupied latrine.

They talked while emptying their bladders. "OK, Doc, I'll be quick, and try to keep this to yourself. The shit's hit the fan, big time. The Japs have taken out Pearl."

"I heard that already."

"No—I mean, taken out! Destroyed! Almost the entire Pacific Fleet was tied up at the docks, and they damaged or sank most of them. There're thousands of casualties. Only good news is that at least a couple of the carriers were at sea."

"I thought—"

"Let me finish, Doc! Also, while we've been sitting up here on our butts sending out patrols trying to find the Jap fleet, they hit us down south. This morning Jap planes attacked our PBYs with the *Preston* down in Davao Gulf. Tillis was killed in his plane."

"Our Ensign Tillis? Dead?"

"Yes! Now stop interrupting—I need to get back. They just now hit us here on Luzon. They bombed and strafed Clark, Iba, and Nichols fields. For some reason, most of our fighters and B-17s were just sitting on the ground and were damaged or destroyed. That means our PBYs won't have air cover when they fly."

This is very bad news. "And the good news is?"

"There isn't any, unless you count Cavite Navy Yard and Sangley Point not getting hit—at least not so far. And one last thing. They're sending Neale back to Cavite, and Preston is moving with some VP-101 PBYs from Cavite to Los Baños. Neale says he sees no sense at all in the moves, but apparently it's part of the war plan."

The abrupt transfer of two squadron commanders within hours of the start of a war surprised Charles. "So, is 102 moving too?"

"Doc, I don't know, and I'm not sure anyone else knows at this point. Just be ready. We could get hit anytime," and he hurriedly returned to his desk while Charles stayed in the latrine, trying to absorb this new, startlingly bad, news.

21

This is Real

Olongapo, Philippine Islands

9-10 December 1941

At dawn a small group of Marines left Olongapo in trucks. They were an advance group to prepare for the entire regiment's transfer to Mariveles Naval Section Base at the southern tip of the Bataan Peninsula. From the old stone dock, Charles stood by watching Marines load their equipment aboard a ship hastily recruited for repositioning the regiment to Mariveles. *Wait! Is that the USS* Vega? *It is! Twenty-six months ago I was aboard that very ship, on my way from San Diego to Mare Island. I had no idea then . . .*

Seventy-six Marines stayed behind as the Olongapo Detachment. Their mission was to protect the Naval Station and augment the fire protection system. Ominously, they also began preparing shore facilities and fuel stores for demolition. The Regimental hospital departed with the main group on the *Vega,* leaving behind a small field hospital and skeleton staff.

The sailors and Marines remaining at Olongapo anxiously waited, expecting the Japanese to attack at any moment.

Charles thought that time had come when a sailor burst through the door yelling, "Doc! Doc!" He held the door open, waving, "Hurry, Doc! The 21 plane got shot up on its way in—they just landed, with casualties."

Charles grabbed his medical pack. "Japanese fighter planes?"

"No, Doc—it was the Filipinos. McConnell and Watson were coming in and setting up for a landward approach to Subic Bay. The anti-aircraft battery must have been nervous and ready to shoot at anything. Gave no warning and opened fire with machine guns. McConnell radioed he had multiple wounded, but he was still able to bring the plane in with a hard landing."

Riding a small launch to the 21 plane, Charles could see bullet holes across its hull. Climbing through the waist hatch, he smelled then saw a mix of water, leaking fuel, and fresh blood sloshing in the bilges. Machinist's Mate Thomas Marbry lay on a cot in the crew compartment, his leg nearly severed at the knee.

McConnell had already jumped from his seat and come aft to help his crewman. He was bent over his stricken mechanic, struggling to staunch the flow with a compression bandage. "It's still bleeding, Doc—" he called, as bright red blood spurted from obviously severed arteries.

"Not your fault—it'll take more than pressure." Charles pulled a tourniquet from his pocket and tightened it above the knee. Once satisfied the bleeding was controlled, he wrapped the wound with more compression bandages. Giving Marbry an injection of morphine, he told two sailors behind him, "Support his leg, and move him out of here on a stretcher. Take him to the Marine Field Hospital."

In the radio/navigation compartment Radioman James Gray sat, crumpled against the bulkhead, fully conscious and bleeding from a groin wound. *Can't put a tourniquet on that. Doesn't look to be bleeding nearly as profusely as Marbry though—at least not on the outside.*

"Easy now," Charles said, lowering Gray gently onto his back, "Let me get a better look." After an injection of morphine to relax Gray's muscles, Charles did a closer examination. "I think you're going to be OK," he reassured Gray. "It's not a deep wound. No major artery was hit, and there doesn't seem to be any bone injury." After packing the wound with gauze, Charles covered it with a pressure bandage, then nodded to crewmen who had arrived with another stretcher, "The Marine hospital for him, too." Squadron members moved Gray to a stretcher and gingerly manipulated it from the plane.

Charles stepped up to the pilots' compartment, noting the smashed instruments and broken glass. "Hey there, sir," he said to Ensign Watson, who was still in his seat. McConnell had wrapped the man's elbow, but the impromptu bandage was already soaked with blood. "How are you doing?" he added as he unwrapped the bandage to inspect the injury. "Need to lie down?"

"No. It hurts a bit, Doc, but don't give me morphine. How bad is it? I don't really want to look myself."

"You're still bleeding, but it's slow. Can you make a fist? Feel your fingers? Definitely Purple Heart, sir, but I don't see any critical damage. You'll be good as new in a couple of weeks." He dressed the wound and put the arm in a sling before helping the ensign from the plane.

Charles accompanied Watson to the Marine aid station, where Gray was resting easy. Marbry, on the other hand, was not doing well. He was in shock, with barely detectable blood pressure. He'd lost a tremendous amount of blood in the short time between the attack and Charles tightening a tourniquet on the leg. The Marine doctor and two corpsmen worked from both sides of the stretcher. Charles watched them push fluid through two IVs, trying to restore Marbry's blood pressure so they could safely attempt surgery. *At best, they'll amputate his leg. At worst, they won't get that far. Not much more I can do here.*

❧ ❧ ❧

Facing uncertainty when, or if, Olongapo would receive more ammunition or food, rationing began by limiting meals to breakfast before daylight and dinner before dark. In the predawn blackout darkness of December 10, Charles listened to an unseen crewman complain, "This food is shit, but I'd still like to see what I'm eating."

A different voice answered. "Just pretend you're having a romantic dinner with your girl, and she blew out the candles."

The much-anticipated replacement ammunition never arrived, leaving almost nothing but boxes with .30 and .50 caliber practice rounds. If the Marines had better, they didn't offer to share.

After watching PBYs lift from the water for dawn patrol, Charles walked to the Marine hospital. The Navy doctor, red-eyed from exhaustion, didn't wait for Charles's question. "Sorry, Doc. Your man, Marbry, never made it to surgery. He died a few hours after you left. Those other two are doing fine, though."

Gray was indeed doing well and anxious to get back to duty. Watson had already talked the doctor into discharging him that day, arguing, "It only takes one arm to fly a PBY." Charles asked the surgeon, "Sir, do you have time for a couple of logistical questions about managing casualties when we're attacked?"

"Sure." The Navy doctor offered Charles a cup of surprisingly drinkable coffee. "What do you need from us?"

"If—or I guess when—the Japanese attack Olongapo, there could be multiple casualties in our squadron, and you'll probably be busy with your own. How should I best coordinate with you when that happens?"

"First, if you haven't heard, we're packing up and moving down the road to a less likely target. We're taking over the Riverside Cabaret and setting it up as an emergency field hospital. I'll still be the only surgeon, but we'll take any of your critically wounded and do the best we can. What else?"

"I think that's it. I'm good for supplies if I'm only supporting what's left here of VP-102."

"Good. We're in reasonable shape ourselves, except for quinine. We didn't have malaria in China. If we're chased into the hills, we'd be in trouble. I don't know if you got the word, quinine has been designated a scarce commodity. I can't even request it without higher approval."

"I have a little, sir. If needs be, we'll share."

Leaving the hospital, Charles could see Marines sandbagging additional .30 caliber machine gun emplacements around the base. *The Japanese won't find us easy pickings.*

He looked around. Above the warehouse roof, the mast and stacks of the decommissioned USS *Rochester* pointed skyward. *Now there's a good position. With a machine gun up there, we could at least put up harassment fire.*

Charles joined a group of somber men gathered in the shade of a building. "You guys don't look too happy. What's going on?"

"We just got word that the Japs bombed Cavite. Their bombers flew higher than the anti-aircraft guns could reach, and we had no fighters in the air. They just took their time and bombed the hell out of the Navy Yard."

A sailor added, "Sangley Point didn't get much damage, but still we lost two, maybe three, of our planes."

Charles's thoughts flashed to Tillie. *Cañacao Hospital's between Sangley Point and the Navy Yard. Maybe the Japanese ignored them? Or maybe they went after the giant communication towers and the hospital was close enough to get hit also?* "What about Cañacao Hospital?"

The group looked at one another for an answer. "Dunno," someone finally acknowledged.

Though Sangley Point had so far escaped the bombings, Wagner foresaw the inevitable. He moved the still flyable planes to Los Baños and transferred PatWing 10 headquarters and his staff to the *Childs*.

A machinist's mate lay prone on the table while Charles stitched a small laceration in the back of his leg.

"Thanks, Doc. Those Jap bastards are going to be sorry they ever thought about attacking the United States of America!"

"I hope you're right, but so far it looks to me like the Japanese are running the show. I haven't seen a single B-17 or American fighter in the air. I expected at least a struggle for air superiority when the Japanese attacked. You have to admit it's a little depressing to see those Betty bombers and Zero fighters fly back and forth all day, unchallenged."

"Someone fucked up bad to put us in this situation, Doc. They must be running around Washington like chickens with their heads cut off."

Charles shared the pessimism, but while treating the injured man he felt obliged to be optimistic. "We're going to be OK—MacArthur's setting up troops on the beaches to push back any Japanese invasion."

"Good luck with that. He'll have to do it with no Navy and no airplanes."

"What do you mean, 'no Navy'?"

"Haven't you heard, Doc? Admiral Hart's ordered the whole Asiatic fleet south, including his submarines."

"Why would he do that?"

"To save his ships. They're sitting ducks without air cover. We've seen the last of them."

"Does that mean PatWing 10's leaving too?"

"We're part of the fleet, ain't we?"

I guess I shouldn't be surprised. "Even if that's the case, everything's on the way. Troops, planes, battleships, and supplies."

"So we've been told, but I'm not sure I believe it, Doc."

"I might have some doubts myself." *I'll hope for the best, but I damn well better prepare for the worst.*

22

The Attack

Olongapo, Philippine Islands

11 December 1941

Thursday, 11 December, three days after the opening salvo of the war with Japan, the Olongapo morning breeze carried a strong aroma of coffee wafting from large vats of boiling water and muslin-wrapped coffee grounds. Charles dropped his two sets of Navy whites, along with his 'Dixie-cup' hat, into one of the vats. *Damn waste of coffee. Even if it is bad coffee.*

"How long do I leave them in there?" he asked the sailor stirring the stew of coffee and clothing.

"Doesn't take long, around ten minutes for the coffee stain to set." After a few minutes the sailor lifted Charles's uniforms from the water and draped them over a line to dry. "There, you have two more sets of khakis."

Charles was unimpressed. "That's not any shade of khaki I've ever seen. It's more like jaundice yellow."

"Don't matter, Doc. It won't make you a target like the bright white did. Coffee-stain brown is the new uniform of the day."

Lieutenant Commander Marcy, the senior VP-102 officer in Olongapo following Neale's departure for Cavite, reviewed their situation with his men.

"We've managed to get three planes out on patrol while we service and repair four more planes. By my count, PatWing 10 has only twenty-one planes still flyable and maybe two more that are repairable. We can't last long if we keep losing one or two planes a day. Also, the parts on hand now are all we'll have for the foreseeable future. Repair rather than replace whenever possible."

Charles stopped holding his regular sick call for the squadron. If someone had an injury or fell ill, they knew where to find him day or night. Instead, he worked with the mechanics, handing them tools or parts, and generally helping wherever he could. He still had no information about the status of Cañacao Hospital, and no convincing excuse to use official radio communication to find out. *Maybe the Marines know something.*

At the Riverside Cabaret, now a 4th Marine Field Hospital, Charles asked one of their corpsmen, "Have you heard anything about Cañacao Hospital since yesterday's attack?"

"No, but we've been told not to ask you to fly patients to Cavite. We're to take them overland to the Sternberg Army hospital in Manila."

"Did they say why?"

"Nope."

There must be some other reason to stop sending patients to the Cañacao Hospital other than it having been bombed or destroyed.

Walking back to the squadron, Charles again looked at the *Rochester* and its superstructure. *Up there is the best field of view on the entire base. I'll talk to Commander Marcy.*

He found the commander and suggested, "Sir, the Marines have their sandbagged machine gun emplacements around the base, but no elevated positions. I think we ought to take one of the squadron's .50 cal machine guns and mount it above the *Rochester*'s bridge. From there a gunner could cover the entire base and sky. Is it OK if I check it out closer? I could get one of the machinists to install a mount."

"Go ahead and check it out, Doc, but I'll find someone else to man the gun. I want you here if there's an attack."

"Yes, sir. It's almost dark, so I'll take a closer look at the *Rochester* tomorrow and report back."

In the predawn hours of Friday morning, 12 December, Olongapo received information from Filipino coast watchers that five battleships flanked by five destroyers were off the Luzon coast and headed for Manila Bay. Marcy ordered the crews to load four bombs on each of the seven PBYs remaining at Olongapo.

By 0600 they were airborne, Marcy flying the lead craft, searching for the reported battleship group.

They found nothing.

Returning to Olongapo around 0900, six of the PBYs moored to the floating buoys along the old coaling dock. Ensign Andy Reid anchored his plane, P-29, in a spot near some trees he thought might provide shelter and concealment. It offered enough shade to allow two crewmen to doze on the plane's broad wings.

Charles joined two other shirtless crewmen smoking in the morning shade next to a shed. "I see you came back with all your bombs—I assume you didn't find anything?"

"Not even a damn fishing boat. No way there were a bunch of battleships out there. You hear anything new back here?"

"I watched a formation of Japanese bombers fly over us at high altitude. They passed out of sight. Either didn't see us or just didn't care."

"Two Jap fighters followed our plane for a while. We readied our guns and flew on a heading for Cavite rather than lead them here. We were shocked when they broke off without attacking. After they were out of sight, we turned back for Olongapo."

With the PBY crews safely home, uninjured, Charles set to exploring the superstructure of the old *Rochester*. *I need a place with a good field of view and some steel to bolt or weld a gun mount to. This railing looks good. The only thing taller is that water tower.* A Marine waved at Charles from the water tower at the edge of the base. *I wonder if he's looking for a gun location himself?* The Marine waved more vigorously, pointing southwest.

Charles turned just in time to see a Japanese Zero flash over the bay. Multiple small-arms fire erupted from the ground, but the Zero flew straight on without firing its guns.

He didn't buzz us just for the fun of it. He was probably testing the strength of our anti-aircraft positions. Only minutes later, Charles heard gunfire from the direction of Fort Wint, an old fortification at the entrance to Subic Bay. Looking that direction, he saw a half-dozen Japanese fighters heading directly for Olongapo.

From high in the *Rochester's* superstructure Charles received his baptism in combat. He pulled his revolver from its holster. *Damn! Another few hours and we'd have had a .50 caliber up here to shoot back at the bastards!*

The Zeros came in fast for their first run. His heart pounding, Charles aimed and fired his pistol. *How far do I lead a 250-miles-per-hour airplane with a Colt 45? More than for a flushed pheasant, I suppose—*

One after another the Zeros dropped low and flew across the bay, ripping the water with .303 caliber machine gun and 20mm cannon fire. Reid's attempt to conceal his PBY in the shoreline trees was a failure. He and the rest of his crew jumped into the water as bullets splashed across the wings and the PBY burst into flames. Some of the men returned fire from their .50 caliber waist guns, but with no effect.

Those pop-pop-pops are the sound of practice ammunition. The tracers arcing up from the PBY guns are just bouncing off those Zeros. Some of our guns have stopped firing, probably jammed by the low-powered rounds.

On the water, PBY crewmen still fighting from their planes knew they were in extreme risk. High-octane avgas poured from holes in their fuel tanks and would sooner or later burst into flames as had the P-29. Compounding the danger, all seven planes still carried the four 500-pound bombs hung onto the wings that morning. The first strafing left three PBYs burning.

A second attack left two more planes in flames.

His pistol empty, Charles scrambled for the dock. A Zero separated from the others and came straight toward him. The Zero's pilot was not interested in Charles though—he was directing his fire at the Navy Base water tower, where the Marine was shooting at the Zeros with his BAR, a Browning Automatic Rifle, from the catwalk encircling the water tank. Every time the Zero pilot came at him, the Marine ran around to the other side as the Zero's bullets riddled the water tank.

Eventually the Japanese pilot gave up and returned to attacking the seaplane base. The Marine resumed firing his BAR, dodging streams of water draining from the bullet holes. The Zeros made a fourth and final strafing run, regrouped above the bay, and disappeared over the horizon.

Charles looked at the squadron's mooring area. *Every damn plane here is sunk or burning—all seven of them! I need to get down there!*

He ran from the *Rochester* to the hangar, where according to plans the wounded should be brought. Several men with minor burns and injuries needed attention, but nothing could be done for two men, both from the P-29 plane. Reid's co-pilot, Ensign J.C. Watson, flying with his patched-up elbow, and Chief Aviation Machinist's Mate George Seeke were both dead.

The survivors gathered at the hangar, reviewing their losses. Some sat silently, waiting for the palpitations and shaking to stop. One crewman stood just outside the hangar, bent over and retching with both hands on his knees.

Another crewman, dripping from his swim to the dock, pointed down the seawall. "Strange that they didn't touch the barge with the aviation gas."

"Not so strange, if they meant to save it for themselves."

After injuries were seen to, Charles joined others at the dock. It was a depressing sight. Smoke hung over the bay, and debris littered the base. The last drops of fresh water dribbled from the punctured water tower.

Nothing remained of the seven PBYs except for scattered bits of wreckage jutting from the water.

"Those didn't fool anyone," someone pointed to the edge of the bay. The two decoy PBYs floated untouched at their moorings, completely ignored by the Zeros.

Captain Wagner flew in to see the damage firsthand, arriving around 1300. After a brief look around, he took Marcy aside. "I have to make a difficult decision. It's been five days, and already half of our twenty-eight PBYs are disabled or destroyed. It's not much consolation, but we've had only eleven killed and four injured. The situation's painfully obvious. Our PBYs are too vulnerable to stay in advance positions."

"What's the plan?"

"I'm going talk to Admiral Hart, or if not Hart then at least Admiral Rockwell, about our options. There's no sense keeping everyone here when we have no flyable planes."

After a short private conversation with Marcy, Wagner left.

Marcy then gathered the squadron. "Listen up, everyone. We're going to have a full meal and then load up our trucks. We're moving to Los Baños tonight. Everyone should have a rifle or a sidearm and extra ammunition when we leave."

Marcy then called the names of eight men, including Charles. "I don't know that we'll have any PBYs coming back here again, but just in case, Captain Wagner is leaving a skeleton crew here with emergency supplies and parts. We won't completely close shop here until we know for certain that VP-102, or another unit, is not returning. The Marines will guard the gasoline stores for us."

Marcy turned to Charles, "Doc, you're staying here with them. If you want to help over at the Marine hospital, that's fine. Remember though, the squadron men here are your first responsibility."

Marcy turned back to the other seven men. "I don't have to tell you that plans are fluid right now. It's my hope to rejoin you soon. If the command decides Olongapo is to be abandoned, we'll come get you. Questions?" He paused in the silence. "No? Good luck, then."

An hour later the trucks rumbled out of the base in fading light. It would be well after dawn before they reached Los Baños.

The eight sailors of VP-102 remaining at Olongapo watched until the trucks were out of sight.

Eventually a voice ventured, "Looks like we've been left behind."

23

Left Behind

Olongapo, Philippine Islands

13 December 1941

Charles woke before sunup on his 21st birthday. *Mary would have made me a birthday cake today if she were here—thank God she's not.*

Through a long history of provisioning ships, Navy tradition required a supply of quality food for its sailors. The Marines' kitchen was now at Mariveles, though. For the present, the squadron's remaining eight sailors would dine from tins of food.

Charles chose canned salmon for breakfast, eating quickly while waving away flies. The meal finished, he assembled his medical supplies, strapped on the belt holding his revolver and Corpsman Knife, and walked through Barrio Olongapo towards the Riverside Cabaret, a.k.a. the 4th Marines Hospital. The establishment was on the road to Manila, a little more than a mile east of Olongapo. Although he intended to offer his services, Charles's real purpose was to get information. The Marine detachment maintained continuous communication with Cavite and Mariveles. Perhaps they knew, or could find out, about Cañacao Hospital.

Passing through Barrio Olongapo, he detoured to a white house near the bay. He knew the occupants. Before the war started, two parents walked onto the base from the barrio carrying a young child with a deep cut in the side of his pelvis. Speaking to the family in his elementary Tagalog, Charles washed, sterilized, and sutured the wound. The child's mother walked back the next day

183

to give Charles three loaves of bread, wrapped in beautiful cloth.

Now Charles paused at the doorway of their white house, pulled the folded cloth from his pocket, and called a greeting in Tagalog.

The smiling family ushered him inside, and, within a few minutes, he was on his way again—without the cloth—but holding a large, still-warm loaf of bread. Charles held his nose to the bread and inhaled deeply. *Not a bad substitute for a birthday cake.* Indulging himself, he broke the loaf open and pulled bread from the soft inside. It reminded him of Indiana, where they'd pull a cold watermelon, stolen of course, from the creek, break it open, and eat the melon's heart.

He enjoyed each bite of bread and soon half of the loaf was gone. He thought about saving the other half for the next day but decided to finish the entire loaf. *What if tomorrow doesn't come?*

He turned down Esteban Avenue, today dry and dusty, towards the Marine encampment. He was between the barrio and hospital when Japanese bombers and fighters, flying low and out of the morning sun, again roared over the base. Charles took shelter in a grove of trees and watched a half-dozen Zeros swoop in, bombing and strafing what they had missed the previous day. They circled back again and again for almost a half hour, leaving explosions and new fires in their wake.

Despite defensive fire from Marine machine guns, the Japanese once again flew away unscathed.

Charles turned and ran back to the base, encouraged to find no new casualties. *I'm happy our guys are OK, but I'm worried about what's happening. Those Zeros flew back and forth, unbothered by any American fighters. Where the hell are MacArthur's planes?*

ᔑ ᔑ ᔑ

The sailors moved their bivouac to the edge of the Olongapo base, away from buildings and other likely Japanese targets. Every day they watched Japanese fighters and bombers fly unchallenged to their targets, taking advantage of the unusually good weather.

When designing and building the Mitsubishi G4M bomber, code-named "Betty" by the Allies, the Japanese traded armor protection, self-sealing tanks, and other defensive elements for better performance. Its 3,750-mile range allowed them to bomb the entire Philippine archipelago from Taiwan bases, and it could fly far above the maximum reach of the American anti-aircraft fire. American and Filipino ground troops could do nothing to stop the unrelenting Japanese bombings.

Just after dawn on Wednesday, 17 December, a military truck rolled into Olongapo.

PatWing 10 pilot Lieutenant Tom Pollock leapt from the truck to an enthusiastic welcome. "Are we happy to see you, Lieutenant! We were wondering if we'd been forgotten."

"It's been a long night," Pollock explained. "We drove the whole way from Cavite without lights and had to talk our way past nervous Filipino guards with shotguns at every checkpoint and crossroad. Throw your things on the truck. Load on all the spares and tools we can carry—we're officially abandoning Olongapo."

While they loaded the truck, Pollock brought everyone up to date with what he knew or had heard. "It's pretty grim, guys. The Japs own the skies. We only put up a plane here and there for reconnaissance, and we don't have many left for that. Admiral Hart's surface ships left days ago. What's left of PatWing 10 is evacuating to Java. The *Childs*, loaded with parts and some of the flight crew, is already on its way to Cebu. They'll refuel some PBYs there and keep going to Mindanao where other planes are waiting. When the *Childs* arrives, they'll refuel all the planes and everyone move on to Surabaja."

"So what's left of us are gathering at Los Baños?" George asked.

"No. We're going back to Cavite. When I left there yesterday, we still had seven planes scattered around Luzon, four of them flyable. I assume those are being held back for evacuating senior officers or other VIPs over the next few days."

Charles's head jerked up. *Evacuating? Does the Army no longer think we can repel an invasion?*

"We're leaving all the avgas and oil here?"

"No. The Marines are abandoning Olongapo in the next day or two themselves. They'll demolish all of it. They're also going to tow the *Rochester* to deep water and scuttle her."

"It sounds like things are bad, or worse?" Charles asked.

"It's not good." Pollock shook his head. "This is strictly my own opinion, but I think we might well lose the Philippines."

Charles voiced a rhetorical question, "If that's the case and we retreat from the islands, how will the Army get out? They can't march to Australia." *Answer that and you'll answer my real question: If our PBY tenders and planes have already left, how will we ourselves escape?*

"The plan is for the Army and Marines to make a defensive stand and wait for reinforcement."

"So, sir, if most of PatWing 10 is already moving south, how will we catch up with them?"

"I'm sure we'll find out when we get to Cavite."

Charles climbed onto the back of the truck with the rest of the crew. Pollock's night trip to Olongapo had been slow and dangerous. In daylight they made better time and arrived in Manila at midday.

In the bay, Charles saw the *Canopus*, a submarine tender, loading torpedoes into the black silhouette of a submarine. There was little other activity. Smoke still billowed from burning fires at the Navy Yard. *Not much left here.*

Passing Cañacao Hospital, Charles's hopes rose. From the road, the hospital seemed intact, though the building and surrounding reservation walkways appeared deserted. Pollock completed his circle around Cañacao Bay and pulled into Sangley Point. The *Langley* was nowhere to be seen. A single, damaged PBY sat in the hangar.

Commander Neale greeted them, "Am I glad to see you!"

"We're even more glad to be back!" Pollock spoke for his group.

"I was afraid you weren't going to be able to get through. Reports had the Japanese landing and moving down from Lingayen Gulf. If it was true, they might have already cut the road from Olongapo."

"Apparently just rumors," Pollock ventured. "The Army people we came across said nothing about an invasion—at least not yet."

Yielding to impatience, Charles blurted, "Sir, the hospital looked abandoned when we drove past. Permission to go and see if there are any supplies I can scavenge?"

"Given. Make it quick."

Charles walked briskly around the shoreline to Cañacao Hospital. He recognized one of the Filipino hospital workers sitting at the entrance. "Where is everyone?"

"Not here."

"Where'd they go?"

"To Manila. I heard someone say 'Sternberg', but there were also other names I did not recognize."

"I'm looking for a nurse, Tillie, or Mary, Finian. Do you know her? Do you know where she went?

"No, sir. I do not."

Inside, the hospital was indeed abandoned and stripped of useable supplies. The pharmacy door hung unlocked and open. The shelves had been swept clean except for some loose papers and a few empty bottles. *They left in a hurry, obviously not planning to return anytime soon. Damn!*

Captain Wagner and his staff had departed earlier with the *Childs*, leaving Lieutenant Commander Frank Bridget, a well-liked and respected officer, in command at Sangley Point.

In the still-dark hours of Thursday morning, 18 December, Bridget addressed the assembled men from PatWing 10 and read seventy-six names from a list.

Charles Beckner was not among them.

"If I just called your name, you are leaving for Australia today on the *Maréchal Joffre*."

"Doesn't sound like an American ship," one of the men commented.

"She isn't. The *Maréchal Joffre* is a Vichy French ship docked in Manila. We took her without opposition, and now she's fully fueled, manned, and ready for departure. She's loaded with evacuees and leaves tonight for Australia."

Charles was ambivalent. *That ship will have to travel through hundreds of miles of Japanese-occupied ocean. The whole way they'll be one Japanese torpedo or bomb away from sinking. I'm not disappointed to not be on her. If my time's up, I don't want to go by drowning. Or by sharks.*

The fourteen officers and sixty-two enlisted men of PatWing 10 selected for the *Maréchal Joffre* loaded onto trucks for Manila. Optimistically, they would be safe in Australia in a few days.

Commander Bridget stayed at Cavite, assuming command of the remaining men from VP-101 and VP-102. With no obvious means of transport out of the Philippine Islands, they, alongside other soldiers and Marines, would have to hold the islands against Japanese invasion, hoping and praying that the military might of the U.S. would soon return in force.

Admiral Hart did not share General MacArthur's optimism that Luzon, not to mention the rest of the Philippine Islands, could be successfully held against the Japanese invasion until help arrived. Nevertheless, Hart did not want to give the impression that he was abandoning the Army by removing all Navy forces from the Philippines. He bequeathed MacArthur the entire 4th

Marine Regiment and the small boats of PT Squadron 3.

He also left behind a mixed group of 500 sailors, including Commander Bridget's 154 men from PatWing 10.

Charles considered his situation. In their latrine discussion the first day of the attack, Neale's clerk told him that the Pacific Fleet was "destroyed" at Pearl Harbor. Though he found that word difficult to comprehend or believe at the time, Charles was now thinking it might not have been an exaggeration. *Why would the entire Far East Asia Fleet flee south for Australia if reinforcement is just over the horizon? I'm beginning to think that the only goal for those left here is to keep Japan's military occupied for as long as possible. Meanwhile our country can regroup and recover from Japan's surprise attack and maybe stop them at Australia.*

That's a bleak big picture, but if it's true, all of us left behind are expendable.

For the briefest moment, a vision surfaced of himself as a Japanese prisoner. He quickly swatted it away.

24

Goodbye, Cavite

Sangley Point, Philippine Islands

19 December 1941

When the Japanese came to bomb the Navy Yard on 10 December, PatWing 10 men watched the destruction from only a few hundred yards across the bay. Now they prepared for the inevitable attack on Sangley Point by stacking sandbags and digging trenches.

One of the sailors paused to rest his arms, "Maybe they'll think our little base here just not worth bombing."

"They're being methodical. First things first," a nearby sailor suggested. "They started by catching as many of our ships sitting in the Navy Yard docks as they could. We know it's only a matter of time till they come for the last of us, so keep digging."

"None of this is going to protect your ass from a direct hit. Not the sandbags and not the trenches. If a bomb's got your name on it, ain't nothing you can do."

"Feel free to take your own chance standing out in the open when shrapnel starts flying. I'm gonna be down flat in this trench."

Adding to the tension was engine noise from the PT boats of Motor Torpedo Squadron 3 moving back and forth on the bay. Each PT boat was powered by three Packard V-12 engines of 1200 horsepower each. When two or three boats cranked up their engines, it sounded all too similar to a bomber formation. Invariably some lookout, nerves already frayed, sounded the air-raid alarm.

Finally, on Friday, 19 December, the alarm was for real. Japanese bombers returned, and Sangley Point was their only target. At the sound of the siren, men ran for cover. Charles had not yet been the victim of a high-level bombing attack, and his curiosity displaced fear, and for that matter, good sense. He stood on the tarmac looking skyward.

"There they are," a sailor Charles did not recognize stopped long enough to point north.

"I see three V-shaped groups."

"Yep. Nine planes in each group. It's how the bastards showed up before."

"There's a burst from our antiaircraft fire now."

"And like always, they're flying a mile above our flak."

"Those dots even higher, above the bombers—are those fighter escorts?"

"Probably Zeros, not that they need escorts. Not one goddamn American plane in the sky, and that's gonna make it even worse down here. After those bombers unload, the fighters will break off, drop down, and begin strafing the base. Don't come out until it's all over."

Charles shook his head. *We are totally impotent. Look at them, they just did a lazy flyover and now they've turned back for the real bombing run. It's as if they are performing on a parade ground.*

The first wave of nine bombers separated from the group and flew towards Sangley Point. They were too high for him to see the open bomb bay doors, but he could see the sticks of bombs they released. Mesmerized by the pattern of black dots falling earthward, Charles hadn't noticed everyone else running away from buildings and towards the trenches or sandbag emplacements.

"Doc! *Doc!*"

Charles turned toward the voice, from a sailor frantically waving at him from a trench. "Who's hurt?" he asked.

"You will be if you just stand there! Get in here!"

Charles ran for one of the zig-zagging slit trenches that were scattered all the way from Sangley Point to the grounds of the hospital preserve. At the bottom of the trench men had reasonable protection from almost anything other than a direct hit, the proverbial "one with your name on it."

The rapid series of explosions shocked Charles physically as well as mentally. They were deafening, and even in the trench, bombs landing closely were like body blows, literally bouncing him from the ground before covering him with dirt and debris. But it was shrapnel that caused most injuries. Like thousands of bullets shooting outward from the bomb burst, some as small as sand and some bigger than a fist, the flying splinters and chunks of bomb casing, wood, and concrete killed and maimed far more men than did the direct explosion.

The staccato of exploding bombs stopped as suddenly as it began. Visible from the trench, rising columns of black smoke were illuminated by flickering light from burning buildings and flaming stores of gasoline and oil.

In a patch of blue sky, a bright rainbow floated, an apparition created by the spray of water thrown into the air by bombs exploding nearby in the bay.

"I'm hit! I'm hit! Help!"

His ears still ringing, Charles stood and looked out from the trench, searching for the source of the voice. Twenty yards away three bodies lay on the ground, one calling for help. "They were probably trying to make it to the trench when a bomb caught them in the open," said a sailor next to him.

"Come on!" Charles crawled from the trench, and the two ran to the nearest man, the one who'd cried for help. He was bloody from head to foot.

"It's OK, sailor. Let's see what you've got," Charles tried to speak calmly. It was obvious from the pattern of injuries that the blast and shrapnel caught the sailor from his left side. Though his face and neck were covered with blood, Charles could not find a large wound. It was possible some bit of shrapnel had penetrated deeper than it appeared.

His companion from the trench called, "This one over here's alive, Doc, but bleeding pretty badly from his arm. He's got some leg injuries too, but they aren't bleeding like his arm. I haven't looked at that other one."

"Put a tourniquet on that arm while I check the other man."

"Don't have a tourniquet, Doc."

Charles ran over, yanked a tourniquet from his pocket, and tightened it above the wound. Since the war started, Charles was never without a small medic's pack on his belt, bulging with bandages, tourniquets, morphine syrettes, and other small items. He carried more bandages and braided cotton tourniquets stuffed in his pockets. "Let me check the third man, and then we'll move them."

A brief check confirmed the third man was already dead. A ragged piece of shrapnel had torn a path completely through his chest.

Returning to the sailor with the bleeding arm, Charles and the sailor half-carried, half-dragged him to the edge of their trench. "Get him in there. I'll get the other one." Charles ran back.

"Come on!" Charles urged the man. "You can walk!"

The ground around them erupted as a Japanese Zero fighter roared over the base. Freed from the necessity of protecting their bombers, Japanese fighters now came at the base from out of the sun, strafing men and buildings the bombing had missed. Charles saw the Zero bank up through the smoke to circle for another attack. *Time to get out of here!*

"I can't see—" the sailor pleaded, his face covered in blood.

Charles started to yell, "Just wipe the blood off your face!" before realizing that shrapnel might have injured the sailor's eyes. He started dragging the man, but it was too late to reach the trench. He shoved the sailor down and tried to push himself into the ground as once again the cracking of the plane's guns passed by. *Didn't hit me again. Either I'm lucky, or it's a lot harder for those pilots to hit a single man than it seems.* He watched the Zero fly west, out of the bay.

"Come on!" He half-led, half-dragged the casualty the rest of the way to the trench.

There was a faint whistle. Charles now understood that sound preceded a bomb's explosion. *Oh shit! That's why the fighters left—more bombers, back for Act Two.*

The second wave of bombing was as intense as the first. Explosions walking across the peninsula hit one of the fuel dumps, erupting into a huge firestorm. The giant radio antennas next to the hospital were left standing, but bombs destroyed a building housing the high-powered transmitters. A direct hit on the Sangley Point hangar demolished it and the PBY inside.

Once the explosions stopped, Zeros again roared in low. This time they concentrated on the trenches.

"I've had enough of this shit!" Charles flipped onto his back, yanked the pistol from his holster and fired vertically from the trench at the Japanese fighters swooping overhead.

"No use in your shooting, Doc. It's a million to one you'll hit it, and even if you do, it'll just bounce off."

Charles paused and then fired at another strafing plane, "Yeah, I know. But I'm pissed off. They're trying to kill us—I can't just lie here and take it!"

Now the third group of nine bombers released their load of death and destruction. Black smoke and flames billowed from burning buildings and fuel. It was twilight in hell, obliterating the sun and leaving men choking and coughing. Everyone stayed in cover until certain that the Japanese fighters had departed along with their bombers.

The sailor dragged to their trench would almost certainly lose his arm. Charles gave him to the gentle arms of Morphia. He turned to the sailor who could not see and used his canteen to rinse blood from the blinded sailor's face.

"I think—yes! I can see!" and he grabbed Charles's shoulder and shook it in joy.

There you go, Bartimaeus. Your sight's back.

The three waves of the attack lasted a full hour. Charles shook away the daze from the explosions and ran with others to the burning buildings and wreckage. The carnage was terrible. Small and large pieces of bodies mixed with debris. It was Dante's hell. Explosions and roaring fires accompanied the stench of burned flesh and stinking smoke from burning buildings, oil, gasoline, and rubber.

Triage and treat. If nothing else, the military fully prepared its medical personnel to manage multiple casualties. Charles had to first do something for those with serious but survivable injuries. Placing a tourniquet on a bleeding extremity or turning a man on his side so blood from facial wounds ran to the ground rather than down his throat was often enough to keep someone alive long enough to receive more definitive treatment.

Some injured were still alive but had suffered obviously fatal injuries. If conscious, they received a quick injection of morphine. The 'walking wounded' with minor injuries he directed to a spot to wait their turn for treatment. The dead, beyond need of tourniquets or morphine, would be seen to later. They didn't mind waiting.

"Corpsman! Over here!" Charles responded to the call from a sailor kneeling next to a wounded man.

The victim, a Filipino civilian worker, lay on his right side, his chest moving with deep breaths. Charles rolled him over and saw, through the blood, bone, and hair, the convolutions of the man's brain pulsing with each heartbeat.

He's beyond pain. Even so. Charles gave him a morphine injection and moved on.

Calls of "Corpsman up!" or "Doc!" rang from every direction. Two more corpsmen joined Charles, and the trio declared a triage zone on the tarmac, instructing others to bring the wounded to them for treatment.

Casualties who could not walk were brought on stretchers, carried in ponchos, or even dragged to the makeshift treatment area. Many were burned, most on their hands and arms. One man had charred skin from his shoulders down. "It doesn't really hurt that much, Doc." *No wonder—his skin's burned so deeply, the pain fibers are gone.* Charles injected him with morphine anyway. Even if the burns were not painful, morphine might alleviate his anxiety.

The three corpsmen packed open wounds, applied compression bandages to lacerations, sealed sucking chest wounds, and injected syrettes of morphine liberally. A Navy medical officer carrying a black medical bag strode from the smoke and assumed command of the triage station. Charles didn't recognize him but was relieved that he'd arrived.

"Let's use this crate as a treatment table," the doctor said, stripping off his uniform shirt and dumping the contents of his bag on the side of the crate.

"One of you corpsmen come help me. The others keep up the triage."

Charles volunteered. "Sir, I don't know where you came from, but, man, am I glad to see a surgeon! I've assisted in the OR, so tell me what you need."

"I'm not a surgeon, just a general medical officer, but right now we're all surgeons. OR tech, you said? Stay close. I'll need your help."

The medical officer, with Charles assisting, worked in the smoke-filled open air to stabilize the injured. They tied off arteries where a tourniquet could not stop the bleeding. Some damaged limbs were held only by strings of tissue, leaving it a simple matter to clip the remaining strands and complete the amputation.

"It's getting slippery with all the blood on the tarmac," the doctor complained.

Charles called to one of the sailors standing near, "Bring one of those sandbags over here, cut it open, and spread out the sand."

"Thanks," said the doctor after the sand was down, "That's better."

"It's something corpsmen used to do on the early warships, sir."

A fourth corpsman joined the impromptu hospital. Sweating in the heat, enveloped by stench and coughing from smoke, they did what they could. For penetrating head, chest, or abdomen wounds, they slapped on a pressure bandage and moved them to the group for transporting to one of the Army hospitals around Manila.

Finally, the casualties stopped arriving. It was over.

"Hey! What're you doing there?" Charles yelled accusingly at an ensign removing a ring from the finger of one of the dead sailors.

"Doc," the ensign replied patiently. "I'm not stealing the ring—I'm organizing a graves detail. This might be the only thing we'll have to identify this poor guy."

The ensign had drafted a dozen sailors and Filipino civilian workers for his graves detail. Fifteen mostly intact bodies were lined in a row, covered by sheets, blankets, or ponchos. They spread out, searching every miscellaneous body part for dog tags or anything else that might help identification. One searcher absentmindedly started to kick a ball out of the road, only to stumble aside when he realized the 'ball' was a charred head. The intact bodies and unmatched body parts were respectfully laid in a bomb crater and covered with dirt and mixed debris.

"Are you just going to leave them there, sir?" a sailor challenged.

"I hope not," the ensign replied. "I've recorded the site, and we'll put up a marker. I'm putting the dog tags, rings, watches, and other items for identification in this canvas bag. By protocol those bodies will be disinterred and buried properly when it's possible. Someday. Maybe."

It was a miserable, depressing job, and one sailor walked away sobbing. A Filipino worker conjured a bottle of whisky which he and two other Filipinos passed around until it was empty.

The remains of many would never be found. Anyone unfortunately next to an exploding bomb or artillery shell simply vaporized, disappearing in bits of tissue too small to identify. These victims might later be identified by exclusion, but that would take time, given the chaos of scattered personnel and destroyed paper files.

The general medical officer-turned-surgeon left for Manila in a truck with the last two patients. Finally able to stop, take a deep breath, and look around, Charles was stunned. The triage site was covered with blood-soaked clothing, strips of bandages, and the stretchers and ponchos used to bring in the casualties. The lingering odor from roasted flesh, incontinent victims, and blood-soaked sand was even stronger than the acrid smoke drifting across the tarmac. *Chief Fahey told me the sight and sound of war cannot be described. He was right. It can only be experienced.*

Charles turned to the other corpsman still remaining at the triage site, "That doctor took off his shirt before I saw his name or rank. Who was he?"

"Don't know, but I'm glad he showed up. Who are you with?"

"Patrol Wing 10 here at Sangley Point, or what's left of it. And you?"

"I'm with a Marine unit trying to secure what's still intact at the Navy Yard. I'm not sure what we'll do with it though. Nowhere to go, is there?"

"Always somewhere to go." Charles looked around at the burning buildings and debris that used to be his base. *There's always somewhere to go, but the options are narrowing pretty damn quickly.*

At dawn on Monday, 22 December 1941, 110,000 troops of the Imperial Japanese Army swarmed onto the beaches of Luzon at Lingayen Gulf and established a beachhead in a valley between mountain ranges. From there, the valley was a natural corridor all the way to Manila. The well-equipped and experienced Japanese troops easily routed the badly equipped, poorly trained, and unsupported Filipino Scouts.

The defenders fought vigorously, but without air support or heavy weapons their lines inevitably collapsed.

The next day MacArthur belatedly activated the decades-old War Plan

Orange 3. WPO3 called for a strategic withdrawal of all Filipino and American troops behind a strong defensive line extending across the Bataan Peninsula. There, they would hold out until the Pacific Battle Fleet and infantry transports steamed from Hawaii to meet and defeat the Japanese army and navy. At least according to WPO3.

Hoping to avoid further destruction of his beloved city and its citizens, MacArthur finally declared Manila an "Open City," as of 25 December. The declaration meant that all American and Filipino troops would immediately withdraw and cease defending the metropolis. Protocol I of the Geneva Conventions required the invading enemy to cease bombing and artillery shelling by that date, thus halting the killing of civilians and destruction of cultural and historical structures. Sometimes the Convention was observed by attacking forces.

On Wednesday, 24 December, the Japanese landed 7,000 infantrymen on Lamon Bay, east of Manila. The Lingayen and Lamon Japanese infantries began a pincer movement to block all roads exiting Manila, including the highway to Bataan.

᠀ ᠀ ᠀

Charles and Joe, the motor mac who introduced Charles on his first day with PatWing 10, watched the sun rise over Cañacao Bay on Christmas Eve.

"This is different," Charles observed.

"What do you mean?" Joe asked.

"Just look out there, at Cañacao Bay. When I left Cavite for Olongapo in October, the Navy Yard was bustling: Men and heavy equipment working on ships at the repair docks, lighters being towed back and forth between the naval supply ships and Cavite, civilian cargo ships anchored or circling in the bay, waiting for their turn to tie up at the Manila docks …"

"Yep. They were busy days."

"Now, the only things moving are a few tugs towing salvaged supplies towards Mariveles. The Navy Yard and Sangley Point are nothing but smoldering rubble."

"We still have two or three more-or-less flyable PBYs, even if they're only still here for VIP extractions."

"Which damn sure isn't us—odds are you and I, and everyone else left here from PatWing 10 will be given to the Marines or even the Army infantry."

"What're you going to do, Doc, if it turns into a situation of every man for himself?"

"Speculation's cheap, so I'm just going to wait and see what happens. By the way, have you heard the news?"

"What news?"

"PatWing 10 remnants, that's us, have orders to move to Bataan."

"Doc, I actually find that encouraging. It means there's still enough organization left to make decisions and give orders."

ﾎﾟ ﾎﾟ ﾎﾟ

Admiral Hart decided it was time for him to rejoin his Asian Fleet.

The *Houston* and other sizeable surface ships had weighed anchor days earlier. Hart was reluctant to depart by submarine since that would leave him out of contact with his fleet for eight days. He approached Lieutenant Commander Frank Bridget, commanding the PatWing 10 remnants following Wagner's departure. "Frank, I'd like you to fly me and six of my staff to Java."

Bridget readily agreed.

When Admiral Hart's entourage arrived at Los Baños for their flight, Hart looked over the beat-up and patched-up PBY, inspecting every element and asking questions of the crew. Then Admiral Hart turned to Bridget. "We have the option of leaving in three days on the submarine *Shark*. It'll take longer to get us there, but in all honesty, this plane is more likely to kill us than the Japanese."

Overhearing Hart's opinion about the beat-up PBY, the plane's crew captain could not disagree. "You know, the admiral has a point there."

After the admiral's visit, PatWing 10 officially abandoned Los Baños. The remaining men loaded onto trucks and moved back to Sangley Point. Swenson, the pilot of the last surviving PBY on Luzon, the P-2 plane, convinced Bridget to let them stay behind, perform additional repairs to the plane, and fly it to Sangley Point.

The same day, 24 December, Japanese bombers made their heaviest raid yet on Manila, concentrating this time on the waterfront.

From Sangley Point, Charles and other PatWing 10 crew listened to the explosions and watched high columns of black smoke billow from uncontrolled fires.

"I can imagine the chaos in the city, with Filipino military and government personnel all trying to get out of the city before the Japanese arrive tomorrow," Charles told one of the radiomen. "Buildings are burning, those streets must be full of debris, and I expect there are wounded and dead people throughout the city."

"And in the middle of all that, our southern forces are trying to move men and equipment right through the city in their rush to get to Bataan."

"We need to leave soon ourselves. I'm ready to move, even if it's only to Bataan."

"Doc, I thought those little Jap bastards had cardboard ships and paper airplanes. How'd they do this to us?"

"Those stories were obviously propaganda—our own. I doubt we've yet seen Japan's full military might." Charles paused, then asked, "Looking ahead, would you rather be killed or taken prisoner?"

"I don't fancy dying, so I guess I would rather be a POW than dead. What about you, Doc?"

"I think I'll take option number three, not dying and not being taken prisoner. Even if reinforcements don't show up."

"What's your plan?"

"Don't have one yet. Haven't thought that far ahead. I just don't like the two more obvious choices."

Charles then gestured with a nod of his head towards the seaplane ramp, "Hear that? I almost forgot it's Christmas Eve."

At the water's edge, a Methodist chaplain led a group of sailors singing *Silent Night*. After the last verse, the chaplain began reading from his bible, "When they heard the king, they departed; and, lo, the star, which they saw in the east, went before them, till it came and stood over where the young child was. And when they were come into the house, they saw the young child with Mary his mother, and fell down, and worshipped him."

"Given our circumstances, I like the next part of the story best," Charles said.

"What part is that?"

"Joseph and Mary heed God's warning and depart for another country."

༂ ༂ ༂

Dawn broke Christmas Day 1941, with Manila officially an open city. American and Filipino forces continued their withdrawal from all the area bases, including Cavite.

Admiral Rockwell formally issued the order for Bridget to immediately move his remaining PatWing 10 men to the Navy Yard at Mariveles, on the southern tip of Bataan. He left it to Bridget to find transportation.

Efforts to salvage any more supplies for Bataan and Corregidor were abandoned. What remained would be demolished. A Marine unit began placing depth charges and explosives at fuel tanks and communication centers, along the railways, and at every other site that might later prove useful to the Japanese. Another unit scattered smokeless gunpowder through the ammunition depot.

ʕ•ᴥ•ʔ ʕ•ᴥ•ʔ ʕ•ᴥ•ʔ

"Listen up!" Bridget yelled to the assembled sailors, "we're going to Mariveles in three separate groups. The first group will be transported across the bay to Mariveles on the minesweeper USS *Quail*. The second group will be towed across on a barge. Lieutenant Pollock will lead a smaller third group overland, driving two trucks that are probably in good enough shape to make it there. We'll regroup, still as PatWing 10, in Mariveles."

Bridget was interrupted by the noise of an incoming PBY. It was Swenson in the patched-up P-2 plane. He had lost his No. 1 engine immediately after taking off from Los Baños.

The remaining engine sputtered as he wobbled over Cavite and splashed down hard near the seaplane ramp.

Once onshore, Swenson reported to Bridget, "Some of my controls were damaged more than I thought in that previous Japanese attack. And a few of our bullet-hole repairs failed, plus we had so much water pouring in we nearly didn't get off the bay at Los Baños."

"I shouldn't have let you try to repair her," Bridget shook his head. "Remove the radios and anything else we might use at Mariveles and destroy her."

"Sir," Swenson pleaded, "I think we can finish our repairs overnight and fly to Mariveles in the morning."

"No!" Bridget said emphatically. "P-2's beyond repair. Sink her!"

Lieutenant Pollock tapped Charles on the shoulder, "Doc, stay with me. You'll ride in the trucks with us at midnight."

"Why are we waiting?"

"The Navy's run out of time and barges to move everything to Mariveles. A Navy lieutenant, Thomas Bowers, has his team preparing both the Navy Yard and Sangley Point for demolition. We won't leave the Japs a damn thing. Fuel tanks, ammunition, food, and anything else that can be used by the Japanese is going up. It's scheduled for 2230 tonight. We'll finish loading these trucks, but then wait at the Pan Am ramp for Bower's team to do their job. They'll join us by midnight and ride with us to Mariveles."

"So I just wait with you, sir?"

"There'll be massive explosions going off tonight. Could be some injuries. Also, we might run into some fighting when we make our way through the city. I wanted a corpsman to stay with us. You're it."

Charles and the rest of Pollock's small group lounged on the Pan American seaplane ramp between the Navy Yard and Sangley Point. The trucks were loaded and waiting.

At 2230, as scheduled, it started.

The ramp shook and their chests resonated with the first deafening explosions. Fireballs rose into the sky, an animated display of light and sound with metal drums, wood crates, and other debris blasting skyward and skimming across the water. Buildings collapsed in flames, and smoke billowed thousands of feet.

When explosions reached the warehouse storing smokeless powder, the spectacle turned into a grand finale. Almost 2,000 tons of instantaneously exploding powder created a rising sun, bringing the brilliance and sharp shadows of daylight across Manila Bay. Gradually the explosions came at longer intervals, and the light faded. Tom Pollock described it as "the biggest fireworks display, the likes of which I'd never seen and never will again."

Fires continued to burn while the group waited for Bowers' demolition team to arrive. An hour past the deadline, they had not appeared.

"It's 0100, Lieutenant. They must have taken off on their own after they set things off," one of the men suggested.

"I hope that's what happened. We can't wait any longer to get out of here ourselves—I'll let Bridget know they didn't show."

It was difficult to predict the situation on the road through Manila, so Pollock's men armed themselves with pistols, shotguns, and a Thompson submachine gun. Anxiety dropped a notch after their two trucks merged with a well-armed convoy of a half-dozen Army trucks also heading to Bataan.

Total chaos met the convoy inside Manila City.

The recent bombing had strewn wreckage everywhere. Debris and fires blocked roads, causing traffic diversions. Filipino troops with their ubiquitous shotguns guarded intersections and bridges, demanding identification. Military vehicles and all nature of civilian transportation choked the roads. *Carabao*-pulled wagons, piled high with personal possessions, mingled chaotically with trucks and cars. Residents escaping before the Japanese rolled into the undefended city clashed with people from the countryside streaming into the city for perceived safety.

Charles leaned into the truck cab and tapped Pollock's shoulder. "Lieutenant," he yelled over the noise, "I need to check on someone from Cañacao Hospital who was moved to Manila."

"Where in Manila, Doc?"

"One of the hospitals. I don't know which one."

Pollock shook his head in disbelief. "In this mess? Doc, you'll never find him."

"Her. She's a nurse."

"Her, him, I don't care—you stay with us! That's an order, not a suggestion." Pollock then added, "Everyone, Army and Navy, is moving to Bataan or Corregidor. That'll include hospital personnel. You can hunt for her there. I'm not explaining to Bridget why I left you behind."

Their convoy crossed the Pasig River and finally exited Manila, heading north on Highway 3. Although headlights were taped to only thin slits and there was little moonlight, the road was so crowded that each driver had only to follow the truck in front.

About thirty miles north of the city, they arrived at Calumpit and the wide Pampanga River. Highway 3 spanned the river with two long, parallel steel bridges.

Charles knew that at some point the Army would demolish both bridges, and probably many others. *I sure hope all our men, and women, get across before they blow them up.*

A few miles farther on, they entered the town of San Fernando. Making a sharp turn southwest in the middle of town, they headed for the Bataan Peninsula. The entire population of Luzon seemed to be going with them. Traffic clogged at every crossroad and at the one-lane bridges that spanned small rivers. Officers acting as traffic cops did their best to give military vehicles the advantage.

Twenty miles south of San Fernando, the column passed through the barrio of Layac. Charles stood up in the truck, realizing he'd been here before. *Straight on is the road to Olongapo.* The convoy turned south, however, rumbling down the peninsula.

A petty officer from the Cavite Navy Yard had hitchhiked a ride to Mariveles on Pollock's truck. He tapped Charles on the shoulder and pointed south, "Won't be long now—next stop Mariveles."

"Sounds like you know this road. Been here before?"

"I had temporary duty in Mariveles for three months earlier this year. Been on this road three or four times. It's the only real road on Bataan."

"Why so few?"

"There's a series of extinct volcano peaks running down the middle of the peninsula. This road, 101, is called the East Road. It goes from Layac all the way down to Mariveles on the southern tip. The road running along the opposite coast of Bataan, called the West Road, is narrow and generally in bad shape. About halfway down the peninsula, a single track crosses the saddle between two peaks and connects the East and West Roads. It's the only real road in the mountains. The rest are just trails through the jungle. A few are wide enough for wagons, but others are nothing more than single-file walking paths."

"So how do we move men and trucks in the mountains?" Charles asked.

"We don't. Nothing up there except for mosquitoes and malaria anyway." He named off the small villages as they passed through: Limay, Limao, and Cabcaben. Intermittently, through breaks in the roadside foliage, they glimpsed fires burning on the Manila docks.

Near Cabcaben two Army trucks with a red cross painted on the hood and canvas left the rest of the convoy, turning onto a small dirt track identified by a small temporary sign, *Hospital No. 1.* Farther south, Charles saw another small sign, *Hospital No. 2*, where three more trucks turned off.

"What are Hospitals No. 1 and No. 2?" Charles looked to the other passengers but received only shrugs. *This must be where they're moving patients and staff to from the Manila Army hospitals. Could Tillie have been in one of those trucks that turned off?*

They entered a long upward curve to the west as the sun rose behind them. At the top of the rise, Corregidor Island came into view. *The first time I saw Corregidor, it was also in the early dawn light, from the deck of the* Chaumont. *When was that? It seems too long ago to remember.*

The convoy slowed and stretched, maneuvering a series of steep switchbacks upward to another ridge. Once across, the trucks coasted down through more curves into the bay at Mariveles.

At the docks, sweating troops unloaded barges with the final transfers of food, weapons, and ammunition from Cavite. Certain that Japanese air raids were imminent, the troops stacked the supplies in camouflaged squares among the trees. The more visible rows of green shacks on the base would be likely targets for Japanese fighters and bombers. Those, they filled with trash.

Charles noted the submarine tender *Canopus* dropping anchor in Mariveles Bay, a Cavite refugee like himself.

In the west harbor, just beneath the water surface, he recognized the USS *Dewey*, the huge floating dry dock he'd first seen on his first flight to Olongapo six months ago. Though she was underwater, he couldn't see any damage. *Maybe, at least I hope, the crew submerged her on purpose, to fool the Japanese into thinking it's a ship they've already sunk."*

They drove through the foothills into the Navy Yard, crowded with sailors, Marines, and military trucks of all sizes.

It was mid-morning 26 December when Charles and the other PatWing 10 men crawled from their trucks.

As they assembled to report to Bridget as a group, Charles looked around, stretched, yawned, and said to no one in particular, "Christmas wasn't a hell of a lot better than my birthday."

25

Circling the Wagons

Mariveles, Bataan Peninsula, Philippine Islands

26 December 1941

Mariveles bulged at the seams with men and materiel.

A platoon of soldiers waited for their lieutenant to arrange ferry passage across the North Channel to Corregidor. Other platoons waited for transportation north, where they would bolster the U.S. troops and Filipino Scouts establishing a line of defense extending west from Abucay.

Commanders, needing to disperse their men before a Japanese attack, spread out their units. The 4th Marines from Olongapo joined the First Separate Marine Detachment from Cavite, bivouacking in cots with mosquito netting along streets and roads among the trees in the foothills above the base.

The PatWing 10 men claimed their own area under the trees. There was less breeze than at the water's edge, but they had shade and would not be an obvious target during Japanese air attacks. As a bonus, they were away from dust and dirt blowing off the main road.

"Make sure to use your netting to keep those tiger mosquitoes at bay," Charles reminded everyone. "We all have enough to worry about already without getting malaria."

Restless, unable to sleep in the afternoon heat, and with no specific instructions or orders to follow, Charles set out to look for familiar faces.

Almost immediately he recognized a corpsman from the Cañacao Naval Hospital.

Skipping social chitchat, Charles immediately asked, "Did you know a nurse, Tillie Finian?"

"Sure. She was a senior nurse on the surgical ward."

"Do you know if she's here?" Charles asked hopefully.

"I don't. When we abandoned Cañacao, most all the staff, nurses and medical officers included, moved to one of the Army hospitals near Manila. I was sent to a special ward set up for Navy patients at Sternberg Army Hospital, and two days ago I was ordered to get on a truck and find a Navy unit over here to join. I don't know where Lieutenant Finian was sent. I haven't seen her since we left Cañacao. She could still be in Manila, or maybe she's at Hospital No. 1 or No. 2 back up the East Road. Maybe she's already over on the Rock."

"The Rock?"

"Corregidor." He pointed to the island. "Honestly, except for you and me, I don't know where anyone from Cañacao is right now."

ᔑ ᔑ ᔑ

Charles drifted to a small group gathered around a Marine whose sleeve wore the triple chevrons and two rockers of a gunnery sergeant. The Marine was sharing what he'd just learned from his captain.

"The Army and Scouts are massing up north, digging in on a line stretching from Abucay in the east, westward across Bataan to the South China Sea at Morong. They're also preparing a fallback position about seven miles south and another fallback line south of that one."

"Sounds like they're already planning their retreat."

"You mean a 'planned retrograde maneuver'?" the sergeant half-smiled. "The Army and Scouts tried to stop the invasion at the beaches on Lingayen Gulf but had no support. They didn't even have machine guns. All they had were old rifles, and it quickly turned into a rout. Some of the Filipino Scouts just threw away their uniforms and blended back into the native populations to avoid capture. Can't say as I blame them, given the circumstances. They're still fighting up there, but our boys are retreating several miles south every day."

"I never thought we'd be running away from a bunch of goddamn Japs."

"Japs or not, they've got artillery, tanks, and air cover. And, unlike us, they have a short supply line for reinforcements, ammunition, fuel, food, and everything else they need."

"—while we're short of everything and the supply line is nonexistent. What do they expect us to do?" an exasperated corporal complained.

"We only have to hold out for a few days, and supplies aren't really that low. Look at all the rations and munitions stacked around this place. The tunnels over on the Rock are also stacked to the roof with supplies. Once we create a defensible line, all we need to do is hold it for a few days or maybe a couple of weeks. Help will be here by that time. I trust my captain, he's a straight shooter."

Indeed, Charles and everyone else at Mariveles and on Corregidor were receiving adequate nutrition. Navy supply had done an excellent job of moving and storing enough rations at the Navy base to support the 1,500 Marines and sailors for six months. Additionally, on Corregidor, usually referred to as either "The Rock" or "Fort Mills," there was even more food and ammunition. Dug into the granite hills of Corregidor, the Malinta Tunnel complex was stocked with enough ammunition and canned and dry food to last 9,000 men six months.

"But I heard a story that our soldiers up north are on half-rations and running out of ammo."

The sergeant paused, considering his answer. "I guess it's no secret. My captain painted the same picture. Logistically it's difficult to move supplies from here up to those lines in the amounts a large army needs, even assuming they had a stable line of defense. The captain thinks MacArthur should have initiated War Plan Orange much earlier."

Charles inwardly nodded. *It seems obvious now. By the time he activated WPO, it was too late. We had to leave tons of ammunition and fuel sitting at the Manila and Cavite bases and watch Tom Bowers' team destroy it all.*

Charles wanted to confirm to himself that Tillie had not been left in Manila. Since PatWing 10 radiomen still maintained a communications tent, Charles asked if he could contact the two Army hospitals and ask about a Navy nurse.

"Damnit, Doc, I wish I could. You'd think that all these units are so closely grouped here at Mariveles that communication would be easy. It's not. Most of our lines are simply laid on the ground. Every Tom, Dick, and Harry at Mariveles seems to have hooked onto one of these communication wires, and it's causing confusion and straining the generators. On top of that, phone lines running north to the Army hospitals and infantry headquarters are being cut almost every night."

"What Filipino would want to do that?"

"Didn't say it had to be a Filipino, Doc—didn't even say it had to be sabotage. It's a known fact in the barrios that our wires make great clotheslines. Don't matter though, I couldn't let you make that call, even if it was possible. Everyone wants priority. There are at least twenty generals and a couple of admirals on Bataan and Corregidor, every goddamn one of 'em wanting instant contact with their units. Don't worry, Doc. It'll settle down soon, and you can go look for your girlfriend."

"You think so? I wish I was that confident."

Official links between headquarters and ground units might have been limited, but information still spread among the troops. Unofficial communication, the jungle telegraph, spread rumors, as well as facts, through the encampment with the efficiency of a flu virus. Besides normal scuttlebutt, personnel moving between various Army, Navy, and Marine commands on Bataan and Corregidor brought with them information generally more timely, and occasionally more accurate, than official briefings.

Charles walked to the Marines' medical tent, hoping to gain information just by standing around and listening.

From outside he heard loud voices.

Arguing voice: "MacArthur's acting like he's commander of the Navy as well as the Army. I never signed up to be in the goddamn Army!"

Calm voice: "Well, Colonel Howard now reports to MacArthur, so you, me, and everyone else in the 4th Marines are going to do what MacArthur wants us to. Don't have much choice about it, do we?"

Arguing voice: "And he's sitting over there in a tunnel with his headquarters staff and President Quezon while we're out here waiting for the bombs to fall. I don't trust him. He's Army."

Calm voice: "The Navy evacuated. No ships left, except for the *Canopus* over there and some PT boats that are too small for the open ocean. I think the subs are gone too since none of them have come to the *Canopus* for torpedoes or fuel."

Confident voice chimed in: "I figure the Pacific Fleet probably now has all their ships loaded and fueled. When the transports from LA and Frisco get to Hawaii, they'll all head here as a convoy."

"They damn well better hurry!"

Charles listened for a while longer before deciding the Marine hospital personnel didn't know any more than he did.

Admiral Hart prepared for his departure, leaving Rear Admiral Rockwell in command of the remaining Marine and Navy units. From headquarters in the Navy Tunnel on Corregidor, Rockwell would coordinate with MacArthur for the defense of Mariveles and Bataan.

Lieutenant Commander Frank Bridget was not one to sit and wait to be told what to do.

He devised a plan, got it approved by Admiral Rockwell, and then shared it with his own men.

"There are thousands of troops on the east coast to meet any bayside attack by the Japanese. Here at the tip of Bataan's thumb, however, we are wide-open to attack from the ocean. I have the go-ahead to organize a 'Naval Battalion, Mariveles' to guard our positions here. Hap Goodall will be my executive officer."

Reactions were less than enthusiastic.

The sailors now on Mariveles and Corregidor had been "shore Navy," not trained in ground combat. Specialists who supported the warships of the Asiatic Fleet, they knew how to keep track of supplies and parts. They could manage communications and even set and monitored harbor mines. They oversaw and performed ship repairs in dry dock and serviced submarines and seaplanes at their tenders. They were trained as machinists, radiomen, quartermasters, clerks, and corpsmen. However, they were *not* trained to be infantrymen.

"Who-all's going to be in this unit?" a sailor asked.

"A bit of a mixed crew," Bridget admitted. "It'll include the bluejackets from the *Canopus*, you men from PatWing 10, and two anti-aircraft batteries of the China Marines. Before you ask, I do realize that we sailors have no infantry training. The Marine NCOs will give us a crash course in tactics, and a Marine will be in charge of each squad."

"So, everyone stays here at Mariveles? With the Marines?"

"Yes and no. The group I just described will stay here. MacArthur ordered Colonel Howard to move the rest of the 4th Marines to the Rock and take over beach defense."

Bridget then added with a half-smile, "His 'Praetorian Guard,' I presume."

"Praetorian Guard?" someone asked.

Bridget ignored the question, "We're also sending fifty sailors to the Rock to form a Corregidor Navy Beach Defense unit. It'll report directly to Colonel Howard."

Charles was among the fifty sailors chosen, randomly it seemed, to move to Corregidor with the main body of Marines. He pulled his gradually deteriorating dictionary from his pocket.

Praetorian Guard
> *n. 1. The elite bodyguard of a Roman emperor.*
> *2. A member of this bodyguard.*

The sailors moving to Corregidor were designated the "Navy Detachment, Beach Defense Organization, Corregidor, P.I." Administratively, they were attached to the 4th Marines, but not otherwise integrated into the Marine ranks. Each sailor in the unit was assigned to a specific detail: Machine Gun Positions 1 & 2, Machine Gun support Squads 1 & 2, Rifle squads 1-3, Tunnel Defenses, and Demolition Party.

Navy corpsmen already with the Marines would stay with their units. Corpsmen who no longer had a unit, like Charles, were simply designated "Medical"—whatever that was.

As a group they assembled at the Mariveles dock for transport to Corregidor. Charles looked around, identified the senior ranking corpsman within their group, and introduced himself, "Charles Beckner. I was with PBY Patrol Wing 10, Squadron 102 at Olongapo. I'm part of what's left."

"Daniel McDougall. I was at the dispensary at the Cavite Navy Yard, part of the 16th Naval District. This 'medical unit' we've been assigned to—is it an actual organizational unit, or just a temporary holding designation for now?"

"I have no idea," Charles admitted. "I'll buy you a drink if you can show me a single one of us with paper orders. It looks to me like you're the senior corpsman here. At some point you'll need to figure out who and where we all report to."

"We have to get there first."

Barges moved the 4th Marines regiment to Corregidor in stages over three nights from December 27th to the 29th, along with a six-month supply of rations for 2,000 men, more than ten units of fire for all weapons, and their 100-bed transportable hospital.

Sailors not otherwise attached to the Marine regiment were told to find their own way across and reassemble with the Marines at Middleside Barracks. Daniel assembled his twelve corpsmen of the "medical unit" at the Mariveles dock the first evening, 27 December.

At one pier, the first group of Marines loaded men and equipment onto barges that would shuttle them across to the North Dock of Corregidor. On the adjacent pier, a PT boat loaded a mixture of soldiers, sailors, and civilians.

"The rest of you stay here for a minute," Daniel instructed, then approached an ensign on the PT boat. "Good evening, Ensign. Can I negotiate a ride for our group? We've got a dozen corpsmen needing to get over."

The ensign turned to the small bridge and yelled, "Lieutenant, OK to take a dozen corpsmen across?" The answer was unintelligible to Charles, but Daniel waved for the others to grab their bags and board the boat.

Charles recognized one of the PT crewmen as a sailor he had met months earlier back on Cavite. "It's Johnson, isn't it? Are you going to have room for all of us?"

"Right, Doc. It's *Bill*, and there's room for your bunch and a lot more," Johnson extended his hand.

Charles found a place for himself and his bag on the foredeck. The PT boat, only seventy-seven feet long, already had seventy-five or eighty men on board and was still loading more.

Once the lieutenant declared the boat at capacity, the crew released from the dock and motored at a sedate, for a PT boat, pace across the channel to the North Dock on Corregidor.

The men on the boat were from various units and took the opportunity to exchange information.

"You hear about Hong Kong?"

"No—what happened?"

"Surrendered to the Japs earlier today."

There was an astonished reply, "No! They lost those two battleships, *Prince of Wales* and *Repulse*, and now Hong Kong? The Brits have been there forever; it's always been 'London East.'"

"Well, it's 'Tokyo South' now. The Limeys are finished here. They've got more'n they can handle in Europe and couldn't send any help."

"So, no French or Brit allies left in Asia? I'm starting to feel a little lonely."

ॐ ॐ ॐ

Halfway across the channel, Bill worked his way between passengers to stand by Charles. "Are you moving permanently to the Rock?"

"If you think anything's permanent in your life, then you're in the wrong Navy. On the other hand, it's sort of the end of the line for my immediate future. I have a question, though. Where are your boats based? I don't see you docking around here."

"I wasn't with RON 3 at the time, but I know the story. The six boats arrived at Cavite last September. In the first bombing of the Navy Yard, they lost all their personal gear as well as all the spare parts and torpedoes. Hart ordered our commander, Lieutenant Bulkeley, to move the squadron here to Mariveles. Bulkeley and his XO, Lieutenant Kelly, felt we were too exposed at the main docks, and found a more protected spot on Sisiman Cove, right over there on the eastern edge of Mariveles Bay. A mostly abandoned fishing village with a usable dock was already there. Bulkeley negotiated a rental deal with the fishermen for their dock, along with some *nipa* huts. We spend nights on patrol. During the day, at least one of the boats is usually assigned to this type of courier duty."

"You called your group RON 3?"

"Short name for MTB 3, Motor Torpedo Boat Squadron 3. Most of the squadron's spare parts and supplies were lost when they bombed Cavite, so maintenance is a challenge. Eventually, we'll run out of fuel, but for now we're still operational. Today, we're running secure messages between Mariveles and the Rock, but the skipper saw no reason not to help get the troops across at the same time."

"I'm impressed with the number of people you took aboard."

"This is nothing! I guess you didn't hear about it, but back before Christmas the USS *Corregidor* tried to leave the bay with a load of civilian passengers. Someone screwed up, and they hit a mine and sank. There were three PT boats docked at Sisiman Cove at the time. The crews heard the explosion, raced to the scene, and found scores of people floating in the oil-coated water. The boats— remember they're designed for only two officers and eight or nine crewmen— rescued almost 300 people before returning to shore. You might find it hard to believe, but one PT boat took aboard almost 200 survivors by itself!"

Before they parted at the North Dock, Charles had an idea, "Hey, Bill, do you guys need a corpsman?"

"Sorry, Doc, we have one, John Balog, rides on PT-41. These are the only surface ships the Navy has left here, and every sailor without a unit wants to join our squadron. Bulkeley is only taking people with a skill we need."

"It was just a thought," Charles admitted, gathering his gear. "PatWing 10 left a bunch of us here when they moved south, and I'm part of this cobbled-together Navy Beach Defense unit."

"Good luck anyway, Doc," Bill called as Charles jumped off the boat onto the dock. He stood on the North Dock, watching the PT boat rumble back towards Mariveles.

Across the channel, faintly illuminated by the first-quarter moon, the extinct volcano Mount Mariveles towered almost a mile above the ocean. Charles looked back at Corregidor. Behind the island, far across the bay, smoke rose from still-burning fires in Cavite and Manila. *We fight on here, looking to the power of the United States to move heaven and earth and come to our rescue. Will it? Even if they do, will it be before we are overrun by the Japanese?*

Moving here from Mariveles didn't improve my situation much, if any. In fact, I feel abandoned and trapped on this island. There's no road off. The officers say dig in and hold on. What if our Pacific fleet really is sitting at the bottom of Pearl Harbor?

I'm beginning to believe we are only a holding action, left behind to slow down the Japanese Army. I'll never give up though—and I'll never surrender to the Japanese.

Never.

ॐ ॐ ॐ

Japanese forces, who had for months been subject to ridicule from Washington, swept in with unexpected tactics, innumerable aircraft, and hundreds of ships. Their war machine had so far proved invincible.

After bombing the Japanese invasion fleet on 10 December, surviving B-17s of the FEAAF moved to one of southern Philippine Islands and a few days later flew on to Australia. The remaining planes and pilots of the P-40 pursuit squadrons bravely continued surveillance and combat missions. They achieved some successes, including several air-to-air kills against Japanese planes, but attrition rapidly depleted their number and effectiveness.

On the ground, American and Filipino troops raced to Bataan, hoping to stop the Japanese invasion there.

26

The Rock

Corregidor (Fort Mills), Philippine Islands

28 December 1941

The small group of corpsmen walked uphill in the dark to Middleside Barracks to billet with the 4th Marines. Though not attached to the Marine regiment, Charles's small group of corpsmen would of necessity have to coordinate with the Marine medical units. Their contact would be a chief pharmacist's mate named Crew.

Crew explained to Daniel and the others the 4th Marine Regiment's medical organization. "It's pretty much the same as we had in China. Lieutenant Commander Thomas Hirst Hayes is the chief regimental surgeon. His offices are now in the Malinta Tunnel where he's establishing lines of communication to the three battalions. The 1st, 2nd, and 3rd Battalions will be responsible for the eastern, western, and middle sectors respectively. Each battalion station has a battalion surgeon and a dental officer working with five corpsmen. Sub-battalion stations are scattered in each section, each with an assistant surgeon and two corpsmen. Individual corpsmen move with their platoons."

"Where are you setting up your hospital?" Charles asked.

"It's staying in the crates. To begin with, there's no room for it up top. Every acre of space up here is already in use. Even if we could find a spot, the Japanese won't wait forever to start bombing and make everything above ground unsafe. For casualties needing hospitalization, we'll tag and move them to the battalion station for ambulance or truck transport to the Army hospital in the tunnel.

"That's pretty much the plan up here. Where's your duty station?"

Daniel looked around his group of corpsmen. "Good question. We were told our small group might be assigned to the Marine hospital, but you say it's not even going to be unpacked. This 'Beach Defense Detachment' was put together verbally, and we're unaware of any written orders for temporary or permanent transfers. At best there's probably a clerk somewhere trying to keep track of all the moves."

Charles had nothing to add. *For those of us who survive, our duty records, paymaster's rolls, and all the other records that constitute an organization will have to be reconstructed and confirmed. I don't know if I'm even still on the roster of PatWing 10. As far as I can tell, this 'Navy Beach Defense unit' isn't even a real organization. The whole fiasco will need sorting out someday. It sure won't be today, though.*

At the barracks, already packed with the Marines, Charles tossed the sea bag holding his combined personal and medical possessions onto an empty cot. "If nobody objects, I'm bunking here, at least for the rest of tonight."

"I can't imagine anyone objecting," replied a corpsman with the Marine regiment. "We only have a couple of nights to enjoy these barracks anyway. Tomorrow, Monday, we'll deploy all over the Rock, digging positions and stacking our sandbags. We'll bivouac in the open. I like being with the 4th, but there's a downside. If there's a shitty job, they give it to the Marines, and I have to go with them. Sleep tight."

Charles dug around in his bag for rations. In the humidity, paper labels identifying the round cans as containing beans, corned beef, or fruit had fallen off. Not wanting to deal with the uncertainty, he dropped the cans back into his bag and reclined on the bunk.

The overhead light was too dim to read by, so he rolled onto his side and fell soundly asleep.

ᔕᐤ ᔕᐤ ᔕᐤ

The next morning Charles ate breakfast at the 2nd Battalion mess tent. Working in nearly pitch dark, cooks boiled water in a giant steel pot and dropped in ten pounds of standard-issue ground coffee sealed in a muslin sack. *At Olongapo I boiled my white uniforms in this stuff. It's the same awful brew, but now I'm expected to drink it.*

Charles filled his metal cup and thanked the cook.

He sat back for a mental word game he devised for himself during nights on the *Langley*. *This coffee is black. It's hot. It's strong. How many other adjectives can I think of? Aromatic, ambrosial, flavorful, delectable? No, none of those apply to this witches' brew. Insipid? Bitter? Yep. It's an unsavory, watery potion, desirable only for its caffeine.*

He drank the coffee watching the sunrise and walked back to the Middleside Barracks. There, the hundred or so members of the Navy Beach Defense Detachment were coordinating placement of their two machine gun units, three rifle squads, and tunnel defense squads with the 4th Marines. Someone had decided that the Medical Unit, such as it was, would be stationed near Lieutenant Hayes's HQ staff in the Navy Tunnel as a reserve unit. During action, they could be sent to any area that needed extra corpsmen or as replacements for wounded or killed corpsmen. Otherwise, they'd stand by as messengers or for general duty needs.

"This won't be so bad," Daniel declared. "At least we won't be out in the open. Since the Navy Tunnel is our duty station, we might even find a place to bunk in there. What luck!"

"I'm not so sure," Charles worried. "How small and how deep is the tunnel?"

Daniel left for Hayes's office to work out the logistics for his group of corpsmen and returned an hour later. "We're dividing rotating ten-hour watches among ourselves, half of us on watch, the other half off. We've been allowed four hot bunks, so in theory we can all get eight hours sleep. We start at 2200 tonight."

Charles's first watch began the next morning at 0800, leaving him nothing to do until then. *I'm probably not going to find a library or any newspapers. I've had a good night's rest, so I'll just explore.*

Asking directions to the Navy Tunnel, he headed downhill to the small barrio on the south shore.

Corregidor was overcrowded. After adding the 4th Marines to Army, Navy, and Filipino troops already on the island, more than 9,000 military jostled shoulders—not including a large civilian population of Filipino contractors. In all, more than 15,000 people were squeezed onto the tiny island. The only departures were the scores of unofficial servants hastily abandoning the island for family villages. Charles noted more than a few soldiers and sailors camping out in the greenery of the island. *I bet they're only waiting for the chow lines to open. Shirkers and malcontents. These men can't be relied on in a fight. And I haven't seen a single military policeman or shore patrolman. Not good.*

He followed the road across Bottomside to the western entrance of the

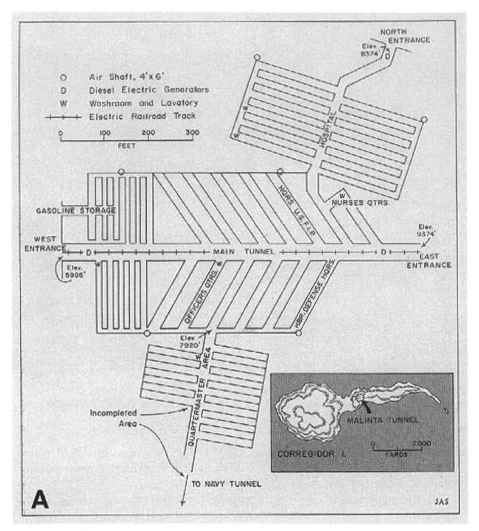

A map of the Malinta Tunnels (elevations in 0.01 foot; i.e. 9374' = 93.74 feet)

Malinta Tunnel, where a single train track ran into the darkness. He peered past the sentries into the dimly lit tunnel, but instead of entering he continued following the road south and east along the shore. After passing through the tiny civilian hamlet of Barrio San Jose, he arrived at the Navy Tunnel entrance.

Before he could ask permission from the sailor guarding the entrance, the sentry asked, "Taking the short cut to the hospital?"

Corpsmen are almost universally trusted by sailors, so he just nodded and walked into the tunnel. He paused before leaving the penumbra of daylight from the tunnel entrance. *No panic yet.*

He continued walking deeper in. *I'm struck by the sheer number of headquarters officers and senior NCOs down here. It looks like they might outnumber actual fighting men up top.*

Two- and three-tier bunks lined a lateral tunnel, providing sparse accommodations along with a few other pieces of standard military furniture. Occasional pin-up calendars or pictures graced the walls. *Hmm, carpets and armchairs—must have been brought from topside quarters earlier.*

A little farther on, another tunnel branched to his left. A sailor sat at a desk next to the entrance, sorting papers. A bookcase against the wall and a steel chair next to the desk created a tiny office space. The word "Queen" was stenciled above the branch tunnel entrance.

"What's the 'Queen' tunnel?" Charles asked.

"This is the HQ for the 16th Naval District. Unless you have business here, I can't let you go any farther."

"No, I'm heading to the hospital. While I'm here though, is there a library in here?"

"No library I know of in the tunnels. You might still find one topside. Anything else?"

"No. Just looking for a newspaper, or maybe a book about this place?"

"No newspapers, but I can show you an information book they used to give all the newly assigned personnel. I need it back." He pulled a thin booklet from his single-shelf bookcase. "It includes a map of the island."

"Thanks." *Might as well familiarize myself with the lay of the land, so to speak.* He sat down in the empty chair, studied the map, and read the booklet.

The rocky island of Corregidor, 'The Gibraltar of the East,' guards the entrance to Manila Bay. This tadpole-shaped island is about 4 miles long and 1.2 miles at its widest point. With American occupation at the turn of the century, four distinct sectors were identified: Topside, Middleside, Bottomside, and Tailside.

Topside is the high point of the largest, western section; the 'head' of the tadpole. Here is located the parade ground, golf course, and tennis courts. The largest barracks building in the world, the Mile-Long Barracks, is on Topside. In reality a little less than one-third of a mile long, it is nevertheless a beautiful three-story building. The sturdy steel and concrete structure is painted white, nicely complementing the red tile roof and green-trimmed seashell shutters.

Middleside is a small plateau interrupting the slope between Topside and Bottomside. It has officer and enlisted barracks, the Army hospital, a Post Exchange, and Filipino and American schools.

Bottomside is the narrow waist of the island between the head and tail. Here the North Dock faces the Bataan Peninsula. On the south side is the barrio of San Jose and another, smaller dock.

Tailside is not an official sector, but a term often applied to the island's elongated tail where Kindley Landing Field is located. While many tunnels lace through the rock of Corregidor, the east-west tunnel through the rock of Malinta Hill is the largest and longest, containing a railroad track connecting Tailside and Bottomside. Carved from solid rock in 1932, it is 826 feet long, and 24 feet in diameter. It has a complex of two dozen smaller lateral tunnels. each about 15 feet wide, 12 feet high, and 150 feet long. There is a long lateral connection to the Navy Tunnel and its laterals in the south side of Malinta Hill.

In military circles, you will hear Corregidor referred to as Fort Mills. The largest of four fortified islands guarding Manila Bay, it is a defensive arsenal with forty-five coastal guns, twenty-three batteries of mortars, and thirteen anti-aircraft batteries with seventy-two weapons.

"Can I ask you a question?"

"If it's short." The clerk laid down his papers and leaned back in his chair.

"I've seen the Marines up top, but not many Army troops. Down here I see mainly headquarters officers and support people. Does MacArthur think the Rock can hold against a Japanese siege long enough for reinforcement?"

"I'm not in charge of strategy here, Doc. I just keep the paperwork moving. I am short of smokes, though." He eyed the cigarette pack in Charles's pocket.

Charles tossed him the nearly full pack. "Keep it. We'll all probably be going without soon."

"Thanks. If you need a favor, you got it."

"I'll remember that. Where's the hospital?"

"Keep on going," he pointed deeper into the tunnel. "Can't miss it. Follow the signs. Ask if you get lost."

Continuing along the main Navy Tunnel another 300 feet, Charles entered a smaller tunnel. *Uh-oh—I'm beginning to sense shakiness and that feeling of doom.* He was about to turn back for the entrance when the tunnel abruptly enlarged again. He looked around. No more Navy. Everyone here was Army.

"Can I help you, sailor?" an Army sergeant blocked his way.

This guy's as pale as a ghost. He must never leave this place. One of those 'tunnel rats' I've heard about. Charles, having increasing curiosity for this fascinating underground city, decided to maintain his bluff. "I'm supposed to check in at the hospital. Never been there—can you help me find it?" It was a small, innocent lie, and "check in" was a nebulous term avoiding need of a more complex story. It worked.

"Your first time in the tunnels?"

"Yes."

The sergeant nodded, understanding. "This is the Army Quartermaster Depot," he explained. "You've come in from the back door. Getting to the hospital this way is not a straight shot. Go to the end of this tunnel, passing all the laterals, until you come to another long tunnel angling slightly to the right. Keep on that, and you'll come to the main Malinta Tunnel where you turn right again. You'll pass three or four laterals off the main tunnel, but just ignore them. You'll soon come to the command headquarter laterals on the right and

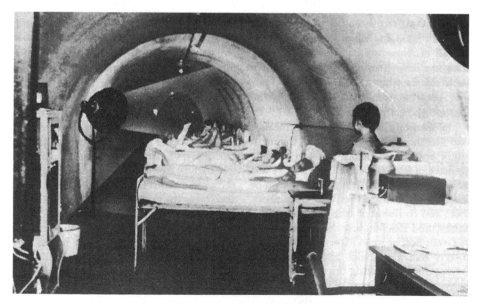

Malinta Tunnel Hospital, 1941

left. One is MacArthur's new HQ—don't even try to go in there. The next one on the left will have the 'Hospital' sign with an arrow. Take that lateral tunnel about 150 feet, and at the end is the entrance to the hospital tunnel."

"Thank you, sergeant." *That was seven or eight waypoints. Hope I don't get lost.*

Following the instructions, Charles worked his way toward the hospital. Even though the tunnels were quite large, the claustrophobia he'd finally admitted to tightened in his gut. The humid air reeked of solvents, sickness, and unbathed people. He also noted unidentified smells, some strange and others downright unpleasant. Scattered bare bulbs gave barely adequate illumination. He passed MacArthur's headquarters tunnel. It appeared recently excavated, and what Charles could see was nicely furnished. He walked faster. *I thought I wanted to explore this place, but now I just want to get out.*

Once he arrived, he realized the hospital complex was huge, and it was crowded. Beds lined the tunnel walls on both sides, almost touching head to foot. There was a narrow aisle down the middle with barely enough room for nurses and corpsmen to pass each other. He walked past a surgical tunnel and another tunnel stacked with medicines, bandages, and general medical supplies. One tunnel was labeled "X-Ray," but he saw no activity. *Is the X-ray machine farther back? Do they still have film and chemicals?*

Charles might have been a sailor wandering through an Army hospital, but the red cross on his arm said, "I belong here." No one questioned his presence. He initiated several short conversations with hospital staff, but no one knew a Tillie Finian or any other Navy nurse.

Disappointed and feeling a cold sweat inside his shirt, Charles knew he'd stayed too long.

These tunnels can't be really shrinking, can they?

He asked the closest person, "What's the quickest way out of here?"

"Go straight, make a right, and you can see the north tunnel entrance from there."

In only a couple of minutes, he was back in daylight. He leaned against the entrance wall, closed his eyes, and breathed deeply.

"You OK, son?"

Charles opened his eyes and looked at the Army major inspecting him with concern. "Yes, sir. I'm fine now. I don't think I care much for those tunnels though."

The major laughed, "You're not the only one. I need to come out here for a break after working in there for a few hours. Want a smoke?"

"Thank you, sir. I just gave my last pack away. I don't smoke much, but this seems a good time." He noticed the major's Corps insignia, a medieval castle. "You're Engineer Corps—you work on the tunnels?"

"For now," the major responded. "We're trying to decide how ventilation, water, and power can be increased and made more reliable. We're expecting even more people to crowd inside."

"Really? It looks pretty full already. How old are the tunnels?"

"Well, it's not a simple answer." The major tapped the ash from his cigarette and took another drag. "We had that 1922 agreement with Japan keeping us from improving our fortifications here, but in 1931 the commander, a General Kilbourne, managed to quietly build a tunnel over at Battery Wheeler. When no one squawked over that, he asked permission for a much larger project."

"The big tunnel, I presume?"

"Kilbourne told his superiors he was only going to build a transportation tunnel through Malinta Hill because the north and south shore roads were always being closed by rock falls, and they approved his 'road improvement' project. He crushed the rock from the excavations for surfacing the roads around the island and claimed the project was a quarry. Damned if he didn't build the entire complex without any extra funding from Washington and with no complaints from Japan. He must have been one smart bastard."

"Right now, I think we could use a few more smart bastards around here," Charles suggested.

"Yep—smart bastards with planes, ships, and guns."

The major flicked his finished cigarette aside, looked up at the sky for a moment, and walked into the tunnel.

27

Leaving the Rock

Corregidor (Fort Mills), Philippine Islands

29 December 1941–6 January 1942

Lee Beckner once told his son, "Always be on time. It's an insult to the other party to be late."

Charles, following his father's advice by habit, arrived for his first shift in Commander Hayes's headquarters forty-five minutes early.

A corpsman at the end of his ten-hour shift stood in front of the desk, arguing with a senior Army NCO while a Navy clerk looked on.

The corpsman pled his case. "Sergeant, I've been here all night. If I go now, I'll hardly get back in time for my next shift."

"I understand, but someone's got to do this right now, and all I see is you."

The corpsman noticed Charles, "Are you one of the replacements?"

"At 0800," Charles replied.

"Why can't he go?" the corpsman asked the Navy clerk.

"It won't wait. I've got a PT boat sitting at the north dock and a driver waiting at Mariveles. The sergeant says this package has to be hand-carried to Hospital No. 1 near Camp Lemay. It's morphine and barbiturate, so it can't be sent in general supply. It has to go right now—who's taking it?"

He looked back and forth at the two corpsmen.

Charles's heart skipped a beat. *Tillie isn't on Corregidor. The only other hospitals are Army Hospitals No. 1 and No. 2.*

"I'll do it."

222

"Better pack some rations," the Army sergeant suggested. "They're stingy with their food up there."

The clerk added, "If the driver can't wait there for you, find another way back."

℈ ℈ ℈

Charles signed for the large, sealed canvas bag, and trotted to the dock where a PT boat waited, identified only by the '35' painted on the chart house.

"I'm Charles Beckner," he said loudly enough to be heard over the idling engine. "I've got some medicine for Hospital No. 1. Are you my ride?"

The seaman waved Charles aboard and then yelled to an ensign at the helm, "It's our package—we can go."

A different voice called out, "Hey, Doc. We keep running into each other."

"Bill! Are you always on this boat? And by the way, I'm still envious. You never did say how you managed to join RON 3."

"First question, yes, the 35's my boat. Second question, I was a communications specialist on the *Canopus*, but they moved that office south when Hart left. After a couple of days, I found a slot as a radioman with this squadron. Yourself?"

"I was with PatWing 10, but now I'm part of the Navy Corregidor Beach Defense. The Marines already had all their corpsmen with them, so for now they're just using me as a messenger. But it could be worse—they could have sent me to the hospital in the tunnel—I don't like the tunnels. Let me ask you again, how'd you get your orders for the PT boats?"

"Didn't wait for orders. When I left the *Canopus*, I was verbally told to report to the Navy communications people. They just took my name and said they'd find a spot somewhere for me. I knew a sailor with RON 3 and asked him if I could join them. Told him I was unassigned, but I could be a radioman or even a general seaman. They radioed Bulkeley, the squadron commander, and for whatever reason, he took me on as a radioman. I ran back for my sea bag and came back to the boat."

"Sounds simple."

"Almost got scuttled. When I got back to the dock, two MPs stopped me. Said I'd been reported AWOL, and they were going to arrest me. I just tossed my bag on the boat and said I couldn't be AWOL because I was assigned to this squadron. I jumped on the boat, and they let me go." Bill grinned. "It was close, but I wanted anything except being given to the infantry. For that matter, when the Japs started bombing, I didn't want to be topside either."

Charles frowned. "Hey, remember I asked you about joining the squadron a couple of days ago, and you told me the squadron already had a corpsman? Didn't they already have radiomen when you joined?"

"Doc, on a PT boat everyone's cross-qualified. I know enough to load and fire the Browning machine gun. Our cook can do the same, and our chief motor mac OJT'd as a torpedoman."

"It was the same for our PBY aircrew." Charles looked at the two machine-gun turrets. "Does your squadron need another qualified gunner? I'm certified on the Browning .50 caliber." He pointed to the twin-mounted machine guns close to the bridge.

"You didn't tell me that before—and, anyway, I didn't know corpsmen qualified on anything but the rifle at basic. You're not even supposed to carry a weapon, are you?" He looked at the pistol hanging from Charles's belt.

"Times are different."

"We're here, Doc." Johnson stood up as they approached the Mariveles dock. "Seems to me we could've taken you on up the coast to Limay, closer to Hospital No. 1. Must be they want to save what's left of the aviation gas."

"If that's the case, Bill, why leave the engines idling while you wait at the dock?"

"Because it's daylight. If a Jap plane drops in on us, we can throttle up and head for open water before they catch us sitting here."

"Makes sense." Charles paused. "I don't want to beg, but let me ask once more. Do you see any chance of my joining this squadron? I feel useless where I am."

"I'll ask around, but don't get your hopes up."

ॐ ॐ ॐ

At the Mariveles dock an Army driver waited for Charles in an "Olive Drab No. 3" Army sedan. They traveled north on the East Road, not stopping until reaching the small sign for Camp Limay.

An Army truck coming south turned onto the hospital road in front of them. They followed it to the hospital, where the truck pulled to a stop. The canvas covers on the back were thrown open, and hospital personnel began unloading stretchers of wounded American and Filipino soldiers.

"Where'd these men come from?" Charles asked the truck driver.

"Somewhere up north of the Layac Junction. Part of the unit that was trying to keep the Olongapo-Manila road open. They were caught by the Japs before they could reach our main defensive lines—there's more on the way. Soon as I load up on stretchers, I'm turning around and heading back up."

Until now, Charles's only combat experience was being bombed and strafed by Japanese planes. *Bombers fly in, do their damage, and leave. Now, since the Japanese infantry invasion, we are in continuous ground combat. If we can't hold a defensive line, they'll push us all the way back to Mariveles. If reinforcement doesn't arrive, they'll push us into the ocean.*

Then the choice really will be death or POW.

He swallowed. *Hard times coming.*

"No hurry with your delivery," his driver said. "I have to wait for some mail bags."

"OK, but go ahead and leave if I'm not back. I'll find another ride."

Hospital No. 1, close to the beach, was a cluster of wood buildings with a few thatched-roof huts and shelters at the edge. "Where's the pharmacy?" he asked.

"Probably you want surgery. It's at the uphill end of the complex, the large building with a sign."

An Army first lieutenant nurse was waiting. "I hope they sent everything. Let's unpack and count this stuff, then I'll sign for it, and you can go." The contents matched the paperwork he'd brought, and the lieutenant signed the copy for Charles to return to the medical supply quartermaster back at Corregidor.

"Thanks for the delivery," she said sincerely. "At the rate we're getting wounded, though, this won't last long."

"Good luck, then. Maybe I'll see you with another batch." He left surgery and looked around. His driver had already left. *Good! They expected me to "find another way back" after making the delivery. Now, I have my own mission.*

Up the slope beyond the surgery building was a short water tower and a generator shack. Downslope was an officers' club and nurses' quarters. A large white canvas sheet displaying a huge red cross stretched horizontally across the open space, clearly visible from the air to identify the complex as a hospital. They apparently didn't trust the Japanese bombers to honor that symbol, and foxholes and trenches lined the periphery of the hospital grounds.

The place bustled with activity. American and Filipino nurses and enlisted hospital staff hurried between buildings. Dirt flew as two men extended a slit trench next to the hospital buildings.

Charles stopped a nurse rushing by, "Excuse me. I'm looking for a nurse named Tillie Finian. Do you know her?"

The nurse stopped, furrowing her brow in thought. "No, I don't think I've met anyone by that name."

"She's got red hair. She's Navy."

"Oh, we don't have any Navy nurses here."

"No Navy nurses? None at all?"

"Not that I know of." She called to another nurse passing by, "Deb, do you know of any Navy nurses here?"

"I think there's one. Isn't that a Navy nurse that works with the Navy surgeon?"

"Is her name Tillie?"

"Sorry, I don't remember her name."

"Where would I find her?"

"I just came from the OR, and she's not there now. Maybe she's in the nurses' quarters, down there. You can ask and see if anyone there knows the Navy surgical nurse."

Charles thanked both the nurses and jogged to the building at the far end from the OR. He stopped a nurse leaving the building. "Pardon me, but I need to find a Navy nurse, named Tillie. Do you know her?"

"Oh yes, we do have a Navy nurse here. I'm not sure that's her name though. I think she's from Cavite. Do you want me to see if she's here and can come to the door?"

"Please. Thank you!" He was elated. *She's here and safe!*

Less than a minute later, a Navy nurse appeared at the door. He recognized her instantly.

"Hi. I'm Liz." She looked questioningly at Charles. "You look familiar—don't I know you?"

"Yes," he responded, struggling not to look disappointed. "I'm Charles Beckner. I was at Cañacao from November to June last year, but I don't think we ever actually worked on the same ward."

"That's right. Now I remember seeing you around. Who are you trying to find?"

"Tillie Finian."

Liz's expression turned serious. "Oh yes, you were a friend of hers, weren't you? She's not here, and I'm pretty sure you won't find her at Hospital No. 2 either."

That's not what I wanted to hear. "Why are you so sure?"

Liz walked with him to a crude wood bench. "I'll tell you what I know. The same day the war started, the sixty or seventy ambulatory patients at Cañacao were sent back to their units. After that, our bed patients were transferred to

Army Hospitals around Manila. I, another nurse, and two corpsmen traveled with half of them to Sternberg. Because they were Navy patients, they had us stay with them. We split twelve-hour shifts until we left."

"So, Tillie—Miss Finian—stayed behind at Cañacao?"

"For only a couple of days, I think. Then the rest of the hospital staff moved out. A few of the staff joined us at Sternberg. At that point some of us were sent to Santa Scholastica, and the rest went to other hospitals, maybe even Balintawak. I don't remember seeing Finian at Sternberg or anywhere else after I left Cañacao."

"So if she's not here, why do you say she's not down south at Hospital No. 2?"

"Charles, I can't be sure of much of anything these days, but I don't think any other Navy nurses managed to get to Bataan before the Japanese took control. Except for me—I was part of an OR team that moved to Bataan on Christmas Eve. A lot of Army nurses moved to Bataan, but as far as I know, no other Navy nurses. I asked and was told that the Navy nurses were still waiting for orders when the Japanese swept into Manila."

They were both silent for a moment. She touched his arm.

"I'm sorry, Charles."

"What do you think happened to them?"

"I don't know, but I assume they're prisoners. I have to hope that as medical POWs, they'd all be treated well under the Geneva Convention."

Bataan Hospital No. 2, 1942.

"I'm sorry, Liz, I mean Miss—"

"I think for the moment calling me Liz is fine."

"I haven't asked how you're managing here yourself?"

"I'm doing fine, except that the Army people here don't want to deal with a Navy nurse for some reason. They've made it clear that I can work with a Navy surgeon, but otherwise stay out of their way. That'll probably change as things heat up. Only this morning we received a message to expect a surge in casualties. Once these wards fill up, we'll extend more cots into the trees and along the paths and put up rain tarps. There's also an evacuation plan that moves us down near Mariveles if—if, well, you know—"

They talked a bit longer, exchanging scuttlebutt and chatting about people they'd known at Cañacao.

Then, after a quick hug, they each walked towards their separate, uncertain futures.

ॐ ॐ ॐ

Most of the East Road traffic moved north, transporting men and supplies to the northern defensive lines. Charles caught a ride on one of the few vehicles headed south, an empty ambulance returning to Hospital No. 2. *This will get me closer to Mariveles, and it will give me one last chance to find Tillie. Perhaps Liz was mistaken about all the other Navy nurses being left behind?*

Slowly making way along the road to Hospital No. 2, the driver droned on with an unending litany of complaints. He hated driving at night, he'd not heard about his promised promotion, his girlfriend hadn't written him since October, and on and on.

Charles tuned out the monologue and catnapped.

"Wake up! We're here." The driver was shaking Charles's shoulder. "Welcome to the Jungle Hospital."

Hospital No. 2 was nothing like its sister. Hospital No. 1 was created from what was previously a Philippine Army Engineering headquarters. Hospital No. 2 was carved straight from the trees and underbrush: Patient beds sat on bare ground, and there were no chairs or other conveniences. The operating bay was the only structure with walls and a wood floor. Rain tarps and mosquito nettings hung beneath trees.

As beds filled, the bulldozers simply cleared another area of jungle for more cots.

Charles listened to mixed groups of medical officers, nurses, and enlisted men discussing a major bombing raid on Corregidor that morning. There were few details, but it seemed to have been a long raid with numerous formations of Japanese bombers releasing their deadly sticks of bombs while, as they had done at Cavite, Manila, and Sangley Point, staying well above anti-aircraft range.

Charles's feelings vacillated between guilt and relief. *Should I have been there for the bombing? So many things are spiraling out of my control! I'll just do what I can, wherever I am.*

A few people glanced at the Navy corpsman walking through the Army hospital grounds but otherwise paid him little attention.

Charles interrupted a group of nurses lining up for their allotted rations in an open mess tent. "Excuse me, are there any Navy nurses here?"

After conferring with the the others, one nurse shook her head, "No, but you might check in the nurses' bivouac area. It's always possible there's been a new arrival."

"Thanks—where's that?"

She gave directions, adding, "You're only permitted in that area during daylight."

He found only two nurses there, one very ill and being fed broth by another nurse.

"Hello?" Charles called from the edge of their area.

"Hi. C'mon over so you don't have to yell."

"Thanks." He walked to the bed where a pale, underweight woman sipped slowly at the broth. "A touch of malaria?" he guessed.

"Yes. This is Diane," said the other nurse. "She's been battling it for a while now. The quinine is helping, but we're all exhausted and what food we are getting isn't all that nourishing. My name's Mary."

It's amazing so many parents chose the name 'Mary' for their daughters. "Nice name. I have a sister named Mary, but right now I'm looking for Lieutenant Mary Finian. She's a Navy nurse, goes by the name Tillie."

"Sorry—there's no Tillie or Nurse Finian I know of, and I'm pretty sure there aren't any Navy nurses or doctors here at No. 2. You're a Navy corpsman. Are you assigned here?"

"No, I'm on my way back to Corregidor after delivering some medications to Hospital No. 1. No insult intended, but in all honesty, they look like a luxury hotel compared to this."

Her face belied her brave response, "It's not all that bad, but it's not that good either. We don't have any hot water, even for bathing the patients. We take baths in the river ourselves. The cooks heat water in big drums to make rice, and we can still taste leftover gasoline or oil when we eat it." She gave Diane another spoonful of broth. "I only wish we had better for the boys, the badly injured ones. I think of them up north, battling the Japanese, and I can't complain about things down here."

"Aren't you missing your supper?" he asked, remembering the nurses in the mess tent.

"No, it didn't take long to eat. We're on two-thirds rations. Both officers and enlisted messes serve an early breakfast and a second meal at 4 p.m. That's it. For lunch all we get is stomach cramps. I did manage to find something for Diane."

Charles felt a wave of shame for taking advantage of the still-plentiful food on Corregidor. "I managed to bring some things—I'm leaving them with you." He opened the bag on his belt and withdrew a can of salmon, a can of beans, and a candy bar.

Mary, knowing thanks would be superfluous, grabbed the candy bar. "Look here, Diane! Think you can get this down?"

Diane weakly smiled. "Only my half of it."

It wasn't far to Mariveles, and Charles considered walking. However, a lone man on the road at night could get shot, with or without being given the chance to identify himself.

He checked with the transportation motor pool. A supply truck from Corregidor was due around midnight and would be returning to Mariveles before dawn. *I'll miss my 0400 rotation, but they sent me here and will figure it out.*

Waiting for the truck, he watched the staff efficiently caring for sick and wounded soldiers in primitive conditions. *These people all deserve a medal. I hope that nurse, Diane, survives the malaria. She looked pretty damn sick.*

At daybreak the truck, with Charles riding in the cab, topped the hill before its descent to Mariveles. Smoke still rose from the previous day's attack on Corregidor.

Most of the 4th Marines were now on Corregidor, and much of the Army had either moved up to the Abucay line or set up coastal positions east and west of Mariveles, leaving it less crowded than on his first arrival.

Charles was not surprised to see the same PT-35 waiting at the dock. He didn't recognize the sailor on deck. "Is Bill Johnson on board?" he asked.

"He is." The sailor went to the day-room hatch and called, "Johnson. You have a visitor."

Johnson looked out the door. Seeing Charles, he joined him on the dock. "Welcome back, Doc. You missed all the action yesterday. Get your package to Hospital No. 1 OK?"

"I did, but I couldn't find someone I'd hoped was there. Seems you have a regular shuttle schedule here. I need to get back over to Corregidor. Are you guys going over soon?"

"We're waiting for some brass. If those Jap planes come back though, we'll run to open water. I'm sure you can ride along, but let me check with Ensign Akers." Bill stooped to talk to someone in the chart house and returned. "No problem—he figures if we took you over, we can return you."

"Great."

Shortly, two Army captains and a lieutenant colonel came aboard. The boat cast off, a few minutes later depositing the passengers at Corregidor's North Dock.

Before getting off, Charles had a question for Bill. "I noticed that yesterday and again today, we didn't go straight to Mariveles but took the same dogleg route?"

"You're observant." Bill pointed at some buoys in the north channel. "Those are markers we use to get through the minefield."

"Minefield? You never told me we were going through a minefield! Is that the same place the passenger ship was sunk a couple of weeks ago?"

"Further west, and that was at night. It's not clear who screwed up, but it's being investigated. Don't worry though—RON 3 is expert at going through the minefields. We do it all the time. Sometimes we have to pass through a second minefield to reach the open ocean."

"It might've been better if you'd left me ignorant."

"You asked. By the way, I did tell Ensign Akers about a corpsman who was qualified on the Browning .50 and looking to join a unit. I didn't follow up because I figured I'd never see you again."

"You're seeing me right now."

"I'll ask again. How will I find you?"

"I'm part of the Navy Corregidor Beach Battalion. For the next few days I'm a standby errand boy at Commander Hayes's office in the Navy Tunnel, near the entrance on the south side of Malinta Hill. If I'm not there, his clerk should be able to get a message to me."

"No promises, but I'll follow up for you. Tell me again, what group were you originally with, if someone asks?"

"Patrol Wing 10, the PBY seaplane unit that was on Sangley Point. When it moved south, a bunch of us got left behind."

Occasional barges still arrived at the North Dock with supplies. From where the cargo came, Charles had no idea. He watched a freshwater barge pump thousands of gallons into the Corregidor water system. The newcomers' booklet noted that Corregidor had little fresh water of its own, relying on regular deliveries from Cabcaben and Sisiman Cove. *That's a weak link if Corregidor comes under siege.*

A west wind blew smoke from smoldering fires away from the island, but the breeze could not clear the lingering scent of explosives and scorched earth. The beautiful topside hospital was severely damaged, Mile Long Barracks was in ruin, and the Navy fuel depot still blazed. A group of men repaired communication lines while others tried to restore power and water lines.

At the Navy Tunnel, Charles asked the waiting corpsman, "How was it?"

"They came a little before noon and hit us good. We lost one Marine, and several more were injured. Probably another twenty or so military and civilians were killed, and maybe a hundred or more wounded. Could have been worse."

"Bad enough."

"After they left, we crammed the Topside hospital patients into the tunnel hospital. The Marines are scattered in positions all over the Rock. Administration and records all moved into the tunnels, probably permanently. It's getting really crowded in here."

"I did notice fewer people standing around outside than when I left. What about us? Any new instructions?"

"Nope. Just sit here like a chigger on a hound's butt and wait for someone to give us an errand."

"Seems a waste of good corpsmen."

"It is, but the Marines know and trust the corpsmen who have been with them since China. They don't want any changes unless they lose their own. Meanwhile, the Army treats the tunnel hospital as their own private club, and they don't want us either."

"That might change."

"Maybe so, but until then don't expect any invitations."

Charles was mentally able to remain in the tunnel so long as he stayed close to the entrance. That proved enough for him to complete his duty shifts. Otherwise he ate and slept outside.

"You know, it's safer inside," an ensign pointed out to him.

"Maybe, sir, but as soon as my shift's over, I'm heading back outside. In here, the power and ventilation blowers keep failing, fresh water is limited, and the sheer number of people have pushed the sanitation facilities beyond their limits. It gets worse every day."

"But it's safer." *This officer's been hiding down here so long, his skin's pale white. He's another nervous 'tunnel rat.'*

"I'll take my chances, sir. The Marines always make room for me behind their sandbags."

Little happened until 11:34 on Friday morning, 2 January, when the Japanese returned. They bombed the island for more than three hours that day and again on Saturday. On Sunday, while religious services were held underground in a tunnel, the Japanese again bombed the island, targeting antiaircraft batteries, large gun and mortar emplacements, and any buildings not already leveled.

At his shift, Charles forced himself to move slightly deeper inside the tunnel, listening. Each cluster of bombs was preceded by four or five seconds of whistling, ending in explosions that were felt as much as heard. When a bomb hit anywhere near the tunnel entrance, the wind whipped at his pants and shirt as shrapnel buzzed around the opening.

On Monday, 5 January, the skies were silent; not a single Japanese plane flew over. Charles was standing outside the Navy Tunnel entrance, leaning against sandbags, when Bill Johnson found him.

"Doc! I've been hunting for you. Do you still want to join the PT squadron?"

"Of course!"

"I don't want this to come back on me. Are you being straight with me about your machine gun qualifications?"

"Straight as an arrow. Anyone can point and push the trigger on an M2, but I can maintain the gun, fix a jam, and know when to back off so I don't melt the barrel. I can shoot pretty well too. I took the course and qualified last year." *Just don't ask me for papers to prove it.*

"OK, then. You're joining RON 3, on PT-34. Your action station will be one of the twin 50s. Lieutenant Bulkeley, the squadron commander, checked with our corpsman, John Balog. John thought it'd be good to have a second corpsman. He'll be your senior." Bill looked hard at Charles. "You have a problem with that?"

"None at all. What next?"

"We just brought Bulkeley over from Sisiman Cove. He reports to Admiral Rockwell in the Navy Tunnel to get his marching orders for the day. After he leaves Rockwell's HQ, Bulkeley's going to the hospital tunnel to go review plans with Kelly."

"Kelly?"

"Lieutenant Kelly's normally the captain of PT-34. He had a finger infection move up into his arm, and he's here in the hospital for a while. Besides being captain of the 34, Kelly is also Bulkeley's XO."

"So, what do I do? Go find Bulkeley?"

"I don't recommend that. You first should talk to Ensign Chandler, a good officer who has command of 34 while Kelly's out of commission. Until Kelly gets back, Ensign Iliff Richardson is acting as Chandler's XO. You'll find no finer officer than either of those two. Like I said, I put my ass on the line and assured both Chandler and Richardson you're fully qualified on the .50 calibers." He looked expectantly at Charles.

"I promise. You'll have no regrets."

"Great. Anyway, now Bulkeley's OK'd it, all you need is your CO's endorsement. Who is that?"

"I'm not sure, but I remember your AWOL story—I'll have something in writing. When and where do I report?"

"We're docked at a small fishing village in Sisiman Cove on the east side of Mariveles Bay. Find either Chandler or Richardson on PT-34 when you get there. I've got to get back—glad to have you aboard, Doc." Bill waved back over his shoulder as he headed for the North Dock.

Charles immediately turned and headed back into the tunnel. The same clerk Charles had talked to on his first foray into the tunnels was still at his desk, still filling out papers.

"Morning. You remember me? I gave you my cigarettes."

"Sure."

"I need that favor you promised. I've been asked to fill a slot on PT Squadron 3. It's been verbally approved by Lieutenant Bulkeley, their squadron commander. Can you get me approval, on paper, to take that assignment? I really don't think I'm being all that useful waiting around here."

"Well, myself, I don't see why not," the clerk replied in his southern drawl and a smile to match. "Who were you with before this?"

"VP-102, Patrol Wing 10. What's left of the unit moved south a week ago. Those of us left here were split up, with most still at Mariveles and a few of us here on the Rock. I've been verbally assigned to the 'Corregidor Navy Beach

Defense unit.' I don't have any paper orders to that effect though. In all honesty, I've been pretty much nothing but a message runner since I got here."

"Let me check with the boss."

He walked a few feet deeper in the tunnel and returned with Commander Hayes, who looked Charles over. "So, the PT squadron needs a corpsman? Nobody said anything to me about that."

"They probably didn't know we were overstaffed with corpsmen here, sir."

"Got any records on this man?" Hayes asked the clerk.

"Not yet."

"Then type out some temporary orders sending him to MTB 3. We can sort it out when appropriate." He nodded to Charles, "Good luck, son," and walked back to his desk.

"Thank you, sir." *And good luck to you too.*

PTs 31, 34, 35, and 41 in the well deck of the tanker Guadalupe, on their way to Cavite in 1941. This might be the only surviving picture of PT-34.

Part IV

28

MTB 3

North Dock, Corregidor Island, Philippine Islands

6 January 1942

Charles arrived at the North Dock with the first hint of dawn. As before, a Navy ensign managed the comings and goings of boats and barges. "Know of any way I can get to Sisiman Cove?" Charles asked.

"Once you get across to Mariveles, it's not a bad walk." Then the young officer pointed at a barge. "That freshwater lighter might be faster. After it's pumped empty, it'll head straight back to the water dock at Sisiman to refill. That's probably your best bet."

"Thanks, I'll wait."

The barge crew gave Charles a ride, no questions asked. A few minutes later they arrived at his new home.

Sisiman Cove was less than a mile from Mariveles but had the advantage of a cliff protecting it from Japanese fighter planes. The cliff was too steep and high for the Zeros to approach from that direction, nor could they attack from the sea without crashing into the mountain. As a bonus, Sisiman had two, if somewhat rickety, wooden piers.

The water barge docked at the westernmost of the two piers to refill from a freshwater cistern near the beach. Without these twice-daily resupply trips, Corregidor would quickly exhaust its water stores.

Four PT boats secured at Sisiman: PT-41 and PT-31 moored about 50 yards offshore, while PT-35 and PT-32 docked at the eastern pier. Near the stern of the 32 boat a group of men in a vigorous exchange alternated between angry yelling and quieter discussion. Not seeing PT-34, Charles walked down the pier to the 35 boat.

"Good morning. I'm Charles Beckner. I'm looking for Johnson."

"Morning. I'm Jimmy." The sailor pointed farther up the pier, "Ensign Johnson is the heavyset guy over there in that group next to 32."

"Not Ensign Johnson—I'm looking for Bill Johnson, a seaman."

Jimmy turned to the hatch behind him. "Johnson! You've got company." Bill Johnson climbed up from the chart house and walked down the deck to where he could talk to Charles, who remained standing on the pier. "Hi, Doc. Did you make it here for good or just a visit?"

"Permanently, I hope. I managed to get typed orders," Charles patted his pocket. "What's going on over there?" he nodded towards the group of men around PT-32.

"Big SNAFU," Bill commented. "They had an explosion in the engine room the day before yesterday. It damaged 32's stern pretty badly and put Shanghai Guyat, their engineer, in the hospital. They're figuring out how to rebuild her. The lieutenant scowling over there, that's our squadron commander, Bulkeley. He's pissed off that we're down to only four boats. Scuttlebutt is that the lieutenant's laying all the blame on Shoe for letting the explosion happen."

"Shoe?"

"It's what everyone calls the boat captain, Lieutenant Schumacher. Anyway, since Bulkeley's in a fouler mood than usual, I'd recommend waiting and introducing yourself to him later. I suggest you'd be better off if you start by meeting either Ensign Chandler, acting captain of the 34, or his XO, Richardson."

"Thanks for the advice. You said 'snafu'? I didn't get that."

Bill laughed. "Someone in the squadron picked it up from the Army guys at Mariveles. It's a new acronym, and you know how much the military loves acronyms."

"What's it stand for?"

"Status Nominal, All Fucked Up."

Charles smiled. "That acronym's going to find a lot of use these days. Where's PT-34, anyway?"

"They're over topping up tanks at the fuel barge."

"It'll be back soon?"

"Hard to say. These things hold 3,000 gallons of 100-octane aviation gasoline. For now, we're having to fill the tanks through felt hats or anything else we can use to strain out rust and wax. Someone sabotaged the gas barge with paraffin, and it keeps clogging our fuel filters. Makes the damn engines stop without warning, even right in the middle of a mission, and it takes fifteen minutes or so to clean the filters and restart the engines. If it happens during an attack or a close-quarters fight, it could be fatal."

"Can't you clean the tanks?"

"We tried, even steamed them out, but the filters still get clogged. Let me get the OK to walk you to the huts, and I'll tell you about your new family." Bill disappeared momentarily into the chart house of PT-35, then joined Charles on the pier.

"Is there a standard routine?" Charles asked as they walked towards the tiny village.

"We patrol mostly at night. Usually two boats. The other boats nest together in the cove for the night, sharing the watch so more men can sleep. At dawn, the nest breaks up. The boats move to various anchorages around the Cove, do shuttle runs for Admiral Rockwell, or move to the dock. Those back from patrol try to get some sleep, while the rest of us work on engines and running

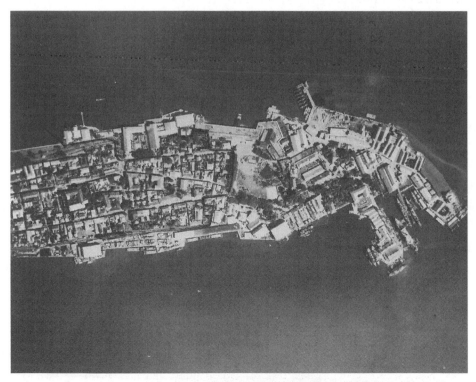

Navy Yard, Cavite Peninsula, 1941. Note the six boats of MTB 3 docked at the small pier projecting north (to the top of the picture).

gear, trying to keep things operational. After leaving Cavite, we started nightly inshore patrols around Manila Bay. Those stopped last week because the Japs now control most of the Bay. Also, our avgas supply's getting low to the point we need to ration it."

Great. I just joined a unit that's about to go out of commission. "You mean you'll soon run out of fuel?"

"Fuel. Oil. Parts. No one can say exactly how long we can continue, but it won't be more than two or three months if we have to rely on what's available now."

At the base of the pier, both stopped to watch a small boat roar into Sisiman Cove and stop near a small dock on the opposite, eastern side of the cove. "That's one of those Filipino boats?" Charles asked.

"Correct. The Filipinos moved three of their Q-Boats here for the same reason we did, protection from Jap air attack. There's some communication between their officers and ours, but they otherwise keep to themselves."

Bill resumed walking. "Let me go over your chain of command. Lieutenant John Bulkeley is RON 3's commander. He commands PT-41, though he often goes on patrols in the other boats. The squadron executive officer is Lieutenant Robert Kelly, the captain of PT-34, your boat. Kelly's still in the hospital for a hand infection, so his XO, Ensign Barron Chandler, temporarily commands that boat. Ensign Iliff Richardson was on PT-33 until she ran onto a reef and couldn't be salvaged. He was moved to Boat 34 as Chandler's XO until Kelly comes back."

"So, I report to Richardson, who reports to Chandler, who reports to Bulkeley?" asked Charles.

"And Bulkeley reports to Admiral Rockwell on the Rock, and Rockwell reports to Admiral Hart who's somewhere between here and Australia. When Kelly gets back, that'll make PT-34 the only boat with three commissioned officers. I don't know how long that'll last. Oh—and somewhere in that chain you probably report to our corpsman, John Balog."

"I'll figure it out. What are Chandler and Richardson like?"

"Both good men, capable and reasonable. Not ring-knockers like Kelly and Bulkeley—not part of that fraternity."

"Ring-knockers? What fraternity?"

"Kelly and Bulkeley are both Naval Academy graduates. At a briefing or a discussion, the Annapolis grads tend, intentionally or not, to tap their class rings on the table as if to remind everyone of that fact. I think that's why Bulkeley trusts Kelly so much. It also explains why the problem with PT-32 irritates Bulkeley even more with Kelly, his XO, in the hospital."

"How long has Bulkeley been the squadron commander?"

"Always. He's been part of PT boats since they started development. In fact, except for you, me, Ensign Richardson, and a couple of others, everyone else in RON 3 was handpicked for this squadron when it was formed back Stateside."

"So, we're outsiders? Especially me?" Charles asked.

"For now, but that'll change. I think all anyone wants is to know they can trust you to have their backs when shit's happening." The two walked past a series of *nipa* huts. "Sisiman Cove was a small fishing community, but over the years most of the young people were lured to larger cities. Now with the war, the few remaining adults left for the hills or less inhabited islands. Probably smart for them not to be here for the Japanese invasion."

"Did they just abandon the village?"

"Not officially. An older woman hangs around, collecting a few pesos from Bulkeley for rent. The small payments give a semblance of legality to our taking over the place."

Like the *nipa* huts near Manila, the huts along the single dirt street were elevated a few feet from the ground. Under two of the huts Charles saw assorted mechanical parts. "Interesting storage technique," he joked.

"We don't store anything on the boats that isn't absolutely necessary. Everything else is here on the beach. Cooking stoves, short-distance radios, rubber mats, electric fans, and even our personal stuff."

"Why?"

"Two reasons. The first is speed. The less weight we carry, the faster the boat is. Back when the first PT boats were still being developed, Bulkeley figured out that the best asset of a small wood attack boat was its quickness. We use that fast maneuverability tactically. Quick attack, dodge return fire, and escape by outrunning anything chasing us. The lighter we are, the faster we are. If we don't use it on the mission, it stays behind."

"Some of those parts look like the same ones we had for the PBY engines," Charles pointed out.

"Our Packard engines are basically aircraft engines, modified for marine use, so that's not surprising."

"You said there's two reasons you keep the spare parts on shore?"

"If a boat goes down, we lose the boat, and maybe some men, but we don't lose spare parts if they're not on the boat. What you see here is all we have left. It's the various bits and pieces we had on the boats when Cavite went up in flames, plus a few parts we salvaged from the 33 before it burned."

"Burned?"

"PT-33 grounded on a reef south of the entrance to Manila Bay on

Christmas Eve."

"It was a tough Christmas for a lot of people."

"I suppose so. Anyway, two other boats worked all night but couldn't free 33 from the reef. Finally, they stripped everything they could and set it on fire. Our four operational boats are still running, but they can't go forever. All the engines are way past replacement hours. Lieutenant McCabe and our motor macs somehow manage to keep them running."

"Lieutenant? You have a commissioned officer for a mechanic?"

"Actually, McCabe is a civilian employee, an engineer. Officially, he's only an advisor who sends reports back to the Bureau of Ships in Washington. PT boat design is still being refined, and there's not really a good manual for maintaining them. He was told to wear a uniform to blend in with the rest of the Navy. To RON 3, he's one of our own."

"Not an outsider like me?" Charles smiled.

"He's earned the squadron's respect. During the Cavite bombing, a fire crew was killed before they could get to their truck. McCabe organized a firefighting unit and got the fire truck into action while bombs were still falling around him."

"Obviously a good man—I'll remember that. I see mats and mosquito netting in some of the huts. Does the squadron sleep here or on the boats?"

"Both," Bill answered. "I prefer sleeping in the huts when I can. The heat below deck on the boats is stifling, especially in the daytime."

"And is there a mess?"

"Each boat has its own cook. We tried to organize a single squadron mess using the sandbox in one of the huts, but that failed when smoke filled the hut. Down there, at the end of the street, do you see that large concrete building about a hundred feet long? That was the next plan for a common kitchen, but it had a terrible stench we couldn't scrub off. Turned out it used to be a goat and pig slaughterhouse. The squadron cooks finally got together and set up a communal kitchen in a tent. For now, we get two meals a day. We're well-supplied with canned salmon, but not much else. The cooks dress it up a bit, when they can. Nobody complains. We know it could be a lot worse."

They stopped in front of the largest hut, and Bill pointed to a hand lettered sign:

SISIMAN COVE YACHT CLUB

"Welcome to RON 3's headquarters," Bill opened the door, looked in, and said, "Hey. I got a new guy you need to meet." He waved Charles inside. "Doc, meet Doc." Bill laughed at his introduction. "Charles here is the new man on

34. Charles, meet RON 3's corpsman, John Xavier Balog, Pharmacist's Mate, 1st Class." After the two corpsmen shook hands Bill excused himself with an admonition to Charles, "Keep an eye out—the 34 will be back soon."

"Glad to meet you and glad to be here," Charles began. "I got here through San Diego, Mare Island, Cañacao Hospital, and Patrol Wing 10. When Japan attacked, I was independent duty with VP-102 at Olongapo. I'd met Bill Johnson back on Cavite and ran into him on PT-35 a couple of times. He got me on board RON 3, a machine gunner on PT-34 as I understand it."

Badly in need of a haircut, John Balog was of average height and weight with a round face outlined by stubble. Like the other squadron members, he'd lost his razors and toiletries and most of his uniforms in the Cavite bombing. He eyed Charles. "Bulkeley talked to me about bringing on another corpsman, but I didn't know anything about a gunner. What's that all about?"

"John, I don't want to complicate things here. It's my understanding that I'm going to PT-34 as corpsman *and* as machine gunner. I'm qualified on the Browning M2. So far as medical duties, I'll be more than happy to follow your directives. I have my medical kit and a few supplies with me. Any way you want to work this is OK. You're the boss."

Balog stared at Charles with a questioning look that changed to a smile before he answered. "Sorry, Charles, you caught me a bit off guard. No, it'll be great having two of us. But, answer something for me though—why, and how in hell, did a Navy corpsman qualify on machine guns?"

After clearing that issue, John brought Charles up to date on the health status of the squadron, including Lieutenant Kelly's finger injury. Next, they discussed how things might change with two corpsmen in MTB 3. Charles soon realized John's unimpressive appearance obscured a wonderful wit and deep intelligence.

"Right now," John explained, "I'm officially assigned to PT-41, Bulkeley's boat. You might have noticed our mascot monkey, Admiral Tojo, running around the deck?"

"Haven't see him yet."

"Anyway, I've been on patrols on other boats at one time or another. We recently stopped patrolling the bay to save our fuel and oil, but the Q-Boats still keep an eye there. RON 3's routine is a two-boat patrol, often up towards Subic and occasionally down the coast south. I obviously can't be on every boat and patrol, so each boat has someone assigned to first aid. On PT-34, it's your cook, Pappy Reynolds. Now there're two of us, I think we could probably manage alternating duty, so that either you or I are aboard one of the two boats for most patrols."

"Do you think that'll fly with Kelly and Bulkeley?"

"I can't ask Lieutenant Kelly since he's still in the hospital. I'll try to talk to Bulkeley later today. That might be interesting," John grinned, "because I got the idea Bulkeley didn't know the corpsman and the gunner were one man."

"I take it you'll always be on PT-41 when it goes out?"

"Usually. The truth is though, my boat only does an occasional patrol. In fact, someone recently called us the 'reluctant dragons.' It was in jest, but I have a feeling that moniker is going to stick," John grimaced.

"Why aren't the patrols shared equally?"

"Bulkeley's offered no explanation for holding the 41 back. Maybe he wants to keep at least one boat in top repair for a critical mission requiring a reliable boat. Nobody could accuse the lieutenant of hiding out though—he often rides with other boats. In fact, he's probably been on more patrols and missions than anyone else in the squadron. I think he's disappointed we haven't seen more action." Balog waved Charles to a table. "Bring your medical bag over here, Charles. What did you bring us?"

Charles emptied his supplies reluctantly. He had carefully assembled a cache of sulfa, quinine, Atabrine, and antiseptics to go along with morphine syrettes, tourniquets, scissors, clamps, sutures, and bandages. *I wasn't planning on sharing my trove of medical supplies. I worked damn hard to get and hang on to this stuff.*

John looked over the items. "My collection pretty much matches yours, except for your giant bottle of quinine tablets." He inspected the bottle of Atabrine. "Why don't we split the anti-malarial pills between our bags? If the Japs deep-six one of us, there'll still be half of it left."

Deep-six? I guess that's a real possibility. "Good idea."

᪣ ᪣ ᪣

Around noon, PT-35 moved from the pier to moor offshore. Within minutes, PT-34, fully refueled, returned and secured at the pier.

Charles was waiting at the dock when the 34's engines shut down. He hailed from the pier, "Ensign Chandler?"

Two ensigns appeared at the side of the cockpit. "I'm Barron Chandler," said the slightly shorter one and gestured toward the other ensign. "And this is Iliff Richardson, my executive officer. What can I do for you?"

"Sir," Charles saluted. "Pharmacist's Mate 3rd Charles Beckner. I'm here with orders to MTB 3. I understand I'll be on PT-34."

Neither Chandler nor Richardson invited him aboard. Chandler looked at Richardson, "Bulkeley said something about approving a transfer, a gunner, but all I see standing here is a damn corpsman."

"I know nothing about a corpsman either," Richardson concurred. "Orders?"

Don't panic, Charles, you can talk yourself past this. "It happened quickly. I'm qualified on the Browning M2s. The corpsman part is a bonus. Here're my orders."

While Chandler looked over the paper, Richardson looked over Charles. Richardson was a thin man with a high forehead and narrow, pointed face. He tugged at his own shirtsleeve but eyed the red cross on Charles's sleeve. "Qualified on the .50 calibers?"

"Fully, sir," Charles stood his ground. "I'm qualified on all versions of the Browning M2. I can maintain it. When it comes to it, I can fight with it."

Chandler handed back the orders. "But you are, in fact, a pharmacist's mate?" He was still confused by this combination of medic and gunner.

"You could look at it as a two-fer, sir?" Charles pleaded his case. "I've already talked with John Balog, and he's looking forward to having another corpsman in the squadron."

The two ensigns looked at each other. "Bulkeley apparently gave his OK, even if he didn't know he was a corpsman," Richardson said to Chandler, "and at the moment Lieutenant Kelly is out of the picture. We can use a qualified man for the Brownings. Clark can check him out."

Chandler thought for a moment, then waved Charles onto the boat. "Welcome to Lucky 34, Doc."

"Thank you, sir!" Charles jumped enthusiastically to PT-34's deck. "Why 'Lucky'?"

Richardson answered, "It's the three and the four. Add them together, and you get seven, a lucky number. I'll get Clark up here to run through the guns with you. After that, you need to meet our cook, Willard Reynolds. He's been our first aid on missions—I'm sure he'll be relieved to have you on board." He turned to the front cabin hatch. "Clark! Need you up here for a moment." A young man stepped up to the deck. "Jessie, meet Charles Beckner. He's a corpsman but says he's qualified on the M2s. Check him out."

"Jessie Clark. Glad to meet you." They shook hands. "Where're you from?"

"The Navy Beach Defense unit on the Rock, and originally from southern Indiana."

"Wyoming myself. So, you're new to PT boats?"

"I rode one back and forth across the North Channel, but that's it."

"Let me give you a tour then," Clark led him to the stern. "You're standing on our best weapon."

Charles looked down. He stood on nothing but the deck. "Seems you keep it pretty well hidden."

Clark pointed down. "Beneath that deck there's thirty-six hundred horsepower driving three shafts. She runs over 40 knots with full throttle and can turn on a dime. We're also a small target as naval craft go. That and speed are our best defense."

"Nimble and quick," Charles nodded.

"Offensively, we are pretty well armed. These four tubes," Clark pointed to the four steel tubes on the deck's edge, "hold Mark 8 torpedoes, each weighing 2,600 pounds, including the 466-pound warhead. Bulkeley's trying to find roll-off brackets for depth charges so we can also do sub hunting." He walked Charles to the bow of the ship, stepping past the .50 caliber turrets. "Up front here, we have our deck-mounted .30 caliber machine gun."

Clark led Charles back to the starboard turret. "The fifty calibers," he pulled the weather protection canvas from the guns. "Chandler wants me to check you out on these. Crawl in there and talk to me."

It was an open question, so after crawling into the turret, Charles began by going over the gun's specifications. "This is a Browning M2, HB—the air-cooled heavy-barrel version. Muzzle velocity is around 3,000 feet per second. On rapid fire each gun fires a dozen rounds per second, or about a hundred rounds with a four-second burst from the pair. The belts are metal links connecting regular, tracer, and/or armor piercing rounds. I've never fired a twin mount, but I see that the guns are set up with opposing left- and right-side feeds. The single trigger between the spade handles fires both guns. Do you want me to talk about maintenance and clearing jams?" He looked at Clark to see if he should go on.

"Had any training on this mount?" Clark waved to the rotating and elevating apparatus and controls in the turret.

"I've never seen this one," Charles admitted.

Pointing out various switches, levers, and pistons, Clark described the Dewandre-Elco electric/hydraulic turret mechanism. "Navy spent a lot of money on this gun mount."

This monster could take some time to master and maintain. "Looks complicated. Is it reliable?"

"Doesn't matter out here. The electrics are disconnected and the hydraulic lines drained."

Whew. That's a relief. "That's so? Why?"

"Bit of a story. The turrets and gun mounts were originally designed with plexiglass covers. In a shipyard they worked fine. On the ocean, the covers are always wet on the outside and fogged-up on the inside, so they were taken off. Without the covers, seawater corroded the electrical components. Even before, with everything working, you couldn't move the guns without the engines running to power the turret. On top of all that, the hydraulics turned and elevated the guns too slowly to track an attacking plane."

"Can you manually move it fast enough?"

"With muscle power, Doc, lots of muscle. Soon you'll look like me," Clark laughed and flexed his biceps.

The conversation continued back and forth until finally Clark said, "Short of seeing you in action with the guns, you're good to go as far as I'm concerned—I'll let Chandler and Richardson know that. Let's meet the rest of the crew."

Taking an open bunk in the forward crew compartment, Charles fell asleep that night as content as possible under the circumstances. *This is great! No more tunnels, and no more standing around waiting for the bombs to explode. No more running off like a dog with its tail between its legs. From what I see, the Japanese will find this squadron's bite is as bad as its bark.*

Realistically though, can four or five small boats make any difference in a war that, so far, we're losing? Is it possible to turn this tide and stop the Japanese?

Will I even be alive to find out?

29

Night Patrol

Sisiman Cove, Bataan Peninsula, Philippine Islands

13 January 1942

Charles still looked to his friend, Bill Johnson, for information about the people and operations of MTB 3. He found Bill in one of the *nipa* huts, bent over a metal box. "Repairing something?"

"Just preventative maintenance on a radio transmitter—don't want it to fail when we need it. I'm reseating the tubes and cleaning all the contacts. Saltwater's not my friend."

"You get any outside news on your radios? It's been nothing but rumors since Radio Manila was taken."

"Nope. Our boats can only talk between each other and with headquarters at Mariveles or the Rock. The official news we get here is what Bulkeley shares with us after his meetings with Admiral Rockwell. I do know the Japanese Navy has a complete blockade, not just Luzon, but now around the entire Philippine Islands. Nothing getting in or out."

"So, we're trapped here. What else?"

"Wake Island surrendered, and so did Hong Kong."

"Before Christmas. I knew that already."

"Did you know that over a thousand British soldiers were killed defending Hong Kong, and after they surrendered, the Japs not only took as POWs the entire garrison of seven or eight thousand soldiers, but they also imprisoned 12,000 civilians?"

"I'm waiting for the good news?"

"If there is any, no one's told me about it."

If Japan's successes weren't depressing enough, RON 3 had to deal with a deteriorating fleet. PT-41, having done fewer missions, was in reasonable shape. In contrast, the 31, 34, and 35 were held together by a host of makeshift efforts. Salvage repairs were still underway on PT-32.

Charles chatted with Velt Hunter, machinist on PT-34, while he cleaned fuel filters. Hunter's giant frame barely fit between the engines, and his hands seemed too big for working with the small mechanical parts.

"When did it happen, that sabotage of the gas barge?" Charles asked.

"We discovered it only after our engines began shutting down from clogged filters—then we found paraffin in the avgas. Boy, were we pissed when we learned that the Filipinos who sabotaged the fuel were the same ones in charge of guarding the barge. Wouldn't admit why they did it. Maybe money, but we'll probably never know."

"What happened to them?"

"I'd have shot the bastards on the spot, but Bulkeley just turned them over to the shore patrol. We cleaned the tanks and fuel lines on every boat best we could, but the engines still quit. It's frustrating because you can't predict it, and sometimes it'll happen in the middle of a mission. There we sit, bobbing helplessly in the sea for at least fifteen to twenty minutes while we clean the filters and restart the engines."

"But isn't there some other source for avgas?"

"Not that we have access to. The Army has some, but Admiral Rockwell told Bulkeley the Army insists on saving their gas for replacement fighter planes. The lieutenant then asked Rockwell exactly where the Army expected to land those planes. He was told they're supposedly going to bulldoze small airstrips from the jungle. I don't know where in hell on Bataan they expect to do that. It's all mountains."

❧ ❧ ❧

PT-41, with Bulkeley aboard, quietly departed Sisiman Cove in the pre-dawn hours on Saturday, 10 January, returning near sundown. John Balog was aboard for the mysterious outing and Charles was waiting when he came down the dock. "You were gone all day. What's up?"

"Interesting day, Charles. I'll tell you after chow. Since we went to half-rations, I try not to miss a meal."

After downing canned salmon and rice, Balog began the story, "We pulled up to the North Dock on Corregidor early this morning. Bulkeley only told us we were taking some VIPs to Mariveles. After a few minutes, a group of Army officers arrived. When the first one boarded, I recognized Douglas MacArthur himself. He stood for a moment in the early morning light, smiled, and said 'Good morning, men.' He then slid those big sunglasses onto his craggy nose."

"Just like in the pictures we've seen of him?"

"Charles, you can't imagine it. He was wearing that drooping field marshal's hat with spaghetti embroidered all over, and he waved around the longest corn-cob pipe I've ever seen. I'll be honest, I was just a little in awe at that moment."

"Did you talk to him?"

"Not personally. Six other officers all came aboard with him, every one of them in clean, new uniforms. Made ours look even more tattered. MacArthur spent the short trip to Mariveles chatting with Lieutenant Bulkeley and Ensign Cox. Their entire group was in a good mood—maybe they know something we don't. At least I hope they do."

"What'd they do on Bataan?" Charles asked.

"They piled into a sedan and a couple of jeeps that were waiting at the Mariveles dock and were gone all day. I got the idea that MacArthur was touring his lines. When they got back with less than an hour of daylight left, they were quieter. Later we heard they were caught in an artillery barrage during the day. One of MacArthur's aides told Cox that during the barrage the general wouldn't take cover, yelling, "There is no Jap shell with MacArthur's name on it!"

"Sounds like he deserves his reputation."

"When we tied up at the North Dock, MacArthur asked our crew to assemble on deck, and he addressed us from the dock. 'Men, the situation on Bataan is shaping up nicely. Japanese forces are attacking the front lines, but we're driving them back. We have ample supplies and can hold out for many months until relief arrives from the United States. Airstrips are currently being constructed on Mindanao, which we expect to be used by aircraft flying up from Australia. Soon we will control the skies and force the Japanese into the sea.' And the whole time he pointed at us individually with that corn-cob pipe."

Charles was skeptical. *At least some of that's not true. Everyone knows our troops are retreating south.* Frowning, he asked, "Did you believe any of that? And another thing—we all know the general's own troops on Bataan derisively call him 'Dugout Doug,' claiming he's hiding out in his headquarters in the Malinta Tunnel. They even have a sarcastic song about it. A lot of men think his headquarters should be closer to the battle lines on Bataan. How does that reputation square with your story about his defying artillery fire?"

"Hard to figure, Charles. He was inspiring today. I want, I *need* to believe reinforcements and supplies are on the way."

"Might be, but not if our battleships are sitting on the mud at Pearl."

On 13 January, Bulkeley acquired another vessel for his squadron. In a mysterious transfer the tugboat *Trabajador* was attached to RON 3. It wasn't equipped as a PT boat tender, and some of the squadron believed that Bulkeley assimilated the *Trabajador* as a "safe harbor" where he could assign men in Squadron 3 without appearing to be overmanned if they lost more PT boats. At first only Radiomen Goodman from PT-34 and Langer from PT-33 were transferred to the *Trabajador,* but others followed later.

Most mornings, Lieutenant Bulkeley took one of the PT boats to the South Dock, walked into the Navy Tunnel, and received verbal orders for the next twenty-four hours, most often instructions for courier or water taxi missions. On the morning of 18 January though, Bulkeley was handed written orders, signed by Admiral Rockwell's chief of staff, Captain Herbert J. Ray:

ARMY REPORTS FOUR ENEMY SHIPS IN OR LYING OFF BINANGA BAY. FORCE MAY INCLUDE ONE DESTROYER, ONE LARGE TRANSPORT. SEND TWO BOATS ATTACK BETWEEN DUSK AND DAWN.

Bulkeley chose PT-31, commanded by Lieutenant Edward DeLong, and PT-34, still commanded by Chandler, for the mission. The boat commanders on receiving their orders were elated to finally strike at the Japanese Navy.

That evening before leaving the dock Chandler briefed his crew, now including Charles. "This is no suicide mission, but it's a risky one. We're going into Binanga Bay, inside Subic Bay, all controlled by the enemy. Japanese ships steam in and out of Subic at will, and their troops infest the surrounding hills and jungles. They've positioned shore guns to protect it all. Intel says there're four Japanese warships anchored there. They are our targets tonight. We're one day past the new moon, so that helps us. Bulkeley's riding in our boat tonight." He looked at Richardson. "Does anyone have questions?"

No one spoke up. Charles had questions but remained silent. *This is my first mission, and it's no patrol or messenger run. We're going in there to attack and sink a warship. They will surely fight back and try to sink us. Am I ready? If I let the boat down tonight, I'll be a long time regaining my crewmates' trust and respect.*

A few minutes later, Lieutenant Bulkeley came on board, carrying an aluminum chair, positioning it just behind the topside command station, beneath the two .50 caliber machine gun turrets.

"Jessie," Charles whispered to Clark before crawling into his turret, "what the hell's Bulkeley doing with that chair?"

"He does this sometimes—rides along on a patrol. Richardson told me Bulkeley's not along just to observe tonight. He's on board as the mission commander."

"Why that chair?"

"It's Bulkeley's usual perch when he rides on patrol with any boat other than his. He calls it his 'conning chair.' From that seat he has an unobstructed view of the boat and the surrounding sea."

"Yes, but isn't he exposed if there's a firefight?"

"Maybe so, but he's probably as safe there as anywhere else. If you haven't noticed, these boats have no armor plating, and the chart house and bridge are made of plywood. Even your machine gun turret is thin sheet metal. The safest place might be below deck, behind the hull's double diagonal Philippine mahogany planking, but Bulkeley would never go below during action."

"I'm sure he wouldn't." *I guess a person could hunker down in the engine room between those big Packards. Makes no difference, though. I don't think anyone in this crew will hide from a fight.*

At 1930, an hour after sunset, the two boats slipped their moorings. They motored out of Sisiman Cove, maneuvered through the minefields, and headed north along the western coastline of the Bataan Peninsula.

Well off the Bataan coast, Clark asked, "Permission to clear guns?"

"Clear guns," Chandler replied.

Clark and Charles each fired a short burst into the empty ocean, confirming the guns were ready for action. "Time to go hunting," a voice announced from the darkness.

Subic Bay extends from the South China Sea northward like an inverted boot. After entering Subic Bay, Binanga Bay would be the first harbor on the east side. At 2330 hours PT-31, with its black kitten mascot pacing the bow, separated from PT-34. The plan was for the two boats to attack from different directions.

All hands stood at battle stations. Charles tried to define the horizon, but found it difficult to separate stars in the dark sky from reflections in the equally dark water. Because engine noise travels far over water on a quiet night, they ran at only eighteen knots. Even so, a mile before reaching the bay, a shore signal light flashed out a challenge.

From the cockpit, just ahead and below his gun turret, Charles heard Chandler ask Bulkeley, "Do we have the codes to respond?"

"No," Bulkeley replied curtly.

Chandler cut speed to ten knots to even further reduce engine noise and turned northwest, away from the Japanese observation post. Bulkeley, Chandler, and Richardson checked their maps against indistinct landmarks along the shore. Belatedly realizing they'd passed Binanga Bay, they circled PT-34 back south, then turned east toward their destination. A field piece began firing from the far shore.

As they approached Binanga Bay, another flashing light challenged them. When they closed on the source, it proved to be a small patrol boat that quickly scooted away. They slowed further to eight knots and continued deeper into the bay. Bulkeley, thinking out loud, said, "Pretty soon someone's going to blow the whistle on us."

He was right. More blinking lights challenged them. Finally, searchlights began probing the bay. Sporadic machine gun and cannon fire came from across the bay.

From his elevated position, Charles watched tracer rounds from shore guns arcing into the water on the opposite side of the bay. *They're certainly not targeting us—are they firing on the 31?*

"Damn nice of them," Chandler commented sarcastically. "It's a helluva lot easier to see where we're going with all this light. Let's hope they keep looking and shooting on that side of the bay."

At 0100 hours they arrived at the rendezvous point. They sat on the water, alone.

"Where's 31?" Richardson voiced the obvious question. An agonizing fifteen minutes passed, with no sight or sound of the boat.

Chandler voiced it: "Something's happened to them."

Bulkeley agreed. "We can't wait any longer. Let's go see what's waiting for us."

Bulkeley manned the torpedo director, Chandler stood ready at the torpedo firing station, and Richardson took the wheel. Five hundred yards into the bay, a two-mast freighter was dimly visible straight ahead. There might be a more valuable target farther in, but this freighter was purposefully anchored to block passage. With a nod from Chandler, the torpedomen immediately readied the forward two "fish" for launching.

Bulkeley spoke orders quietly. "Right a bit. Steady. Steady—" Richardson repeated each of Bulkeley's orders as he followed each command. Bulkeley glanced at the other two officers to reassure himself they were ready. He took one more sighting, then calmly said, "Fire Two." Chandler repeated the order, "Firing two," and hit the firing key. With a *bang-swish-plunk*, the torpedo ejected from the tube, powering into the water with its prop furiously spinning.

Bulkeley continued the attack. "Right a touch. Steady. Steady. Fire One."

The same moment that Chandler sent Torpedo One from its launching tube, the 34 was bathed by an intense white light. The freighter's searchlight had them dead on. Machine gun fire erupted from the freighter.

"Shit! I can't see!" Charles had been staring at the ship's superstructure when its million-candlepower light blazed on, unfortunately pointing directly at Charles in PT-34. He blindly fired a short burst towards the searchlight and stopped shooting. "Goddamn it! I can't see anything!" He pulled off his glasses, looked away, and shielded his eyes, but it was too late.

All hell broke loose as enemy guns unleashed fire at PT-34 from both ship and shore positions. Bullets from the Japanese ship splashed in the water around them. Richardson rammed the throttles full on and turned the boat hard to port, escaping the searchlight beam. The Japanese knew they were under attack, but in the confusion had not imagined it was by only one tiny American boat.

Chandler tracked the run of one torpedo. It ran straight and hit the freighter at the waterline, exploding in a fireball. "The first one hit square," he yelled. "Where's the other one?" For the moment, no one could answer that question.

Charles's vision finally returned. He looked for a target, but Clark had already stopped firing. "Hold it, Charles!" Clark yelled. "They've lost us for now, and your muzzle flashes will only give the shore guns a target."

Running at high speed, PT-34 was out of Binanga Bay before the Japanese realized their attackers were gone. A crewman stumbled onto the open bridge, soaked with seawater and out of breath. "Sir, I know where the second torpedo went —nowhere." Breathlessly he continued, "Port torpedo didn't eject, sir. She's making a hot run in the tube."

Chandler and Bulkeley swung out of the cockpit to have a look. The second torpedo had ejected only two-thirds from its tube and was indeed running hot, howling like a banshee. Smoke and air spewed from the front of the tube. Without surrounding seawater for cooling, the engine casing was glowing hot.

Chandler called to Richardson, "Back off the throttle."

Bulkeley verbalized what everyone knew. "If that torpedo engine explodes, the shrapnel will save the Japs the trouble of killing us."

The crew stood momentarily frozen by the shrieking beast. Torpedoman First Class John Martino considered every torpedo his responsibility and reacted without hesitation. Crouching to avoid the plume of steam and, with the calmness and deliberation of a surgeon entering someone's belly, he opened an access hatch on the torpedo's side. He reached in and carefully closed a valve on the air line to the combustion pot. The racing engine came to an instant halt.

Charles couldn't see what was happening from his starboard position, but in the silence, he gave a long sigh of relief. Jessie Clark, who was watching events from his port-side turret, and thus closest to the danger, leaned back in relief, "Martino! You're a good man. Thanks for saving my ass!"

"Haven't saved anyone's ass yet—prop's active." Martino yelled back, knowing he'd completed only the first half on the job.

"Prop's active." Charles repeated Martino's pronouncement. *I remember Martino describing how his torpedoes work. He's talking about that small induction propeller at the nose of the torpedo. As it runs towards the target, seawater rotates the blades until, after a certain number of rotations, the explosive charge is armed.* Charles stood on the edge of his turret so he could see the torpedo better. *The nose is splashing in and out of the waves, and the prop turns a little each time. Once it's armed, the damn thing will explode at the next wave hitting with enough force. There'll be nothing left of us but splinters and an oil slick.*

Martino ran between Jessie and Charles to the forward head and returned with a roll of toilet paper. Straddling the rocking torpedo like a bucking bull rider, he scooted down to its tip and stuffed toilet paper into the small blades, jamming any further rotation. The arming sequence was blocked for the time being, giving the crew time to work the torpedo from the tube. Soaked in seawater, Martino calmly slid backwards off the torpedo as if his heroic actions had been a routine part of any torpedoman's job.

The crew tried unsuccessfully for a half hour to remove the torpedo from the tube. Knowing that if they delayed any longer, the Japanese were bound to find them, Bulkeley ordered, "Let it ride," and Richardson smashed the throttles forward.

At around 0600 hours, PT-34 crossed a large wave, jolting the boat. The dangling torpedo jarred loose from the tube and fell harmlessly into the sea.

At 0645 they arrived outside the minefields at the north entrance to Manila Bay. Still, no PT-31. While they waited, looking northward for the missing boat, PT-41 appeared from the south. While the other two boats were at Binanga Bay, the 41 was reconnoitering the south shore of Manila Bay, near Ternate where heavy Japanese gun emplacements were reported as being installed. They found no heavy guns but did strafe a unit of Japanese shore troops with machine gun fire. Both boats waited another half hour. PT-31 did not show up, and at 0715 they crossed through the minefields back to Sisiman Cove.

John Balog met Charles at the dock. "Don't tell me we lost the 31 boat?"

Charles's face clouded over, "Don't know what happened to it. The mission was to attack in Binanga Bay, and we did sink a ship there. We separated from the 31 before entering the bay. We never saw or heard from them again. There was shore fire across the bay from us that might have been directed at the 31, but no one knows."

"At least for the 34 it sounds like a successful mission?"

"For myself, John, not really." Charles went on to describe their attack and escape, including the close call with the torpedo. He then leaned back and closed his eyes. "I was nervous from the start. Once the searchlight blinded me, I was plain scared. No other way to say it."

"Charles," Balog spoke quietly and directly at his friend, "And how does that make you different than me or anyone else?"

"This was my first action. Oh, I was bombed at Cavite and watched the attack on our PBY base at Olongapo, but those were different. I was supposed to be the one shooting them this time, and after that first short burst, I didn't fire another single round. I should've known better than to be staring at the superstructure of that ship, right where a spotlight would be. It blinded me, and by the time I recovered vision, we were running for the open sea."

"That was just bad luck, Charles."

"That may be so, but I feel like I was nothing but a passenger the entire night. And as bad as I feel about myself, the 31 didn't come back."

"We all get depressed—"

"John," Charles interrupted. "I'm not depressed—I'm pissed off and angry! I'm angry at myself as much as the Japs that were shooting at us. I'm also angry about the 31 boat. You've known those guys longer than I have, and whatever I feel, I know you feel it worse."

Balog squinted at the morning sun, "Most of us feel exactly like you, Charles. But just like us, you'll keep doing what you can, when you can, until there is no RON 3 left."

30

Barge One

Sisiman Cove, Bataan Peninsula, Philippine Islands

19 January 1942

The three-inch healing incision in Lieutenant Robert Kelly's finger still required daily dressing changes, but he was otherwise out of danger. He was champing hard at the bit to be released from the hospital and reclaim command of PT-34 and his status as Bulkeley's XO. Under pressure from Bulkeley pointing out his loss of another boat and two good officers, the doctors finally agreed someone else could make better use of Kelly's bed.

Before leaving the hospital, Bulkeley mentioned to Kelly, "I'm sure 34 will be in top shape with you back at the helm." Kelly must have interpreted this statement as, "PT-34 has languished and declined in your absence. I need you to get the crew back in shape." While the squadron generally celebrated Kelly's return, the good mood of the PT-34 crew soon soured.

"Congratulations on your successful mission," Kelly said, before dismantling that compliment. "It was a good thing Bulkeley was along with you. Chandler, I know you and Richardson are well-qualified, but you both need more experience."

"Sir," Chandler protested, "I've been with RON 3 since it was formed."

"Yes. But it's a matter of training, isn't it?" Kelly said. "I'm sorry I was out so long, but we'll get things back into shape soon. I want to see 34, and each of you, ready for a formal inspection in twenty-four hours."

Kelly paused and frowned at Charles. "Who are you?"

"Pharmacist's Mate Charles Beckner, sir." Charles stood eye to eye with Kelly. The men were equally tall, lean, and stood straight with self-confidence. "I'm your gunner, on the starboard 50s. I also assist John Balog."

Kelly looked at Richardson and Chandler who both nodded affirmations. Chandler deflected further interrogation of the new man, saying, "He's fully qualified—I'll fill you in later."

Charles was unhappy with his introduction to the returning PT-34 skipper. *Kelly views me as the ultimate outsider. He doesn't know me and therefore doesn't trust me. If I make a mistake, he'll kick me straight back to the Rock. I'll have to make sure he doesn't get that chance.*

The crew knew Kelly was serious about the inspection. They scrubbed every surface and touched up paint where needed. Someone even flushed and scrubbed the bilges. Using a shared pair of scissors, they trimmed hair and beards. They washed uniforms, stitched loose seams, and shined shoes. All this activity pleased Kelly, since he was convinced that in trying times the Navy tradition of keeping things shipshape and standing for inspection would give the men comfort. Maybe it did.

That evening Balog teased Charles, "You did hear what I said about Kelly and the Annapolis traditions, didn't you?"

"I heard you, but I thought you were talking about his relationships with other officers. Even so, I actually don't mind spit-polishing the boat and myself. In fact, I think it's generally a good thing to take pride in yourself and your equipment. But it doesn't sit well with me if it's only to feed someone's ego. Use plain language next time, John."

꙳ ꙳ ꙳

On 20 January, two hours after Kelly's inspection of PT-34 and two days after the Binanga Bay mission, nine PT-31 crewmen, led by Lieutenant Edward DeLong, walked into the Sisiman Cove base, unannounced.

"Thank God! Where the hell you guys been?" A chorus of questions came from the RON 3 men.

"That damn sabotaged gas finally cost us the boat."

No one was surprised at that. "We all knew it would sooner or later—what happened?"

"Bad luck at the wrong time," DeLong began. "After separating from the 34, just as we were entering Subic Bay, the filters clogged and shut down both wing engines. While we were cleaning the strainer and carburetor jets, the center engine sprang a coolant leak, and we had to shut it down as well. It was bad luck on top of bad luck." DeLong shook his head in disgust.

The engine problems needed no further explanation. Clogging of the filters happened regularly and unpredictably, and they all understood that running the center engine without coolant would have instantly overheated the engine and turned it into a thousand-pound lump of scrap metal.

"We drifted for about five minutes, working to clean the filters. Before we could restart, a big swell lifted the boat and gently set us down on a reef. By the time we had the engines running again, it was too late," DeLong shook his head again. "We worked in and out of the water for three hours trying to power off the reef. Finally, we burned out reverse gear."

"So, you were stranded. And in Jap territory."

"We were screwed. The Japanese heard our engines and knew we were out there. They were shooting towards the noise, but without seeing us it would have taken a lot of luck to hit our boat. On the other hand, I knew that if they decided to put up illumination flares, we'd be fish in a barrel. I ordered all twelve men into a raft we made using the engine room canopy. Someone brought our black kitten on the raft as well. I stayed behind, blew holes in the hull with hand grenades, and set her on fire. I didn't want the Japs to get so much as a goddamn splinter from her." The tremble in DeLong's voice betrayed his emotion.

"My plan was to swim to the raft, but I couldn't find it in the dark. I swam to shore and hid out the rest of the night. After dawn I followed tracks in the sand and found these men hiding in the trees along the beach. We knew we were behind enemy lines and would have to make our way south to find friendly forces. We ended up stealing two *bancas*, those double-outrigger canoes. It was windy, and the seas were running high. It wasn't long before both boats capsized and sent our gear to the bottom. We righted the boats and used makeshift paddles for several more hours. Eventually we were just too exhausted to keep going, so we beached. I was leading our group through the jungle, when I suddenly came face to face with a soldier pointing a bayonetted rifle at me. I was too surprised to move or say anything. Then he said 'Hello, Joe,' the sweetest words I ever heard. He was with a unit of Filipino Scouts, and they passed us on to the US Army."

While DeLong told the story, one of the sailors did a mental roll call of PT-31's crew. "You're missing three."

They all waited silently. DeLong paused to clear his throat. "I don't have any information on Plant, Ballough, and Dean. When the raft with these guys drifted close to shore, Ensign Plant told everyone to swim to shore before the raft drifted back out to sea. Ballough and Dean said they couldn't swim. Plant ordered the rest to head for the beach, and he stayed with the two non-swimmers. None of us saw them again, and there's been no word that they've been found or made it to our lines."

DeLong stopped speaking. The men were silent.

Charles looked around. *We're down three good men, and now we only have three serviceable boats, 34, 35, and 41. I'm sure the mechanics and carpenters at Mariveles are doing their best to rebuild 32, but from what I saw, there's no way they can make her like new. We're shrinking by attrition. At this rate I'll soon be without a squadron. Again.*

The Japanese had already failed once in their attempts to land troops behind the U.S. lines on Bataan. Other landings were expected, most likely somewhere along the southwestern coast of the peninsula. With no aircraft to search, offshore patrolling with Squadron 3's PT boats had the best chance of detecting an incursion before the Japanese could set foot on the beach.

On Friday night, 22/23 January, PT-34 with Kelly now back in command cruised north along the western coast of Bataan. Bulkeley was along, sitting in his aluminum chair. "Just for the hell of it," was his explanation for joining this time, but everyone knew that Bulkeley wanted to be in the thick of the action, if and when it happened.

PT boats had until now patrolled in pairs. Bulkeley convinced Admiral Rockwell that could not continue. They were rationing avgas, and RON 3 was reduced to only three seaworthy boats, each needing time between missions for maintenance and repair. Tonight PT-34 departed for patrol in the company of USS *Fisheries II*, a District Patrol Vessel. *Fisheries II* provided moral support, but little in the way of firepower.

PT-34 and *Fisheries II* motored slowly north in the South China Sea under a first-quarter moon. Even though they were well off the coast of Bataan, friendly forces on the Bataan shoreline heard them and nervously fired towards the engine noise. Moving a little farther off the coast, the two boats continued patrolling.

Reaching Morang, just south of Subic Bay, around 0200, Bulkeley declared, "Nothing out here tonight. Let's turn around and go home."

Bulkeley and Kelly took the watch, sending Chandler and Richardson below to rest. Charles relaxed at his station in the turret. *The gentle rocking of the boat tonight is soothing. It's tranquil. Can't let myself go to sleep—I've got the starboard watch. Damn, I have to clean the salt spray from my glasses again. I can get away without glasses in daylight, but not so well at night.*

Around 0215, Clark brought Bulkeley's and Kelly's attention to a dim light close to the water. *Fisheries II* was signaled to hold her position while the 34 cautiously moved forward to investigate. All sense of tranquility vanished.

Charles tensed at his guns and his pulse quickened. *Friend or foe, I need to know.* He pointed his guns at the light, but otherwise kept his eyes focused below the waterline. *Not going to be blinded by a searchlight again.* He felt along both guns to check the belts of armor-piercing .50 caliber rounds. *I'm ready.*

Bulkeley had to be cautious. The light could be one of the small American or Filipino supply ships from Cebu that occasionally penetrated the Japanese blockade. Slowly, the partial moon revealed a dark shape moving slowly, about five or six knots.

As the 34 closed on the vessel, a light began to blink on and off. It looked like the dots and dashes of Morse code, but otherwise made no sense. Bulkeley whispered to Kelly and Chandler, "Recognize any of that?" Both shook their heads.

Charles felt rising adrenaline pulsing in his chest. His hold on the gun grips tightened. The light stopped blinking and went out.

Bulkeley stepped around the wheelhouse to the foredeck, straining to identify the vessel, but still could make out no identifying markings. It was time to find out. He hailed the other craft, "Boat ahoy!"

The answer came suddenly. *Burrrrrrp*—a burst of machine gun fire pelleted Charles's side of PT-34.

Oh shit! Simultaneously hearing the shots and feeling the rounds hitting their boat, Charles instinctively swung his guns a few degrees to target the flashes from the other boat. He released a three-second rapid-fire burst, sixty or seventy rounds, at the incoming fire. Return rounds again thumped through the wood of the PT boat. Anger and adrenaline surged. *Those bastards are trying to kill me!*

Chandler and Richardson, startled awake by the firing, ran up to the cockpit. Machine guns, rifles, and even handguns exchanged close-quarter fire in a wild and frenzied shoot-out from both sides. The enemy boat proved to be a barge packed with Japanese troops. The Japanese soldiers lifted rifles over the side rail and joined their machine gunner in firing at PT-34. The barge pilot maneuvered his clumsy craft to keep either his stern or bow, the heavily armored sections, pointed at the Americans.

It was a hopeless effort against the nimble PT boat.

Chandler opened the throttles and took PT-34 roaring back and forth along the barge, alternating the field of fire into the barge for his .50 caliber guns. Each time the barge was starboard of the PT boat, Charles fired repeated short bursts, the yellow-purple muzzle flash from his own barrels briefly hindering his vision.

Someone started firing from the .30 caliber gun on the foredeck. Even Bulkeley was firing at the barge with his pistols.

Charles finished loading a new belt of ammunition just as a round in one of Clark' guns jammed. Chandler reversed his circle to clockwise, giving Charles, on the starboard turret, an open view of the enemy. *I have a perfect field of fire. I'm also square in the line of Japanese return fire.* Muzzles flashed from the entire length of the Japanese landing craft. In the midst of flying bullets, Charles lost any sensation of fear or anger. In the back of his brain he recalled something Richardson had told him only days earlier, "In a close-quarters fight, as long as you're firing, the enemy won't fire. It's difficult for any gunner to stay at his post when he's staring at a stream of incoming tracers and hearing the impact of hits all around him. Even when he does fire, he's usually anxious and without much aim. In short, your best defense is offense."

Charles continued pouring bursts of rapid fire up and down the length of the landing craft, each short burst slamming fifty to sixty rounds through the sides of the Japanese boat. It took all his willpower to not fire continuously. *I hope I'm letting the barrels cool enough. I can push it as long as I don't melt them completely. We can replace the barrels later.*

Return fire from the barge slowed, but Charles could still hear the *thump* of bullets hitting his boat. Then he heard someone in the cockpit, it sounded like Chandler, say, "Boy, that was close," followed by the same voice, "Ahhhh! Damn! I'm hit." Charles turned in time to see Chandler collapse on the deck. He yelled, "Reynolds! Wounded up here!"

Reynolds came to the cockpit and examined their skipper. "Chandler's been shot in the foot, Doc. Keep shooting—I'll take care of him."

The barge increased speed to about ten knots and headed for Bagac Bay on the Bataan coast. Bulkeley was furious, "Shall we ram the little bastard, Kelly?"

Kelly didn't respond to Bulkeley, assuming the comment was neither a serious question nor an order. He continued giving orders to Richardson, who had assumed the wheel when Chandler was hit. "Come hard left—right—steady."

Richardson repeated each command as he followed Kelly's orders. The topside crew could still see flashes coming at them from the barge with an occasional thump of a bullet impacting the PT boat, with a few ricochets whining away.

Return fire from the barge slowed, and Richardson circled closer. Between bursts, Charles could see their enemy was a fourteen-meter motorized barge packed with Japanese troops, but only a few of them were still firing over the armored sides.

His guns cleared, Clark resumed firing. The four .50 calibers poured streams of armor-piercing rounds into the barge, literally chopping it to bits. The barge sank lower and lower into the water until finally, weighed down by its armor plating, it gave one last gurgle and vanished under the surface. Kelly switched on their small searchlight. No survivors or casualties floated with the debris on the water. Every Japanese soldier had sunk under the weight of their weapons and packs.

Bulkeley said, "Send a radio message to HQ that we just sank a fourteen-meter Japanese barge with estimated one-hundred equipped infantry aboard. No survivors. Give the location." Richardson passed the order down and the message was sent.

Charles checked the time. *What? Only 0230. That firefight lasted less than fifteen minutes, but it seemed like an eternity!* He suddenly remembered. *Chandler!* He crawled out of his turret to inspect Chandler's wounds. The .27 caliber Japanese bullet had penetrated the wood cockpit wall and passed through the skipper's right foot at the ankle before lodging in the instep of his left foot. Chandler moaned in pain.

Reynolds pressed bandages on the wounds. "I poured iodine on the bullet holes and put tourniquets on both legs. It looks like I stopped the bleeding, Doc."

"You sure did—good job." Charles knelt down, pulled a syrette of morphine from his belt kit and injected it into Chandler's thigh. "You stopped it before he lost a dangerous amount of blood. If we wrap pressure bandages on his feet tight enough to stop the bleeding, we can release your tourniquets and let some circulation return. They'll fix him up like new back at Corregidor." He said the last sentence loudly, for Chandler's benefit.

Charles stood up to speak quietly to Kelly and then Bulkeley. "Both his feet are damaged pretty badly. We need to get him to Corregidor as soon as possible."

A look passed between Kelly and Bulkeley. Kelly spoke, "It's going to be a few hours, Doc. They don't expect us to negotiate the minefields before 0700 hours. If we try any earlier, the gunners on Corregidor will shoot first and ask questions later."

Bulkeley added, "Doc, we'll get him there as soon as we can. You and Reynolds get him below and make him comfortable. Then we finish the patrol."

Charles gave Chandler another syrette of morphine and, with help from both Reynolds and Richardson, carried him below deck. Chandler stirred from his morphine haze and asked quietly, "Can I have a smoke?"

"I'll check with the commander." Richardson squeezed Chandler's hand. Smoking was possible above deck but strictly forbidden below because of the gasoline hazard. Richardson returned moments later and handed Chandler a glowing cigarette. "Here you go. It's your brand—Bulkeley lit it for you himself."

Reynolds stayed with Chandler. Charles and Richardson returned to their stations. Kelly turned around to face Charles in the starboard turret and glared. "Beckner, you and I are having a little talk back in Sisiman."

What's that all about? I put more rounds into that barge than anyone, but he's angry with me? What's with him?

Bulkeley radioed a brief report of the action to Navy command. For another half hour PT-34 and *Fisheries II* searched the darkness for more Japanese landing craft. Satisfied no more enemy vessels were in the area, they turned south for home. Those close by heard Bulkeley say, "I now understand why soldiers in the Great War prayed for dawn to come."

31

Barge Two

Off Bataan Peninsula, Philippine Islands

Pre-dawn, 23 January 1942

Charles checked once more on Chandler. He was comfortable enough, needing no additional morphine. Charles crawled back in the starboard turret, keeping watch on the dark ocean. *I still can't figure out what I did to upset Lieutenant Kelly.* Those ruminations were kicked back into the sea when tracer bullets appeared about a mile away.

"Go!" Bulkeley called out, and Richardson gave full throttle to the three Packard engines. PT-34 leapt across the waves trailing a giant rooster tail in her wake.

Closing on the action, Bulkeley identified a converted American pleasure cruiser, *The Mary Anne,* firing from a distance at another Japanese landing barge. The barge pilot, making about ten knots, turned in a futile attempt to escape the oncoming PT boat. Unlike the previous barge, only sporadic return fire came from the barge.

PT-34 closed on the landing craft and began firing at 400 yards out. Richardson passed starboard of the barge, allowing Clark to rake the length of the Japanese craft. Richardson reversed his circle to bring the starboard guns to bear, this time at lower throttle, since return fire from the barge had almost stopped.

Charles watched the barge come into his field of fire. *This one's riding much higher in the water. It must have already unloaded its men or equipment.*

Clark put hundreds of rounds into it, but it's still going. Same configuration as the other one with the engine at the stern. The fuel tank is probably back there somewhere—yes!

Every fifth bullet in the .50 caliber ammunition belt was a tracer round, a bullet with a small incendiary charge attached to the base. When fired, the glowing bullet could be followed with the naked eye, allowing gunners to adjust their aim. Sometimes, tracer rounds started a fire in the target.

Charles ignored the occasional muzzle flash from the barge and instead concentrated his fire on the barge's stern, releasing repeated bursts until one of the tracer rounds did its damage. A dramatic flash of orange and red fire enveloped the entire stern of the landing craft. Billowing black smoke poured from burning fuel draining from the barge's tank. Return fire from the barge ceased.

Though his boat was mortally damaged, the Japanese pilot used his final momentum in a futile attempt to ram the PT boat. With twenty feet still separating the boats, Bulkeley pitched two fragmentation grenades into the hold of the landing craft. It finally drifted to a complete stop, burning quietly in the water.

From his elevated position in the turret, Charles could see the barge was in fact nearly empty. A lone Japanese soldier stood in the boat with his arms upraised. Two more soldiers, one obviously dead, lay in the mixture of diesel fuel, water, and blood sloshing in the bottom of the barge.

Bulkeley crawled aboard the rapidly sinking barge with his .45 pistol in hand. The soldier standing in surrender, a captain, dropped to his knees. "Me surrender! Me surrender!" *So much for the noble Japanese soldier, choosing death before surrender. At least some of them are just like us. They want to live.*

Bulkeley looped ropes around the officer and the injured soldier so they could be pulled to the deck of the PT boat. He commenced pitching guns, equipment, and document cases onto the deck of the 34 until the barge literally sank underneath him. He grabbed Kelly's outstretched hand and was pulled aboard the PT boat as the second barge disappeared into the sea.

Charles examined both Japanese soldiers. "The captain here has three wounds, but I think he'll survive. This second soldier has at least seven wounds—not sure he's going to make it."

None of them had seen a Japanese soldier this close. Curious, the crew took turns to come look at them. Charles had his own thoughts. *Ten minutes ago I was trying my best to kill these guys, hating every Japanese in the world. Now, like everyone, I'm feeling sorry for these two abject little men. Our smallest crewman towers over them. Kelly even gave the captain a cigarette—to the officer's complete surprise. He must've expected us to interrogate him and then shoot him before rolling his body over the side.*

"These are awful wounds, not simple bullet or shrapnel holes," Reynolds observed as they tended to the more severely injured soldier.

"Back at Cañacao I heard about what these guns can do. A .50 caliber bullet has tremendous muzzle velocity, and the rifled barrel gives it a high rate of spin for stability and accuracy. When it penetrates armor plate, it comes out on the other side deformed, like a corkscrew. It's slowed down by that time, but when it hits a body—" He didn't need to say more.

Reynolds turned away. "That's more than enough information, Doc. I'll go below and check on Chandler."

Charles looked down at the two injured Japanese soldiers. *I probably did this to them, and I probably killed more than my share of the soldiers on that first barge. But how strange—I don't feel sorry about that. After all, they were sure trying to kill me. Back then I was raging with anger and hate, but at this moment I don't feel much of anything. I actually hope these two fellows survive. Should I hate their emperor and his generals? Should I hate the Japanese race? Is there even a right answer?*

I do know there's a pragmatic answer for every soldier and sailor thrust into battle: there is a time to kill, and for me, tonight was that time. Even so, I'm a corpsman, and I think it's now my time.

ॐ ॐ ॐ

The welcome red light of dawn outlined a familiar horizon at 0700. Under radio and visual contact from the shore, PT-34 and *Fisheries II* passed through the minefields. Richardson steered PT-34 to the Corregidor dock. In addition to an ambulance and surgeon for Chandler, several Army Intelligence officers waited. They took possession of the Japanese document cases and debriefed Bulkeley and Kelly on the night's action.

Before leaving Corregidor, the 34 crew fastened a bayonet and silver helmet taken from the second Japanese landing craft onto their mast to signify victory. They then docked at Mariveles for the wounded Japanese soldiers to be moved to an ambulance and taken to Army Hospital No. 2.

After returning to Sisiman Cove, the 34 crew assessed damage to their boat. More than a dozen bullet holes pierced the chart house and cockpit. It seemed miraculous that Chandler was the crew's only casualty. Charles found two marks on his turret where rounds had deflected from the curved surface. *If one of those had been a few inches higher . . .*

Two men cleaned the mixture of blood and seawater from the cockpit deck, the motor macs serviced their engines, and Charles and Jessie retrieved more ammunition. After a trip to the fuel barge around noon, PT-34 was ready for her next mission.

Bulkeley made his morning trip to Admiral Rockwell's headquarters. On returning he went straight to PT-34. "Kelly," he yelled. "I'm coming aboard."

"Yes, sir." Kelly popped out of the chart house.

"I received a follow-up to last night from the Army. Those Japanese barges we sank were part of a larger landing. They did manage to deliver several hundred troops to shore, but our early message to headquarters gave the men on Bataan time to organize resistance. It was actually a Navy unit, commanded by someone named Bridget, who ultimately repelled the Japanese landing."

Charles overheard Bulkeley's report. *Bridget? He must be talking about Frank Bridget, PBY pilot and commander of the Bataan PatWing 10 men. I knew he was a good man!*

Later, Charles was in the charthouse sorting and restocking his medical pack when Kelly came down the steps and stopped in front of him. Charles jumped up, "Sir?"

"Doc, got something to put on this?" Kelly raised his sleeve to reveal a superficial burn about four inches long on his upper arm.

"Sure, sir. Let me get some ointment and a bandage."

Kelly pulled his shirt sleeve back down and fingered a burn hole in the fabric over his injury. "It actually doesn't need bandaging, Doc, but I'd told you during the night that we'd be having a talk when we got back here."

Uh-oh. "Yes, sir. How can I help you?"

"After we sank that first barge, I left the bridge. When I passed your turret, your guns were not stored."

Then it dawned on Charles. After the shooting, he had jumped down to take care of Chandler and hadn't locked his guns in the normal storage position with the barrels pointed upward. Kelly must have burned his arm when he passed by the red-hot gun barrels. Not only that, if a round left in the chamber "cooked off," fired spontaneously from barrel heat, it would not have done so with the gun pointing harmlessly straight up. *I'm mortified—no wonder he was upset with me!*

"Sir, I'm sorry, sir. My mind was on Ensign Chandler. It won't happen again."

Kelly looked at Charles for a moment. "I'm sure it won't. Now, can you change the dressing on my finger?"

"Yes, sir."

As he removed the old dressing and cleaned the wound, Charles commented, "I thought Balog was changing these dressings between your hospital checkups?"

"You're on my boat, Doc. You'll take care of me. And, one more thing—I don't think I said it earlier, but welcome aboard Lucky 34."

It had been a long night and morning. After noon, Charles found an empty bunk in one of the *nipa* huts and stripped to his shorts and undershirt. Before he could lie down for a nap, John Balog stepped in.

"What's that in your hand, John?"

"What's it look like, Charlie?"

"It looks a lot like a bottle of Old Crow rye whiskey, John."

"And two glasses."

"I've heard it's medicinal. Effective for general exhaustion."

"I thought we should do a quality control inspection, Charlie. Sample it. You know. Just to make sure it's still effective. This stuff can go out of date."

"'Charlie'? Not Charles, or even Doc?"

"Yep. Me John, you Charlie."

They clinked glasses.

32

Flash of Red

Sisiman Cove, Bataan Peninsula, Philippine Islands

25 January 1942

Early Sunday morning, Charles walked out the Sisiman Cove dock with a canteen of hot coffee and two cups. One was for himself, the other for John Balog, due to return from night patrol on PT-41. From radio contacts he knew PT-41 had seen action with the Japanese during the night, and John would give him the details. When the 41 motored into the cove, a broom, the universal symbol of a clean sweep, a successful mission, waved proudly from the boat's mast.

"Here you go," Charles handed Balog a cup of coffee as he stepped to the dock. "At least Bulkeley manages to keep us supplied with coffee. He usually brings it back after a trip to Mariveles or the Rock. What happened last night?"

As they walked down the dock for their morning meal, Balog said, "I'll tell you about the night, but since you brought it up, I'll let you in on something about Bulkeley's trips—he gets more than coffee. If he goes to Mariveles instead of Corregidor, he's really going to the *Canopus*."

"That old submarine tender? The one that survived the bombing of the Cavite Navy Yard and moved to Mariveles? They bombed her a couple of times around New Year's Day—she's a burned-out hulk, listing against the shore, still billowing black smoke."

"I've been aboard her with Bulkeley, Charlie. That smoke comes from smoke pots on the deck and superstructure. The disguise is working. She hasn't been hit since they first attacked Mariveles. Below decks machinists and mechanics are working every night making replacement parts and repairing small Navy craft, including PT-32. You didn't know all this already?"

"Nobody bothered to tell me. Still doesn't inform me as to why Bulkeley goes there so often."

"Here's the secret, Charlie. The *Canopus* has a huge freezer—and it's full of ice cream!"

"What? He's never brought any ice cream back for us!" Charles closed his eyes, trying to recall the sweet taste and creamy texture he loved.

"Of course he never brings any back, you idiot. It would melt," Balog laughed. "Either Bulkeley has friends aboard, or maybe he has an old Academy buddy assigned to the *Canopus*. Every time we go there, he and our other officers get treated to giant servings of chocolate or vanilla ice cream. If he stays through the evening, it's because he's been invited to their supper. Cox went with Bulkeley once and told me they had fried chicken, mashed potatoes, carrots, and peas."

"Oh my God," Charles's imagination ran with that image.

"And," John pointed his finger at Charles, "with strong coffee and chocolate cake à la mode for dessert." Balog spoke almost reverently.

"John, my mouth is watering. But while you're talking about all that food, doesn't it bother you just a bit? Our guys are trying to hold back the Japanese Army only a few miles north of here, and we both know they're getting desperate. What little food they have is left behind for the Japanese when they have to retreat. On top of that, most of them have either malaria or dysentery—or both."

He paused, the vision of chocolate cake fading. He shook his head. "It simply doesn't seem right to have all that ammunition and food stored down here but not getting to the troops."

"I suppose the skipper on the *Canopus* figures it won't be long before either our forces arrive and relieve us, or the Japanese take it all. Either way, you can't send them the ice cream, so no need to hoard it. And you're right of course. We've both seen with our own eyes all that food that MacArthur has in the tunnels. Is he preparing for a last stand on the Rock after Bataan falls? Maybe. It makes no difference to you and me though, so I'll stop talking about food."

"OK—what happened last night? When you left the cove, I saw DeLong was also aboard, standing next to Bulkeley and Cox."

"Charles, when the sun came up this morning, I was just happy to see another day. Were we good or just lucky? Who knows? But we're back."

"So, again, what happened?"

"We made a run into Subic. Bulkeley moved us in quietly on only one engine until we spotted a loaded transport, around 5,000 tons. We then started our torpedo run at full speed a half-mile out. Thank God for Chief Hancock's young sharp eyes—he started waving and yelling 'Propeller nets ahead!' Cox was at the wheel and just whipped the boat to port with one hand and pulled back the throttles with the other. Bulkeley damn near went in the water, but Hancock saved our ass."

"The Japanese must have heard you by then."

"They had. Searchlights came on, but fortunately they were scanning the sky."

"As usual. Everyone's looking for American planes to appear in the sky. We just have different reasons."

"While they searched for planes, we worked our way through the floating nets and restarted our run. Bulkeley fired one torpedo from around 800 yards. He fired a second about 500 yards out, but that one barely cleared the tube and deflected straight down to the bottom of the bay. Then the Japanese transport searchlight found us, and they opened up with fore and aft machine guns. Cox ran us in under the bow so close to the ship that their machine guns couldn't follow us. Meanwhile, our .30 and .50 calibers raked the superstructure. Bulkeley was firing his automatic rifle, DeLong was blasting away with a Thompson sub-machine gun, and even Hancock had grabbed his rifle and added his two bits to the madness. We were firing almost straight up. Finally we knocked out their searchlight."

"Did you get a torpedo hit?"

"I'd totally forgotten about that first torpedo during the gunfight, but Ensign Cox was tracking it in his head the whole time. He was bringing us about in the blind spot just ahead of their bow when it hit with a red flash below the waterline. A moment later a huge secondary explosion with boiling black and orange flames rose hundreds of feet into the air. Wreckage began raining down all around us, so we got the hell out of there. Cox did a speedy ballet back through the nets, and we ran like hell for ten minutes. They were still shooting, but never hit us. DeLong had a good look back as we were leaving. He thinks it looked more like a seaplane tender than a freighter."

"No injuries?" Charles asked.

"Not even a barrel burn on Bulkeley's arm." Balog laughed while dodging the last drops of Charles's coffee.

That evening, Watson Sims interrupted their meal, waving a paper over his head. "Hey, guys! Listen to this."

Sims, the radioman on PT-32, believed he was destined to become either a famous journalist or successful novelist. He spent much of his time listening to "Radio Fort Mills," the Armed Forces radio station on Corregidor. The station tried to boost morale with stories of success and sometimes a bit of humor. Sims transcribed many of the stories into a newsletter for the squadron, sometimes adding his own commentary.

Charles closed his now well-worn copy of *Meditations* and joined the gathering group. "What do you have, Sims?"

"This is an occasion, gentlemen," Sims teased his audience. "We were the big story on the radio today. It was about those Jap dive bombers that made a run at us a few days ago."

"OK, now you've got our attention, so you can drop the grandstanding."

"When they announced the story as being about the Torpedo Boats, I grabbed pencil and paper and got it all down."

> *When General MacArthur planned an Offshore Patrol for the Philippine Army composed of Motor Torpedo Boats, his plan was met with almost universal misgiving and some laughter. During the present war the Motor Torpedo Boat has been re-markably successful and now is accepted by all. Two days ago, when two of these boats observed two waves of dive-bombers approaching the shore for an attack, they could have easily sought cover. Instead they increased speed and placed them-selves in the line of flight of the second wave and engaged the planes with fire. All three planes were hit, the formation was dispersed, and with smoking motors each plane limped away, rapidly losing altitude. Officers and men of the crews have been cited for gallantry. This exploit, following closely on other daring and successful forays of Lieutenant Bulkeley, definitely establish-es the value of the Motor Torpedo Boat in this Theater of War and confirms the wisdom of its selection for local defense.*

When Sims finished, spontaneous self-congratulations and back-slapping followed. No one engaged in combat for glory, but it was nice to be recognized for doing a job well.

Following up this report, Captain Herbert James Ray, Admiral Rockwell's aide, sent Bulkeley a simple handwritten note:

Dear Bulkeley:

I really think your gang is getting too tough. The latest report is that "three dive bombers were seen over Mariveles Mountain, chased by a PT boat." Don't you think that is carrying the war a bit too far!

Sincerely,
Jimmy Ray

The afternoon of 25 January was sunny and even muggier than usual. PT-34 floated at anchor in Sisiman Bay, away from the mosquitoes. With avgas reserves reduced to critical levels, routine patrols were halted, and vital missions were carried out by single PT boats. After an hour of inserting tracer rounds into belts of .50 caliber ammunition, Charles leaned back against the hull and closed his eyes, imagining a lazy Indiana summer day. Small waves slapped rhythmically against the hull, and he drifted off.

Voices and footsteps of crewmen on deck slowly awakened him. *Sounds like Martino, Clark, and Reynolds, and maybe Hunter or Owen.*

"Wow! Look at that!"

"I almost forgot what they looked like!"

"Let me have them—it's my turn!"

"No! I'm next!"

"Where'd they come from?"

"I don't know, but I'm damn glad to see them."

"My turn! Hand them over."

Wonder what they're all excited about? It's a strange conversation. I'd better go up and see what's happening. What he saw was just as strange as the conversation: Crewmen lined the starboard side, gazing towards the beach about a hundred fifty yards off. A pair of binoculars was the subject of contention, with Martino currently maintaining possession.

"What's got you guys so worked up?" Charles asked Reynolds.

"See the beach?"

"Yes."

"Look closely."

Charles squinted and with one hand shaded his eyes. "OK, people on the beach. Big deal—hey! Women! In swimsuits!" Now Charles was as excited as the others. "I can't see from here, but are they American women? Who are they?"

"See the 41 boat over there, anchored about fifty yards from the beach?" said Reynolds. "One of their crew actually swam over and asked. They're officers from Hospital No. 2, and the women are nurses. There more than a dozen of them! They've been there for a couple of hours, but the bastards on the 41 boat didn't bother to radio us about them until a few minutes ago."

Nurses? Tillie?

"Let me see the binoculars," Charles asked.

"Sorry, Doc. My turn next," and Clark yanked the binoculars from Martino's reluctant hands.

Charles used his T-shirt to clean his glasses and stood on the rails of the machine gun turret for a better view. The people on the beach were packing up to leave. The men carried boxes to the trail leading back into the overgrowth, while the women, all in bathing suits, departed by a different path. He caught just a flash of red hair, and his chest tightened. *Could that be Tillie? Damn! She's behind the trees now.*

"Shit! They're all leaving." Clark announced.

"Jessie! Let me have a look. Please, just for five seconds—" Charles pleaded. Clark made no move.

"Hand me the goddamn glasses!" Charles demanded with a fierceness that surprised everyone, including himself.

Clark handed them over. "Keep 'em, Doc. They're all gone anyway."

Charles quickly scanned the beach and tree line. He watched the women appearing here and there, as if playing peek-a-boo through the trees. There! Another flash of red hair! It disappeared, then for a moment reappeared. *Yes! That must be Tillie. Please, turn and look this way.* Then once more, the woman with red hair passed from sight, this time for good.

Charles kicked off his shoes and started undoing his pants.

"What the hell are you doing, Doc?" Clark asked.

"I think I know one of those women. I've got to be certain, so I'm swimming over to find out."

"Whoa, Doc—you're a good swimmer, but they'll be long gone by the time you get there. Besides, you do remember there're sharks in this bay, don't you?"

Damnit, he's right.

Charles collapsed on the engine compartment cover. *If that redhead was in fact Tillie, at least she's alive on Bataan, not a prisoner in Manila.*

277

"Hey, Jessie."

"Yeah, Doc?"

"Sorry about the binoculars. It was important to me. OK?"

"I could sort of tell that," Clark chuckled. "Your face was as red as that cross on your shoulder. Remind me to never really piss you off."

🐦 🐦 🐦

Two days later RON 3 received more news from Captain Ray. The crewmen of PT-34 who took part in the attack in Binanga Bay on the night of 18 January had been recommended for commendation. Rockwell recommended Bulkeley receive the coveted Distinguished Navy Cross award.

"John?"

"Yes, Charlie?"

"Didn't you say that Hancock's sharp eyes and quick warning saved your boat from getting tangled in the propeller nets the other night?"

"Yep."

"And you remember me telling you about Martino saving the 34 from that partially ejected torpedo doing a hot run?"

"Yep—saved the boat and your entire crew."

"Seems to me that without men like Martino and Hancock, PT-41 and PT-34 would both have been lost, and Bulkeley's Navy Cross would have been awarded posthumously."

"You're trying to make a point?"

"Yes. Bulkeley goes on most of our missions and puts his ass on the line. He deserves recognition for that leadership. On the other hand, why is it that when an NCO saves the day, the officer gets the big medal?"

"Charlie, only the senior commanders like Admiral Rockwell, can recommend the Distinguished Navy Cross. He knows Bulkeley and he knows MTB 3. He doesn't know Hancock or Martino, or, for that matter, you or me. There are exceptions, but we sailors first have to get ourselves killed, doing something heroic, while some officer's watching. Then, maybe, someone might take notice. I'd rather stay alive than get an award that way. Let it go, and don't lose sleep over it, because it's never going to change."

33

Look Again

Sisiman Cove, Bataan Peninsula, Philippine Islands

10 February 1942

"Wake up!"

Awakened from sleep in his crew bunk on PT-34 by footsteps on the decks and voices through the boat, Charles opened one eye. Jessie Clark stood in the middle of the crew room pulling on his pants. "What the hell, Jessie—it's my night to sleep."

"Sorry, Doc. We got a call to escort a supply boat through the minefields this morning. Could be our lucky day!"

"What's lucky about interrupting my sleep?"

Hunter was starting up PT-34's engines, and Clark had to raise his voice. "The message said it's a small Filipino supply vessel."

"What's so great about that?"

"We'll see."

Four lines of underwater mines protected the entrance to Manila Bay, two set by the Army and two by the Navy. Half the of them could be remotely turned off and on from an electric control station on Corregidor. The longest field extended from the west end of Corregidor south to Carabao Point, blocking the main channel into Manila Bay. Three other lines blocked access to Mariveles Bay and the north channel. A narrow path allowed shallow-draft boats to pass without turning off electric mines, but the pilot had to know the exact route and marker codes.

After the mines were in place, MTB 3 often drew the task of leading inbound ships through the mine fields. Manila and Cavite were now occupied by the Japanese, but these smaller supply craft still needed to reach the docks at Mariveles or Corregidor.

Fifteen minutes later, from his station Charles watched Kelly and Richardson work PT-34 past the marking buoys. Clark seemed eager, if not outright excited. "What's the big deal here, Jessie?"

"These small Filipino supply ships work their way north from the southern islands, hiding from enemy planes in small bays or inlets during the day and playing cat and mouse with the Japanese ships at night. One of them made it here overnight and is waiting for us to escort them safely through to the north dock."

"So?"

"We'll know soon."

PT-34 turned south at a coded buoy marking the entrance to the safe channel, a path less than a quarter-mile wide and almost three-quarters of a mile long. A half-mile outside the minefields they greeted the new arrival.

As PT-34 approached a small cargo boat floating low in the water, Clark grinned at Charles and gave a thumbs-up.

Huh? I still don't get it.

The Filipino crew waved, greeting the American sailors in broken English, Tagalog, and something else, possibly Bisaya. "Hello! *Kamusta*! Happy! Japanese not see us, and we bring lot of food." They began opening crates on the deck as PT-34 drew close.

Holy cow—look at all that fresh fruit, vegetables, and meat!

The Filipino crews saw the PT boat sailors as their country's defenders, the men for whom the supply boat crew had risked their lives. Besides that, PT-34 was about to lead them through the dangerous minefields. Generous armfuls of pineapple, durian, mango, banana, avocado, and papaya were passed from one crew to the other until Lieutenant Kelly finally halted the transfer. "I think we have as much as the squadron can eat before it spoils."

"Thank you! *Salamat*! Thanks!" The PT-34 crew acknowledged the gifts and waved as they pulled ahead to lead the way.

"OK, Jessie, I'll admit I was more than a bit tired of eating rice, coconut, and canned salmon," Charles quipped between bites of a ripe durian fruit. "In fact, this might be even better than ice cream from the *Canopus*."

Japan stationed troops in and around Manila and the Americans settled in at Mariveles and Corregidor. While these troops watched each other across the bay waters, occasionally exchanging artillery fire, fierce fighting raged along the Abucay line.

Repeated Japanese bombing reduced the topside of Corregidor to little more than a rubble field.

The Malinta Tunnel complex remained intact, but MacArthur couldn't hold the island indefinitely. If the Japanese were able to defeat the American Army on Bataan and surround Corregidor, the Rock would also fall—and that was exactly the Japanese strategic plan. With China and the Philippine Islands in its hands, Japan would possess island stepping stones all the way to Australia. Every soldier and sailor on Bataan and Corregidor asked themselves the same question: Would the U.S. and its allies mount a response to this imminent threat? Could they?

MacArthur thought it imperative that his Army believe help was coming.

A month earlier, on 15 January, Bulkeley had assembled the squadron to read them a message from General MacArthur. He stood on a crate as fifty crewmen gathered closely. "Men," Bulkeley spoke loudly so all could hear, "MacArthur has requested all field commanders—and Captain Ray says that includes me—to read you this message." He read flatly, giving no inflection or emotion to his voice.

> *Help is on the way from the United States. Thousands of troops and hundreds of planes are being dispatched. The exact time of arrival is unknown. They will have to fight their way through Japanese attempts against them. It is imperative that our troops hold until these reinforcements arrive. No further retreat is possible. We have more troops in Bataan than the Japanese have thrown against us; our supplies are ample; a determined defense will defeat the enemy's attacks. It is a question now of courage and determination. Men who run will merely be destroyed, but men who fight will save themselves and their country.*

After Bulkeley finished, the assembled men were quiet.

Finally, a voice called out, "Is it true, sir? That part about the reinforcements?"

"MacArthur talks to President Roosevelt," Bulkeley replied. "I presume therefore that MacArthur has accurate facts." Then he added, "Time will tell, I suppose."

"Do you believe all that?" Charles asked Bill Johnson.

"Do we have a choice?"

"No, we don't. I'm not ready to fulfill that 'death before dishonor' motto. I'm going to survive—"

"—to fight again." Bill finished the sentence.

Now, more than a month later, MacArthur's words rang hollow to most American servicemen, Charles included. *His encouragements that reinforcements will arrive any day now simply are not true. Every Japanese attack drives us farther south. Our soldiers are plagued with malaria, severely malnourished, and riddled with dysentery.*

I don't understand why MacArthur's holding onto the food and ammunition stored in the tunnels when Americans and Filipinos on Bataan are running out of both. I don't fancy surrendering, but the mountains on Bataan are too easily isolated to sustain a guerrilla force. I'm between a rock and a hard place, but not about to give up.

Seeing that red hair flash between the trees on the beach the previous week was for Charles a cruel tease. Every scheme he could think of to leave and find Tillie was flawed, against regulations, or potentially fatal. Then serendipity intervened.

"Doc!" It was still dark when Richardson returned to PT-34 after a pre-dawn meeting with Kelly and Bulkeley at the squadron's small *nipa* hut headquarters. "The 32 boat's making a daylight run this morning to Cabcaben with supplies for Hospital No. 2. On the return, they're bringing back three special patients to Corregidor. Balog said to send you with the boat."

"PT-32?"

"Yep, she's back in service, at least for courier duty. Shoe has her at the pier, ready to leave. He's just waiting for you."

Charles wanted to shout, "Thank you!" but managed a restrained "Yes, sir." His previous trip to look for Tillie at Army Hospital No. 2 had been unsuccessful, but new-found hope had sprung from that flash of red hair on the beach.

The engines were already rumbling when Charles jumped aboard PT-32. Repairs from the engine room explosion could not restore her previous speed, but she was still a reliable and well-armed courier. Thirty minutes later they tied up at Corregidor's South Dock. Soldiers quickly loaded her deck with medical supplies and several dozen cartons of food.

Charles signed for the bag containing morphine, pentathol, and procaine.

Before they cast off for the short trip to Cabcaben, a dozen Army soldiers heading to the front line came aboard. They silently took seats on the cartons of food, stoically accepting their duty.

Lieutenant Schumacher motored east at half-throttle, paralleling the "tail" of Corregidor. Once past the island, they turned north for Cabcaben, arriving as sunlight slowly flowed down the peak of Bataan's Mount Mariveles. With daylight came danger from Japanese air attacks. All eyes scanned the sky, though PT boats had so far fared well in open water encounters with Japanese aircraft. So far.

Waves whipped by the wind caused delays in securing PT-32 to the Cabcaben dock. The soldiers helped move cartons of food and medicine from the deck to handcarts at the pier and wheeled them to the shore.

"Transport from the hospital should arrive soon," Schumacher told Charles, "It'll drop you, the medical supplies, and the soldiers at Hospital No. 2. One of the patients is from there. If the other two patients are still at Hospital No. 1, have an ambulance or truck take you to pick them up."

"Are you saying Hospital No. 1 is close to No. 2 now?" Charles asked.

"Right—they had to move back with the rest of the defensive line. It leapfrogged past Hospital No. 2. It's supposed to be less than a mile further west along the river."

"OK. What's special about these three patients?"

"I don't have any details, Doc. I'm sure you'll find out when you get there."

"How much time do I have?"

"Plan to be back here with all three patients by 1900. Meanwhile, I don't want to be sitting around if the Japanese decide there's something here worth attacking. I'll circle offshore and come back for you."

So, if Tillie's not at Hospital No. 2, I'll have a chance to search No. 1. I'm certain that was her leaving the beach at Sisiman.

The truck arrived, and with Charles and the soldiers perched on top of the supplies, it rumbled south on the East Road for about three miles. There was no sign for Hospital No. 2, but at a 162.5-kilometer marker, the truck turned onto a well-worn dirt track branching off from the main road. The smell of sickness and rot hit almost immediately. Once into the jungle canopy, the misery of smothering humidity was accentuated by swarms of biting flies and other insects too small to see. At least the mosquitoes would wait for dusk in their search for human blood. Charles smelled the stench long before he was able to see the source.

Since his previous visit Hospital No. 2 had expanded like a starburst artillery round. Bulldozed paths snaked into the jungle canopy in every direction. Steel and wood patient cots, abutting end to end, bordered both sides of the dirt paths. It was as if a pale green caterpillar had wrapped itself into a chrysalis and emerged a giant, ugly brownish-green moth.

This reminds me of the print hanging on the wall back at the Mare Island Library, that Florentine painting of Dante's Inferno, his "Nine Circles of Hell." Charles turned to the soldier next to him, "This has to be Dante's seventh circle. Violence."

The soldier returned an uncomprehending, blank stare, shrugged, and returned his attention to a dragonfly riding the toe of his boot.

The truck pulled into the main compound and cut its engine. Cries, moans, and occasional screams replaced the diesel's deafening rattle. Hospital No. 2 had held only a few hundred patients when Charles was here more than a month ago, searching for Tillie. Now it was a giant complex, extending hundreds of yards along the Real River, hosting thousands of patients. Stores of pain killers, sulfa drugs, and other medicines were desperately low or exhausted. They had even run out of simple bandages. After changing dressings on a wound, staff were forced to wash and boil the dirty bandages for reuse.

On my last visit, I was led to understand that Hospital No. 1 was to receive battle casualties from the front lines. After surgery, those patients, alongside the patients with dysentery, malaria, or dengue fever, would be transported south, here to Hospital No. 2, for convalescence. It sounded good, but that plan has obviously disintegrated. I bet the battle plans fell apart just as quickly.

A corpsman checked off the inventory list of medicines and signed for the morphine and anesthetics. "I'm to tell you that your three nurses are in the medical ward."

"Nurses?"

"Right. The two sick nurses from Hospital No. 1 arrived here last night. All three are ready and waiting for you to take them to Corregidor."

Nurses! So that's why they're "special" patients.

"Our boat, PT-32, isn't meeting us at the dock until this evening. I'll come back for the nurses in a few hours. Meanwhile, I need to find a Navy nurse. Know of one here?

The corpsman thought for a minute. "Nope. We haven't had a lot of time for meeting new people. Ask one of the nurses—I think most all of them know each other."

Charles walked through the giant compound, interrupting nurses and doctors rushing between tents and huts. "I'm looking for a Navy nurse, Mary Finian, goes by 'Tillie.' She's got red hair."

"Nope. Haven't heard of any Navy nurse."

"Don't know anyone by that name."

Hope reappeared in the form of a dark-eyed nurse smiling and pushing strings of hair from her sweating forehead. "Yes, I know an Irish nurse. She's not Navy, though."

Charles considered. *Has Tillie been transferred to the Army?*

"Where can I find her?"

"You're looking at her."

Charles was too confused to speak.

"What's wrong? Were you expecting a pale redhead with green eyes, high cheekbones, and freckles?"

"Well, actually, sort of. She is Irish," Charles stammered.

"And so am I, buddy."

Charles was momentarily speechless. *This woman is lovely. Of course, by now every American female I encounter is a goddess.* He only said, "I'm sorry. No offense intended."

"Apology accepted. For your information, most of us 'Irish lasses' are dark-haired. Some of us are dark-skinned too. You might have heard of 'Black Irish'? It has something to do with Spanish soldiers sent to Ireland a couple of centuries ago. Some of them decided to stay, and so—here I am."

"I'm so sorry, ma'am, I'm just disappointed—I mean, I was looking for someone else."

"My name's Trish. And as a matter of fact, there is one other Irish nurse here. I know her pretty well. She's a redhead, and she's Navy."

Tillie!

"Where can I find her?" Charles struggled to control his voice.

"I think she's still working the gas gangrene unit. Go upriver a hundred yards or more. Stay on the road and away from the posted area on the river. That's where we nurses bathe and do our laundry. Gangrene's a separate section, isolated from the rest of the patients for obvious reasons. It's another hundred yards uphill from the river. Just follow your nose."

"Thank you! Thank you!" Charles turned quickly and headed upriver.

"Hey, Corpsman—" the nurse called to him.

"Yes?" he stopped and turned toward her.

"Is your name Charles?"

"Yes."

"Thought it might be."

"Gangrene" was little more than a cross-hatched path among the trees. As elsewhere, the cots lay end to end, each holding patients with horrible wounds. Charles was used to the stench of sickness and rot, but here it was overwhelming. He was on the verge of retching but forced it back. Several Filipino assistants and a corpsman moved among the patients, kneeling beside cots elevated only a foot above the ground. The buzz of flies was audible. At least half of the patients had no protective netting.

At the far end of one path, a figure wearing oversized coveralls knelt next to a patient.

34

The Promise

Hospital No. 2, Bataan Peninsula, Philippine Islands

13 February 1942

Charles stared at the kneeling figure, facing away from him. Red hair, untidily pinned up, shone as a bright beacon against the monochrome jungle background. He walked slowly down the path, pausing a few feet away. *It's a woman with red hair, but the coveralls hide everything else.*

The woman said something reassuring to her patient, stood, and turned. A cloth tied across her nose and mouth gave scant protection from the surrounding miasma. She stared at Charles for a long time. Her hand slowly pulled her mask down. Gaunt, with hollow cheeks, she stared at him through dark, sunken eyes.

Tillie.

"Oh my God!" Tillie wrapped her arms around him. For a long time, they silently held each other tight.

Tillie finally let him go. "Have they transferred you here, to the hospital?"

"No, I'm only here for a couple of hours. Was that you with the hospital staff on the beach at Sisiman Cove a few days ago?"

Tillie's eyebrows furrowed. "How'd you know that?"

"I was on one of those PT boats moored in the bay, the one furthest from you. We're part of what's left of MTB 3, Motor Torpedo Boat Squadron 3. I saw someone with red hair at the beach. I was sure it was you, but you all left before I could get to the shore. After I was told the group was nurses and doctors from the hospital, I knew it *had* to be you. I hoped for a chance to come here and look for myself. I was considering going AWOL when I got lucky and was sent here to transport some sick nurses back to Corregidor."

"As if you would ever go AWOL!" *It's so good to see her smile.* "Yes, it was me at the beach. General Homma has eased up his attack for the moment. It's still terrible here, but with the interruption in fighting, surgery slowed down. Someone took advantage of the pause and organized a few hours on the beach to try to recover our humanity. It worked—for about an hour."

"I like the new nurse's uniform," Charles gave a tug on the sleeve of the coveralls.

"I washed blood and other stuff from my nursing uniform so many times the seams fell apart. Air Corps people gave us these things to wear. They're durable, but the smallest they had was a men's regular. We're grateful, considering the limited alternatives. How long will you be here?"

"Not long. I delivered some drugs and now I'm taking three sick nurses back to the tunnel hospital on Corregidor. As much as I want to, I can't stay. How'd you get here anyway?"

"We moved the Cañacao Hospital patients to a separate building in Manila before Christmas. A few days later they separated all the men who could walk and loaded them in trucks. They knew the Japs were coming soon and wanted to move every patient possible to Bataan. A couple of corpsmen and I were assigned to bring a group of stretcher patients to Hospital No. 1."

"But how'd I miss you?" Charles asked. "I searched both hospitals—I think it was a Sunday, maybe December 28 or 29?"

"I don't know, Charles. That was around the time I moved from No. 1 to No. 2. Been here ever since. It's painful to think that we might have passed in the night—but I'm glad you didn't give up. How did you wind up on those boats? Weren't you in that seaplane squadron?"

"I was. It would take a while to tell the whole story."

"Charles, I'd so love to sit and talk, but I just can't stop right now. Walk with me while I do what I can for these men."

Tillie stooped to hold the hand of a man with an open, putrid wound from his knee to his groin. Tillie waved ineffectually at flies attracted to the exposed tissue. The stench was hardly bearable, but she didn't replace her mask. The soldier grimaced with closed eyes and pleaded through his pain, "Take it off—I can't take the pain. For God's sake, *please* take it off!"

"No, no, Sergeant, you don't want that," Tillie squeezed the soldier's hand. "You're going to need that leg when you get home."

"But the pain! Please help me!"

"I'll try to find you something that'll help." Tillie stood and told Charles quietly, "Like everything else, we ration our pain drugs."

Charles opened the medical pack on his belt and handed Tillie eight of his nine syrettes of morphine. "Here. It's not a lot, but it's something."

Tillie talked while moving from patient to patient, all with horrifying, open, stinking gangrene infections in various stages. "When shrapnel or a bullet passes through dirty clothing and mud-caked skin, it carries germs of every type deep into the body. When the germ is *Clostridium perfringens*, it hides deep in the tissues and literally eats its way to the center of the body. This is what you get, gangrene."

"I know."

"How stupid of me. Of course, you know all this. Sorry. Anyway, this is where we isolate them from the other patients."

Charles again forcefully swallowed the bile that rose to his throat. *Is it even possible to get accustomed to the smell of so much rotting flesh?* "I remember lectures about gangrene in Corps School, but I could never have imagined this. I do remember the infection can spread through the bloodstream to the rest of the body—then it's fatal. Soldiers in every war have dreaded it. I'm surprised that most of the men I see here don't have amputations. I thought that was the only treatment that could save them."

"Amputations save a lot of men from dying from gangrene, but of course it's devastating to go home that way. Sulfa was going to be the miracle drug, but it almost never stopped gangrene. The surgeons here are using a new, highly aggressive approach that, so far, seems to be effective. They excise every bit of infected tissue, often going right down to the bone and up the entire leg or arm. It's takes them longer than a quick amputation, and it's one reason we are running out of anesthetic. They swab the remaining tissue down with peroxide but don't close the wound. The incision's left open to the air, uncovered except for mosquito netting—well, until we ran out of netting. Sun and oxygen kill the Clostridium bacteria. We're seeing many of these men recover, at least as many as did after amputations. They'll have deep scars, but be happier for it."

Charles looked at her. "These men might not have a lot to look forward to, even if they heal."

Tillie's face clouded over. "You're right, of course. If we're not already dead, we'll surrender unless the Bataan Army finds some way to hold back the Japanese."

"There'll be some way to get you nurses out before that happens," Charles tried to sound confident. "I know for a fact that submarines still regularly reach Corregidor and leave for Australia the next day. They always pack in one or two dozen passengers, including women, before departing. You *will* be OK, Tillie—I know it."

"I'm not so sure, Charles. People here are acting like it's the end of the world. There are about fifty of us nurses here, and men are proposing right and left. Because they think this is the end, people find it easy to say, 'I love you' and 'Will you marry me?' without really thinking. Everyone's assuming there's no future."

"And are they?" Charles spoke flatly.

"Are they what?"

"Getting married."

Tillie paused, hearing what he hadn't said.

"Yes. Maybe a third of the nurses have accepted proposals. I'm among those who realize that to do so would be giving up hope, abandoning thoughts of any future beyond this hell. Charles, I dream of home during the little sleep I manage. The rest of the time I take care of these men and try not to think that I might never have a life in Chicago, Philly, LA, or some other city. I am not going to give up—" Emotion quavered in her voice, "And surely our country will not give up on us, Charles!"

"Of course not. They'd never abandon us." *But it sure feels like they have.*

Tillie gathered her strength and stood erect. "Charles, I have to be realistic. We're all going to die someday, but none of us knows when that'll be. Even though the hospital itself hasn't been attacked, the fighting is close. Even now shrapnel falls from the sky. The other day a Filipino kitchen worker was killed by a stray .50 caliber round that came from nowhere. Death, in all its apparitions, stalks every path here."

Tillie locked eyes with Charles before continuing. "The Navy somehow keeps track of all of us. Whenever this thing is over, promise me you'll find out what happened to me. Write to me if I'm still alive. And, I want to know that if I don't survive this war, you'll remember me and the good things I did."

"Tillie, I'm sure you'll make it out of here."

Tillie didn't let him off the hook. "No, Charles, you can't be sure, and you know it. Just like I can't be certain that you'll be OK, no matter how much I hope you will."

"OK," was all he could manage to say. He'd never shared his deepest emotions, let alone his darkest fears, with anyone. So far, he'd moved through the war without dwelling on his own death. Deep down, he assumed he would survive, and he remained as certain of that as ever.

When she understood that Charles wasn't going to say more, Tillie continued. "I think of you every day. When I get back, I *will* write to you. And if you don't make it, I will remember you to my own dying day. I swear that to you. I *need* you to do the same for me."

His emotional shell giving way, he said, "Tillie, I can't *not* think of you. I do now and will for as long as I live. I will not forget you. Please know that without my even having to say it. At the same time though, I'll tell you that I've got a strong feeling, a certainty actually, that you will survive this war."

She took his face in her hands and kissed him, lightly, on his lips. "We both have work to do. Now, go back and do whatever it is you have to do on those boats. I pray both of us survive to see each other again."

Tillie abruptly turned and walked back up the path to kneel at a patient's side. She did not look back.

35

The Reporter

Corregidor Island, Philippine Islands

16 February 1942

Reluctantly, Charles walked back to the central hospital zone. Three nurses lay on adjacent stretchers for their transfer to Corregidor. A nurse introducing herself as Betty handed him the patients' medical folders and quickly reviewed each patient.

"This is Pat. Her recovery from dengue fever has been slow and difficult." She gave Pat's hand a squeeze, "Enjoy Corregidor, Pat. I hear they have some really good-looking doctors there."

"Hi, Pat," Charles smiled at her. "We'll make sure the ride is smooth as glass for you."

Pat looked up at Charles and said softly to Betty, "This guy's not so bad-looking himself."

Betty ignored Pat's comment, continuing, "And this young lady over here is Marilyn. The mosquitoes love her, and so does the malaria. She's special, Doc, take good care of her."

"Hello, Special Marilyn. Unfortunately, they've had a lot of experience treating malaria on Corregidor, but for you that's good—they have all the medicines and know how to use it."

Betty patted the shoulder of the nurse on the third stretcher. "Charles, this is our very precious, but very sick little bird, Diane. She had malaria and got better, but relapsed."

292

Charles looked at his third patient. *I know this one.* "Remember me?"

Diane turned her head to look at Charles with her yellow eyes. "Are you the Corpsman who gave me the candy bar?"

"Yep, the one and only," Charles gave Diane the best grin he could muster. *This woman looked very sick when I saw her before, but she's in even worse shape now.* "I'm sorry, I didn't bring one this time, but I promise you'll get one at Corregidor. Chocolate's good for malaria, you know." He turned to Betty. "Let's load up. Our magic carpet should be waiting."

A week passed. PT-34 bobbed on the gentle waves at Corregidor's South Dock. Lieutenants Bulkeley and Kelly had walked to the Navy Tunnel, presumably meeting with Captain Ray, if not Admiral Rockwell himself. Ensign Richardson remained as officer in charge on the boat.

"Sir. Permission to stretch my legs on the dock?"

"Given. Don't stray off."

Charles climbed from the boat but stayed close. He knew Bulkeley and Kelly might return any moment, and if air raid sirens sounded, Richardson would immediately take PT-34 to the relative safety of open water. After walking a few yards up and down the dock, he chose to sit in a small patch of shade, in sight of PT-34. Even though it was still "dry season" in the Philippines, the humidity remained merciless. Road dust hung in the air behind moving vehicles before settling on sweat-soaked skin and clothes, creating a thin layer of mud. He opened his pocket dictionary to the bookmark and focused on an unfamiliar word.

Misanthrope /mɪs ən̩ θroʊp/
n. A person who hates or distrusts mankind.
First use 1653. Origin Greek.

I've never heard that one used before, but I think I've met one or two. Charles concentrated on memorizing the word, repeating it to himself several times.

Over his shoulder a voice with a drawl, not southern, but possibly Oklahoma or Texas, said, "That's a good book, but the story is inconsistent, and its organization is dislinear." The man, in civilian clothes, moved to face Charles directly. He was thin, like everyone else on the Rock, but not to the point of appearing sickly. A pencil mustache complemented a smile that most women found handsome. Add the amiable drawl, and he was instantly likeable.

"Mind if I share your shade?" he inquired.

"Have a seat." Charles was happy for the company. "I have to admit it is a pretty shallow plot," Charles raised his dictionary. "On the other hand, I would argue that its organization is impeccable." He extended his hand to the stranger. "Charles Conrad Beckner."

"And I'm Nathaniel Crosby Floyd. Most everyone just calls me Nat." He accepted the handshake. "Impeccably organized, you say?"

Charles accepted the challenge. "Highly organized, I'd say. In sequence, in order, in succession, or as a chain, train, or string."

"I see. Is a dictionary the only thing you can find to read?"

"No, but it helps when I read other books. And talk. And write."

"Are you a writer as well as a medic?" Nat pointed toward Charles's red cross insignia.

Charles leaned back. "You're a civilian, so instead of letting you choose between swords or pistols at dawn to allow me satisfaction from that insult, I'll assume you're only ignorant." He flashed a grin to take the sting out of the comment, then went on, "I'm *not* a 'medic.' Medics are Army. I'm Navy. I'm an IDC, an Independent Duty *Corpsman*. Addressing me, a Navy Corpsman, as 'medic' could be construed an insult. If you don't know the difference, I can explain that to you."

"Sorry, *Corpsman*. No insult intended," Nat raised both hands in apology.

"OK, I apologize too, Nat. As to your question, no, I'm not a writer. I've worked to memorize this dictionary for months now. It was given to me, and if you keep a gift, you should use it. I do think articulating one's thoughts clearly and precisely makes a good impression on educated people. They're more likely listen to what you say and give credibility to your ideas."

"That's certainly true, and I can't possibly criticize your efforts, Charles. Who is it you are trying to impress though? Officers?"

"And others, including educated people like yourself. What exactly is it you do here?"

"Oh, I'm one of the civilians who didn't leave when I had the chance. Let me ask you something, Charles. I saw you on that boat." Nat pointed at PT-34. "I assume you're with the PT squadron, are you not?"

"I am," Charles nodded.

"Might I ask what is your role with that unit?"

"I'm one of the squadron's two corpsmen. My action station is the starboard machine guns there on PT-34." Seeing Nat's raised eyebrows, he added, "It would take too long to explain."

"OK, let me ask you something else. When are you getting out of here?"

The question puzzled Charles, but rather than admit so, he answered the question with another question. "When, and where, do *you* think I'm going, Nat?"

"There are rumors."

"There are lots of rumors, Nat. There are rumors that our Pacific fleet broke the Japanese blockade and steamed into Manila Bay, but I don't see any U.S. warships out there. What rumors are you talking about?"

"The one I'm talking about, Charles, is that some people, Navy people, plan on leaving here soon."

"And where are they going, Nat? You and I and every other American here are strictly 'Title A.'"

"'Title A? What does that mean?"

"It's a quartermaster's term. It identifies inventory items that'll be eventually be consumed and need to be replaced. It means we're expendable. Replaceable. No one says as much, but we all know it's true."

"Come on, Charles," Nat cajoled, "I've heard the rumor about your China trip—you can tell me."

Huh? China? I don't know anything about a trip to China, or anywhere else.

"Tell me again who you are, Nat?"

"I'm a journalist. Write for *The New York Times*. I've been following the war out here. I could have left a month ago, but, like I said, I stayed too long and got stranded. Now I'm in the same situation as the rest of you."

"How do you get your stories back to New York?"

"The Army lets me file stories through their long-distance radio communications center, but only after the General strikes out the bad news."

"In that case, you must be good at writing short stories."

"I give 'concise' a whole new meaning."

"Is MacArthur afraid to let the world know how bad the situation is here?"

"No. The general is happy to let me tell the world about hungry undersupplied soldiers fighting valiantly against the Japanese Army." He paused, then went on. "I'm just not allowed to say we're losing that war—he won't even let me comment about our daily visits from Japanese bombers. I don't know if he has secret information about reinforcements, or if he's only saying whatever it takes to keep the soldiers fighting. My suspicion is that MacArthur's mission is to slow the Japanese Army as much as humanly possible. While he does that, the Allies will be pumping men and materiel into Australia. That'll be our Pacific fortress. We're on the verge of losing Bataan along with the rest of the Philippine Islands. We and our allies will eventually attempt to stop the Imperial tsunami and turn the tide at Darwin. It's too late here."

He paused again. "That's where I see things, Charles. Your turn."

As Nat spoke, Charles was thinking of how to glean more information. "China trip, you asked? I'll make a deal with you. Tell me what you already know about this China trip, then I'll tell you everything I know. Before I say anything else, though, you have to swear not to share what I tell you."

Nat paused, then agreed. "OK. I accept that bargain." He leaned towards Charles and spoke quietly. "What I've heard is that you guys, the entire PT Squadron, are going to fill up with the last of the gasoline, load up on ammunition, and make a breakout run through the Japanese blockade for Chiang Kai-Shek's unoccupied China."

With a non-committal tone Charles replied, "That's pretty specific information. When is this supposed to happen? I mean, according to what you've heard."

"I don't know when—that's what I'm trying to find out. I want to talk Bulkeley into letting me come with you. I know a little already, and if I know the rest, he'll have to let me come along."

"You mean Bulkeley might invite you along just to keep you quiet about our secret?"

"That's my leverage, isn't it? Your turn now. When is this going to happen?"

"I have no idea, Nat. In fact, I hadn't heard a thing about any China trip until you sat down here."

"Damn it, Charles! You agreed to tell me everything you know!"

"And I just did, Nat. In fact, I knew nothing. Maybe you sniffed out a real plot being hatched by Bulkeley and one or two of his officers, probably Lieutenant Kelly. I can't be 100 percent sure, but if there are any such plans, it's a very tightly held secret. I haven't heard a single word about a plan for the squadron to run for China, at least not yet. I am delighted to hear that Bulkeley might want to save the entire squadron before the boats are reduced to empty shells with no ammo or gasoline, only waiting to be sunk. Truth is, I don't know how you're going to verify it other than by talking to Bulkeley himself. You might still not know, even after you do that."

Nat stood and looked Charles in the eye. "I do believe you're telling the truth, Charles, but you are one son of a bitch. I'm the reporter, and you weaseled the story out of *me*. I do have to say good luck to you, whatever comes to each of us. You and I have an agreement though. If you learn something, I expect you to share it with me. True?"

"True. I never break my word."

Nat Floyd sealed their agreement with a handshake before walking away.

Could Nat's information be correct? That plan would have RON 3 fight through the Japanese naval blockade of Bataan and Corregidor, followed by a dangerous, open-water run to China. If we managed to reach the Chinese coast, we'd have to again make our way through Japanese coastal defenses. Ditching our boats between Japanese strongholds, we might be able to fight our way overland to Nationalist Chinese territory. What an ambitious and audacious plan! I like it, but I need to find out if Nat's information is true and accurate.

Bulkeley and Kelly eventually returned from their briefing, and PT-34 motored back to Sisiman Cove. Once they'd tied up to the pier, Bulkeley left the boat. Charles watched Kelly and Richardson hold a private conversation, then Kelly also left the boat, leaving Richardson the only officer aboard. Charles moved close to the ensign and stood gazing west, as if to try and see some distant coast. Casually, he tossed the question into the air.

"Sir, how long would it take for this PT boat to reach China?"

Richardson was still for a moment before slowly turning to look at Charles. "That's a strange question, Doc. Why do you ask?"

Richardson's reaction was the only answer Charles needed. "Just thinking out loud, sir."

"You need to think silently in the future."

"Yes, sir."

"You will not say the word 'China' again."

"No, sir."

Nat Floyd's rumor is true! Something is definitely afoot. Hmm, a run to free China is a logical plan. Surrender and imprisonment would be as abhorrent to Bulkeley as to anyone else in the squadron.

Charles again looked to the western horizon, for real this time. *I wonder what it's like, China?*

36

What in Hell's Going On?

Sisiman Cove, Bataan Peninsula, Philippine Islands

28 February 1942

The entire crew of PT-34 spent Saturday cleaning, repairing, and repainting their boat. As sailors, it would be unusual if they were not constantly repainting something. It was curious, though, that this time Lieutenant Kelly, like the other boat commanders, had them repaint their entire vessel using dark green camouflage paint. The sailors followed orders, using mops and brushes to spread the thick paint.

"Why are we using this? I know there's some grey paint left."

"Lieutenant said to."

"Why'd he say to?"

"Don't know. Don't care. Keep painting."

The spare engines that originally arrived at Cavite with the six boats were all lost when the Navy Yard was bombed. The engines, three on each boat, were now many hours past scheduled replacement, and the motor macs were caring for them the way nurses hover over newborn babies. Innovation substituted for replacement parts. Gaskets that previously had been scraped off, discarded, and replaced were carefully removed, handled as gently as precious lace , and laid back in place when the components were reassembled.

Their problems were not only worn-out engines. When Charles first rode the deck of PT-35 from Mariveles to Corregidor, he thought the PT boat simple in construction. After joining RON 3, he quickly learned the reality that there were pumps, switches, bearings, plumbing, electrical cabling and circuits, radios, and running gear to maintain, not to mention management of the torpedoes, guns, and ammunition. The same pounding waves the crew absorbed with flexed knees strained the boat's joints, leading to cracks and leaks. Only through continual inspecting and repairing could they maintain a literally tight ship.

While others finished painting, Charles and Jessie Clark stripped, cleaned, and reassembled the .50 caliber machine guns. "Doc," Jessie said, "my old instructor told me it wouldn't be my fault if a bad round caused my gun to jam—but it would be my fault if the gun malfunctioned because I left it poorly adjusted or failed to keep it clean."

"Yep, I was told the same thing. What about these barrels, Jessie? We have six replacements and these are pretty worn."

"Let's swap out all four. No reason to hold 'em back. We'll soon be out of ammunition, avgas, and everything else anyway."

Kelly returned from one of his frequent meetings with Bulkeley and called for his crew's attention. "Before tomorrow morning clean yourselves up as best you can. We have an awards ceremony to attend."

Martino, the torpedoman, couldn't resist speaking up. "Sir, that's no simple matter. I'm down to only one complete uniform, and the threads on it are barely holding. I've got stains on my stains with no way to wash 'em out—and I'm not the only one."

"That's right, sir," Reynolds agreed. "The one razor blade we enlisted men are sharing is so dull it's not sure where my beard stops and my skin starts. Most of us are following Lieutenant Bulkeley's lead and just letting our hair and beards grow."

Lieutenant Bulkeley had indeed set the standard. His beard was the bushiest and longest in the squadron, and the matched .45 caliber pistols Bulkeley carried on each hip contributed a dramatic touch. In addition, his eyes were perpetually bloodshot from lost sleep due to night missions and daytime meetings or briefings. Bulkeley was not entirely displeased that his appearance was more pirate than squadron commander—or that at Navy headquarters on Corregidor they referred to him as "Wild Man Bulkeley."

"I know we're all getting a bit ragged," Kelly nodded. "But do the best you can."

The next afternoon, Sunday, 1 March, all four boats of MTB 3 motored from Sisiman Cove across the North Channel and tied up at Corregidor's North Dock. The Army's last four flyable P-40s circled overhead. At 1700 the crews were shocked to see General MacArthur, several members of his staff, and the general's wife, Jean, arrive at the dock. Crews from the other boats watched the general's group board PT-41. A few minutes later, Bulkeley, with Cox at the helm, roared off into the channel.

"Admiral Rockwell isn't here. These are only MacArthur's Army people. What's going on?" Clark asked Charles, quietly enough as to not draw the attention of Kelly and Richardson, who also watched Bulkeley's boat circling to the bay.

"Beats me," Charles replied. "I feel like a mushroom."

"Kept in the dark?"

"I don't know what's happening, but I can smell the manure they're feeding me."

PT-41 took the general's party only a thousand yards east of the North Dock before circling back and returning. While the crewmen of MTB 3 stood at attention, General MacArthur presented Lieutenant Bulkeley with the Distinguished Service Cross (DSC) for his actions in the Philippines to date. He specifically mentioned the actions in Binanga Bay on 18 January and in Subic Bay on 24 January.

Still wearing his aviator's sunglasses in the twilight, the general addressed the squadron.

"You have carried the fight to the Japanese as true warriors. Your actions have given heart to myself and to every American and Filipino on these islands who today holds the Japanese at bay while our combined Allied forces gather to attack, repel, and defeat them on land and at sea. We are all eternally grateful for your courage and strength. Remain ready and alert, we are depending on you."

MacArthur's staff gave a pack of American cigarettes to every man in the squadron. Then the general and his staff disappeared from the dock.

"What the hell was that all about?" Hunter, the burly senior machinist on PT-34, had the temerity to ask Richardson before climbing down to his engine room.

"I'm really not sure," Richardson ignored Hunter's profanity and the missing "sir." Ensign Richardson was not an original member of the squadron, having joined MTB 3 in December. He tended to be less aloof from the enlisted crewmen than Kelly and Bulkeley, and he was seldom offended by such bold inquiries. "That was definitely the strangest awards ceremony I've ever seen."

꙳ ꙳ ꙳

Charles shared Nat Floyd's information about the China run with Balog, Johnson, and Clark, receiving their promise to keep it confidential. Within hours the rumor spread through the squadron and was now accepted fact. The crew began to interpret every order and instruction from Bulkeley and Kelly in that light.

In early March, Carpenter's Mate Joseph "Chips" Boudolf oversaw the reinforcement of the aft deck of all four PT boats. His instructions were to "make the decks strong enough to carry three and a half tons in rough seas."

Machinist's Mate Hunter did the calculations and then announced with a wink, "That's equivalent to the weight of about 1,200 gallons of avgas, enough to get us to the China coast."

Bulkeley had RON 3 load their last sixteen torpedoes into the four PT boats' firing tubes. The crew assumed this was a good sign, further confirming the rumored breakout for China.

On 5 March, one by one, the four boats visited the fuel barge, PT-34 last. The usual practice was to pump avgas from the barrels directly into the fuel tanks and depart. This day was different. After topping up with avgas and oil, and with Kelly and Richardson supervising, the PT-34 crew manhandled twenty barrels of fuel onto the boat's deck. They were fitted into a 7-6-7 pattern from stern to midship.

"That's all twenty. Eleven hundred gallons." Hunter reported to Kelly. "Should we tie them down?"

"Not yet," Kelly replied. "I think we're riding too low at the stern. See if there is enough room to crowd them from forward to aft in a 6-5-6-3 pattern." After the rearrangement, Kelly walked his boat, stopping at points to sense how she sat in the water. "OK, that's better. Lash them down tightly, and we'll test her ride on the way back to base."

With eighty barrels of avgas transferred to the boats, only a hundred or so barrels remained on the fuel barge. Based on RON 3's past use, that was only enough to last a few weeks. Once that was gone, the squadron would be useless, nothing but floating lumber.

Back at Sisiman, PT-34 tied up at the pier and shut down her engines. Kelly disappeared to a short boat commanders' meeting with Bulkeley and returned with surprise orders. "Don't ask why—but we now have to unload all this gas. We're moving it to shore and storing it all under camouflage."

Rolling twenty heavy barrels from the boat, down the pier, up the sandy beach, and into the trees was a hot and nearly impossible task. Protest was muted. Complaining would not change anything. It was not the first time, nor would it be the last, that orders made no sense.

"Why did we just do that?" Martino was dripping sweat and panting after he, Charles, and Hunter rolled the last barrel up the beach. "If we need to use this gasoline, now we'll just have to take these back out on the dock. If we'd left them on the fuel barge, we could just pump it directly without moving the barrels."

"My old PBY squadron set up aviation fuel caches like this at various coves all around the islands. If some of our seaplanes fly back in later, maybe they can use this to refuel."

Hunter disagreed. "This stuff is scarce. I think Bulkeley's hiding it for a special purpose—probably for getting us to China."

"A logical assumption," Charles agreed. *Thank God I haven't run into that reporter again. On the other hand, I really don't know any more now than I did before.*

The sailors of MTB 3 expected departure on the now all-but-certain breakout at any moment. Speculation increased when Reynolds and the other boat cooks were told to load enough stores to feed a full crew for four days.

"Think this means we're taking the whole squadron, Pappy?" Charles asked.

"I assume we'll take everyone who wants to go—we've sure got enough food, and there's plenty of room."

On Tuesday, 10 March, a sequence of unanticipated events brought their assumptions into question.

Storekeeper 1st Class Morey was moved from the Navy's paymaster team in the tunnel to the *Trabajador*, now commanded by Lieutenant Edward DeLong and crewed by ten men from MTB 3. Further confusing the sailors, the *Trabajador* itself was transferred to the Inshore Patrol, removing the boat and its crew from MTB 3. Six other men of MTB 3 were transferred to the section base at Mariveles. In addition to these departures from the squadron, three men were still missing from PT-31, and Ensign Chandler was still in the hospital on Corregidor, recuperating from his ankle and foot wounds.

Charles and John both remained with the now smaller MTB 3.

One of the transfers out of the squadron was PT-34's mess attendant, a Filipino named Grimes. Everyone liked him for his cheerful demeanor and good food. He and Charles had spent hours together, Grimes helping Charles practice Tagalog, and Charles doing his best to improve Grimes's English.

After preparing breakfast for the crew, Grimes approached Charles. "*Kailangan kong makipag-usap sa iyo.*" Grimes wanted to talk with him.

Charles paused a second to shift into Tagalog. "*Tungkol saan*? About what?"

"I am leaving you. The US Navy has assigned me to Mariveles. I leave right now."

"*Bakit*? Why?"

"They say I am too old. I say I am healthy, and the men like my food. Then they say things will get harder, and I am transferred."

Charles worked out a halting, flawed response. "*Ikinalulungkot ko, kaibigan. Paalam.* I am sorry, friend." Grimes waved a final goodbye from the west dock while waiting for a ride to Corregidor on the water barge. *Damn! I'll probably never see him again. There are too many changes, all coming too quickly. Something is about to happen.*

"Come on," Charles tapped Jessie's shoulder. "Let's go grab Balog and see what we can find out." Assigned to PT-41, Bulkeley's boat, Balog often overheard, and sometimes shared, high-quality information about squadron matters.

"What do you think?" Charles asked when the three of them were alone. "If we were to leave right now, by my count, twenty-one men from MTB 3 are going to be left behind. That wouldn't be right."

Balog agreed. "I don't know what's going on, except it's super-secret. Bulkeley and Kelly stop talking when anyone comes close. Whatever it is, I can't believe Bulkeley would voluntarily leave anyone from the squadron behind."

"Then what the hell's going on?" Jessie looked at his companions.

"Something big, really big." Charles offered. "We stashed all those barrels of avgas for some purpose. All four boats are set for action, full of torpedoes, ammunition, and food. John, do you think you can find out anything?"

"I'll try, but don't hold your breath. I do know that the motor macs all got together and decided that with an extra twenty barrels of gasoline per boat, the squadron could reach China even if there were fifty people on each boat. If that's the case, it makes no sense to leave with only basic crews on board." John looked at Charles. "You saved me from having to go find you. Bulkeley left instructions for you and me."

"And—?" Charles prompted.

"We're to split up all the medical supplies and drugs equally and pack them into two bags, one for each of us. You're to leave your bag aboard PT-34, and I'm to keep mine on the 41."

"When? Today?"

"Yes. That's all he said, and, no, he wouldn't tell me a thing more than that. I agree with you, though. Whatever's going to happen, it's close."

Tuesday, 11 March, Lieutenant Brantingham, who had skippered the PT-33 before her loss, came aboard PT-34 and informed Ensign Richardson that Bulkeley had just assigned him to the boat. This made PT-34 once again the only crew that included three officers.

Kelly returned around 1100 hours with new orders after yet another meeting with Bulkeley. "OK, boys, it could be a late night. I'm moving my stuff into the forward enlisted compartment. Brant, you and Iliff do the same. Everyone else pack anything from your bunks in your sea bag. We have a couple of free hours. Take care of anything you need to do now." He then added without explanation, "You won't have time later."

He looked at Charles, "Doc, have your medical stuff aboard?"

"Yes, sir," Charles nudged his bag with his foot.

"Stow it in the chart house where it won't get soaked, but where it's accessible."

After all the rumors, personnel shifts, and days of waiting, the crews were thankful that something, whatever that something might be, was finally about to happen.

At 1300, PT-34 motored to the fuel barge and topped off her tanks with avgas, even though they were already nearly full. They returned to the cove, and, while cursing the afternoon heat, rolled back out their twenty barrels of aviation gasoline.

Two hours later the barrels were lashed down in the 6-5-6-3 pattern approved earlier by Kelly.

Other boats followed suit.

At 1630, PT-41 led the other three boats to the water pier and each boat filled its freshwater tanks.

Ross, PT-34's quartermaster, looked around and then at Richardson. "Sir, this is weird. The water barge is here, but I don't see the crew anywhere. The cove is deserted. Even the Filipino Q-boats are gone. Where is everyone?"

"Must've gone to supper." Richardson looked away as he spoke. "Cap those tanks, and let's get back to our dock."

At Bulkeley's "suggestion," everyone took a soap shower, before dining as a group at the onshore mess tent.

Back on their boats at 1730, several men took the opportunity to smoke, Charles included. *After all, doctors insist smoking is a means of reducing stress, assisting digestion, and maintaining alertness—even the Surgeon General says so. I can buy a pack for almost nothing at base exchanges. At military hospitals cigarettes are free for patients and staff. Coffee and cigarettes. That's how the Navy keeps moving.*

Kelly walked to the bow of PT-34 and scanned the bay.

Looks like Kelly's saying goodbye to this place. Maybe I should too.

At 1830, PT-41 and 32 cast off and quietly motored out of Sisiman Cove. PT-34 and PT-35 remained at the water dock. Richardson did a last-minute inspection of the boat and reported to Brantingham and Kelly, "All watertight doors closed and ready for getting underway."

Charles and Jessie removed and stored the weather covers from their guns and crawled into the turrets. Long belts of .50 caliber ammunition were readied. It was the best of their remaining ammunition: all armor-piercing bullets, with a tracer inserted every fifth round.

From his elevated position at the starboard turret, Charles watched a man in civilian clothes appear at the base of the water dock and walk towards the boat. The man was wordlessly greeted by Lieutenant Kelly and quickly taken below. Kelly returned to deck scowling silently at the crewmen with a look clearly saying, "Don't you dare ask!" No one said a word.

Charles didn't need to ask who the civilian was. *Nat Floyd! That son of a bitch, he did it! He must be one silver-tongued devil. When we get there, wherever 'there' is, I want to hear his whole story.*

Everyone, except for the reporter, waited topside, sweating in the oilskins they'd been told to put on. Jessie leaned over towards Charles, "You know what this means?" He flapped his oilskin collar.

"What?"

"It means we're leaving the bay for open ocean."

After dark, around 1900 hours, the Admiral's Barge, used by Admiral Rockwell since Admiral Hart's departure, entered Sisiman Cove and approached

PT-34. Men dropped fenders over the side, and the barge tied fast to the PT boat. A cloth bag was passed across to Kelly, who handed it to Richardson, instructing, "Stow this in the cockpit." A Navy officer emerged from the barge, stepped across to the PT boat, and was silently welcomed aboard PT-34 by Lieutenant Kelly.

The crewmen who recognized their visitor were aghast. *That's Admiral Rockwell, Commandant, Sixteenth Naval District!*

Following Rockwell, three more officers, these from MacArthur's Army staff, were welcomed by Kelly: Brigadier General Richard Marshall, Colonel Charles Stivers, and Captain Joseph McMicking, a Filipino.

The barge then moved to PT-35 and quietly transferred three senior Army officers and a master sergeant to that boat. After disgorging its high-profile passengers, the barge departed Sisiman Cove as quietly as it had arrived.

Rockwell himself is standing right under me in the cockpit, and some of those who went below are probably members of MacArthur's staff. Does this mean that Lieutenant Bulkeley left to pick up the General himself? Are we taking the entire United States command to China with us? Is this why we are leaving so many men from MTB 3 behind? What in HELL is going on here??

Charles caught Jessie's attention in the opposite gun turret and gave him a questioning stare.

Jessie just shook his head and shrugged.

37

Departure

North Channel, between Corregidor and Bataan Peninsula, Philippine Islands

11 March 1942

At 1940 hours the sun was only a faint orange glow behind the hills west of Sisiman Cove. In a half hour there would be only starlight. A sliver of moon would not rise until after midnight.

"Status?" Kelly looked at Richardson.

"Sir, all watertight doors are closed, and she's ready for getting underway," Richardson repeated again the report he had given Lieutenant Kelly before the passengers arrived.

"Start our engines."

With all three engines idling smoothly, Kelly turned to Brantingham. "Cast off now, Lieutenant. I need to address the crew before we leave the cove."

Maintaining barely enough speed for steerage, Lieutenant Brantingham kept the bow pointed at the entrance to the cove. PT-35 followed thirty yards behind. Ensign Richardson stood with the rest of the crew on deck.

Kelly looked at all the faces, one by one, as if taking a mental roll call. Admiral Rockwell stood at his side but said nothing. He was letting this be Kelly's show. For now.

"Listen up," Kelly began. "The mission we are about to undertake is not the rumor you've been hearing. We're not going to China." The crewmen exchanged glances until Kelly continued, "That said, the next days will be long, hard, and dangerous. The fact that Admiral Rockwell is standing here should be convincing evidence of the importance of this undertaking. This mission has been carefully planned, and although I am confident in the outcome, I cannot guarantee our success. Backup plans are in place for completing this mission if we ourselves, MTB 3, fall short. I know I'm being vague and maybe confusing. I'm saying this is a volunteer mission. If there is one or more of you who wants to stay here, come forward and I will deposit you on shore. You will be kept in confinement for two weeks, then released without prejudice."

There were no raised hands; no one was about to stay on Bataan when there was a way to leave, even if it carried substantial risk. Kelly continued. "Hunter, I suspect we have a stowaway. Would you go check the lazaret, and if someone's in there, bring him up."

"Yes, sir" Hunter disappeared below and reappeared a few seconds later with a grinning Nat Floyd.

"Mr. Floyd," Kelly announced without anger or surprise, "is a reporter for *The New York Times*. We are at sea. We could throw him overboard, but I doubt he can swim. I have no choice but to take him with us." Smiles broke out all around. Floyd's presence was obviously pre-planned, or Kelly would have never let him on the boat. He continued with a wry grin, "The offer to stay behind does not include you, Mr. Floyd. If you try to leave this boat, I'll have to shoot you."

Kelly continued, "We've been honored with a critical mission, perhaps the most important of the war. We are providing transportation for critically important passengers to the southern island of Mindanao, where further transportation awaits them. Can I tell them, Admiral? We've cast off."

Rockwell nodded and shrugged as if to say, "Why not?"

Kelly continued, "You've seen the passengers we have on 34 and 35. If you haven't already figured out who's on 41 with Bulkeley, you're slower than I thought. Shoe of course has his own complement of brass on the 32."

Ross had been doing rough mental calculations and spoke up, "Mindanao, sir? That's what, 700 miles away?"

"Not quite. Yes, our engines are long past due replacement, and ours is the only boat that didn't get its hull cleaned, so it's hard to guess our exact range and speed. With these twenty barrels on board, we should do it with a hundred gallons or so to spare. It's not the most comfortable of margins, but it will have to be enough."

Richardson leaned to Brantingham with a quiet question. Brantingham turned and asked Kelly, who nodded and resumed speaking. "I'm letting you know up front that our boat will be the 'minesweeper', looking for stray floating mines as we pass through the minefields to open water. Once out, we'll travel in 'ball diamond' formation with PT-41 leading at second base. We will be in back at home plate. The 32 will be at first base and the 35 at third base. With four torpedoes and a thousand gallons of gas on deck, we'll do well to make thirty knots."

"Weather, sir?" asked Harris.

"High seas are forecast, so it might be difficult to keep formation. Also, clogged fuel filters or some other unforeseen mechanical problem could result in a boat dropping from formation. If that happens, the remaining boats will not stop, but will continue on. We've agreed on an 0700 rendezvous location in the Cuyo Island group, about 250 miles south of here. After arriving there tomorrow, we'll transfer gasoline from the barrels to the main tank and do whatever maintenance the boats require. Hopefully, we can get a few hours sleep during the day. From there we'll make our final run to Mindanao tomorrow night and arrive Friday morning. Questions?"

"So, sir, China's no longer in the plan?" a sailor asked.

"I'm sorry, but no. If it makes you feel any better, Bulkeley did have a plan for the entire squadron to make a run for the Chinese coast. When the directive for tonight came through, it was easier to maintain secrecy of our new plans by letting the original rumor run."

Charles considered the startling news. *OK, I'm not going to China. I'm a little disappointed, but maybe this is better. This small squadron is transporting the mythically famous General Douglas MacArthur and his staff through enemy waters, all the way to Mindanao. I'm amazed to be two feet from Admiral Rockwell. What in the world must John Balog be thinking if he's standing next to Douglas MacArthur?* A realization struck him. *Now I know why those twenty-one crewmen were transferred out of RON 3. Damn it! We're leaving them all here on Bataan.*

"Admiral. Do you wish to say anything?" Kelly asked.

Rockwell looked around. "This is my first cruise on a PT boat. Impress me."

"One more thing," Kelly turned back to the crew. "The Japanese control all Philippine waters. Everyone will remain ready at your action stations through the night until we reach the Cuyos in the morning. We'll tuck in during daylight to avoid any Japanese planes. On the other hand, if we are spotted by a Japanese warship—I don't care if it's a heavy cruiser with three escorts—we, PT-34, have the privilege of attacking and sinking it while the other boats evade and escape." He gave Rockwell a side glance. "Our primary duty, above all and at any cost, is to see that Bulkeley in PT-41 delivers his passengers to Mindanao."

He gave them a moment for that to sink in. "Assume General Quarters. Expect to remain so through the night."

Kelly turned deferentially to Rockwell. "We have your bag below on my bunk. Would you like to get some rest?"

"Lieutenant, you command PT-34. That given, this is a Navy mission. Do you really expect me to be anywhere but on the bridge?"

❧ ❧ ❧

The four PT boats rendezvoused west of the turning buoy at 2000. The buoys marking the entrance to the safe channel through the minefields could barely be seen in the moonless dark. For a few minutes, the boats floated expectantly. Suddenly a steady volley of artillery began. "That's our cover, we can leave now," Kelly said to the officers with him on the bridge. "It's the guns on Corregidor drowning out the sound of our engines."

Motoring slowly, PT-34 led the way through the minefield, keeping to the safe channel. To be heard above noise from the three Packard engines, compounded by exhaust noise from the six unmuffled pipes at the boat's transom, the four officers on the bridge spoke loudly. From his position in the starboard turret, Charles stood just behind and a little above the officers on the bridge, hearing almost every word.

Kelly explained to Admiral Rockwell the sequence he and Bulkeley had agreed on to maximize MacArthur's safety. "First, PT-34 leads through the minefields. If there are any loose mines or we get out of the safe channel, we'll find them first, not Bulkeley. Second, as you see on the foredeck, we have two men with long bamboo poles ready to push away any stray mines. The third safety action I thought we'd see by now." Kelly pointed up into the darkness on his port side. "Up there on Battery Point, the No. 1 searchlight of K Battery is supposed to light up the water ahead of us until we're clear—"

From exactly where he had been pointing, a blinding light pierced the darkness. Instead of illuminating the water ahead of PT-34 as planned, it was pointing directly at PT-34 itself. Their PT boat was bathed in such brilliance that any casual observer from the shore could not help but see it making an escape to the sea. Through simple misfortune, or through ineptitude, when the operator switched the powerful searchlight on, it happened to be pointing directly at PT-34.

"Goddamn bastard! Shut off the fucking light!" Kelly cursed through clenched teeth. The searchlight went dark before his words were finished. "That son of a bitch just compromised this whole rescue mission."

Charles was startled by Kelly's explosion. *That's an intense release of anger, even for Kelly. Maybe this really is the most important mission of the war.*

"An inauspicious beginning," Admiral Rockwell quietly agreed, "but only time will tell to what extent it mattered." He then added, "By the way, Lieutenant, I would not let the general or his staff hear you call this a 'rescue' mission. Officially, we are executing a 'breakout maneuver.' MacArthur points out that he has been ordered by the president to leave. He is not being 'rescued,' and it is only with great reluctance that he, and the rest of us for that matter, are leaving while so many others battle valiantly on. What we are engaged in here is a breakout through enemy lines—a breakout that will allow re-establishment of a new command from which to organize and lead a relief force to retake the islands."

"Yes, sir," Kelly responded. "I misspoke. This is definitely a breakout."

38

An Inauspicious Beginning

South China Sea

0100 hours, 12 March 1942

The squadron emerged into the South China Sea, shaken by the mistake with the searchlight. Maneuvering into the diamond formation allowing the four boats to maintain visual contact, PT-41 moved into the lead. No longer a sacrificial minesweeper, PT-34 dropped to the back position. The formation turned and accelerated south. Ocean swells were high, ten feet or more, limiting the heavily loaded boats to around twenty knots. At this speed, it would be impossible for them to make the Cuyos before daylight.

Charles, the designated starboard lookout, searched the ocean. He could barely see faint outlines of land against the stars. *If these swells get any higher, I'll lose the horizon every time we drop down.* His eyes stayed on lookout, but his ears were tuned to the officers conferring in the cockpit. Four Navy officers occupied PT-34's bridge: Rockwell, Kelly, Brantingham, and Richardson. They continued speaking loudly to be heard above the engine noise and waves pounding against the hull.

I presume Jessie, like me, can hear every word they're saying. It's amazing how an enlisted sailor, standing still and silent among officers, will not even be noticed. Stay invisible, listen, and learn.

"Our planned route is to steer due south, far enough off Batangas so we're not spotted or heard." Kelly told Rockwell. "After fifty miles, we turn due west for the Calavite Passage between the small island of Lubang to the north and the larger island of Mindoro to the south."

Rockwell frowned, "That will put us in open ocean for half the night, and it could mean even heavier seas."

"Yes, sir. This route's an end run avoiding the Japanese picket ships between Batangas and Mindoro," Kelly explained. "Bulkeley made that decision even though Japanese destroyers have been spotted somewhere southwest of Mindoro. But as you know, it's a big ocean. We'll keep a sharp lookout."

"And hope for good luck," the Admiral added. "Before we get to the passage, I'd like to see the charts of that area."

"Don't have any, sir."

"No charts? What if we get separated from the formation? What do you have?"

"I have some oil company road maps of the islands." He paused. "We're a coastal unit of small boats, sir. We've never required much in the way of ocean charts. The few we could locate are with Bulkeley."

"Good God, Lieutenant!" Rockwell exclaimed. "Does this mission ride on anything more than a hope and a prayer?"

"Admiral, almost fifty men from the squadron, including myself, are betting our lives on this mission. If anyone can do this, we can."

From the start, PT-34 had difficulty maintaining its place in formation. Bulkeley had originally been told that the departure would take place on "The Ides of March," the 15th. Boats 41, 32, and 35 each had their turn for hull scraping and mechanical repairs in the floating dry dock. When the date was unexpectedly moved up to 11 March, PT-34 lost her chance for the same maintenance. The encrusted, dirty hull increased water resistance, reducing her top speed. The three engines suffered from carbon fouling in the cylinder heads after weeks of running errands at slow speeds. Only after running at full throttle in wet air for several hours would the cylinders be steamed out.

Kelly's separation from PT-41 gradually increased to fifty yards, and then 200 yards.

Admiral Rockwell was unable to remain silent. "Don't you think we're getting a little far apart?"

"We'll close in gradually," Kelly replied.

They did not. In fact, PT-41 finally disappeared from their vision.

"Damn it," the admiral yelled at Kelly. "Close up!"

Charles could see the throttles were wide open already, confirmed by the engine sounds and vibrations through the hull. He watched Brantingham whisper something to Richardson. The ensign nodded and disappeared below. After a couple of minutes Richardson reappeared and gave a subtle nod.

The crew, knowing what had happened, felt the very slight increase in engine RPMs. In the engine room, Chief Machinist's Mate Velt Hunter used a trick to squeeze slightly more speed from the engines. He disconnected the throttle controls from the cockpit, pushed the carburetor levers as far as possible, and then wired them tight in that position. It was not the gentlest treatment of the already overworked engines, but PT-34 increased speed by a couple of knots.

At first, it was hard to discern any change in speed. "We're closing pretty slowly," the Admiral grumbled.

Five minutes later the gap between the two boats abruptly narrowed. Bulkeley had slowed so that Kelly could catch up, but by the time Kelly realized they were overtaking PT-41, it was too late. Belatedly, Richardson carried the message to Hunter to unwire the carburetors and reconnect the throttle cable. PT-34 was now well in the lead, adding to Rockwell's frustration. "Just what the hell is going on, Lieutenant?" the admiral demanded.

When Kelly explained the dirty hull, the condition of his engines, and Hunter's trick with the carburetors, the admiral exclaimed, "My God! I told the general that the Navy, meaning Bulkeley and these PT boats, could pull off this mission. I hope to God that's our last problem."

Charles listened to the exchange between the two officers. *Rockwell sure is unhappy. Maybe he thinks as the second-highest ranking officer on this operation, he should be on PT-41 with MacArthur. Putting him here, on PT-34 with Bulkeley's second-in-command, was a smart distribution of senior force— Bulkeley didn't want all our eggs in one basket. As logical as it seems, it may not have been a good idea. Rockwell is challenging Kelly's command of PT-34.*

ᔓ ᔓ ᔓ

A half hour later, Clark called to the cockpit from his position, pointing to a small light that flickered and then brightened. "It could be a fire, sir."

Richardson agreed. "Someone's lit a fire at the top of a hill on a small island. I think it's Fortune Island, and I'm pretty sure it's Japanese-controlled."

"If they heard us, then the fire is a warning to the mainland," Kelly agreed. "If they think we're anything more than a small supply or fishing boat, they'll probably send out planes at dawn, or even send a destroyer this way."

"How far are we from that island, Kelly?" Rockwell asked.

"About four miles, sir."

"Looks farther than that to me. Take a bow-and-beam bearing."

Kelly paused for a beat. The admiral was giving orders, despite his earlier promise to Kelly that "you command the boat"—and there was little Kelly could do about it. "Aye, aye, sir."

The distance estimate Rockwell requested was ordinarily done using a Pelorus, a simple instrument with two movable sighting vanes. With no Pelorus aboard PT-34, Kelly had only one option. He extended his hand to a point on the island. He sighted along his thumb and forefinger, spread at an approximated 45-degree angle. Knowing they were running around twenty-five knots, when they came abeam of that point, he could calculate their distance from shore, though it would be a very rough estimate.

"Where's your Pelorus?" Admiral Rockwell demanded.

"We don't have one, sir."

"You mean Bulkeley's flagship has the only one?"

"No, sir, he doesn't have one either. Like I said earlier, our missions have all been in the bay or closely offshore. We've never needed more than a basic map and compass to know where we are."

The admiral once more uttered his profanity of choice: "My God!"

At 2200 hours, now heading west, the men on deck heard an engine skip a beat. The passengers may not have noticed, but every crewman on PT-34 tensed. Charles looked at Clark, both of them holding their breath. *Which boat was that?*

The answer came a minute later. The engines on PT-32 sputtered and shut down, leaving the boat bobbing in the ocean.

"It's probably clogged filters. That damn sabotaged gas has struck again," Kelly told the admiral as they watched PT-32 drop behind. "Assuming that's it, they will dismantle, clean, and reassemble the main fuel strainers. It could be a half hour before they can get underway again."

"And if that's not the problem?" Rockwell asked.

"Then it could be longer. Lieutenant Schumacher's a solid man, with a good crew. Still, that particular boat has patches on its patches, so it could be anything."

"There are four generals on that boat, Lieutenant."

"Yes, sir, and I'm sure they're as worried as we all are."

PT Boats 34, 35, and 41 continued crashing across the swells. PT-32 would have to rejoin them in the Cuyos—if it could.

PT-32 dropping out, even temporarily, unsettled Charles. *Only two hours into the mission, and we've already lost a boat. What next?*

The passengers would have been worried too, if they weren't so preoccupied with finding somewhere to throw up. The rolling and pitching of the small boats on the ocean swells quickly threw the Army officers into prolonged, severe bouts of seasickness. They'd have been draped over the rails vomiting, but for the fact that PT boats didn't have railings. Admiral Rockwell, of course, stood in the cockpit unaffected. Navy men don't get seasick. Ever.

He leaned over and asked Kelly a question, who answered by pointing to Charles. The admiral took a step and looked up. "Corpsman, I don't suppose you've got anything to give our passengers?"

Since the first person stepped on a boat or rode on a camel, men had been hunting for a cure for motion sickness. There were a thousand remedies because none of them were effective. Pharmaceutical companies around the world, anticipating massive profits, still searched for an effective drug.

Answering the admiral's question was easy. "No, sir," Charles responded. "Nothing that works. Letting them empty their stomachs is probably the best thing short of a calm sea."

The admiral nodded. It was the answer he expected.

Charles remained at his action and lookout station through the night. He was soaked by saltwater spray splashing onto his face every time the hull hit a succeeding swell. Having put away his glasses after threading the minefield, he squinted into the darkness. Around midnight, his full bladder couldn't wait any longer. Army officers had permanently laid claim to both heads, dry-retching into the toilets, so Charles turned his back to the cockpit, stepped high in the turret, and, with some awkwardness, tried to aim away from the wind. What scattered onto the boat was quickly washed into the sea.

In the early morning hours, the crew and passengers were startled by a sudden quiet. Within a few seconds, not one, but all three engines shut down. Richardson ran below to investigate while the other three officers watched the other boats, PT-35 and 41, disappear into the darkness. In less than a minute, Richardson returned. "Hunter thinks it's nothing but lost gas suction, maybe when we pitched up on that big wave." As Richardson finished reporting, the first engine rumbled to life. A minute later all three engines were running smoothly, and PT-34 again making her best speed. The stop had been brief, but long enough that the other two boats were out of sight and sound.

"I assume you have a plan for this contingency, Lieutenant?" Rockwell asked Brantingham, who was standing closer at that moment.

Kelly answered over Brantingham's shoulder, "Yes, sir. It's an annoyance, but every boat captain has gone over the plans. We will regroup at dawn or as soon thereafter as possible at Tagawayan, one of the Cuyos islands."

"I've seen that island group on a map, Lieutenant. As I recall, it looked like thirty or forty flyspecks. Am I to assume you don't have a detailed map?"

"No, sir, but Bulkeley has one. Before we left, I used it to draw a pencil sketch of Tagawayan."

"And you think you can find it without a chart and without navigation instruments?"

"Yes, sir."

"I'm skeptical, Lieutenant. But it's not about me. It's General MacArthur for whom this mission has to succeed."

"PT-41 will make it, sir. She's been recently overhauled, and her engines have half the hours of the rest of the boats. More importantly, Bulkeley is the best officer in the Navy as far as I'm concerned." Too late, Kelly added, "Present company excepted. Sir."

At dawn, the Cuyo Island group hove into view. Hundreds of small islands lay scattered across the seascape. Some were nothing more than bare rocks jutting from the sea. Others were low islands with pristine cream-colored beaches fringed with palm trees. Several had small coves protected by hills on three sides. Tagawayan Island would be one of these uninhabited flyspecks. It was fifteen miles northeast of Cuyo and about as far off the beaten path as possible without getting lost.

They motored through the Cuyos archipelago in full daylight. Around 0800 Kelly pointed to an island and showed Rockwell his drawing.

"I'm sure that's it."

"Yes, the hills and bays match your sketch almost perfectly. I agree, that must be Tagawayan."

They entered the sheltered cove. It was calm and beautiful, but empty. They left the cove and circled the island. No sign of the other PT boats. They were alone.

"Where are the other boats?" exclaimed Rockwell. "We fell behind and we're late, yet no one else is here. *Where is General MacArthur?*"

39

Complications

Tagawayan Island, Cuyo Island Group, Palawan Province,
Philippine Islands

0837 hours, 12 March 1942

PT-34 dropped anchor in the large cove on the east side of the island, just off the beach. They were one hour and thirty-seven minutes late. Floating motionless in the sheltered cove, the Army passengers slowly regained some degree of appetite. One made his way to the bridge and asked, "Any breakfast available? Perhaps with some coffee?"

"Can't do that yet, sir," Brantingham informed him. "We're about to transfer that fuel in the barrels to our main tank. Reynolds can't use the galley until we finish."

"And we need to get some camouflage cover," Kelly added. "If they heard our engines as we left last night, and that fire we saw makes me think they did, they'll be trying to find us."

Many tasks required attention before the exhausted crew could rest. Kelly assigned refueling and camouflage details and sent two lookouts with semaphore flags to the top of the island's 500-foot hill. Their job was to search the horizon for Japanese warships, as well as the missing PT boats. Charles watched the men depart. *That hilltop must be at least a half-mile hike from the beach. If they do see Japanese ships, Kelly will have the engines running before they finish signaling. We'll be long gone by the time they can get back to the cove.*

I hope they have fishing lines and hooks with them.

Charles started cleaning saltwater residue from his machine guns. Richardson came over and asked, "Doc, you still got that machete?"

"It's not really a machete, but, yes, I've got it."

"I'm going with the shore party to get greenery to cover the boat. We need your—what do you call that big knife?"

"Hospital Corps Knife."

"Yeah, that thing. We need it to cut down palm fronds."

"I know you'll get it back to me, sir." It was the first time Charles had willingly loaned his knife to anyone. But even though Richardson was an officer, he was a good man. He knew his business, trusted the crew, and respected honest reasonable suggestions from enlisted men. These characteristics positioned him as a buffer between the crew's sailors and Lieutenant Kelly.

The detail transferred barrels of avgas to the main tanks, tossing the empty barrels over the side. Two men stripped, jumped into the water, and sank each barrel by filling it with seawater. Floating barrels might easily be seen by Japanese aircraft. With refueling completed and tanks sealed, Kelly gave permission to fire up the galley. Soon everyone was drinking hot coffee and filling empty stomachs with Pappy Reynold's breakfast. His version of canned-salmon omelet made with government-issued powdered milk and dried eggs was a crew favorite. There was little speculation over the missing PT boats. What would be, would be.

Unsurprisingly, the night's pounding had taken a toll on the boat as well as the men. Hunter made and supervised repairs in preparation for another night's pounding. Richardson's camouflage crew completely covered the boat with palm fronds. From a few yards off, PT-34 looked like a low mound of vegetation in the bay.

Brantingham set a two-man watch, fore and aft. Repairs finished, the crew desperately needed sleep, even catnaps, but finding room to stretch out was a problem. Admiral Rockwell had retired to Kelly's bunk, and General Marshall was in the XO's bunk. The other army officers claimed the remaining crew bunks. Wedging themselves into the available clean deck space, the sailors dozed off.

Charles had remained at his station from the time PT-34 left Sisiman Cove until she dropped anchor at Tagawayan. Now, satiated by Reynolds's generous breakfast, and jammed into a sliver of space below deck, he drifted into a light sleep. Gradually, he became aware of a low voice whispering his name. It was Reynolds, poking his head down through an open hatch.

"Hey, Doc!" he whispered, "Want to see something interesting?"

"What, damnit?" Charles whispered back. "I really need some sleep."

"Just come look, but be quiet."

Charles stepped up and stuck his head and shoulders out of the hatch. Kelly and Richardson were prone on the deck, Reynolds next to them. He pointed to the mouth of the cove.

Whoa, that's a lot more than just 'interesting.'

Only a few hundred yards offshore, three Japanese destroyers steamed south at high speed with smoke pouring from their stacks. *Those guys aren't pleasure-cruising, they're steaming full ahead toward something over the horizon. I hope it's not one of our boats—*

The lookouts on the hill had indeed spotted the ships and signaled Kelly that enemy ships rapidly approached the island, but were coming on so fast there was little time for PT-34 to escape.

Kelly immediately sent back, "Where is 41?"

The lookout immediately responded, "Unknown."

Kelly had orders to launch a diversionary, even if suicidal, attack if it was necessary so that PT-41 and Douglas MacArthur might escape. Since PT-41 was nowhere near, it was pointless for Kelly to now attack the Japanese group. They hid in place.

Charles held his breath. The minutes ticked by as the enemy armada, one by one, passed the entrance to the cove. If only a single Japanese lookout pointed out a suspicious structure in the cove, their guns could pulverize PT-34—and her passengers and crew—without even slowing down.

Finally, the last Japanese vessel steamed out of view. The camouflage had worked. The men crouching on deck breathed in relief.

Well, that's the way things work out. Charles dropped back through the hatch, wedged back into his resting spot and tried to go back to sleep.

At 1500, the lookouts on the hill began signaling. This time it was the message they'd all been waiting for, "Friendly craft, closing our position."

Minutes later PT-41 rounded the island and cruised into the cove. Bulkeley pulled abeam of Kelly's boat, and they lashed together. Breaking protocol,

Admiral Tojo, PT-41's mascot monkey, leaped to PT-34 in search of food, not bothering to wait for an invitation or permission.

General Douglas MacArthur stepped up to the deck of PT-41 and stood next to Lieutenant John Bulkeley. "Wow," Charles whispered to Clark, "I know he's sixty-two years old, but he looks closer to eighty."

"Probably had a bad night—I bet he was as seasick as the other soldiers."

Admiral Tojo notwithstanding, even on this remote speck in the ocean Navy etiquette remained in force. Admiral Rockwell asked permission and was invited to board PT-41. The three officers, MacArthur, Rockwell, and Bulkeley, moved down to the chart house, dropped their voices, and began a private discussion.

Charles watched, disappointed he couldn't hear these most senior of military officers. *There must be interesting personal dynamics flowing back and forth over there. Technically, MacArthur's the senior officer. On the other hand, this is a Navy mission carried out under Rockwell's command. But Bulkeley's the squadron commander with the responsibility for successfully executing the mission.*

John Balog, topside on PT-41, caught Charles's eye and pointed aft. Both corpsmen walked to the stern of their respective boats and sat on the torpedo tubes. There, only a few feet from each other, they conversed with almost as much privacy as the three officers in the chart house.

"Glad to find you here, Charlie! We all wanted to cheer when we saw you guys anchored in the bay. We were just hoping the others would be here with you."

"We've had no sign of the 32 or 35. In fact, you're the first PT boat we've seen since we sucked air into the fuel line around 0400 hours this morning. Where've you guys been?"

"Bit of an unfortunate story, and I'm sure it's part of the discussion going on up there." Balog glanced toward the cockpit where the three grim-looking officers were still talking. "When 32 fell out last night, it was more than dirty gas. Their center shaft strut came loose, causing the engine to vibrate, and that eventually separated the main fuel line. They had to try to catch us with only the two wing engines. On top of that, the repairs made after that fuel explosion in January didn't hold up in last night's pounding. Seams opened up all over the place—it's been a constant bailing effort for them to keep the aft compartments from flooding."

"Can they make it through another night?"

"They're not even going to try."

Balog held up his hand to stop Charles from interrupting. "This is the really unfortunate bit. Somehow during the night Schumacher got ahead of us. Around 0530 we spotted a PT boat ahead. Bulkeley added a touch of speed and made for it—it was the 32 boat all right." He glanced forward toward the cockpit.

"But Schumacher thought we were a destroyer—I guess with those barrels of gas on deck our outline could have looked like the superstructure of a Jap ship. Shoe had his crew push their barrels of avgas overboard, hoping that would give them enough speed to escape. By the time they realized who we were, they had already rolled off a dozen barrels."

"So, they don't have enough gasoline to make it to Mindanao? We already transferred all our gas to the tanks and sank the barrels, so it's a little late to share."

"I overhead discussions about their trying to make Iloilo, but one of the generals said if it's not already overrun by Japs, it would be in the next day or two."

"Why didn't they just retrieve the gasoline?"

"The fuel barrels floated, of course, and they did try. The barrels were just too heavy and slippery. After almost an hour they hadn't managed to heft a single barrel back on board. Bulkeley called it off. We sank the barrels with the .30 caliber and took off."

"Where is the 32 now?"

"We took on their four generals and Bulkeley sent Shoe ahead, maybe he was using the 32 boat as a decoy. Whatever the reason for doing that, we haven't seen them since. Soon we were running in daylight and expecting a Japanese plane to appear any minute. Around 0700 we anchored at Pamalican Island. Beaches straight out of Hollywood—no real cove, but shallow water extended 360 degrees. Bulkeley thought that would keep Japanese destroyers away."

"Well, they might have stayed away from you, but a destroyer group passed close by here just a few hours ago. Didn't spot us, obviously. Go on."

"Bulkeley was antsy all day. Hoping all three boats had made Tagawayan, he wanted to get here before you left. We hadn't seen any planes all day, so I guess he thought leaving in daylight was worth the risk."

"What's the plan? Are we going to wait here for Shoe and the 32?"

"I think that's probably one of the questions they're discussing in the chart house right now."

Charles looked forward as three Army generals stepped across from PT-41 onto PT-34. "Are those some of the brass from PT-32?"

"Yep. Looks like they're yours now."

"If tonight's like last night, our toilets are going to be in high demand. By the way, John. I understand that we're headed to Mindanao so this bunch can catch a plane. Is that true?"

"Far as I know."

"And then what? What happens with the squadron?"

"Beats the hell out of me. We still have four torpedoes on every boat and a fair amount of ammunition. Maybe there's more fuel on Mindanao. I'm sure it'll involve something more than sitting on the beach with a pretty girl and a glass of rum."

Charles's reply was interrupted by a shout from Ross. The three newly arrived generals were standing expectantly next to Albert Ross, PT-34's quartermaster, while Ross yelled down through the hatch. "Reynolds! We got three hungry generals here who missed supper—how's about bringing up three rations?"

The reply was loud and clear. "Tell 'em to come down and get it before I throw the goddamned stuff overboard." Reynolds was well-liked by everyone. He talked bluntly, and he was king of the galley. Limited to monotonous ingredients consisting mostly of canned salmon, a few cans of fruit, dried eggs, and powdered milk, the meals from his domain were nevertheless hot and tasty. Taking advantage of the occasional availability of fresh meat or fish, he prepared healthy meals of surprising variation.

Charles and John, along with the other enlisted men, chuckled at his brash response to the generals. "Charles," Balog said, "This may be the only time in this war where an enlisted man tells not one, but *three* general officers to go to hell."

"And he's getting away with it—look at those generals laughing as they head down to the galley!"

🐬 🐬 🐬

The deep-throated sound of big engines turned everyone's attention to the lagoon entrance.

PT-32 motored into the bay and joined the flotilla. Three boats. Three-fourths of the squadron and passengers were safe and accounted for. *Perhaps PT-35 will appear any minute.*

After PT-32 tied to the flotilla, Kelly, Cox, and Schumacher joined MacArthur, Rockwell, and Bulkeley on the crowded bridge of PT-41. After about five minutes, a decision made, Kelly and Schumacher returned to their boats.

"Signal the men down from the hill, and toss the greenery overboard," Kelly said before sharing MacArthur's and Rockwell's decision. "As part of the backup plan, a submarine is scheduled to arrive here in the morning. MacArthur, Rockwell, and Bulkeley discussed having us hold up here overnight and leave it to the sub to finish the mission. Instead, they decided to continue on tonight. The weather's supposed to improve, and the sub would take four days to get to Mindanao, assuming it makes it here in the first place. We're getting the hell out of here. Right now."

"Even though it won't be dark for a couple of hours?" Brantingham asked.

"It was Bulkeley's decision. We'll have to run in daylight for a couple of hours either now or in the morning. The consensus was that it's better to do that today, out here in the middle of nowhere, than tomorrow near Mindanao where we're more likely to encounter Japanese ships or planes."

"What about the 32?" Richardson voiced the concern on everyone's mind.

"She's going to wait for the submarine. If they show up, Schumacher can pass on the status of the mission."

"And then?"

"I overhead something about the 32 probably having enough gas to reach Iloilo for repairs. I'm sure Bulkeley told Schumacher what to do after the sub leaves."

That was not a satisfactory answer. The men felt they were abandoning those on PT-32 to an unknown, dubious fate.

The sentries returned from the hilltop and inhaled the meal Reynolds was holding for them. At 1745 hours PT-34 and 41 cranked up their engines. Bulkeley yelled "Good luck!" to Schumacher in the 32 as they pulled away.

Charles crawled into the starboard turret and checked his guns. As PT-34 passed out of the lagoon, he looked back at a forlorn PT-32 bobbing gently in the departing wake of the other two boats.

Good luck, guys.

40

A Bad Night

South of the Cuyo Island Group, Palawan Province, Philippine Islands

1800 hours, 12 March 1942

Overheard discussions suggested that MacArthur's decision to remain on the boats instead of waiting for the submarine was made in part on a weather prediction. Bulkeley and Rockwell had assured the General that this night's trip would likely be smoother than the previous one. That prediction proved overly optimistic. The trip from Tagawayan to Mindanao began badly—and then got much worse.

Leaving the lagoon, the tiny flotilla immediately encountered ten-foot swells. A westerly wind sprang up, adding a rolling motion to the boats' constant pitching. Conditions were barely tolerable above deck due to the continuous saltwater spray. After taking on the three additional officers, PT-34's passenger manifest now included an admiral, four generals, a colonel, and a captain. All but the admiral immediately, again, fell victim to severe seasickness.

Charles thought about the surprising frailty in MacArthur's appearance that afternoon. *The General isn't a young man, and it looks like he's already suffered greatly on that first leg of the trip. I can't imagine he'll do better tonight.*

Bulkeley had the same thoughts. Attempting to minimize General MacArthur's discomfort, Bulkeley told Kelly to take lead. Keeping PT-41 in PT-34's wake would, perhaps, smooth the ride a bit for PT-41.

Kelly, Brantingham, and Richardson took their normal stations. Rockwell again took his post close to Kelly, unwilling to relinquish the bridge.

It's obvious Rockwell doesn't see himself as a 'desk jockey' admiral. From the time we departed Sisiman Cove until we arrived at Tagawayan, Rockwell only left the cockpit for a brief trip to the head. The whole time he was questioning Kelly about our location, navigation, fuel status, and contingency plans. A couple of times he even gave direct orders to Brantingham or Richardson, bypassing Kelly. It's more than tradition that gives the captain of any boat or ship absolute command of his craft and crew when at sea. Kelly must be smoldering over Rockwell's intrusions on that authority.

"Lieutenant, veer a little west," Rockwell said. "If there are Japanese ships out here, they'll probably patrol the shipping lanes. Let's avoid them."

It was a reasonable thing to do, and Kelly could not object. "Yes, sir," he responded and passed the order to Richardson at the wheel. Though irritated that Rockwell's statement was clearly an order, not a suggestion, Kelly could do little about it.

Charles shifted his weight from foot to foot in his turret, preparing for another long night. He and Clark were again the designated starboard and port lookouts. Rain gear gave only partial protection. Both men continually squinted and wiped the stinging salt spray from their already tired eyes. Tonight wind blew spray from the port stern. Charles kept his back to the wind with his oilskin hood pulled far forward. *As long as the wind doesn't shift, I might be able to keep my glasses on tonight.*

Less than thirty minutes out of Tagawayan, still running in full daylight, Charles thought he saw something—a dot—break the horizon when PT-34 topped a swell. He stared at the spot waiting for the next swell. *There it is again … and again!* The spot was definitely a vessel, its superstructure appearing and disappearing with each rise and fall of PT-34 on the water.

"Ship sighted!" Charles yelled down to the cockpit. "Starboard bow!"

Kelly was momentarily below deck, making the XO, Lieutenant Henry J. Brantingham, officer of the deck. Brantingham scanned with the binoculars. "It's a vessel—not sure what kind," he agreed and yielded the binoculars to Admiral Rockwell's outstretched hand.

"Maybe," Rockwell demurred and handed the glasses on to Ensign Richardson. "What do you think?"

Richardson held the binoculars to his eyes as the boat crested three consecutive swells. Finally, he said, "Yes sir. It's long. It's low and grey. It's probably a destroyer."

After another swell, "It's definitely a destroyer, sir, and not one of ours."

Brantingham mentally calculated the relative headings and speeds of the PT boat and destroyer, "It'll be a close intersect if we stay on this course."

"Come hard right," Rockwell ordered.

Wow, Charles thought while keeping his eyes on the distant ship. *The admiral didn't even consult Brantingham. With Kelly off the bridge, he's taken over as boat captain.*

Kelly, down below, felt the sharp turn. Negotiating hatches and stairs at record speed he returned to the bridge. He made out with bare eyes the Japanese warship. PT-34, with PT-41 following in her wake, raced west. Shed of the twenty barrels of extra gasoline on deck, the boats traveled almost five knots faster than when they first left Corregidor.

Rockwell took back the binoculars. "She's holding course—must not have seen us," he noted.

"We're small enough to be lost between the swells and the spindrift," Kelly said.

"It feels like we're running away," Richardson complained as he watched the Japanese destroyer disappear below the horizon.

Kelly shot back, "My mission is to get our passengers to Mindanao, not sink a destroyer."

The admiral quickly corrected Kelly, "It's our mission, Lieutenant Kelly. *Our* mission. This breakout is perhaps the most critical event of the Pacific war to this point." Rockwell stood tall on the bridge of his small flagship, disregarding the saltwater streaming down his face.

🦢 🦢 🦢

Wind and seas worsened. Swells surpassed fifteen feet. Seasoned crew members' flexed knees absorbed the pounding, rolling, and pitching deck. The prostrate, seasick Army officers threw up Reynolds' afternoon meal. Some claimed their space in the head. An Army general, hanging on to keep from being tossed into the sea, vomited on the rainswept deck in misery. Clark leaned out of his turret, motioning Charles to lean closer. "Too bad he's got such a weak stomach."

"You're wrong about that," Charles said with a grin. "He's heaving it out with the best of them."

Another Army general staggered from the cockpit, worked his way between the turrets in the dark, and draped his body over the forward starboard torpedo tube. He retched and dry-heaved through the continuous pelting of saltwater.

Charles leaned over and shouted, "Do you need help, sir?"

"No," the general moaned. "Just let me die here."

With an estimated correction for the detour past the destroyer, PT-34 again headed south. Off the coast of Negros Island, Charles got a whiff of burning sugar cane. *We're too close to shore*, he thought. Not long thereafter, searchlights probed the night sky. *Sound carries a long way on water. As usual, they think we're aircraft.*

PT-34, still in the lead, steered their little convoy away from shore to safer water.

Clouds turned from grey to black before disappearing completely into the night's darkness. Around 2200 hours, the wind shifted to the west and strengthened. With PT-34 cresting a tall swell, a sudden flash of lightning from the enveloping clouds illuminated the seascape.

In that brief moment, Charles saw whitecaps breaking from huge swells across a heaving sea. Sheets of spindrift flew across their boat. A deafening thunderclap and smell of ozone followed them down into the trough between swells. A few pelting drops turned into sheets of torrential rain. Lightning flashed and thundered about the small boats. Wind howled across the deck. Swells rose to over twenty feet. One moment Charles was looking down into a deep trough, the next looking up at a wall of water higher than their antenna mast. Charles repeatedly wiped salt spray from his glasses, although it was a losing battle. *I can still see reasonably well by squinting*

Kelly ordered everyone below except the topside crew, including the general draped over the torpedo tube. The seasick brass would have to do their retching in the safety of the cabin, below deck.

Kelly asked Brantingham, just returned from a quick visit to the officer's head, "How're they doing down there?"

"Not so well. They're bracing themselves, holding on for dear life. One general was thrown completely from his bunk to the deck. He just stayed there, praying out loud for the journey to be over. It's wet, miserable, and crowded. The stench of vomit is overwhelming. It's a wretched hell."

"At least no one's washed overboard," Kelly said, justifying his orders forcing their passengers to endure the misery below.

Charles was not much better off in his machine gun turret. He was forced to remove his glasses, fearing they would be blown away. *I'm in a damn Edgar Allen Poe novel, bobbing like a cork passing through unending rapids! Richardson is doing his best to keep us headed into the next swell, but if he lets us get broadsided, we'll go over. No way any of us would survive.*

I've read about drowning—the instinct to breathe is too strong for anyone to hold their breath forever. At the point of losing consciousness there's so little oxygen in the brain it triggers an involuntary breath, underwater or not. Then you breathe, and one of two things happen. Your larynx spasms from contact with cold water and you die, or your lungs fill with water, and you die. Either way, you choke to death.

Admiral Rockwell shouted through the storm, "Kelly! I've sailed every type of ship in the Navy except one of these PTs, and this is the worst bridge I've ever been on. I wouldn't do duty on one of these goddamned PTs for anything in the world!"

Charles thought the Admiral sounded shaken. Perversely, this made him feel better. *I'm not the only one who's scared.*

The seemingly unending storm continued through the night, bringing everyone to a breaking point. Just before dawn the sky cleared. The seas calmed, and the swells shrank to less than five feet. The sun's rays chased the last star from the western horizon. Their ordeal was over.

Charles put his glasses back on and searched the surrounding ocean. *PT-35 is still nowhere in sight.*

Without the storm-induced adrenalin rush, exhaustion took over. Charles fought to keep his eyes open. The officers in the cockpit shared his struggle.

Like a summoned apparition, Pappy Reynolds appeared on deck waving a pot of cold coffee in one hand and cups in the other. "How about some cold mud?" he asked. "Those Army officers below don't seem interested in my coffee for some reason."

"Thanks, Pappy," Charles said when Reynolds handed him a cup.

"Any excuse to get away from the puke smell below—them's the sickest men I've ever seen on a boat."

Kelly advanced the throttles. With carbon burned from the cylinders and lightened by more than five tons of gasoline, PT-34 skimmed over the water. PT-41 kept pace, still following in 34's wake.

Sailors settled into the monotonous rhythm of the sea. Slap, the hull crosses the swell. Saltwater sprays over the deck. Props vibrate in the swell. Knees flex like a racehorse jockey. Wave after wave—ad infinitum.

Charles, dripping and salt-encrusted, turned to welcome the first rays of sunlight on his face. *Life … it's good.*

41

Landfall

Approaching Cagayan Province, Mindanao Island, Philippine Islands

0530 hours, 13 March 1942

The orange sun had not yet cleared the horizon when Jessie Clark yelled, "Lieutenant Kelly, navigational light dead ahead!"

All four Navy officers crowded into the cockpit, conferred, and agreed: It was the Macabalan Point light. A few minutes later, the wide mouth of the Cagayan River appeared a hundred yards west of the light. A hundred and fifty yards east of the light was the Cagayan wharf, their destination.

Even with the storm, Kelly's adjustments for the wind and seas had been perfect. With virtually no navigational fixes, charts, or advanced instruments, they arrived dead on target.

Admiral Rockwell, who had not given Kelly a single compliment for the past two days, could not hide his amazement. "A perfect landfall, Kelly—perfect! I have to admit that your dead reckoning navigation was spot on. I wouldn't have believed it possible."

Charles silently agreed with the admiral. *That was a stunning accomplishment, and I bet for Kelly it was also a huge relief!*

Bulkeley had the navigation charts and pulled ahead of PT-34, knowing MacArthur would expect them to be lead boat on arrival. He sent word to the general and his family that their ordeal was at an end.

MacArthur soon stepped topside. Although the strain of the journey showed in his face, he was dressed in his distinctive field coat, famous gold-braided cap, aviator's sunglasses, and the corn-cob pipe with its overly long stem. Secrecy may have permeated this mission from the beginning, but MacArthur had no intention of sneaking ashore incognito.

Charles watched the general take a position next to Bulkeley on the bridge and point towards the dock. *No one, including Admiral Rockwell, will be allowed to arrive before General MacArthur!*

In PT-34, Ensign Richardson bent down to a compartment in the cockpit. Standing up, he held out to Kelly the same bag that had mysteriously been stored aboard during the final minutes at Sisiman Cove. "What about this stuff?"

Kelly waved it away. "Give it to MacArthur's aide."

When Richardson left the cockpit, Charles leaned over and quietly asked, "What's in there, anyway?"

"Army secret." Richardson then grinned and opened the bag, revealing a floppy field marshal's cap, dark glasses, and corn-cob pipe. He closed the bag and quietly said, "Kelly explained that if the squadron encountered an enemy ship, we were to attack it while the other boats ran for the hills. If that happened, Kelly would don this stuff. He's close enough to MacArthur's build that hopefully they'd fall for it, give chase, and ignore the other boats."

"Pleasant thought—would it have worked?"

"We'll never know, thank God. We're still the Lucky 34."

🦢 🦢 🦢

The city of Cagayan de Oro bordered the river a short distance up from the coast. The Cagayan River at that point was still wide and shallow with shifting sand bars. The town itself had no sizeable dock; those wanting access to the open ocean had to bump along a two-mile road through mangrove swamps and a coconut grove, eventually reaching the sizeable wharf at Macabalan.

Throttled down to five knots, and with considerable trepidation, the two PT boats approached. The wharf and small buildings looked eerily vacant. At the time the squadron departed Corregidor, U.S. forces still occupied Cagayan, but that could have changed. The crews stood at battle stations.

Charles pointed his guns at the dock and nearby tree line, watching for movement. A vehicle broke from the trees. His thumb twitched on the trigger. *It's a US Army sedan.* His thumb relaxed.

The car was followed by three more American sedans, then by two trucks, and then a group of civilians. General William Sharp, the US Army commander on Mindanao, stepped from the lead vehicle. Soldiers leapt from one of the trucks and brought improvised gangways to both the 34 and 41 boats.

The civilians were local citizens who'd heard the PT boats' engines long before the boats themselves docked. Failing to see any bombers in the sky and then seeing Army vehicles heading to the wharf, everyone knew something unusual was happening. Cagayan's town leaders, including the mayor, several merchants, and a priest, followed the Army vehicles to the dock, but two soldiers stopped them from approaching the PT boats.

General MacArthur stepped from PT-41 and strode down the gangway. He and General Sharp, old friends, greeted each other warmly. With MacArthur having officially arrived, the other passengers could now disembark. They were wet, tired to the point of collapsing, and desperately pleased to be alive and on solid ground again.

Nat Floyd came on deck, giving Charles a nod.

Charles nodded back. *I never got a chance to ask him how he talked his way aboard.*

Without pausing, Nat walked straight to the group of civilians on shore, undoubtedly intending to gather local color, write his scoop, and plead with the Army communications center to send it to New York.

Rockwell, hugely relieved that his Navy had successfully delivered MacArthur from Corregidor, was the last passenger to depart. "Lieutenant, Lieutenant, Ensign," he formally addressed each of PT-34's officers in turn. "We can be proud of our success. I hope and pray that PT-35 with Ensign Akers and his crew and passengers will find their way safely here as well."

The admiral then departed to join the rest of the entourage. MacArthur stood by the lead sedan but turned to the PT boats. Flanked by his security guard, he walked back onto the wharf and asked Bulkeley to assemble the crews from both the 34 and 41 boats.

As the men gathered in anticipation, Torpedoman Martino quietly shared with his crewmates what he'd heard while carrying the passengers' bags to the trucks.

"I talked to a sergeant, the truck driver. Know why the docks were deserted when we arrived?"

"No. Why?"

"Because they thought our engines might be Japanese bombers, everyone went to shelter, even the Army guys. Only after a lookout confirmed it was us did they all rush down here."

"That's happened before—no surprise there."

Martino kept the best for last. "Know what else?"

"OK. What?"

"We're standing on more than a ton of dynamite. This dock is ready to be blown at the first sign of Japs."

"Shit!" The men shifted nervously, imagining the explosives under their feet.

"Attention!" Kelly called out.

The men stood in a crowded, but reasonably straight formation. They had been in the same tattered clothing for three days and looked more like desperate castaways than elite sailors. Still, they stood straight and proud.

"General MacArthur would like to address MTB 3," Bulkeley announced and then joined his men at attention.

MacArthur was brief. "You have performed in true Navy style. It gives me great pleasure and honor to award each of you the Silver Star for gallantry and fortitude in the face of heavy odds."

He then turned to face Bulkeley. "You've taken me out of the jaws of death, and I won't forget it!"

Bulkeley, surprised and a bit embarrassed, murmured, "Well, thank you, sir," and shook the general's outstretched hand.

Before the security guards could whisk MacArthur away, Bulkeley quickly asked, "One more thing, General? What are my orders?"

MacArthur, no longer a seasick old man but now the "Old Soldier" back in command, gave a quick and pointed answer. "You will conduct offensive operations against the Empire of Japan in waters north of Mindanao."

"Thank you, sir. As you know, we brought minimal supplies and munitions. I will be making requisitions." Bulkeley was not going to pass on the opportunity to enlist MacArthur's help on obtaining everything from torpedoes to fuel.

"Of course, Lieutenant," MacArthur affirmed. "I will have directives drawn up for General Sharp's Mindanao Force and General Chynoweth's Visayan Force on Cebu. They are to provide you with full support in materiel, communication, and, should you need any, men."

The two officers exchanged salutes, and MacArthur's convoy roared back through the coconut grove towards the Army base. Bulkeley dismissed the PT crews from formation.

"I'm stunned!" Charles looked at Martino. "MacArthur himself just gave Bulkeley carte blanche to wage unrestricted warfare against the Japanese at the time, place, and manner of his choosing. On top of that, the Army has to provide us with unconditional support!"

"After all," Martino quipped, "we are the entire American Fleet in the Philippines."

The discordant image of this rag-tag, unshaven, and stinking group of Navy men sailing out to confront the Japanese Imperial Fleet was difficult to fathom.

Eichelberger, not prone to loquaciousness, surprised everyone by speaking up, "It would seem to me, given that we all look the part, MacArthur decided to officially declare MTB 3 a pirate squadron, with Bulkeley as our captain."

No sooner had the dignitaries departed than a fuel truck from the Del Monte airfield pulled onto the dock with enough avgas to fully refuel both boats. PT-34 stood off 300 yards while PT-41 had her tanks filled. Then the 34 returned to the dock for her turn.

Richardson, Charles, and Hunter managed the refueling. Safety procedures for handling aviation gasoline on a PT boat were not all that different from those when refueling a PBY. "I see we're using only a mesh filter," Charles commented to the Army sergeant with the fuel truck, "That's a nice change. We've been using felt, or at least cloth, filters for months because our avgas was sabotaged with paraffin."

"No problem with this stuff—it's sweet. We've got plenty to share since the B-17s stopped regular flights."

"You're saying there's no more flights out of here?"

"No regular flights. A plane still flies in now and then."

Kelly inspected PT-34, making a list of maintenance needs. Stresses encountered in the high seas had loosened joints and broken fittings. Under normal circumstances, most of the parts would be replaced, but of course no such spares were to be had. They would continue to improvise and manage as they'd been doing for months.

Charles and Hunter waited on the dock while Richardson signed for the avgas. There may have been a war going on, but that didn't stop the ubiquitous military accounting of materiel and supplies.

Sudden shouts from PT-34 made all four men turn and look.

"What!" Richardson exclaimed. Then he saw the crewmen pointing north. A boat was heading straight for them at full speed.

It was PT-35.

Ensign Anthony Akers slowed his boat, allowing his crew to receive welcoming congratulations from Ensign George Cox and the other crewmen on PT-41. Once he had PT-35 secured to the dock next to PT-34, Akers met his senior passenger, Colonel Willoughby, with a huge grin and a sharp salute at the gangplank. "Welcome to Mindanao, sir."

Lieutenant Colonels Le Grande Diller and Francis Wilson, and Master Sergeant Paul Rogers followed Colonel Willoughby from the boat. Exchanges of "Thanks!" and "Good luck!" echoed off the boat hulls until an Army sedan arrived to whisk the soldiers away.

Bill Johnson waved to Charles from PT-35's foredeck. Charles asked Richardson, "Sir, permission to go over and speak to Bill Johnson?"

Richardson simply waved Charles toward the 35.

"Hey Bill, what happened? You guys stop along the way for drinks and girls?"

"Probably would have, Charles, but we couldn't find any bars. Of course, it was that goddamn gasoline again. We got behind and never caught up—until now."

"Bill, I first met you, standing right here on this very boat, back at Mariveles. I had no idea what all would happen to bring both of us here."

"Stick with me, Doc. We're going all the way to Australia—maybe even San Francisco!"

"I like your thinking." Charles said before turning serious. "Did you see the 32?"

"We reached the rendezvous island yesterday afternoon, just after you guys left. Akers and Schumacher talked for only a few minutes. Then we took off, trying to catch you. I don't know what Schumacher's orders were, but it was a dejected bunch of guys watching us from PT-32's deck when we left." Johnson looked down and shook his head. "I know they can't make it here, and it's real iffy for them to make Iloilo." He then looked back at Charles. "What's the plan here?"

"You and I don't make plans, Bill—you know that. We just wait for orders. General MacArthur did tell us we're all getting a Silver Star. Then he told Bulkeley and MTB 3 to go sink the Japanese fleet, or at least that part of it between here and Cebu."

"Between you and me, Doc, I was visualizing R & R on the beach, downing fancy drinks, surrounded by Army nurses." Johnson feigned disappointment.

"Maybe adulterated rum at a cheap bar, but no, no nurses."

"Doc!" Charles turned to see Jessie Clark waving him back. PT-34 was casting off.

Charles leapt back onto his own boat. *Moving away from a dock still wired with explosives seems like a wise plan.*

337

Bulkeley left with the last sedans for General Sharp's command center, leaving his XO, Kelly, in charge of the squadron. Once the 35 was refueled, Kelly moved all three PT boats to shallow waters in a small cove about four miles up the coast, near the village of Bugo. Crewmen walked anchors out from the boats, away from outcroppings of coral. The last thing they needed was to lose another PT boat on a reef. The machinist's mates saw to mechanical repairs while others scrubbed down every surface. Charles joined a detail gathering fronds for camouflaging the three PT boats.

MacArthur sent the crews an unexpected treat for their evening meal, a load of fresh pineapples. The ravenous crew devoured the piles of deliciously sweet, juicy fruit. The shock to their bowels triggered repeated hasty trips to the head.

At dark, leaving one crewman on watch, the men settled in for much-needed and long-overdue sleep. Charles and Pappy Reynolds took blankets to the foredeck. Offshore, with a continuous ocean breeze, mosquitoes would not be a problem. Pappy was assigned the mid-watch beginning at midnight. Charles had the morning watch at 0400 hours.

He stretched his long frame and closed his eyes, but immediately felt someone shaking his shoulder.

"Up, Doc. Come on, get up," Reynolds kept shaking Charles.

"What the hell, Pappy—I need to sleep before my watch."

"It's eight bells, Doc. I put up with your snoring for the past four hours. My turn now."

Part V

42

Absolution

Bugo, near Cagayan de Oro, Mindanao Island
Philippine Islands

1000 hours, 14 March 1942

After arriving, Bulkeley spent most of his time at General Sharp's headquarters or with civilians in Cagayan. On Saturday morning he returned to Bugo to meet with Kelly and Akers, the commanders of PT-34 and PT-35, as well as his own XO on PT-41, George Cox, and bring them up to date on the immediate plans for MTB 3.

Kelly relayed the information and plans to his crew. "Any PT boat action in the area might alert the Japanese and lead them to suspect MacArthur is here on Mindanao. Until we get word that the general is safe in Australia, we will suspend all operations and remain under cover."

Eichelberger, who had lately turned absolutely chatty, asked Kelly, "Sir, do we just stand ready on the boat in case the Japanese show up?"

"No. Bulkeley agrees that we all need some down time. The squadron is on holiday routine until further notice. We'll work out a schedule giving shore time for everyone, but here's a warning: Not one word—not to your priest or your whore—about who we are, where we've been, or what we just did."

He paused to glare at all the men.

"You will be arrested and thrown into the Army brig—and then something bad will happen. Got it?"

Eichelberger was on a roll. "Sir, shore leave won't be much fun without any money. I don't know about the rest of the crew, but I'm broke."

"Bulkeley's ahead of you. An Army officer from the paymaster's office agreed to work Saturday, if you can believe it. He should be here any minute. Each of us will sign for a hundred dollars cash. Uncle Sam will eventually sort out the pay records."

As the men dispersed, Reynolds said quietly to Charles, "I was thinking about finding a poker game with some Army grunts."

"I hope you can find one, Pappy. I've seen you in action, and I know what you can do with a pair of deuces. You have a sixth sense for holding, betting, bluffing, and folding."

"Aw, Doc."

"No, it's true. While we were waiting, back in Sisiman, I watched you clean out everyone in the crew and then give it all back just so you could keep on playing."

Reynolds grinned sheepishly. "Yeah, well, at the time I needed entertaining more than money. But I'm serious about finding some soldiers for a game—they know nothin' about betting. You know, Doc, the military could skip the middleman by simply giving the soldiers' pay straight to us sailors."

At 1130, an Army sedan arrived on the shore at Bugo. An Army paymaster's clerk and two MPs set up a table in the shade of a tree. Both MPs had pistols, and one held a Thompson submachine gun.

The sailors divided into groups, ferried ashore, and stood in line at the table to sign for their cash. The clerk brought enough U.S. dollars for everyone, but offered to give them ten dollars of their pay in Filipino pesos. As a U.S. territory, dollars had always been accepted throughout the Philippines. Now that the Japanese had invaded, some Filipinos began to think pesos a better bet for the immediate future.

Charles's turn came. "Can you just hold it for me? I have enough cash already, and I don't need to be carrying more."

The clerk shook his head. "I wouldn't advise that—this could be your last payday for some time. On top of that, if records get mixed up, you might never get it."

Charles thought for a moment. "OK, in that case, I'll take it all in pesos."

"All pesos? No dollars?"

"Unless you have Australian—what is it—pounds? I've already got plenty of dollars." In fact, he had more than a hundred dollars with him, half in his pocket and the other half tucked away in his sea bag.

"Don't have any Australian currency. Why are you asking?"

"I'm going to need it. Hopefully sooner than later. But since you don't have it, just make it all Filipino money."

The clerk shook his head, counted out one hundred dollars in Philipine pesos, and shoved the thick stack of colorful bills to Charles.

The Army scheduled shuttle bus transportation to the base, giving the sailors the opportunity to eat hot meals with the 28th Bombardment Squadron. The sailors divided into "port" and "starboard" sections, and half of each crew remained with their boat while the other half ate.

That night, Bulkeley sent a message for the entire squadron, "A Protestant chaplain will conduct a service, just for RON 3, in Bugo tomorrow morning. For our Catholics, a bus will arrive at 0915 and take you to the 1000 Mass in Cagayan. You will later mess with the port section on base and return to the boats with them."

Seven Catholic crewmen accepted the invitation to Mass. Charles boarded the bus with them. "Didn't know you were Catholic, Doc," one commented.

"I'm converting," Charles smiled.

"Since when?"

"I was thinking, about, maybe this coming Tuesday, Saint Patrick's Day."

"Doc, you're as Irish as General Tojo."

"Bulkeley's gonna be pissed if he finds out you aren't Catholic and you don't actually go to Mass," another said.

"I wouldn't think of missing my first Mass."

"Right—" the other two laughed, shaking their heads.

The truck passed a large school campus in the center of Cagayan with tree-lined avenues and paths. What looked to Charles like a large dormitory was fronted by a large statue of Saint Ignatius. In addition to the centrally positioned church, Charles took note of a relatively modest chapel to the side. Its door stood open, inviting. Two blocks farther, the driver deposited the seven sailors at the elongated Plaza Divisiora in the center of Cagayan.

"I'll meet you back here at 1600," the driver instructed. "You're going to be disappointed if you were planning on finding a place to eat. Most everything's closed on Sunday, so don't hurry to rush through your Mass thinking about a party afterwards. Cathedral's that way," he pointed.

Charles broke away from the other six. "I'm going to that chapel back at the college we passed. Anyone else want to go?" The others declined, making their way to the century-old San Agustin Cathedral, anticipating that it would be more interesting and perhaps more inspiring than the small chapel.

Charles backtracked to the school. The open chapel door fronted the wide avenue. Taking off his cap, he paused before entering the dark cool space. Only three people sat on the benches, each with head bent in prayer or meditation. He saw no clergy. He did see a table with candles, five with flickering flames, perched in an iron rack. He recalled Father Francis in Cavite City explaining to him that, for Catholics, lighting a votive candle was an act of Christian prayer. A hand-lettered wood box holding small candles was labeled, "10 P."

Ten pesos. That's about 20 cents. He reached into the pocket of his worn pants and pulled out his smallest Filipino bill, a hundred-peso note, and slid it into the slot on the top of the box. He took a candle, paused, and then took a second candle.

He thought of Tillie. Not the Tillie of the infectious laugh in the Cañacao hospital, but the Tillie with the thin face, hollowed eyes, and quiet voice working the gangrene ward at Hospital No. 1. *Are you still caring for the men in the jungle, Tillie, or are you now on Corregidor? Are you ill? Injured? Or …* He refused to follow that thought any farther. He lit one candle and placed it among the others flickering on the table.

He lit a second candle. *This one's for you guys: Simms, Grizzard, and the rest on PT-32. I hope you make it home safe.* He put it next to his first candle.

The three original worshipers finished their prayers and departed while Charles was lighting his candles, leaving him alone in the chapel.

Solitude is a rare commodity for sailors. Taking advantage of the cool, quiet space, Charles sat on a chair and stretched out his legs, relaxing as tension left his body. He stared at the flickering candles, the quiet stillness of the chapel enveloping him.

After a few minutes he suddenly stood, abruptly interrupting the moment of reverie, disappointed at his brief loss of mental discipline.

Whatever that was, I guess it was as good as actually attending a church service.

"I'm sure it was," a voice said in English behind him.

Was I talking out loud?

Charles turned around, feeling embarrassed and guilty.

The priest behind him looked European or American. Robust, but not fat, he smiled calmly.

"I'm Father J. Edward Haggerty."

"Charles Conrad Beckner, US Navy. I apologize for my appearance, but I've been at sea. To be truthful, I'm not a Catholic. I hope I didn't do anything wrong by lighting your candles."

The padre laughed. "No, so long as you put money in the box. I take it that you were on one of those three small boats that arrived two mornings ago?"

"Uh, yes." Charles said uncomfortably. *His English sounds one-hundred percent American, but I can't discuss anything about our presence.*

"Welcome to Ateneo de Cagayan de Oro. It seems you are a believer, but perhaps not a Catholic—maybe not even a Protestant? In any case, I am grateful to see an American sailor in our chapel. I know many of the Army men. General Sharp and I do much work together for mutual benefit. I would even say we are friends."

"Thank you." Charles was no more comfortable discussing his personal religious thoughts than he was their completed, but still super-secret, mission. *I better change the topic to something else.* "This building seems to be part of a large school or college, but I don't see many people around?"

"I named it for the great *Ateneo*, or place of learning, in Manila. I'm the rector. If you'd been here before that first day of war in early December, you'd have seen a thousand khaki-clad cadets standing at attention on our lovely green lawn. We've grown rapidly, even though we are a young institution. In fact, we're all young here. Not a single member of the faculty is over forty years old."

"Is this the only such school on Mindanao?"

"Hardly. Christians have long wanted to save the Mohammedans and others. We've been establishing missions and schools here for centuries. The Irish Columbians are in the west. The Dutch missionaries of the Sacred Heart are in the east. The Canadians of the Quebec Foreign Mission are in the southeast. In the southwest are the latest arrivals, the American and Canadian Oblates of Mary."

"And here, in the north, is you?"

"Yes. We are the American Jesuits."

"Where are your students now?"

"Scattered throughout Mindanao or to other islands. We had 200 residential students, but almost all of them returned to their families. A few of the older boys reported to their Filipino Scout Reserve divisions. Some entire families have retreated into the hills. As you probably are aware, the Japanese recently occupied Davao City, down on the southern coast."

He shook his head. "We are uncertain if MacArthur can gather more forces and return in time to save the rest of Mindanao."

Charles was taken aback. Davao's occupation was news to him, but the priest's casual talk of MacArthur "returning" stunned him. "You are talking about General Douglas MacArthur?" he whispered.

"Of course—you brought him here. We saw him get off your boat Friday morning at the wharf. I even talked with him!"

Charles vacillated between shock and amazement. "You talked to Douglas MacArthur? When?"

"Yesterday. It was remarkable. Would you like me to tell you about it? It's supposed to be some secret, but of course you know he's here anyway. I assume you are sworn to secrecy as well?"

"Sort of. Well, yes."

The padre gestured for Charles to join him on a bench. "About ten o'clock on the day you arrived, I went to Del Monte. I had business there with General Sharp. The guards seemed unusually alert that day, but I passed by without challenge to the reception room. I noted strangers with the insignia of generals and admirals were about. General Sharp was nervous and preoccupied, and he seemed eager for me to leave."

He smiled benignly. "So, I became bolder and asked for authorization after authorization to help me in a project preparing for evacuation of American citizens. He quickly granted all my requests."

"He must have wanted you gone."

"Indeed so. But, as I was finally leaving, an air alert sounded. A handsome four-star general walked calmly from a bedroom and inquired about the alert. Seeing me, he came straight across the room, shook my hand and said 'Father.' It was, of course, MacArthur himself."

"That was amazing—for you to shake his hand."

"There's more. It was too late for General Sharp to keep me from seeing the famous man, so he began anxiously making and answering telephone calls and did not order me to leave. MacArthur apologized, went back to his room, and brought out his wife, his son, and the Chinese *amah*, and placed them safely in a dugout. When MacArthur returned, he walked over to where I was sitting.

"'Would you like to go to a shelter, Father? I am told there are only two planes. I never bother about so few.'

"'No,' I chattered, 'Your calmness makes me feel brave.' He sat down beside me, and we were absolutely alone. I noticed his worn khaki, his tired eyes, and an unshaven face. But he looked vital, young—and somehow aloof and personal at the same time. Without a question from me, he took me into his confidence in a way that made me his firm admirer, and I will be impervious

348

hereafter to any criticism against him."

Charles said nothing, waiting to see how much more there was to this padre's story.

"He continued talking to me. 'Bataan cannot be taken, if food holds out. We have food for less than two months. The men on Bataan are splendid. They have proven their valor far beyond my expectations, beyond the expectation of friends and, especially, of the enemy. I have been ordered by President Roosevelt to Australia to begin the offensive. If the Jap does not take Mindanao by Easter, all he will receive is bullets.' Then the all-clear sounded, and Sharp hung up his telephone. MacArthur went for his wife and boy, without a word of secrecy to me."

Charles remained silent, and the padre continued. "Sharp, though, said 'Padre, I think you've scooped a few of us. Please consider everything secret, even his presence here.'"

Haggerty patted Charles's arm. "Of course, since you obviously know even more of his presence than me, I feel I have broken no promises." He paused, this time looking to Charles for a response.

"How did you come to know General Sharp so well?"

"Shortly after he first arrived here from Cebu as a brigadier general, we had the opportunity to meet socially. Later, he invited me to his headquarters. He said, 'Padre, I am not a Catholic, but when the real fighting comes, I want a Catholic priest around as chaplain because I know you'll be here when we need you.' Of course, he was right, and we have been friends since, something I hope he has not regretted."

"It must be a difficult time for him now."

"Yes. He enjoys my confidence, and perhaps that has helped a little in these dark days. He has a deep intellect and is a rock of morality." The priest looked more intently at Charles. "Now, is there anything I can do for you? As a priest, or just as a friend?"

"Do you have a library, perhaps with some newspapers in English?"

"We moved the books of our library into a hiding place in the hills. Some of them are quite old, written in the native language and very rare. Even if Cagayan is occupied by the Japanese, they will be safe until they leave. I have not seen an English newspaper since our war started. Where are you from, son?"

"Indiana, Father."

The priest thought for a minute. "That's close to Wisconsin, I believe?"

"It's not that close, but not that far either."

"We now hold only the early morning Mass at this chapel, and I am without obligations for a few hours. There is a family here that often honors me with a meal after Sunday Mass. I think they would enjoy meeting you. They have a long familiarity with America, particularly Wisconsin. I am sure the family would welcome your presence today. Could you join us?"

"I have to be back at the Plaza Divisiora by 1600. But I'm free until then."

"That's four p.m.? I believe there is plenty of time. A large family named Paradies owns the hardware store across the way. The upper story is the family home. It's quite large, six bedrooms, I think. The patriarch, Richard Paradies, emigrated from Germany to America, and then came to the Philippines during the Spanish-American war. He married the daughter of the governor of Bukidnon Province, stayed here, and started the hardware business. Sadly, he has passed on, but he left ten children, and eight survive. His son, Fred Paradies, and his wife, Emilia, left for America some months ago, when it was still possible. Bill, Dick, Walt, Carmen, and their families are all living here in Cagayan. They are wonderful people. Let me get something, and we will walk over there."

Padre Haggerty disappeared for a few minutes and returned with three boxes. "Here—Mr. Beckner, was it not? Carry these, please, but keep them upright."

"Sure. What's in the boxes?"

"A surprise!"

43

The Paradies

Cagayan De Oro, Mindanao Island, Philippine Islands

Noon, 15 March 1942

Charles followed the padre across the broad avenue separating the Ateneo from a concrete building on the opposite corner. The Paradies hardware store occupied the ground floor, leaving the entire upper floor as the residence. A man called from an upper level window, "It looks like you bring a young friend, Padre. Come on up."

Great! He's speaking English. Do I even hear a bit of Midwest accent?

Inside, Father Haggerty and the man greeted each other as long-time friends. The padre introduced Charles. "This is Mr. Charles Beckner—he arrived on those small boats the other morning. Mr. Beckner, meet my esteemed friend and leading citizen of Cagayan de Oro, William Paradies."

"Please, call me Bill, Mr. Beckner. Is your family German?"

"I have been told so. Thank you for speaking English, and please call me Charles. Am I to take it that you are German?"

"Through my father, yes. My generation, though, is far more American and Filipino. My brother Richard and I both went to the University of Wisconsin. Cold in the winter for sure, but we remember it only as a wonderful place and time." He pointed toward the living room. "Come and meet more of my family."

Bill introduced Charles to Richard, another brother named Walt, his sister Carmen, and Carmen's husband John "Jack" Barker. He waved toward some children running in and out of the room, "I have seven siblings, so there are many children, so many that I lose count. If Fred was still here, there'd be even more. The children will be eating separately. Even if they were old enough, there aren't enough places in the dining room."

"Most of the kids are mine," Richard proudly proclaimed. "And it's possible there might be one more before we finish our meal. This is my very pregnant wife, Myra."

"I'm glad to meet you, Myra." Charles extended his hand, feeling a need to bow ever so slightly to the beautiful woman in colorful dress. The men, Bill, Richard, Walt, and Jack, each wore variations of a beautifully embroidered shirt that buttoned only on the top half. Charles had seen similar dress by the men and women on Luzon. He recalled from his Tagalog lessons that Myra's dress was called a *terno*, and the men wore untucked *barong tagalogs*, or simply *barongs*.

Charles smoothed his trousers. *Even though they're not in coat and ties, I'm feeling underdressed.*

Bill continued, "My brother Fred managed the hardware store for many years, but last year he emigrated to Madison with his wife, Theodora, and their three children, Barbara, Fred Jr, and Arlene."

"Emigrated? That sounds permanent."

"Yes. He saw the war coming and left when it was still possible. I'm afraid the rest of us have missed that opportunity."

A Filipino woman appeared at the door and announced, "The meal is ready."

While the men waited for Myra and Carmen to take their seats, a handsome Filipino man arrived in time to take the last chair. He also wore an embroidered white *barong* made of cloth so light it was transparent.

"This is my future brother-in-law, Enrique Aboitiz," Bill said. "His sister, Carmen, and I are to be married soon. He represents the third generation of a prominent shipping family in Cebu. You know Cebu?" Charles nodded. "The Aboitiz family donates generously to many good causes there."

"A family of philanthropists. I am honored to meet you." Charles shook the proffered hand. "Please excuse my appearance, Mr. Aboitiz. My uniform is the worse for wear, but I assure you it is clean."

"Of course. Meeting you is entirely my honor. I know of the fierce fighting the Americans are engaged in against the Japanese on Bataan. We will be forever grateful for your valor. The Japanese will be repelled, and the Philippines will have our independence as promised in 1946. There is an American Navy base at Cebu, on Mactan Island. If you are ever there, you must visit my family.

Anyone in Cebu can direct you to our house."

"Thank you." *It must be a big house, if 'anyone' knows where it is.*

Father Haggerty, giving the sign of the cross, offered a brief invocation, "Bless us Lord, and these, your gifts ..."

Charles watched the others cross themselves but decided it would be best not to imitate. His discomfort increased farther when the padre immediately directed the table's attention to the guest. "Tell us about yourself, Mr. Beckner."

Painfully conscious of his worn uniform and aware he was dining with educated people of means, Charles sat straight and used his best enunciation. "I am from Princeton, Indiana. I joined the US Navy, and after a year of medical training in San Diego and then Mare Island—it's near San Francisco—I arrived in Cavite in 1940. I was in Olongapo with a PBY—a seaplane—squadron, when the Japanese attacked Manila. Many of our planes were destroyed before Christmas. The few remaining planes flew to Australia. I remained at Cavite, then moved to Bataan, and then to Corregidor. In January, I joined a squadron of small boats."

"Ah yes—we saw your PT boats arrive on Friday morning," said Bill.

Please, don't anyone mention MacArthur. Charles accepted a bowl of meat bathed in an aromatic, red-brown sauce. Putting a spoonful on his plate, he realized good manners required him to give someone a compliment. "Your dining room and these dishes are beautiful, and this meat smells wonderful! Is it the adobo sauce I had the opportunity to enjoy in Manila?"

Bill had just taken a bite, so Richard Paradies answered Charles's question, "I would think it the same vinegar-based sauce you sampled on Luzon. It's used for almost any meat or fish throughout the Philippines. You mentioned medical training. Are you a medic on the PT boats?"

Charles answered tactfully. "Yes. I'm actually a Navy corpsman, what you might know in the Army as a medic, but with more training and responsibility."

"Will you still be here when the Japanese arrive?" Richard asked.

Before Charles could compose an answer, Bill interjected, "It's possible that they'll think this island too large and too sparsely populated to occupy, and they must know the Moros will not welcome them. Nevertheless, we can't afford to be unprepared. In fact, Enrique is here to discuss the situation between Cagayan and Cebu. He tells me that the number of Japanese warships in Visayan waters grows daily, and travel between our cities is becoming hazardous, perhaps not even possible. Even my wedding is threatened."

Conversation drifted from Charles's presence to speculation over when and where the Japanese would next invade and how to deal with Moros in the southern islands.

"Can you tell me more about the Moros?" Charles asked.

Enrique spoke up. "The Moros are Mohammedan. They resisted the Spanish Christians that colonized the islands centuries ago. Now the Moros resist you American Christians for the same reasons. You must *never* travel through Moro regions alone or without weapons. If the Japanese invade Mindanao and force you Americans to retreat into the mountains, you will be living among Moros. It will be difficult."

The family spoke mostly English for Charles's benefit but occasionally shifted into other languages. Charles picked out patches of Spanish. When house staff were present, they spoke Cebuano, also called Bisaya, the common native language of the middle and southern islands. Charles noted some similarities to Tagalog, but the Cebuano was almost as hard for him to follow as the Spanish.

After four courses, helpers cleared the table. The same woman who had announced the meal came to the room and looked at Father Haggerty. "You bring?"

"Ah, Vena, yes we did. Charles, would you hand me those boxes we carried here—thank you. As you all know, most of the students have gone, and the cooks in our kitchen have had to look for ways to occupy themselves. The American soldiers bring us ingredients for our cooks to turn into pies, cakes, and cookies. We sometimes keep a small amount for ourselves." The priest feigned a guilty look.

Opening the first box with a flourish, he withdrew a coconut-banana cream pie to a round of applause. The second box contained a fruit pie, and the third a nut pie.

Vena brought in a carafe of strong coffee and a tray of cups and milk and sugar. She said something that Charles loosely interpreted as either "enjoy it while it lasts," or maybe "while you can."

Only to be polite and to demonstrate that he possessed as much self-control as his hosts, Charles reluctantly turned down a second serving of pie. At 1530 he excused himself. "I am most thankful for meeting you and sharing this wonderful meal, but I must leave or risk missing my bus."

"I will see you to the door," the padre said, rising.

Sincerely grateful for the meal and experience, Charles spoke first to Father Haggerty. "Thank you so much for inviting me to meet this wonderful family." He turned to the rest of the table and added, "I pray you and your families remain safe and that your homes are spared from whatever may come."

Vena had already combined the remains of the three pies onto one pie plate. Father Haggerty put them into one of the boxes and handed it to Charles.

"Please share this with your friends on the PT boat. I will come to Bugo in a day or two and, if you are still there, retrieve the plate."

He said Bugo! I never told him or anyone else we were anchored there. This priest must have contacts everywhere!

"I have a question," Haggerty said as they walked to the door. "I knew you were a medic—pardon me, corpsman—but during the meal I remembered seeing you in the gun turret of the boat when you arrived. Was that correct? Perhaps that explains the candles you lit this morning?"

He's as observant as he is intelligent...

"Padre, I'm not an expert on the Bible, but somewhere in there doesn't it say there's both a time to heal and a time to kill?"

"Close enough," Haggerty nodded.

"Maybe we can leave it at that?"

44

On the Coral

Bugo, Mindanao Island, Philippine Islands

16 March 1942

Monday morning Kelly spoke to his crew. "It's been a tough month, and we've made our boats as fit as possible under the circumstances. Until we're released from this stand-down, Bulkeley is giving alternating shore leave from 1600 to 2400 hours. We'll stay in the same port and starboard groups as before. We'll find transportation to take you to the camp or to Cagayan. We start with the starboard section this evening." His stern gazed focused on each man for a moment before continuing. "Behave, and keep your mouths shut."

By design, the two corpsmen were in separate groups, so Charles and John wouldn't be able to share a drink ashore. Nevertheless, it was an opportunity to stretch one's legs and have a beer with crewmates. At 1600 sharp, punts took Charles and the rest of the starboard half of the crew to shore.

A sedan waited to whisk officers Brantingham, Cox, and Murray to dine at the small Officers' Club on the Army base.

A bus waited for the enlisted crewmen. "Where are we going? Base or town?" the bus driver asked.

"Town!" the men yelled in unison. As they piled off the bus in Cagayan, Charles announced, "I'm going to stretch a bit. Walk the town. Maybe have a beer someplace before figuring out where to eat."

"I'll go with you," Machinist's Mate George Shepard said, falling in step with Charles. As they passed by the chapel at the Ateneo, Charles considered

356

going in and lighting another three candles. *No. That's too personal unless I'm alone.*

They ended up having a beer at a bar at the far end of town and afterward found a small open-air restaurant. Charles tried to order in Tagalog. The proprietor answered in broken English. *I'm not sure if he just wants to practice his English, or if my Manila version of Tagalog doesn't work so well down here.*

After dinner they joined two other crewmen from PT-34 also wandering in search of a post-prandial drink. They stopped at a store selling beer and local whisky and where patrons drank in an adjacent small room faintly illuminated by low-watt bare bulbs. Four sailors from PT-41 waved for Charles's group to join them.

Henry "Jocko" Rooke, PT-41's cook, was entertaining a beautiful young Filipino girl. She sat on his lap, shared his drink, and laughed at everything he said. When she spoke, Charles was pretty sure it was Cebuano sprinkled with Spanish, a mixture obviously incomprehensible to Rooke. For that matter, she probably couldn't understand a thing Rooke was saying to her either.

Charles's beer was at his lips when the lights went out.

"What the fuck!" a voice came from the dark.

Then came the ear-splitting crack of a gun and flash of light that froze everyone. In the moment of silence that followed, footsteps scurried from the bar before pandemonium erupted. "Lights! Get the goddamn lights on!" one of the sailors yelled. More scurrying and the dim lights returned.

The pretty Filipina was still sitting on Rooke's lap. Her head was a bloody mess, and gore was scattered over the table. Rooke looked at Charles helplessly. "Doc?" was all he could say.

Charles lifted the girl from his lap and laid her on the floor. Confirming there was no pulse and she was not breathing, he looked up. "Sorry, Jocko, there's nothing I can do."

"Check your guns!" Shepard yelled.

Rooke's .45 pistol was not in his holster. A search found it just outside the door where someone had discarded it while making their escape. A Filipino policeman arrived and Army MPs soon followed. It seemed the lovely young girl had a jealous Filipino lover, likely galled by his fickle girlfriend's attraction to the Americano. The MPs sent the sailors packing, minus Rooke's .45, and left the matter in the hands of local authorities. The subdued crewmen crawled back onto the Army bus and rode quietly back to Bugo.

Am I dreaming? Charles sat up and opened his eyes just after 2300 hours. He was not dreaming. The sound was real, the unmistakable rumble of American-made radial engines on a B-17 bomber coming from the southeast, the direction of the Del Monte Airfield.

"Doc, you up?" Jessie Clark came over.

"Yes—were those B-17s landing at Del Monte?"

"Sounded like two, maybe three of them. I bet they're here to pick up MacArthur."

Charles was fully awake now. "If that's why they're here, it'll only take them an hour or so to refuel, load up, and take off. I'm too awake to go back to sleep. I'm waiting up to see if they fly back out."

Around midnight Ensign Richardson joined the vigil.

At 0130 the engines restarted. A few minutes later, the men listened as two bombers took off to the southwest, avoiding the Japanese garrisons thirty miles south at Davao.

"You think they just picked up the general, sir?" Clark asked Richardson.

"Had to be. That means our stand-down is ending—we'd best get some sleep."

The next day, Saint Patrick's Day, Bulkeley gave two new orders. Because of the incident involving the starboard shift the night before, the crewmen could not wear their sidearms when on shore leave. Second, all crewmen would now mess on base with the soldiers and stay away from town. Lieutenant Brantingham accompanied the starboard section first. On their return, Lieutenant Kelly and Ensign Richardson took the port section to a later mess, not returning until after dark.

The port section had barely re-boarded PT-34 when the gangway watchman shouted, "We're dragging anchor!" This was a shock, as the 34 had been securely riding at anchor for days, maintaining a seventy-yard separation from the coral shelf.

Ross and Clark ran forward and pulled on the anchor cable, but it would not hold.

"Fire 'em up!" Kelly yelled.

The first engine roared to life, but not before the boat hit the coral with a loud *crunch*. Kelly engaged forward gear and advanced the throttles. Instead of roaring to open water, a rapid thumping vibrated through the boat.

Then the engines stopped.

"Goddamn it!" Kelly yelled, running forward to pull on the anchor line himself. The end of the line dangled in his hand, no anchor, and nobody to blame. The connecting shackle pin had broken and fallen out—yet another consequence of limited maintenance and no spare parts.

"Signal the 41 to get underway immediately and tow us off this reef," Kelly ordered. "Till they get here, let's try to push her off."

Charles, along with other hands, jumped into the water. Ignoring cuts and scrapes from the sharp coral, they lifted, shoved, and pushed. The boat was too big, and the waves too strong. Each succeeding wave pushed PT-34 a little farther onto the coral. PT-41 arrived and tossed cables to the 34, but even with PT-41 giving full throttle the 34 didn't budge from her coral trap.

Ebb tide, at dawn, left PT-34 sitting high and dry on top of the coral. Discussion among officers and crew discarded formality in their search for ideas.

"We're twenty-five yards from deep water."

"Maybe we can float her off at slack high tide."

"If we clear some of the larger rocks out, it'll be easier."

Lieutenant Bulkeley returned mid-morning and was surprisingly sanguine, considering his serviceable squadron now consisted only of boats 41 and 35. "Kelly, I'm sorry, but you'll have to get help from the Army. We've been given a critical mission, and I'll be taking both the 41 and 35 boats. I'll fill you in later."

Help arrived from the Army that afternoon in the form of laborers, picks, crowbars, shovels, and dynamite with fuses and caps. While the Army was clearing a passage for PT-34 through the coral, the crew took the opportunity to scrape five months of marine growth from her hull.

The Army lieutenant in charge came aboard. "We've got a tug, the *Misamis*, coming to pull you off at high tide."

"Great." Kelly's frustration eased, minimally.

The *Misamis*, when it showed up near sundown, was a disappointment. Smaller than the PT boat, and with a single-cylinder diesel engine, no one was surprised when later that evening at slack high tide, the diminutive tug couldn't budge PT-34. The tug's captain gave the cable some slack and tried to jerk the boat off the coral, but only succeeded in snapping the attachment post from the tug. The crew abandoned any further effort until daylight.

Lieutenant Brantingham spoke quietly to Ensign Richardson, "Déjà vu?"

"It's a goddamn nightmare that keeps coming back." Richardson shot back. The same two men had been commander and executive officer on PT-33 when she'd grounded on a reef on Christmas Eve. All efforts to extract her had been unsuccessful, and they'd ultimately had to destroy the boat.

"The Army lieutenant's trying to round up a bigger tug. Not much we can do until then."

The next day a second tug was conscripted, but it was only a little larger than the *Misamis*. The engineer that regularly ran her diesel engine had not been located, so Machinist's Mates Shepard and Eichelburger, both with diesel experience, were dispatched to run the tug's plant.

"God, show me some mercy," Shepard exclaimed. "This thing is ancient!"

"1905 two-cylinder Kinoshita Japanese marine diesel," Eichelburger read the plate. "I'm sure it has its share of idiosyncrasies, but all these diesels are basically the same. We can run this thing."

The sun was long gone by the time lines were secured to PT-34 at maximum high tide. With billowing smoke from its exhaust, the tug pulled slack from the tow ropes. After about five minutes, the 34 had moved only six inches and was stubbornly refusing to move farther.

Near midnight, while the tug strained, a punt with three men approached in the dark. "Who goes there?" the watch on PT-34 called out.

"Major Joe Webb and Major Robert Bowler."

"Who's the third man?"

"I'm only a padre," a deep voice shouted.

"Father Haggerty?" Charles recognized the voice. "Have you come for your pie plate?"

"No," the padre laughed, "but we thought we might be able to help in some way."

David Goodman, the boat's radioman, arrived at Charles's side and intoned in a deep voice, "Glory be to God, Father. We've tried dynamite, curses, and tugs on this tub. How about a blessing?"

"Of course," the padre replied, raising his hand. "We pray for your strength to be added to that of these men in their hour of need."

The boat gave a small jerk forward.

"She moved, Father! Give us another one!"

"Help us, Lord, in this endeavor. One more push is all we ask," quickly adding, "but we need it right now."

PT-34 at that moment slid smoothly from the coral into the passage dug for her the previous day.

"By God, Padre, you did it!"

Father Haggerty, a bit surprised himself, looked to the sky. "Thank you, Lord. We stand most grateful for that gift."

"So long, Padre," Charles shouted over the engine noise as the boat floated into deep water. "Is this your first miracle?"

"Possibly so. I'll try to visit you in—" but the straining engines drowned out the rest of the priest's response.

I don't know myself where we're going next, but I bet that priest does.

ᔐ ᔐ ᔐ

The jubilation of getting off the coral was short-lived. PT-34 was no longer the powerful swift war boat of only hours earlier. The propellers, struts, and shafts were little more than mangled bits of metal, and the squadron possessed not a single replacement unit. Highly crafted phrases of profanity wafted over the water.

The tug deposited PT-34 at the small Bugo dock, next to PT-35, at 0100 hours. When he heard the 34's story, Bill Johnson applied to PT-34's situation still one more acronym he had adopted from the soldiers at camp. "It's FUBAR." Charles could only nod in agreement.

At first light, a fuel truck arrived and topped off the tanks on all three boats. Late that afternoon, PTs 35 and 41 departed for a mission apparently of some importance, though Bulkeley kept the details to himself.

At 1700 the *Misamis* arrived, attached a line to PT-34, and with the PT boat in tow, headed immediately for Ginoog Cove, roughly sixty miles east. Reportedly, Ginoog had a shop capable of repairing 34's running gear. It was a fourteen-hour journey and the slowest sustained speed PT-34 had ever travelled. At last they anchored offshore of Anakan, a *barangay*, or neighborhood, across the bay from Ginoog until daylight.

At 0700 a small tug from the Anakan Lumber Company towed them to a pier along a lumber corral. The manager of the company, a Mr. Walters, explained to Lieutenant Kelly, "Please leave as soon as you can. Japanese planes fly over almost every day. If they decide to bomb your boat, we don't want to lose our pier at the same time."

Lieutenants Kelly and Brantingham left Ensign Richardson in charge while they went in search of the boat repair shop, taking with them the two machinist's mates, Eichelberger and Hunter. Mr. Walters from the lumber mill accompanied them as interpreter and facilitator.

"What's happening?" Charles asked Hunter after they returned.

"That so-called machine shop's nothing more than a small blacksmith's shop. Its main function is to keep the local sawmill in working order, along with keeping their horses and mules shod. It's basically a backyard garage with a homemade forge. There was an older Filipino man who claimed to be the boss. Walters translated, and with Kelly's stash of dollars and pesos from Bulkeley, they reached an agreement. The Filipino promised to put our boat back in working order—and to do it quickly. I told Kelly I have a lot of doubts about them, but he didn't see any other options."

Repairs on PT-34 began immediately. The bow was anchored in the bay and the stern held in place by ropes tied to wood pylons near the shore. This kept the running gear in shallow water for the blacksmith's workers. Kelly ordered his crew to take advantage of the opportunity by disassembling, repairing, re-assembling, and adjusting every working fixture on the boat.

Hunter personally performed a one-day rebuild of the auxiliary generator. It was the boat's only source of electricity when the main engines were shut down. "You want hot meals?" Pappy Reynolds demanded, "Give me a damn generator that works."

On 20 March, the vernal equinox, PT-41 motored into the Anakan lumber corral with an hour of daylight remaining. Bulkeley made straight for Lieutenant Kelly and without preamble, asked, "When can 34 be ready for action? We've lost the 35."

45

The Reluctant Passenger

Anakan, Ginoog, Mindanao Island, Philippine Islands

20 March 1942

While Bulkeley and Kelly talked, Charles approached Ensign Richardson, "Sir, permission to find Balog and go over some medical issues?" *John will tell me what happened on the mission and what happened to PT-35.*

Charles carried his medical bag to PT-41, and the two corpsmen went to the chart house. Worried that "lost" meant something terrible had happened to PT-35 and its crew, Charles skipped formalities and asked, "John, where's the 35—and where's her crew?"

"They're all OK, Charles. It was one of those goddamn coral reefs again! Want to hear the whole story?"

Charles breathed a sigh of relief.

"All of it. I have time—the 34's not going anywhere soon."

"Last night's mission was to pick up Quezon on Negros and bring him to Cagayan so he can be flown to Australia."

"President Quezon? He's here?"

"He was at Corregidor with MacArthur for a while, but he moved down here when Bataan looked vulnerable in January. The Japanese want to capture him, probably to force him to publicly surrender the islands and tell his people to stop resisting. Last night we were sent to pick up him and his entourage and bring them back to Del Monte. A guy named Soriano went with us as a guide for the channel and port at Dumaguete, on Negros. He was also to be

363

our liaison with Quezon. For some reason, Bulkeley thought Soriano might be leading us into a Japanese trap. He put guards on him with instructions, 'Any monkey business, and Soriano goes down first!' Turned out though that Soriano was OK."

"So, what happened to PT-35?"

"Hold on, Charlie. You wanted the whole story?"

"I do."

"OK. Before we left Cagayan, we received a report that as many as seven Japanese destroyers had been seen in the area. The Japs might have learned that Quezon was down here and were hunting for him. That's probably why finding Quezon was harder than we thought. At Dumaguete, the tide was too low to use the dock, so Bulkeley, Soriano, and the two Army officers waded ashore. A local constable challenged them and wouldn't answer any questions. Every time Bulkeley demanded, 'Where is Quezon?' the constable kept insisting, 'I cannot tell you that.'"

"Let me guess—Bulkeley didn't accept that answer."

"Of course not. He pulled back the bolt on the Tommy gun he was carrying, put it to the constable's head, and said, 'The hell you can't!' Oddly enough, the constable changed his mind. He admitted that the president was up the coast at a village called Bias. Time was getting critical, so our group waded back on board and we roared up to Bias."

"Both boats?"

"Only us. Bulkeley left the 35 to patrol the shoreline and watch for enemy ships while we went to the dock to pick up the president. Our engines attracted several locals to the Bias dock, and they readily admitted that Quezon was in a small *nipa* hut a few miles down the road." John yawned, responding to a day and a half without sleep, then continued. "Bulkeley borrowed some vehicles and took some of our crew to where Quezon was hiding, but the president didn't want to come with us. I'm sure he was frightened and threatened by all the military men carrying submachine guns, rifles, and pistols, not to mention the grenades and various large knives draped on, over, and around their bodies. You know how we all look now, especially the lieutenant with that bushy black beard, two semiautomatic pistols on his hips, and filthy clothes. Quezon must have thought he was being kidnapped by bandits. Somehow Bulkeley convinced him, and he finally relented. They made it back to our boat and loaded up."

"What then?"

"While all that was going on, PT-35 radioed that they'd hit a reef at near-full speed and were taking on water through a major breach in the hull. We had to go back and pick up 35's entire crew. Space was tight, and seas were running high between Negros and Mindanao. With the added group of soldiers, Quezon, his wife and three children, his personal priest, the vice president, his chief of staff, and two cabinet officers, their baggage had to be left on the dock. From the way those bags were being guarded when we left, I think they contained something important, maybe the entire Philippine treasury—though it made no difference. It was after 0300 already. We found the 35 and stuffed their crew on top of everyone else. We left PT-35 anchored at the beach, and she's still there, I presume."

"That was quite a night," *I'm sorry I missed it. Well, almost sorry.*

"It wasn't over yet. I didn't think I'd ever again have as miserable a night as we did that second night on the run from Corregidor, but this one was no better, if shorter. We were bashed side to side while motoring up and down through massive swells. The passengers were all instantly seasick and puking everywhere below deck. I tried to help Quezon as much as I could. I had to laugh though—the president actually asked his priest to perform last rites on him and his family. Bulkeley told the priest they could use the chart house. It was cramped with everyone in there, but the priest made it work. After that, Quezon asked Bulkeley to take him to the closest landfall, so we headed to Oroquieta. Bulkeley radioed General Sharp in time to get an honor guard there to meet the president."

"Where's 35's crew now? I don't see any of them here."

"PT-35's out of action and will be for a long time, maybe forever. After we left Quezon with the Army reception team at Oroquieta, Bulkeley dropped off the PT-35 crew at Cagayan. He made arrangements with General Sharp for them to move as a group up to a high mountain lake, where they're supposed to form a 'lake defense force.'"

"No surprise. If the Army finds a bunch of sailors sitting around, they create a Navy defense force for this or that—gives them something to do."

"Maybe. Ensigns Akers and Murray have charge of the unit. The Army on Negros agreed to salvage the 35 and move her to a boatyard at Cebu for repairs. After that, the crew will still be together and can be brought back as a unit to bring the 35 back into action. Meanwhile, we're going back tonight to pick up Quezon's baggage."

"So you *were* right. It's important baggage."

"I'm sure it's more than Quezon's spare underwear."

Once the crew fixed as much as was possible with limited parts and tools, it became a matter of waiting while the blacksmith workers forged and reshaped damaged props, shafts, and struts. The men were given alternating days of shore leave, though Gingoog didn't have much in the way of diversion, and the incident with Rooke and the Filipino girl was still fresh in everyone's memory.

When the crew did go to town, they wore their best threadbare uniforms. Charles still wore the same whites he had dyed with coffee back at Olongapo. Dress on board was another matter. Physical closeness aboard PT boats precluded formal standards in ordinary circumstances, and much more so in wartime. Kelly permitted the crew, himself included, wide latitude in dress to allow greater comfort in the hot and sticky tropical humidity.

The sawmill provided a small launch that daily brought water, food, and workers to PT-34. Late one afternoon the launch arrived with passengers as well as the usual provisions. Mr. Walters from the lumber company brought with him four other visitors from town. One was an American, accompanied by his wife. It was a show-and-tell visit by Mr. Walters.

Lieutenant Brantingham was officer of the deck that day and called down through the hatch, "Mr. Kelly, Mr. Walters has come alongside in the launch."

"Very well," Kelly responded from below and arrived on deck clad in his undershorts and slippers. Nothing else.

Without the slightest bit of embarrassment, he extended his hand to the lady as she stepped from the launch. "Welcome aboard PT-34, ma'am."

Mr. Walters then introduced the four male visitors which Kelly acknowledged as each came aboard.

After the introductions, Kelly said, "Lieutenant Brantingham, will you begin a tour of our vessel for our guests?" Then, turning back to the visitors, "If you will excuse me for a moment, I will rejoin you in more appropriate attire."

Charles thought the encounter interesting as well as entertaining. *Kelly didn't even bat an eye, and that lady was most gracious the way she made light of his appearance. Both of them showed class.*

After ten days, the blacksmith crew declared their work complete. They admitted it wasn't a perfect repair, but it was the best they could manage. A trial run in Gingoog Bay was disappointing, even at low throttle. One sailor aptly described it saying, "her stern wiggles like a shipwrecked sailor's dream of a French musical comedy star."

At the end of March, PT-41 returned to Anakan. Bulkeley came aboard the 34 and brought Kelly and the crew up to date. "The Army pulled PT-35 off the reef and towed it to a civilian shipyard at Opon, on Mactan Island. She's been pulled up on a marine railway for repairs, and I've been told she'll be seaworthy in two to three weeks. I'm sure they can manage your shaft and propeller repair in a matter of days, if you can get your boat there."

"I honestly don't know if she can make the trip or not," Kelly answered, "but we don't have any other choice. It's time for us to leave. These people have treated us well, but they know the Japanese are coming, and when they do arrive, it's going to be hard to explain having an American warship in their harbor."

"Then let's leave tonight. We'll accompany you in case of trouble."

The 150-mile trip, even in calm water, took almost twelve hours. Because vibration from the still bent props and shafts stressed his engines, Kelly intermittently shut down power and allowed PT-41 to tow them for an hour. The strategy was cumbersome, but it worked.

"Where the hell is this Opon?" Clark asked Charles while they were under tow.

"It's basically part of Cebu, the second largest city in the Philippines. Opon's on Mactan Island and separated from Cebu City by a narrow channel. We have a small Navy base and some oil and fuel tank farms on the island. The private shipyard is run by an American from Minnesota, 'Dad' Cleland. He's apparently well known around the Philippines."

Clark stared at Charles. "How do you know all that? What else?"

"Back at Cagayan I was introduced to a man from Cebu who knew Dad Cleland. That's pretty much it."

"No," Clark said. "I've been around you long enough to know when you stop before you've finished."

"There's a little history to Opon. I just didn't want to seem like a wise-ass."

"Too late, Doc—we all already know you're a wise-ass. What's the rest of the story?"

"OK. A priest took me to a local home that first Sunday we were in Cagayan. There I met this man, Enrique, who's from Cebu. He told me about the city. A couple of hundred years ago a chief named Lapu-Lapu got pissed off at Magellan when he tried to land there. I don't know the details, except Lapu-Lapu's warriors drove the invaders away, killing Magellan in the process. What we call Opon used to be named Lapu-Lapu, after that chief. Enrique said the locals are proud of their ancestor's dark deed, yet inexplicably they also revere Magellan as an historical figure."

He paused, then grinned. "Do I need to tell you who Ferdinand Magellan was?"

"Go to hell, Doc!" Clark sat down and closed his eyes. A shiver passed through his body.

"You OK, Jessie? Are you coming down with something?"

"Nah. I'm good. Just tired."

The two PT boats reached the entrance to the Cebu channel in the dark. They waited until daylight to navigate through the shoal waters, pass up the channel, and moor alongside the pier at Opon. The four officers were greeted by Dad Cleland himself.

Kelly wanted to know how long it would take to repair PT-34's running gear and hull. Bulkeley was equally interested in the status of PT-35. "I'm down to one boat, Mr. Cleland. What's our best time frame for having these boats back in action? I have been assured by General MacArthur himself that money's no object."

"Money's not an issue," Cleland answered. "I'm doing the repairs, and doing them as quickly as we can, without charge for parts or labor—it's the least I can contribute here. Time? Repairing the hull incursion in the 35 boat will take another twelve to fourteen days. While we're doing that, the entire hull gets cleaned and repainted. After that, she'll need to sit in the water for at least forty-eight hours for the wood to soak up water and swell the joints tight."

"What about this one?" Kelly pointed to PT-34 at the dock.

"If it's no worse than what you described, eight or nine days, plus a day or two in the water to soak the joints."

"Thank you for everything you're doing for us," Bulkeley sincerely shook Cleland's hand. "I'll check in daily to see how it's coming, if you don't mind."

With the help of the shipyard, the PT-34 crew constructed a framework of timber over the boat's bow to hide its pointed contour. They draped the decks, guns, and torpedo tubes with leaves, branches, and gunny sacks. Hopefully, the square shape would look like a barge to Japanese reconnaissance planes. If all hands bent to the task, they could make the PT boat action-ready or return it to camouflage in a matter of minutes.

PT-35 sat at the top of the marine railway on blocks, topped by similar camouflage. The initial plan had been to bring back PT-35's normal crew from Lake Lanao if their boat could be salvaged and repaired. With all the boats now at Cebu, Bulkeley felt that plan was no longer practical. Instead, he made up a new PT-35 crew from men on PT-34 and PT-41. He moved Lieutenant Brantingham from PT-34, where he was XO, and gave him command of PT-35. Chief Machinist's Mate Regan would serve as Brantingham's XO. That still left the 34 with two officers, Lieutenant Kelly as the boat commander and Ensign Richardson as his XO. Hunter and Harris would move with Brantingham from PT-34 to PT-35. Five crewmen from PT-41 would join them. The shift was to take effect as soon as PT-35's repairs were finished. The shifts would leave crews of eight sailors and one or two officers on every boat, a reasonable wartime complement.

Within twenty-four hours, PT-34 was out of the water and blocked next to PT-35. The four torpedoes were removed, and repairs to propellers, struts, and shafts commenced. A separate work crew began scraping and cleaning her bottom. Dad Cleland estimated repairs on the 34 would be finished a few days before PT-35 was back in service.

The crews stood down to wait for their boats' repairs to be finished. The Army quartermaster supplied the waiting crews with food, tobacco, and even some candy. The easy times lasted less than forty-eight hours.

Friday, 3 April, Bulkeley gathered all hands at the dock where PT-41 tied up. "From this point, say absolutely nothing about what you do or what you see tonight." Bulkeley paused for effect. "All civilians have been restricted from the Cebu dock, but there will be an Army contingent waiting there. I've assigned two men to stay here as guards for our boats. Everyone else jump on board. You'll get further instructions when we arrive."

PT-41 deposited Kelly and most of the crewmen onto a small ancillary dock on Shell Island. They were a short distance from the main dock, but still on the main channel. Lighters loaded with food and medical supplies and a group of Army and Navy men were waiting there. A harbor pilot joined Bulkeley in PT-41, and they disappeared down the channel.

Kelly explained to his perplexed crew, "The 41 is leading a submarine up the channel. When they get here, we're going to unload her and then pack in the supplies from those lighters. I presume they'll deliver them to Corregidor or Mariveles. Martino, to make more room for supplies, the submarine is going to unload its torpedoes, and I'm claiming them. You're in charge of transferring the torpedoes to that empty steel barge and getting them back over to Opon."

Kelly gestured to a Navy officer standing nearby. "This is Ensign Ross Hofmann. He's in charge of this operation tonight and another one tomorrow night." He turned to the ensign. "Any instructions while we wait?"

Hofmann strode into the gathered squadron like a coach gathering his team for a huddle before a game. "In case you're wondering, we're using this small island dock to avoid the attention we would draw in Cebu at the main docks. Like you, I was on Bataan a few weeks ago, and we all know how much those guys need this stuff." He paused for a moment before continuing. "How do I say this? I've tried to work with the Army down here, and they are—well, I'll just say they do things differently. Let's show them how the Navy works."

At 2100, PT-41 returned to the dock, followed by the long, dark silhouette of the USS *Sea Dragon*. The sailors threw their backs into unloading the submarine. Even the *Sea Dragon's* crew, who hadn't breathed fresh air for days, worked hard moving materiel from the submarine and loading the supplies into it. Charles decided the soldiers were all too willing to let the sailors lead the way. *Maybe they're just uncomfortable around things that float.*

Around midnight, Martino talked to Ensign Hofmann. "Sir, it's going to be slow going with the torpedoes. The crane here is small and doesn't have a long reach. Moving their torpedoes to the barge is going to take all night. Just letting you know, sir."

Adding to the other difficulties, the fuel barge pump broke down with the submarine's tanks only partially filled. Before daylight, PT-41 led the *Sea Dragon* back down the channel to the Olango Channel where she could hide in deep water through the day. That night the *Sea Dragon* returned to the dock, finished filling her tanks from the now-repaired fuel barge, and took aboard thirty-four tons of rice and flour in 100-pound sacks.

While Cox, aided by the local pilot, led the packed and refueled *Sea Dragon* back down the channel to open water, Hofmann spoke to Bulkeley. "We, the Army and I, made a mistake. This small dock didn't work as well as I had hoped. Tonight, I'll need you to lead the submarine *Snapper* straight to Cebu's main Dock No. 1. I think it's a fair swap of secrecy for speed. With the proper cranes and equipment I think we can finish in a single night."

The next day, 5 April, was Easter Sunday. The tired sailors chose their bunks and sleep over an impromptu sunrise service. That night Charles and the rest of MTB 3, along with a few soldiers, unloaded the *Snapper* and filled her with forty-six tons of rice and flour, and 29,000 gallons of diesel fuel, finishing well before dawn.

Snapper followed PT-41 down the channel to open water and headed for Corregidor.

Ross Hofmann thanked the squadron. "If successful, both submarines will dock at Corregidor, unload, and proceed from there to Australia with two dozen or more passengers jammed into each submarine. Unfortunately, people don't pack as efficiently as sacks of rice."

The work of Squadron 3 at the docks was not without reward. In return for their labors, they appropriated fourteen more precious torpedoes. The submariners didn't give them up happily but were at least kind enough to charge them with compressed air before transferring them to the barge.

On the way back to Opon, John Balog found Charles looking down the channel from PT-41's stern. "You're quiet this morning, Charlie."

"I'm thinking, John. We loaded about eighty tons of food on those submarines, right?"

"More or less."

"OK, that's 160,000 pounds. We've got what, roughly 80,000 men, on Corregidor and Bataan?"

"About that."

"That's about two pounds per man. If you ration it at six ounces per day per man, that's maybe five days of food, assuming no waste in the process?"

"There are a lot of *ifs*, Charlie. *If* both subs reach there, *if* all the food is offloaded, and *if* it's efficiently distributed. It's more likely only two or three days of starvation rations."

Charles nodded, then looked at Balog, "Those men on Bataan are finished, aren't they? Their backs are to the ocean. Nowhere left to retreat. It's not like Dunkirk two years ago—no boats are coming to take them off the beaches. They're going to be killed in the fighting, die from starvation or sickness, or be surrendered as prisoners. It's not right, John. Why were they left in that situation?"

"I think you know the answer to that, Charles. We're not on Bataan, but that doesn't mean we aren't just as expendable as them. Our purpose is to give our forces more time. We are the acceptable losses in battle, buying time now for the war to be won later. Since the first recorded history, war's had its cannon fodder, Charlie. This time it's us."

"I still have to ask, why are we all in this mess? Whose fault is it?"

"Japan, I would say," John grinned for a second or two. "OK, I know that's not what you meant. Perhaps it's MacArthur's fault. Or Congress or the president's. It doesn't matter really. I overheard Ray telling Bulkeley that intelligence thinks Japan intended to wrap up occupation of these islands by early February. Now it's April, and they're still fighting us for control. Every day we keep their army tied up in the Philippines gives the allies more time to build up forces in Australia. The Japanese can be stopped there."

"John, there's still a chance you and I might get to Darwin. Bombers are still evacuating people from the Del Monte field, and MacArthur said he would make sure that all of us, every man in Squadron 3, got to Australia."

"C'mon, Charlie—you've been in this man's Navy too long to fall for every bullshit promise an officer makes. Mark my words, even if Bulkeley, Kelly, and the other officers fly off to Australia before the end, you and I probably won't rate that same ticket. We're stuck here until the surrender, if we're still alive then."

"I'm not surrendering, John. Never! I'm coming out on the other side of this with my body and mind in one piece."

"You say that with confidence."

"John, since my war started in Olongapo I've known it. I am one-hundred-percent sure I'll finish this war alive and well."

46

Fever

Opon, Mactan Island, Philippine Islands

7 April 1942

"Doc, I think you need to take a look at Jessie. He's burning up with fever, and he can't get out of his bunk."

Clark was indeed seriously sick, in the throes of a violent rigor and shaking uncontrollably. His temperature was 104, and he had difficulty answering questions. *Damnit! He's got malaria, a very bad case.*

Kelly was in Cebu City, so Charles went to Brantingham. "Sir, Clark needs to be in a hospital."

"Can't you treat him here, Doc?"

"I could try, but he's in bad shape. He needs a hospital."

"How long is he going to be out of commission?"

"Ten days, two weeks minimum—if he doesn't die."

Hearing that, Brantingham arranged immediate transportation for Charles and Jessie across the strait to Cebu City and an ambulance to the city hospital.

Southern Islands Hospital was the most modern and best equipped Philippine hospital outside of Manila, and most of the staff were American trained. As in every other Philippine hospital, the doctors were knowledgeable and experienced in dealing with malaria in all its clinical forms.

There was nothing else Charles could do but squeeze Clark's hand, offer words of encouragement, and leave it to the hospital staff to take care of him.

ॳ॰ ॳ॰ ॳ॰

Charles walked out of the hospital's main entrance and looked up and down the street. *No need to hurry back. Enrique did tell me I could ask anyone.* He went back inside the hospital and found an authoritative-looking woman behind a desk. "Por favor, *quiero*—I want to find the house, *la casa,* of Enrique Aboitiz."

"Ah, the Aboitiz house. Of course," she replied in perfect English. "I am Maria." She extended her hand but did not stand.

Perhaps Enrique wasn't exaggerating. "You know him?"

"Everyone in Cebu knows the Aboitiz family. They are a major benefactor of this hospital. Do you know Enrique Aboitiz?"

"I met him in—on another island, and he asked me to visit him if I came to Cebu."

"Is that so?" Maria looked doubtful as she eyed his tattered uniform. "It's close to here. A very short walk." She gave him directions and added, "If you get lost, which you won't, but if you do, ask anyone, and they will point the way."

Arriving at what he thought must be the Aboitiz house, Charles hesitated momentarily before pulling the bell chain. A house boy opened the gate. Behind him Charles could see manicured grounds. "I am here to visit Mr. Aboitiz?" Charles heard uncertainty in his own voice. *Is this really a good idea?* "Please tell Mr. Aboitiz that I am the American sailor, Charles Beckner, who met him in Cagayan recently."

"Yes, but which Mr. Aboitiz is it that is expecting you?"

"I'm sorry. I'm looking for Mr. Enrique Aboitiz."

"Of course. Please come with me." He ushered Charles into a small sitting room. The house seemed almost American in construction and appointment. Moments later Enrique strode into the room with a broad smile and a two-handed welcome. "Mr. Beckner! It is so kind of you to honor me with a visit. How are you, and how did you get to Cebu?"

"I'm not sure I'm permitted to share the details, but I am here for a while on Mactan Island."

"Yes, of course. I understand that two of your boats are now at Mr. Cleland's shipyard. He runs a good shop and will quickly have your boats in perfect shape."

Good Jesus Christ! This country is like living back in Princeton—there are no secrets! Then he remembered that the Aboitiz family was in the shipping business. Enrique would of course know Dad Cleland personally.

374

"You must stay for dinner, please. I insist."

Charles knew that dinner would likely start late in the evening and might last beyond midnight. "I only came to the city to bring a crewman to the Southern Islands Hospital. He has a severe case of malaria. I would be in trouble if I stayed so late."

"Could you not stay here for the night? I know the repairs are not completed on your boats."

Amazing—he knows as much or more than I do about our PT boats. "I would need official permission, Mr. Aboitiz. Otherwise I would be considered AWOL, absent without leave."

"Enrique, please. And Charles, if I can obtain permission, would you agree to stay? My family is acquainted with General Chynoweth. If we obtain permission from your commander through the general's office, will you agree?"

Bradford Chynoweth was Commander of the Visayan forces. If Enrique was willing to obtain approval from the general, Charles could hardly decline.

"Of course. I would be grateful for a cooked meal. You must understand I didn't bring any other clothes." *Not that I have anything better.*

An hour later, word arrived that Pharmacist's Mate Charles Beckner had a 24-hour shore leave.

Later that evening, freshly bathed and clean-shaven, Charles joined the family. Enrique loaned him an embroidered shirt, a *barong*, which he wore over his undershirt, untucked as instructed.

Their dinner guest, a priest, claimed the chair next to Charles and gave a blessing to the gathering before turning to the young American. "I'm Father Luke, with the Redemptorists in the Philippines. We have a house outside of Cebu and run the Eversley Children's Leper Sanitorium."

"Do you know a padre in Cagayan, Father Haggerty?"

"We have a small house there, and I might have heard the name. Though we are all Brothers in Christ, each of the orders tends to be somewhat insular in pursuing our missions. How do you know him?"

Charles summarized his meeting Father Haggerty in the Ateneo and the dinner with the Paradies, where he'd met Enrique.

Then, remembering that MacArthur was safely in Australia, he decided he could freely share stories of his journey. He told the story of the "miracle" of Father Haggerty's blessing to release PT-34 from the coral reef at Cagayan. Father Luke and the others roared with laughter at Charles's dramatic rendition of the event.

The meal and the conversation were both long. It was well after midnight by the time Charles made it to the guest room. He was tired to the point of exhaustion, and the food had not settled well. A thin coating of perspiration dampened his forehead. *Am I coming down with something? No chills or shakes, so it's probably not malaria like Jessie. I'll feel better in the morning.* He crawled into the bed.

Horrific visions filled his sleep. He watched PT-32, with its crew desperately waving for help, slowly sink beneath the water. Why weren't they rescuing them? Day turned to night, and swells on the dark sea lifted him up and dropped him down. He was aware of explosions and flashes of light and realized he was shooting into a barge that moved closer while he continued shooting. Then he saw, with horror and revulsion, the deck piled high with American sailors, the faces on their emaciated corpses staring back accusingly. He tried to scream but in the paralysis of sleep was unable to move or cry out.

The worst pain he'd ever known erupted in his head and spread down his spine and to every part of his body. *This must be a dream.* He tried to wake himself but fell back into the abyss of nightmarish hallucinations. *Am I dead? Is this Hell?*

Eventually everything went black, and the dreams, along with all awareness, faded away.

Consciousness gradually returned. Every muscle in Charles's body screamed in pain, and he had no strength to move.

He opened his eyes. It was dark, but he could make out a bedpost. A man sitting in a chair next to the bed spoke very quietly, but he couldn't understand the language.

Am I dreaming? I'm confused. Oh yes, I am—was?—at the Aboitiz home.

"Hello. Who are you?" he quietly asked the figure next to the bed.

"It's Father Luke. Do you remember me?"

"Yes. You sat next to me at dinner last night."

The priest chuckled and drew open the shutters, letting light into the room. "Partially correct, Mr. Beckner. That dinner was two nights ago. You have been quite ill. The doctor was going to move you to the hospital last night, but your fever and spasms finally dissipated."

Charles digested that information for a moment while he inspected the surroundings. He was in a different room than the guest room he remembered. He shifted in bed, but his right hand was caught on something. He saw it was tied by a cloth bond, and fluids were dripping from a glass bottle through a tube into his arm. Thankful to be left-handed, he used that hand to untie the knot. The priest observed but did not interfere. "How do you feel?"

"Like shi—umm, I feel weak. No strength. Every inch of my body aches. Dinner was—" Charles paused to think, "Tuesday night?"

"Yes."

"So today is Thursday?"

"Correct again. You seem to have recovered. At least your mind is working."

Panicked, Charles sat up straight, ignoring the pain shooting down his spine. "I'm AWOL! I have to get back to my squadron right now!"

"It's OK, it's OK," the priest calmed Charles. "Your unit has been informed that you are extremely ill with dengue fever."

"Dengue fever?" *That explains it.* "When I woke up, you were mumbling something I couldn't understand. Was that Latin?"

"Yes."

"Were you giving me last rites?"

"I do admit we had a slight concern yesterday that you might succumb. I chose not to wait until you took your very last breath. The tradition of offering the sacraments to the dying has always been part of the Catholic faith, including the opportunity for Reconciliation, the administration of Viaticum, Anointing of the Sick, and the Apostolic Pardon. The Sacrament is part of our Catholic tradition."

"Back in Hospital Corps School, in San Diego, Navy chaplains of different faiths talked to us about their role in caring for the mortally wounded. I don't recall everything, but I thought the sacraments were only for Catholics. Would your church approve of offering them to me, a non-Catholic?"

"I believe so. We Redemptorists follow a path of social justice. In that same vein, we believe our Lord and Savior died to save *all* people—even an American sailor." He chuckled. "Jesus Christ won grace for us by His death on the cross. The church teaches that a person must be in a state of grace when he dies in order to get to heaven, and an effective means for grace is the sacraments. So, I try to do whatever I can to provide those sacraments to all the baptized, Catholic or not. And, from the stories you told, you seem to have acquired as friends a number of Catholic priests. You were in danger of death, and I was hoping for an opportunity to receive your confession before proceeding. Then your temperature came down, and you lapsed into a very deep sleep."

The door opened, and a man Charles did not recognize walked in. He looked at Charles, then at a smiling Father Luke, then back to Charles. Though obviously Filipino, he spoke in English. "I am Doctor Ortiz. Mr. Aboitiz called for me early yesterday. You were quite sick."

"So Father Luke has been telling me."

"How do you feel?"

"General myalgias, but minimal arthralgia. No chest or abdominal pains, and no rigors or sweating. Extreme fatigue."

Dr. Ortiz raised one eyebrow. "Ah, yes. Enrique did say that you are a Navy corpsman. It was dengue fever, of course. You have scattered bruising and small scleral hemorrhages, but it stopped short of full hemorrhagic progression. I expect there'll be complete recovery, but be aware that fatigue will persist for days, sometimes weeks."

"At the moment, I have a very full bladder. Can we take this thing out?" Charles lifted his right arm with the intravenous tubing.

"I will, if you can demonstrate you are able to stand long enough to empty your bladder. Anything else?"

"Right now, I think a cup of strong coffee would be the best medicine you could give me."

47

The Fall of Cebu

Cebu City, Cebu Island

Morning, 9 April 1942

Enrique entered the library where Charles, still wrapped in a light blanket, had been moved. A Filipino helper followed with a full coffee service on a tray. "I will bring you up to date," Enrique began.

"First, if I may interrupt?" Charles had thought carefully about what he wanted to say. "I have to thank you and your family, as well as Father Luke and Dr. Ortiz, for everything you have done for me. This was much more than you bargained for when you invited me to dinner, and I am very grateful. I do hope you understand that I must get back to Opon and join my boat and crew? PT-34 will be ready for action soon."

Enrique smiled at the eager young sailor. "I appreciate your kind words, but there are some things you need to know. First, the Army has informed your superiors of your illness and that you were being cared for here." He held up his hand when Charles started to speak. "Let me finish. Your boat was returned to the water last night, and with another boat was engaged in some sort of action against the Japanese."

Oh my God, they went on a mission without me! Jessie Clark's in the hospital—he and I should have been on the machine guns—

Enrique continued, "One of the boats, I do not know which one, was attacked by Japanese planes early this morning. It was destroyed in the channel south of Cebu. There were casualties, and four of your men were taken to

379

the Southern Islands Hospital. I am sorry, but one crewman was taken to the hospital morgue. I do not know any of the names. The other boat did not return, and I have no additional information on that boat."

He paused. "There is more bad news."

Charles just stared at Enrique.

"Though Corregidor still holds out, Filipino and American forces on Bataan have surrendered."

"My God! That means tens of thousands of our men are now prisoners." *That would include Commander Bridget and our PatWing 10 men. What about Tillie? She was working in the jungle hospital—was she part of the surrender? Certainly, the nurses would have been moved to Corregidor before a surrender.*

After a moment, Charles asked, "What about down here? Cebu, Negros, Mindanao?"

"Negros, as far as I know, is free of Japanese incursion. In Mindanao, they occupy Davao on the south, and assemble forces to move north. Here at Cebu, unfortunately, the Japanese Navy and soldiers are already positioned for invasion of the city, expected to begin within a few days. General Chynoweth has already moved most of his men to Mindanao. Those left here are placing demolition charges around the harbor to slow the Japanese and to destroy all supplies, munitions, and fuel. That includes those on Mactan Island."

"What will you do, Enrique?"

"My grandfather was Basque," Enrique said with pride. "Our family thrived under Spanish rule, as we have done under the Americans. The Japanese, though? It will be difficult, and our family could lose much. Fortunately, we were able to remove some assets from the islands earlier this year. But, I am certain of this, the Japanese will be driven out, and we will rebuild our business."

"Will you leave Cebu?"

"The Japanese do not have enough soldiers to occupy the entirety of every island. All I can say is that we are survivors. When the Japanese do take this city, I advise that Cebu is not an island where an American could escape the Japanese soldiers for long. Food would be difficult to acquire and hiding for a long time impossible. Mindanao and Leyte both have regions I doubt the Japanese can ever control, and food and shelter can be found. On Mindanao, of course, one would have to come to accommodation with the Moros."

"Sir, I need to go to the hospital now, to see my injured crewmates. A friend is also there with severe malaria. I want to find out how they are doing and what has happened to my squadron."

"Of course, but you are weak. Though it's not far, I will have someone drive you there."

Charles pushed himself up from the chair with some difficulty and extended his hand. "Once more, thank you again, for everything."

"No," Enrique took his hand. "It was my privilege to serve as host to an American sailor who is fighting for our country. You are welcome to return here at any time in the future, under any circumstances. Even tonight, should that be necessary."

"That's kind of you. Maybe I will."

"Your clothes are clean and waiting in the room where you woke this morning. A driver will be waiting on the street in front. *Dios te Bendiga.* God bless you."

$$\text{🐦 🐦 🐦}$$

At the hospital entrance, Charles thanked the driver, then pointed to a map on the car seat. "Can I look at that road map for a moment?"

The driver handed the Texaco automobile road map of the southern islands to Charles. "Keep this one. I have another."

"Thank you." Charles stuffed it in his pocket. *Boat's gone. Japs are coming. If I have to, I'll walk to Australia. At least I'll have a map.*

The hospital had special wards for leprosy and malaria, but the staff chose to keep all of the American sailors together in their own ward. Charles found Jessie Clark sleeping in the corner bed, and then saw the others, Hunter, Martino, and Ross. Even as he rushed in to see his PT-34 mates, thoughts crowded through his head. *These are my crewmates. It must have been PT-34 destroyed in the channel. That means it's PT-41 that's missing. Enrique said one man was killed and four injured men were brought here. Where's the fourth injured crewman, and who was killed?*

Clark, limp with malaria, remained only semiconscious. Hunter, his huge frame draped across the hospital bed, struggled to balance a right arm buried in a mound of bandages. Martino's thigh was wrapped from groin to knee. Ross had bandages on both legs, both arms, and his head.

Ross was groggy but the first to recognize Charles coming through the door. "Doc! They moving you up here with us?"

"I'm not a patient—just came to see why you deadbeats aren't back scrubbing the decks."

"I don't mean any insult, Doc, but maybe you should be in one of these beds. Frankly, you look like shit. Right, John?"

"Like roadkill on southern blacktop in the noonday sun," Martino agreed.

"Is that blood in your eyes? We got word that you were real sick, about to die in some local house. Malaria?"

"Dengue fever, the doctor told me. Worse than malaria when you're sick with it, but then you recover. It doesn't keep coming back like malaria. My eyes might look terrible, but they don't hurt. Seems like the people here are taking great care of you?"

Hunter pointed to Clark with his good arm, "Jessie's not doing too well. He's sleeping most of the time 'cept when he wakes up to moan and shiver. Why's he so yellow, Doc?"

"It's jaundice. The malaria breaks up his red blood cells, releasing hemoglobin, the protein that carries oxygen. All that hemoglobin overloads the liver and causes that yellow color in his eyes and skin. It'll go away." Charles pointed to an unmade vacant bed. "I heard there was a fourth injury?"

"Pappy—" Martino stopped.

Hunter finished. "He went to surgery right away. Didn't come back."

A sinking emptiness opened in Charles's gut. *My God. Reynolds is gone.* Charles cleared his throat. "Anyone feel up to telling me what happened?"

Hunter looked at Martino, "Why don't you tell him, John? You were topside and saw everything."

"It was all very fast," Martino began. "Yesterday afternoon they finished repairs on the 34 and put her in the water to soak for two or three days. Bulkeley came tearing down to the shipyard and told Kelly 'Round up your crew and load the 34 with fuel, torpedoes, and ammunition. We're going hunting.' You and Clark were both out sick, and half the crew was on liberty in town. We dragged Ensign Richardson out of a bar. He was a little rough, but he performed well. Never found Shepard or Eichelberger, but we had enough to man the boat. Reynolds took the port .50s and Harris took your starboard turret. Ross and I were on the .30 caliber up front on and off."

"What was so important that Bulkeley couldn't let the hull finish soaking, or at least get a full crew together?"

"Bulkeley got word there were a couple of destroyers heading south through the channel between Negros and Cebu. Just before a ship comes out of there, the channel narrows and turns east. Bulkeley figured if we could get there before midnight, our two boats could set up an ambush as they made that turn. The idea was perfect 'cept it wasn't two destroyers, it was a damn cruiser, the *Kuma*, and she had four destroyer escorts with her."

"And you attacked anyway?"

"We did. Bulkeley fired his torpedoes first. Both missed. Our first two torpedoes were fired at a thousand yards, but the cruiser turned, and they both missed as well. While Kelly came about, we started another run. Richardson took us straight into the searchlight that had us locked in—must have been six or eight guns firing on us from the cruiser. Pappy was firing at the searchlight and Harris was raking the superstructure. Ross and I were by this time firing away on the .30s. Some geysers lifted from the water, but they were misjudging our distance and their shells were hitting long.

"I was beginning to think Kelly was planning to board her when we finally launched the last two torpedoes from less than 300 yards. We came about hard right. I counted, and then saw both torpedoes hit amidships. The cruiser slowed, and the searchlight dimmed."

"Fantastic!" Charles exclaimed. "Did she sink?"

"Last I saw, her stern was down, and the bow was raised. She must have sunk, but we had the destroyers to worry about. While we were making that second torpedo run, Bulkeley ran the 41 back and forth with harassing fire, trying to draw their attention. Two or three of the destroyers went after them."

"That's when we got separated from the 41," Hunter interjected.

"Haven't seen or heard from them since," Martino resumed. "Then one of the destroyers turned and came after us."

"Who got hit first?" Charles asked.

"Reynolds was our first casualty. Right after hitting the *Kuma*, we got raked with fire on the port side. It took out the port turret, and Pappy took a round through his neck and shoulder. It looked real bad, but he was talking to us the whole time—even smoked a cigarette after the action. He tried to drink some water, but it ran out the hole in his neck. Would have been comical under other circumstances."

Once more, Charles felt guilt grip his midsection. *Damn, damn, damn! Reynolds was our first-aid man. He went down, and I wasn't there for him.*

Jessie moaned and started shaking. Charles went to get one of the nurses. A few minutes later they had Clark again resting quietly.

Martino continued the story. "It took a couple of hours of cat and mouse, but we finally lost the destroyer. Even though it was still pitch dark, Kelly tried to navigate the channel to Cebu. He wanted Reynolds to get some medical care. It didn't work. We got hung up on a tower of coral about 200 yards offshore and lost the middle strut and propeller. We did forward/reverse and rocked the boat, but she was stuck. Kelly had Ross and Shepard row Richardson to shore in the punt with instructions to find and send back a doctor for Pappy. Then Richardson was supposed to find a craft that could pull us off. Never saw a doctor, and Richardson never made it back."

Charles's gut constricted. Trying to hide his feelings, he asked, "How'd you three get hit?"

"Around 0500, near high tide, the boat just floated off. We still could use the outboard engines and there was just enough predawn light to see our way through the channel. 'Bout that time, out of nowhere, a seaplane flew in over our stern and let loose a bomb that exploded about ten yards off the port bow. It blew out all the chart house plexiglass and made a hole into the crew's head big enough to walk through. The port machine guns were already out. Ross ran to the .30 caliber, and Harris started firing from his starboard .50s. Then came four more planes, each one coming in with guns firing, and dropping their bombs. One exploded close to starboard. Harris was shooting up at the plane at that moment, and a small splinter of shrapnel went through his chin into his brain. Hardly any blood, he looked like he'd only slumped down for a nap. Thank God he never knew what hit him."

Harris was in the starboard turret—that should have been me.

Hunter picked up the story. "After their bombs were all used up, they kept strafing. I was with the engines when a bullet blasted through my elbow and came out my forearm, I tried to put on a tourniquet, but with only one hand it took me a while. By then we had a couple of feet of water in the engine room. I stuck my head up and informed the lieutenant it might be a good time to find some shallow water and beach her. Going back to the engines, I saw Reynolds on the officer's bunk. He'd been hit again, this time by shrapnel in the belly. He was holding his gut with his hands. Wasn't much a one-armed machinist could do, so I told him, 'Hang on, we'll be on shore soon,' and went back to keep the engines going as long as I could."

Finished with his part of the story, Hunter nodded to Martino to continue.

"I saw Harris drop and pulled him out of the turret. I climbed in, but the guns were hit and useless. Right then I took one in the thigh and fell down in the turret myself. After I crawled out, I watched Ross do some good shooting on the .30 caliber. One of the planes he hit trailed smoke and dropped into the trees on the mainland. Just as I cheered him on, he took a couple of hits and went down himself. Those same bullets took out the last machine gun, leaving us nothing but our sidearms. Only three of us weren't dead or wounded, Kelly, Goodman, and Shepard. Lieutenant Kelly knew we were through and grounded her on the sandy beach of one of those small islands in the channel."

"Shepard tightened the tourniquet on my arm," Hunter resumed. "Then he, Martino, and I helped Kelly and Goodman get Ross and Reynolds ashore."

Charles looked at Hunter, the largest man in the squadron, a machinist's mate well-liked by everyone. *I can see him ignoring his own pain and taking care of his wounded crewmates. His arm was practically shot off, and still he kept the engines running so Kelly could beach the boat, and with only one good arm, he then helped the rest of the crew abandon ship.*

"Not long after that," Martino said, "Richardson and an Army officer arrived in a *baroto*, one of those small local fishing boats. They retrieved Harris's body, then made a raft to tow us to the mainland. An ambulance brought us here."

Martino was winding up his story when Ensign Richardson strode into the room.

"Doc! You're alive! Two days ago we got a message you were taking your last breaths."

"I feel half-dead, but I'm still on this side of the grass. Hunter and Martino have been bringing me up to date." *And I'm filled with guilt, having been lying in bed during the whole thing.* "Sorry for the loss of your boat, sir."

"Me too, Doc. I watched from the docks while those goddamn Jap planes sank her. Never felt so helpless in my life. By the way, you look like shit."

"Thank you, sir. Dengue fever. I don't recommend it. The doctor said it'll take days or weeks to get my strength back, but I'll recover fully."

"Good, Doc." Richardson turned back to the others, "I collected ID tags from Harris and Reynolds. The Army rounded up a small honor guard to bury them and found a local priest to say the words. It was supposed to be today at 1600, but they just changed it to 1000 tomorrow morning."

Richardson turned to Charles, "Kelly was coming to the burial and bringing Eichelberger and Owens with him. I was supposed to meet them at the American Club, and we'd all walk to the cemetery. Are you in good enough shape to make your way there and tell them about the new time? Tell Kelly I've been requisitioned by the Army for a job. If not before, I'll see you at the funeral in the morning."

"Yes, sir. Watch those Army soldiers, or you'll end up doing all the work. What're the plans after that?"

"You'll have to ask Lieutenant Kelly. Nobody's heard from Bulkeley and the 41. For now Kelly's the boss."

Walking slowly, Charles reached the American Club, finding Owens and Eichelberger waiting outside. Charles told the doorman he had a message for Lieutenant Kelly from Ensign Richardson. A few minutes later, Kelly emerged along with the vice-president of the American Club, who wanted to attend the funeral himself.

"Ensign Richardson said to tell you that the funeral has been postponed until 1000 tomorrow, sir."

"OK." Kelly thought for a minute and pulled from his wallet the pack of emergency money that Bulkeley had given each of the boat commanders at Bugo.

He handed each man a wad of pesos, saying, "Go get drunk. We'll meet you at the cemetery in the morning."

Kelly obviously has his own plans for tonight.

"The thought of booze turns my stomach right now," Charles told the other two. "I'm going back to Opon, check my stuff, and get some sleep. Have fun."

Owens and Eichelberger looked at each other, and Owens said, "Hell, Doc—you don't look like you'd make it halfway there. We'll go back with you. The beer at Opon is just as cold as anything here in the city. Come on."

Ensign Richardson was already at the Cebu dock waiting for a ride to Opon himself when the three sailors arrived. As they crossed the narrow channel, Richardson asked, "Where's Lieutenant Kelly?"

"He told us to meet him at the cemetery in the morning," Charles answered. "From what else he said, I think he's staying in Cebu with businessmen from the American Club."

"Damnit. I'll have to talk to Lieutenant Brantingham then. I've made a decision, and he's not going to like it."

48

The Burial

Opon Island, Philippine Islands

Evening, 9 April 1942

"You son of a bitch!" Charles looked around as if a recipient worthy of his wrath would magically appear.

Back at Opon he'd found his medical bag open.

Probably after the narcotics. Curiously though, they'd left half of his morphine syrettes. *Two other things are missing though: the large bottle of quinine and small bottle of Atabrine.* Almost as distressing, his *Rand McNally Pocket World Atlas* had also been taken. It must have been another corpsman or a medic, or maybe even a doctor, scavenging for medical supplies— otherwise they wouldn't have left any of the morphine. Whoever had taken it was probably preparing, like everyone else, for evacuation or escape into the hills where mosquitoes waited for American blood. The Philippine Islands map in his atlas wasn't detailed, but perhaps someone thought it better than no map at all.

Charles slumped on the cot and closed his eyes.

I'm upset to lose that atlas—Susan gave it to me. But I've got the Texaco road map, and for these islands it's more detailed than that atlas. More importantly, I've got to replace my quinine, and soon. I assume John Balog still has some— where the hell IS John? We still haven't heard anything from PT-41.

There's nothing I can take care of tonight, though, and I'm so, so tired.

ᔓ ᔓ ᔓ

Early the next morning the twelve MTB 3 crewmen at Opon assembled with full canteens and carrying backpacks loaded with rations. Four men had scavenged rifles and the rest carried pistols. Kelly had not yet returned, leaving Brantingham the senior officer and acting squadron commander. Under him were Ensign Richardson and ten sailors: Goodman, Shepard, Eichelberger, Owen, Regan, Napolillo, Tripp, Shambora, Devries, and Charles. With ratings of machinists, radiomen, torpedo mates, gunners, and corpsman, Lieutenant Brantingham had a full crew, but PT-35 still sat on blocks. The shipyard men had labored feverishly and done their best, but the hull repairs were still incomplete.

Dad Cleland apologized to Brantingham. "The Japanese have almost reached Cebu City. Most of my workers left last night for the countryside. I'm sorry, but we'll have to leave PT-35 on the blocks."

"Richardson, where the hell is Lieutenant Kelly?" Brantingham demanded.

"I don't know, sir. The last I knew, he was at the American Club. He told Doc and two others that he'd meet us at the cemetery for the burial this morning. I don't know what his plans were in the meantime."

Richardson chose that moment to make his request to Brantingham. "Sir, I'm needed with the Army. They're getting set to blow the entire docks and warehouse blocks when the Japs get here. Colonel Edmands asked me to help. We're moving medical supplies, food, and munitions up into the hills."

"And then what?" Brantingham challenged.

"We have to assume that PT-41 was lost last night. If—when you destroy PT-35, that's it—there's no MTB 3 left. I could be of more use staying here with Edmands than anywhere else."

"I could just order you to come with us."

"Yes, sir, you could. But I respectfully beg your permission to stay and help the colonel, for as long as I can."

Brantingham considered the request for a minute. "OK, Ensign. Mainly because I don't really have a clear-cut plan myself, I'm not going to stand in your way. When we get to the Cebu docks, you have my verbal permission to be of whatever help you can with General Chynoweth's army."

"Thank you, sir."

"PT-35's old crew should still be on Mindanao, at Lake Lanao. As far as I know, Bulkeley, with or without PT-41, might already be there himself. If the opportunity arises, I suggest you rejoin the squadron there."

"Thank you, sir."

Brantingham then prepared his crew for something they needed to do, no matter how repugnant. "I regret to say this. We must make sure there's nothing left of PT-35 for the Japanese." *Our last PT boat. Damn, this is depressing.*

Brantingham pried off the 35's aluminum nameplate and stuck it in his pocket. He ordered combustibles placed in all corners of the boat. At the last minute, DeVries and Napolillo pulled a small cart loaded with a heavy box to the boat. "We thought we'd put this down in the engine compartment, sir."

"What is it?" the lieutenant asked.

"The explosive warhead from a torpedo, sir," DeVries announced with a broad grin. "Won't be a thing left for the Japs to salvage!"

Several hundred yards north, an explosion preceded a giant fireball rising into the night sky. The Navy was waiting no longer to destroy the fuel and oil tank farms on Mactan Island. Brantingham looked at his watch. "They're doing it early—the Japanese must be here already. Let's go."

The men donned their backpacks and followed their lieutenant to the dock. DeVries held back, and moments later came running up. "I lit two fuses to make sure." A tremendous explosion and flying debris from the shipyard saluted the destruction of PT-35. The warhead from the torpedo had done its duty.

Brantingham walked to a nearby tree. Using a stone, he nailed the aluminum nameplate to the tree. "A marker?" someone asked.

"Yes. PT-35 died and was cremated here. When the Navy comes back, I hope they'll see this and remember us."

They boarded a small launch for the short crossing to the Cebu dock. Smoke and stench from burning fuel tanks darkened the channel.

Richardson took his leave from the lieutenant and exchanged brief goodbyes with several of the men. "Doc, you better have finished that dictionary next time I see you."

"Yes, sir. That's a promise."

Charles watched Richardson stride purposefully back into town. *He's a damn good man. I'm going to miss him.*

"Lieutenant Commander Simmons is the senior Naval officer still on Cebu," Brantingham briefed his crew. "He's taking a boat with his men to the island of Leyte, and we're invited along. The boat is docked near his office—let's go."

Simmons was indeed loading his boat when they arrived. The boat was small. Too small. It was clear there would not be enough room for eleven additional men. "Go ahead, sir," Eichelberger encouraged. "We're a tough and devious lot. The Japs will never lay a hand on us." Others agreed and encouraged

Brantingham to leave with Simmons.

"No," Brantingham said. "We're all going home together. We'll work out a plan." *What a prince of a man! He didn't even think about leaving us!*

Charles had always liked Brantingham, and now, watching the boat that Brantingham could have boarded slip her lines and depart, he felt new admiration for this lieutenant.

A runner from Lieutenant Colonel Edmands's command post reached the group of sailors. He was looking for Lieutenant Commander Simmons.

"You missed him. He just left, and I don't think he'll be back."

"Colonel Edmands needs a Navy officer for the next few hours. Who's the senior officer here with Simmons gone?"

Brantingham looked around, "Anyone seen Kelly yet? No? Damnit, I guess it's me."

"Lieutenant Commander Edmands needs you to help identify and give information about Japanese ships as they come up the channel. That's probably an order, unless you have a superior close by. Also, your men need to leave here. Edmands will give the order to blow up the docks and buildings as soon the first Japanese ship lands."

"Give me a moment." He turned to the crew. "I have a plan, but I need one of you to find me a map while I'm gone. I know Bulkeley and Kelly had one, but neither of them is here."

"Sir, would this one help?" Charles pulled the Texaco road map from his pocket.

"It's better than a stick and sandbox." Brantingham laid the map flat and gathered the men around. "Simmons told me that the Japanese have already landed at Toledo, on the other side of Cebu, so we have to avoid that area. They'll probably move east on the main Cebu-Toledo road, coming through Cantabaco. There's another route, this dotted line on the map, here. It crosses the island north of the main road. Looking at the map legend though, it might be nothing more than a wagon path."

"How far is it across there, sir?" Owens asked.

Brantingham made a rough estimate from the map's scale. "It looks to be about twenty-five kilometers as the crow flies, but it'll be fifty to sixty kilometers in reality."

"Thirty-five miles or so—"

"About that. We can follow that road, path, whatever, to the west coast, find some native craft, and sail or paddle across the strait to Negros. By the last reports, the Japanese are ignoring that island, at least until Cebu is taken. Once on Negros, we make our way south along the coast to Dumaguete. From there, it's only thirty or forty miles by boat to Mindanao. We can buy, rent, or commandeer a crossing. If any of our planes are still landing at the Del Monte Plantation, we should be able to take one to Australia, since MacArthur promised us priority transportation out of here."

"What time? And where do we meet?" Owens asked.

Brantingham pointed to the last intersection where the northern road left Cebu City. "Head to that intersection now. If you see any working vehicles on the way, take a minute to disable or destroy them. We regroup at that intersection no later than 1100 and leave immediately. If I'm not there, hold until 1200. If I don't show by then, the senior man takes charge and you leave without me. I'll catch up somewhere between here and Dumaguete. We have to be out of this city by nightfall."

"Sir?" Charles asked. "Someone took the supply of quinine tablets from my bag while I was sick. While crossing the mountain we'll be in malaria country. I have enough in my small kit here for a couple of us, but not enough for everyone. I'd like to go the base and maybe the hospital to get more."

"OK, Doc. Don't be late. I won't wait for you."

Charles tried the Army dispensary first. The medic, even younger than Charles, was reluctant to give Charles any quinine. "I'm really not supposed to give away our supplies to the Navy."

"But the Japanese are here, and you're going to run for it any minute now. Can you carry everything in your pack?" Charles pressed.

When it became obvious that Charles would not accept no for an answer, the medic finally parted with one of his four small bottles of quinine, taking them from a medical field chest that was already packed for departure.

"Where are you going?" Charles asked.

"I don't know—I'm just waiting for transportation to show up."

"I suppose you'll be heading into the hills. Good luck, and thanks for the quinine."

With a dozen of us, this small bottle won't last long. Charles headed for the Southern Islands Hospital. It was unlikely he'd be able to obtain any more quinine there than he had managed to get from the medic, but it was worth a try. Before he reached the hospital, a Japanese plane flew low over the city, dropping leaflets. Charles picked up one. It was a message, printed in Cebuano and Spanish. The Japanese were offering a bounty for any American soldier or sailor. The payment for an officer, dead or alive, was huge. *Time to see who our friends really are?*

At the hospital, Charles went straight to see his crewmates. Clark was again sleeping. Ross was alert now. Martino and Hunter were still cheerful.

"How's Jessie? He looks to be sleeping better than yesterday, and you look better too, Ross."

"I feel better than you look, Doc." Ross agreed. "I heard you had dengue fever. Was it that bad?"

"You can't imagine. How're you doing, other than being bandaged from head to toe?"

"I can't walk, and I'm tired of bedpans. On top of that, I can't scratch my balls when they itch. I've told the nurses, but they just ignore me."

Charles laughed, "Good to find you back to normal."

A distant explosion came from the direction of the Cebu docks, bringing an end to the jokes.

Do they know that the Japanese are at our doorstep? I'd better be honest.

"The Japanese are here, and we've started demolition. Colonel Edmands's men set charges throughout the docks and warehouses, the fuel tanks, and everything else. They'll be blowing it up as the Japanese advance into the city. We're evacuating—our Army will have backed into the hills by dark." He paused, looking at the four injured and ill men. "Has anyone said when they're moving you guys out?"

"Doc. Look at us," Hunter said. "We're not in shape to take to the hills. We'll just have to wait for them right here."

"Your legs look OK to me," Charles looked at Hunter.

"Yeah, but then who would scratch Ross's balls?" They laughed, despite the grim circumstances. "Anyway, this arm would just be a burden for anyone I was with. Everyone's better off if I stay here. So, what about you? Where are you going?"

Charles told them of Brantingham's plan to walk out of the city and work their way across land and water, back to Mindanao. They all looked towards the window at the sound of another explosion.

Then John Martino handed him three thin letters. "We were hoping for the Red Cross to send these out, but they haven't been back. If you get a chance, give these to someone leaving on a boat or plane—or mail 'em yourself when you get out."

He paused. "You better be moving on now, Doc."

After handshakes and hugs, Charles left the four men without looking back. Along with the letters, he carried a large lump in his throat.

Only a skeleton staff remained at the hospital, enough to care for patients too ill or too injured to be moved. The other patients left with families for homes in the city or elsewhere on Cebu.

The hospital pharmacy was closed and locked. At the main reception, sitting calmly at her desk was the same woman he met before. "Maria!" He took her hand. "You're still here?"

"Yes, I live very close. You don't look so good. Did you find the Aboitiz house?"

"Yes, thank you again. Now I need to find someone with keys to your pharmacy. I'm hoping they will share some medicine that I need."

"You need drugs?" Maria furrowed her brow.

"No, not pain drugs. I need malaria pills. Quinine."

"Let me call someone. Go wait at the *farmacia* door."

A young Filipino doctor met Charles at the pharmacy. "I am Doctor Torres. Maria said you needed quinine? Are you a doctor?"

"No, I'm a US Navy corpsman." Charles showed his now tattered Geneva card with the red cross imprint. "We're leaving Cebu City. On foot. Someone stole my supply of quinine, so I was hoping you could sell me some. I have eleven sailors in my group, but in the countryside, I might have many more."

"You will be a guerrilla?"

Charles was not sure why the doctor was asking this, but he gave a truthful answer, "Maybe."

The doctor unlocked the door and motioned Charles in with him. "In that case, you will need a lot of quinine. I prefer to give it to you than wait for the Japanese to take it." He handed Charles two large bottles of quinine tablets, then added, "Take this too. We have only two bottles here. I have hidden other bottles outside the hospital. We give it only to those patients with the worst cases of malaria." He handed Charles a bottle of tablets labeled "Mepacrine/Atabrine."

"I know about this drug, but it's only been available in our big hospitals. I can pay you for this." Charles reached for his fold of money.

"Do you have 100 pesos?"

"Yes, but I know 100 pesos has to be much less than it cost you—"

"No matter," the doctor said quickly. "Now I have legally sold you the medicine. *Magmadali*. Hurry on your way. God go with you."

"*Salamat!*" Charles thanked him once more and left the hospital. He glanced upward. *OK, God. Twice in the last twenty-four hours you've been asked to 'bless me' or 'go with me.' OK with me—I could use a good partner right now.*

He still had time to make the burial, to be in a cemetery at the edge of town.

Charles found it at the end of a dirt road. The graveside service was already underway. The promised Honor Guard and American flag were nowhere to be seen. Three civilians bowed their heads as a priest said words over the two graves.

The explosions from the docks are coming faster—and there's small arms fire now. I suppose that can serve as a twenty-one gun salute for these guys. Charles walked up and stood with the civilians. The padre nodded at him and read another scripture. *It's Father Luke! I keep running into these damn priests.*

Charles stared at Harris and Reynold's rough wood coffins. He gave the two a final salute while the priest led the tiny assembly in prayer. The brief service over, two Filipino workers with shovels began to close the graves.

Father Luke's greeting was only to apologize, "I must hurry back to the House. I can tell you that the Aboitiz family is safe. When you return, God willing, I will be here. Now we both must hurry on our own way."

Charles jogged back down the road into town. At the first intersection, he was stopped by two Army military police. "You can't enter the town." One guard held a Thompson machine gun at the ready. "Sorry, sailor, but all military in the town are under evacuation orders."

"Here's my I.D. My unit's in town. They're regrouping to walk out, and I'm their corpsman."

"Your squadron's probably left already. The Japs are here, and there's a delaying and harassing action underway. On the streets you could easily get killed. Everyone's ordered to leave, and no one gets back into the city."

"But—"

"No exceptions. Strict orders."

"Can you call Edmands's headquarters? My commander, Lieutenant Brantingham, is with him."

The senior guard just shook his head, "Lots of stray soldiers are separated from their units."

"Then how am I supposed to get to one of the other roads leaving the city? This road only goes to the cemetery, and my unit's in town."

"Sailor, our orders are strict with no leeway. Turn around. Now!" The man with the submachine gun didn't point it at Charles but lifted it enough to threaten.

Can't talk my way past these guys. I've got a problem.

49

The Long Walk

Just outside Cebu City, Philippine Islands

Midday, 10 April 1942

Charles walked a few yards back up the road and sat down on his bag. His muscles still ached, and sleep deprivation amplified his fatigue. *Damn dengue fever!* Staring down at his feet, he realized the inside sole of his right service shoe was beginning to separate from the upper. *I'll be in real trouble without shoes.*

Opening his medical kit, Charles removed his largest curved needle and thickest, strongest suture thread. Using a rock to help force the needle through the leather, he placed the suture through the edge of the sole and into the upper leather, keeping it unexposed to the sole's bottomside where it would quickly wear through. It was not a permanent repair but should endure a few more hours of walking.

While doing the repair, he thought about his options. The rendezvous intersection Lieutenant Brantingham had selected was north of the cemetery. If Charles skirted the city northward, he would eventually intersect the road, follow it back toward the city, and meet the crew at the intersection to wait for the lieutenant. But he'd have to hurry.

Backtracking past the cemetery, he followed a series of dog-leg paths and dirt roads, always moving north. Finally, he came to a narrow dirt road extending from the city into the jungle-covered hill. He turned towards town, hoping Brantingham and the others would still be there.

Charles encountered no soldiers as he walked back into town—and no one from MTB 3. It was almost noon before he reached what he thought to be the correct intersection. No one was there. *The guards' refusal to let me into to the city delayed me too long. It's my own fault for leaving the group. The upside is that now I have a supply of atabrine and quinine. I don't regret seeing the guys at the hospital before leaving, and it was important for one of us to be at the cemetery for Reynolds and Harris. I can't go back and undo any of that, so move forward, Charles.*

A paper fluttered on a nail in a wood post. Printed on the outside was "MTB3." Charles pulled it from the nail and unfolded the note.

DeVries, Beckner, Napolillo.
Unable to wait. Proceeding as planned.
Rejoin RON 3 when possible. Good luck. Lt. B

Charles marked a line through his name and returned the note to the post in case DeVries and Napolillo showed up later.

I'm not the only one who missed the rendezvous. Should I wait around for the other two? Or leave and try to catch up? The explosions and gunfire are intensifying—and much closer. In my weakened condition and on these narrow paths and trails, it's unlikely I can walk more than three miles an hour. It'll take me a minimum of ten, maybe fifteen hours nonstop to cross the mountains and reach the west coast of Cebu. DeVries and Napolillo could be anywhere.

If I don't leave now, I might never catch up with the lieutenant and others.

An Army sergeant and a civilian walking out of town watched him put the note back on the nail. "Is that letter to the Japs or to your girl?"

"Neither. My squadron was going to meet here at 1100, but I missed them. From this note, I wasn't the only one."

"I'm in the same boat. My name's Bob," the sergeant extended a handshake. "I've been on temporary duty with Chynoweth's army here for the past six months. When most of the others were sent to Mindanao, I was told to hang around until someone cut orders for me. Never came."

"Lost in the shuffle."

"Exactly! My sidekick here is Ed. He manages a sugar cane operation on Negros and needs to get back to his business. The Tañon Strait between Cebu and Negros is less than ten miles wide at some points. Ed says we can probably get a fisherman to take us across. I'll head south from there and maybe find a boat to Mindanao."

"That outlines my commander's plan. The rest of our squadron's already on

Mindanao. If worse comes to worst, I'm sure a resistance group will organize there."

"Join us?" Ed offered.

"Sure—but I'm not stopping until either I catch up with my squadron or I'm standing in the ocean," Charles warned the other two.

"Sounds good to me," Bob said. Ed nodded.

Charles, anxious to catch up with Brantingham, set the pace, despite his heavy pack and residual fatigue. A week without rain left dust flying from the trail with each footstep. The jungle was generous with shade, but also with humidity and mosquitoes. Charles swallowed two of his quinine tablets that morning and offered some to the others. Ed claimed he had been in the islands so long he was immune to malaria, and Bob silently declined the offer with a shake of his head.

The three walked uphill, alone in silence, encountering no other refugees.

Two hours later, the road curved around a rise in the mountain, yielding a view of the embattled Cebu City and its harbor. The trio stopped for a minute to watch the harbor buildings burn. Japanese troops filed from barges to begin the ground invasion. Each time the Japanese soldiers advanced a block, Edmands's men set off another round of demolition charges in the next group of buildings. Fuel oil splashed through the buildings the night before burst into an inferno of black smoke and flames. American Army soldiers and Filipino Scouts pelted the Japanese troops with unrelenting rifle and machine-gun fire from hidden perches. Edmands might not be able to repel the Japanese, but he was managing an excellent and well-executed retreat from the city. By nightfall the Japanese might occupy Cebu City, but Edmands's men would be entrenched in the mountains, having left behind nothing useful for the enemy.

"I'm getting thirsty," Bob stopped to drink from his canteen.

Charles pulled his canteen from his belt and drank from it without breaking stride. "We need to keep moving."

Bob and Ed silently caught up and fell in stride.

As a young man hunting in the Indiana woods, Charles developed a habit of constantly observing movement, patterns, and color in surrounding growth. He did so now. Several times he was certain that something else moved with them, but remained hidden in the surrounding bush.

Something, or someone, is following us, but staying just out of sight.

Charles stopped their march at a small spring in the hillside. "We can refill our canteens here. I have some purification tablets." He dropped one in each of their canteens. "You'll also want to use this vitamin C tablet. Wait thirty minutes for the purification tablet to work, then add the vitamin C and shake the canteen. It'll remove the chlorine taste."

"Sun's setting in a half hour or so," Bob said. "As long as we're stopped, I have some rations."

"Good! I need something to eat," Ed agreed.

"Ever heard of SPAM?" Bob asked.

Charles and Ed looked at each other, then both shook their heads.

"It's canned pig meat. Comes from Minnesota. They've been sending it to England for the past year, and now the Army's buying it for our troops. The quartermaster here at Cebu received several thousand cans before the Japanese blockade and handed some around. It's not bad—I'll share a can with you."

Ten minutes later, Bob tossed the empty SPAM can aside. "What do you think, Doc?"

"Ham that failed the physical."

Charles stood, slung his bag over his shoulder and started walking. "Let's get going."

"Why not just stay here for the night?" Bob called him back. "The road's deserted, and the Japanese are back in Cebu. It's going to be pitch-black anyway."

"I think the moon will come out around midnight."

"What's the damn hurry?"

"I want to catch up with my unit."

"They'll have to stop when they reach the sea anyway."

Charles looked from Bob to Ed and back. He tried another route of persuasion. "Did either of you notice something out there, following us for the past two hours? I did. It could be a leopard. It might be a man. Or two. Even on Cebu it could be Moros. I've never met a Moro, but I know they never liked the Spanish, and they like Americans even less."

"That's exactly why we should keep together," Ed said.

"I agree, and I'm staying right here," Bob stated firmly. "We can rotate a watch through the night."

"My feet hurt, and my legs are tired," Ed said. "I'm staying with Bob."

"You do that then. Like I told you—I'll stop when my feet hit the sea, unless I find my unit first."

Charles unfolded a large square of mosquito netting, draped it across his exposed head and neck, and tucked it under his collar. "Do either of you have any netting? This is the time of day the mosquitoes wake up for their dinner."

"No," said Ed, looking at Bob.

"Me neither," Bob acknowledged. "Go ahead. We'll survive."

Charles nodded, turned, and walked up the path into the darkening jungle, stepping around a pile of *carabao* dung. He pulled his pistol from its holster. The Colt model M1911 .45 caliber he carried was introduced after the Moro rebellion that followed the Spanish-American War. Moro warriors, numbed from pain by religious fervor and/or drugs, continued fighting after being shot once, or several times with the smaller .38 caliber slugs the Americans used at the time.

It was thought, with some justification, that the mass of a .45 caliber slug was more likely to incapacitate a man immediately.

It's a hefty gun, but the weight's reassuring.

Starlight twinkling through the trees provided barely enough illumination to define the path. Armed and ready, Charles walked quietly, with heightened vigilance. Periodically he stopped abruptly and listened. If something, or someone, had indeed been following him earlier, it was gone now. Maybe it/ he/they had given up or were back watching Ed and Jim.

Even so, he continued walking with his gun in hand.

Around midnight, Charles heard faint voices. *Great! I'm catching up with my squadron.* He walked a little faster until the voices were more distinct. *Wait, that's not English. It's not Cebuano either—shit! I think might be Japanese!*

He stood still.

The talking was louder, moving towards him. He had two choices: turn and flee back towards Cebu City or move perpendicular from the trail. Charles looked around and quietly moved into the thickest undergrowth visible in the starlight. He dropped flat onto the fecund mixture of rotting leaves and damp earth. Peeking through undergrowth, he pointed his pistol towards the trail. *Now to be perfectly still until they pass.*

A patrol of seven Japanese infantry troops appeared from the darkness. With rifles slung on shoulders and talking normally, it was obvious they anticipated no encounter with U.S. or Filipino troops on this trail.

They must be from the forces landed at Toledo. I guess they're clearing this path while the main force moves towards Cantabaco on the Toledo-Cebu road. The Japanese army is cutting Cebu Island in half. Enrique was right, this island's no good for an American guerrilla operation.

About thirty yards after passing Charles's lair, one of the soldiers spoke loudly, and the patrol stopped. The Japanese soldier unslung his rifle and looked about. Charles willed his body to sink deeper into the jungle floor.

The soldier walked a few feet back on the road and stepped from the trail into the jungle. He looked around, his eyes pausing on the shadowy thicket where Charles lay.

The man leaned his rifle against a tree, dropped his trousers, squatted, and proceeded with an explosive evacuation of his bowels.

Charles watched two other soldiers put down their rifles and relieve their bladders at the side of the trail. *Christ! It's a piss-and-crap break . . and that squad leader's making no effort to hurry his soldier. Is that a bug crawling up my leg? Please, guys. Move on!*

After five minutes that seemed like hours, the Japanese soldier pulled up his trousers, slung his rifle, and rejoined the other men. The patrol continued down the road.

Charles waited until he no longer could hear their voices—then waited several more minutes.

Standing, he brushed debris from his clothes, confirmed that whatever had crawled on his leg had moved on, and holstered his pistol. There was a dirty-white object next to the same thicket where he hid. Looking more closely, he recognized it as a standard US Navy-issue canvas bag, but could discern no name or initials in the darkness. Inside were two empty U.S. ration cans. *It could be from the squadron. If so, it means I'm following their route. Unfortunately, I just lost another half hour, and my leg muscles are turning to jelly. Unless they stop, I won't catch them.*

Returning to the path, he thought about warning Jim and Ed, but couldn't think of a way to do that.

The quarter moon finally rose, its light filtering through trees. The path climbed steeply through the night, but at first light Charles sensed he had reached the crest.

The rest of the way is going to be more downhill than uphill. Thank God. I'm really, really tired. What is today anyway—April 11? It must be Friday, or is it Saturday?

Doesn't matter.

ॐ ॐ ॐ

After sunrise, the path crossed a small patch of cultivated crops. A farmer waved from a *nipa* hut, speaking what Charles thought was some dialect of Cebuano. Using his limited Tagalog and corresponding hand gestures, he asked the farmer if a group of American sailors had recently passed. Fortunately, the farmer understood enough to indicate that, yes, the Americans had passed his farm during the night. In fact, the farmer fed them. Would Charles also like some food?

After wolfing down a bowl of cornmeal and chicken, Charles extracted pesos from his pocket. "I will pay you for the food," he said in Tagalog.

The farmer waved back the bills. "I grow what I need. I trade for what I can't grow."

Charles thought for a moment, then pulled a small cylinder from his bag. "For the food?"

The farmer's face brightened. He grabbed the waterproof vial of matches before the offer could be withdrawn.

Charles struggled with a decision. *Can I trust this man? Brantingham's group can't be far ahead, but my muscles ache from the dengue fever, and I haven't slept since night before last. I simply don't think I can continue at this pace.*

"Can I sleep here for an hour?"

"Yes."

"No Japanese! See Japanese, wake me. One hour!"

"Yes. No Japanese."

50

Reunited

Jungle road, Cebu Island, Philippine Islands

Afternoon, 11 April 1942

Charles opened his eyes but didn't move. He was lying under a small lean-to. Judging by the sun and shadows, it was somewhere near mid-day. *I've slept several hours. No matter, I needed it.*

His body still ached, but the muscle soreness and fatigue were in retreat. Slowly, his thoughts cleared, and he stood.

The farmer-host, seeing his guest rise, disappeared into his hut.

In a moment he returned with his wife and three young children and introduced each of them to Charles. He took a small bundle, wrapped in leaves, from his wife and handed it to Charles, explaining that it was food for his journey.

"Thank you," Charles touched his heart with sincerity. "Did any Americans or Japanese come by here while I was asleep?"

"Nobody come today. Only you."

"Thank you again for helping me." There was nothing he could offer beyond gratitude, so Charles shouldered his bag and walked into the afternoon heat.

A mile past the farm, a stream crossed the road. Charles turned, walked upstream out of sight of the path, and stripped off his clothes. Using soap from his kit, he bathed in the subdued light of the forest. He decided against washing his clothes; there was no time or open sun in which to dry them. *My clothes may still be dirty as sin, but underneath I'm clean, as they say, body and soul.*

Physically and mentally renewed by the bath, Charles was tempted to abandon all caution and jog downhill. *When Brantingham reaches the coast, he might take the squadron up or down the coast to find a boat. I might have to guess which direction they took. They might even have found some* bancas *immediately and already be on Negros. I'll walk quickly, but not so carelessly that I stumble into another Japanese squad. Hopefully, that patrol last night was the only one.*

By the time the path widened into a real road in the low foothills, night had fallen. After another hour of walking, he could see flashes of moonlight on the ocean between shoreline trees.

At the beach, his road intersected the larger coastal road. Beyond was a small village, sleeping in shadows of moonlight. *Brantingham could have the squadron in that village, or they could be anywhere up or down the coast from here. It's too dark to look for them, and it's far too dangerous to enter the village this time of night.* Charles retreated north to a hill where, hidden, he could observe the village at sunrise.

Life stirred in the village at first light, well before the sun rose above the central mountain mass. Smoke rose from an early morning fire. Charles stood up. *There's only one way to find out if the squadron's hiding here, or if they passed through and continued up or down the shore. I'll just walk down there and ask.*

Charles picked up his bag and glanced once more at the village. He froze in place. Filing out from the village were eleven Japanese soldiers. The officer in charge separated out five men and sent them up the road Charles had just walked. Five more were sent up the road going north along the coast. The officer turned and disappeared back into the village.

Shit. There's no way I can wander through the village or explore the beach. Patrols are on the roads north and east, and the road south leads straight to the Japanese garrison at Toledo. That leaves west, the sea, as my only option. No sign of the squadron. I'll have to get to Negros on my own.

He looked beyond the village. On the sandy shore were four *bancas*, native outrigger boats. The largest *banca* had a mast with canvas. *It might be possible to sail that one by myself, assuming I could push it to the water. It'd be easier to take a smaller one, but could I paddle to Negros on my own? Maybe.*

I have money, but with the soldiers around, I have no way to negotiate with the villagers to take me across. Besides, they might have seen and be tempted by those Japanese bounty offers—so stealing a banca *looks like my best option. Well, maybe not steal. I still have a few dollars in my pocket, as well as the pesos from the paymaster at Bugo. I'll leave a reasonable amount somewhere they'll find it.*

Charles contemplated the theft, decided it would work, and began planning. *I have to assume the Japanese stand a rotating watch through the night, so I'll need to do this before the moon comes up. That'll be after midnight. If I circle around the village to the shore after dark, but before midnight, and if I'm careful, they'll never see me.*

Charles settled back against the tree. He unwrapped the ball of food the farmer's wife had given him for the journey. *Rice. Spices. Some sort of dried meat? Wow! This is good!*

He ate it all, licking the last grain of rice from the leaves. Charles's mind wandered as he waited and watched. He realized, with some irritation, that he had lost track of the days. *Let's see, now. If it was Thursday the 9th when I woke up at the Aboitiz house, that would make today—the 12th. Sunday.*

That's good. I could sure use a day of rest.

Both Japanese patrols returned to the village before sunset. At 2230, with only starlight outlining the village and ocean, Charles worked his way down from the hillside.

He looked and listened towards the trail he had taken from Cebu. *Still no sign of Jim or Ed. For that matter, no sign of DeVries or Napolillo.*

Charles circled north of the village to the shore. The background of breaking surf at the sandy beach drowned out his footsteps on the soft sand. Reaching one of the smaller *bancas*, he examined it inside and out. *I can easily push this one into the surf, but it has no mast or sail. I would face the daunting task of paddling across the strait.*

He searched the *banca* again.

No paddles. Eliminates that option.

He moved on to the large *banca* with the mast and furled sail. *The rigging seems simple enough, but getting it to the ocean could be a problem. It's at least three times the size of the smaller* bancas, *and it's heavy. On top of that, it's low tide, and it's more than twenty yards to the water.*

I'll try anyway.

Charles threw his bag in the big boat, put his shoulder into the bow, and pushed with all his might.

The *banca* didn't budge.

Damnit. It'll be daylight before the tide's in enough for me to float this thing off the beach. No choice now—it'll have to be one of the small boats, if I can find something to use as a paddle.

Charles searched the big *banca* for something to use as a paddle, then stopped. *Shit—something just moved in the starlight. Down the beach.*

He stared at the spot. Gradually he made out the shapes of several men moving up the shore towards him. *Friend or foe?*

He pulled out his .45 and crouched close against the stern of the *banca* to watch. A man, apparently the leader, gave a series of hand signals, and the group split into three. Two men each went to one of the smaller *bancas*, while another four approached the large *banca*, Charles's hiding place. Charles heard a man whisper. *That's English. In fact, I know that voice! Oh my God, it's my squadron!* He holstered his pistol but remained quiet and hidden in the darkness. *I don't want to startle them.*

Spreading out to launch the large *banca*, a man went to each outrigger, and two men put their shoulders to the boat's hull. A low voice that sounded like Brantingham, said, "Now!"

It was not the time for a surprise reunion, so Charles slowly stood up, grabbed the side board, and helped shove the *banca* to the surf.

When the boat was halfway into the water, Charles said quietly, "OK, we're floating back here."

A second of silence was followed by, "Who's that?"

"Can I join you guys now?" Charles whispered.

"Who the hell's there?" the low voice demanded.

"It's me, Beckner. I know your voice even when you whisper, Eichelberger."

"Doc! You bastard! You scared the shit out of me."

Brantingham waded over to Charles. "Welcome back, Doc. Are DeVries and Napolillo with you?"

"Haven't seen them since we left Mactan, sir."

"OK—no time to talk. Let's get a line to those two small *bancas*. Two men get in each of those and the other five in this one. Say goodbye to Cebu."

ʕ•ʔ ʕ•ʔ ʕ•ʔ

A light and steady wind blew from the south. With full sail and a steady southern breeze, the larger *banca* easily pulled the two smaller ones across the strait.

Charles took a silent roll call. *Goodman, Shepard, Eichelberger, Owen, Regan, Tripp, and Shambora. Plus Brantingham. Man! It's good to be back with these guys.*

After checking their course, Brantingham leaned over to Charles. "OK, Doc. What happened to you?"

"The Army hospital would give me only a small bottle of quinine, so I went to the Southern Islands Hospital and managed to secure a good supply of quinine as well as a newer antimalarial drug, Atabrine."

"Great, but why'd you miss my deadline?"

"Reynolds and Harris, sir—I went to their burial. It was just me, a priest, and a couple of civilians I didn't recognize."

"Thanks for that. I'll note for the record that they had a proper Christian burial."

"I would have met you at the intersection on time, but the Army closed down the city. Armed road guards wouldn't let me back in, so I had to work my way around through farms and paths to the road you were taking. I was late but saw your note."

"Do you know what happened to the other two?"

"No idea, sir. I put your note back on the nail before I left to catch up with you. What about Lieutenant Kelly?"

"He never showed."

"Are we still heading for Mindanao?"

"Yes, and from there we're going to Australia. Together. One step at a time, though."

51

Return to Mindanao

East Coast of Negros Island, Philippine Islands

13 April 1942

They beached the *bancas* on Negros after dawn on Monday, 13 April. "Pull the *bancas* high onto the sand so they won't drift away," Brantingham instructed. "We stole them, but at least we can make sure someone else can use them."

"Where to now, Lieutenant?"

Brantingham pulled out a map that Charles recognized.

Was it only two days ago I gave him that Texaco map?

The lieutenant looked at the map and began walking inland. "The coast road should be somewhere just beyond those trees. Looks like it's a little over a hundred miles down to Dumaguete. Hopefully there's still enough commercial traffic on this island for us to beg or hire a ride. Grab your gear."

Charles looked at Shepard. "You guys are traveling light."

Shepard snorted, then explained, "On the first day walking out of Cebu, Brantingham set a fierce pace. Walking uphill in the heat was exhausting. Most of us dumped everything we could. By the time we made it to the coast, all we had was our guns, ammunition, and canteens."

"I didn't see that stuff along the road when I was trying to catch up?"

"The lieutenant said if we weren't going to carry it, we had to hide it away from the road. He didn't want the Japanese to stumble across it and start looking for us."

"Oh, right—" *That explains the bag with the empty ration cans in the thicket where I hid from the Japanese patrol.*

༺ ༺ ༺

At the coast road Brantingham waved down a farm truck. The driver happily gave them a ride twenty miles south. From there, the lieutenant hired another truck for the next thirty miles, paying from Bulkeley's pesos. One more paid truck ride and the nine men stood on the Dumaguete dock.

"I think it better if only a couple of us wander through the village and hunt for transportation to Mindanao," Brantingham announced. "Chief Regan will go with me. The rest of you stay here together until we return." Chief Machinist's Mate Richard Regan was not only Brantingham's second in command, he was also considerably older than the other men.

Brantingham and Regan had barely disappeared into the village, when Owen exclaimed, "Hey, look at that!" pointing to the ocean.

"I think they're Japanese ships."

"Yep. At least three destroyers and a bunch of transports."

"I wish one of our cruisers would show up and sink the bastards."

"Or at least a submarine. I feel so goddamn helpless just standing here!" It was a universal sentiment.

A half hour later, Regan trotted back to the group. "We might have two fishing boats for tonight, but the owners want more money, and they'll only take pesos. The lieutenant used the last of his for the truck ride, and he wants to know what the rest of us can put together."

The other men pulled pesos from pockets, together totaling less than three dollars' worth—not nearly enough.

Regan looked at Charles, who sat on a post, rummaging through his pack. "Don't try to tell me you got no money, Doc."

Charles stood and handed Regan a thick wad of pesos. "That's nearly a hundred dollars in pesos. It's the pay I took in Bugo. See if it's enough."

Using Charles's pesos, Brantingham reached an agreement with four fishermen to transport them in two boats to the small Mindanao harbor of Dipolog.

The fishermen unloaded their day's catch of unrefrigerated fish and gave the hold a quick rinse with seawater. Brantingham ushered his men aboard the fishing boats in two groups.

"Want fish?" One of the Filipinos offered Eichelberger a dried fish.

"No, thank you," Eichelberger replied. Then he said quietly to the others, "I'm not as tired of coconut as I thought."

The boats sailed out of Dumaguete harbor with their passengers crowded in the bottom of the hold, out of sight, in case a searching Japanese vessel appeared. The splintery wood reeked of old fish, a smell almost as rank as the sailors themselves.

Sailing across familiar and mercifully calm waters the fishermen delivered their passengers directly to the small dock at Dipolog shortly after sundown. Pocketing the second half of their payment from Brantingham, the fishermen fled back to the ocean, relieved to be rid of their dangerous cargo.

"This is eerie, Lieutenant," Regan said, listening and looking at the dark and soundless town.

"Blackout status, I presume. Can't go storming in there in the dark. We'll share the beach with the sandfleas until morning and then decide what to do next. First, though, I'm going to that creek and try to wash this stink off."

Daybreak and a quick walk through Dipolog revealed disarray bordering on madness. Stragglers arrived on the Mindanao coast from all over the archipelago, among them sailors without ships, aviators without airplanes, and soldiers without rifles. Civilians, both American and Filipino, wandered the streets without homes. The US Army formed newly arrived military men into ad-hoc combat units—even though they had run out of weapons for them.

"Sir?" asked Owens, looking at the refugees crowding the village, "Do you think it's like this along the entire northern coast of Mindanao?"

Brantingham pondered the question, then answered. "Not the entire coast. But Leyte's a short sail from the northeast coast of Mindanao, so I suspect it's the same situation over there. At any rate, we obviously can't stay here. Army resources are already running out."

"So, where do we go?"

"The Del Monte Plantation. Hopefully, B-17s are still making it into and out of the field there. Time to see if MacArthur can deliver on his promise to bring MTB 3 out. Keep everyone here, Regan. I'll find us transportation."

"You're staring into space, Doc. What are you thinking?" Owens asked.

"Just wondering."

"Wondering what, exactly?"

"Hundreds, actually thousands, of men, women, and children are all gathering here on Mindanao—all waiting."

"Yes?"

"They think they're waiting for American planes and ships to arrive, but, really, they're not."

"Then what are they doing, Doc?"

"They might not realize it yet, but they're really just waiting for the Japanese, and the Japanese most assuredly will arrive—soon."

ॐ ॐ ॐ

Brantingham returned and handed Charles a hand-written receipt. "Here, Doc. It's a chit for your money. I had to spend the last of your pesos hiring a bus to take all of us to Del Monte."

"And here I was about to buy new uniforms at the base exchange."

"The Army Post Exchange doesn't sell Navy uniforms or take pesos, Doc— you'll just have to wear what you've got."

This bus is old and dilapidated, but at least we have it to ourselves. We delivered MacArthur to this island last month, and here we are, right back again. It's been a long and hard journey, but maybe tonight we'll fly to Australia. I'm finding it hard to stay awake—maybe I'll just let my eyes close for a moment—

The rocking bus carried its sleeping passengers west of Mount Malindang before reaching the bridge across the Cagayan de Oro river. At Bugo, the driver turned inland, towards the Del Monte pineapple plantation.

Near sundown, they reached the Del Monte airfield.

Soldiers and a few sailors loitered about. Brantingham and Regan disappeared into the control building, emerging half an hour later. Brantingham gathered the men around him.

"First, Bulkeley flew out on a B-17 last night, so PT-41 must have survived." The men cheered.

The lieutenant smiled and continued, "I don't have any information about the rest of the crew, but as far as I know they're somewhere here on Mindanao. Second, I've put all of our names on the standby passenger list."

A murmur of anticipation ran through the crew.

Bulkeley flew out, but none of his crew? That bothers me. Where's John?

"And third?" Charles asked.

"Right. There are 400 names on the standby list, and several dozen have priority status for evacuation. All of those will be boarded before any of us."

"But they will eventually get to us?" Eichelberger asked for confirmation.

"Eventually," the lieutenant looked at his men, "but maybe not soon enough. They're calling about forty names a week. Even if it continues at that pace, it'll be weeks before our names rise to the top—and it'll be even longer if flights slow down."

"Sir?" Charles asked, "If Bulkeley got out, surely your name must be already on the list."

Brantingham glanced at Regan, then continued, "No reason for us to wait here. There's an Army base, Camp Keithley, next to a resort town in the mountains where they said we can secure bunks. I can check from there every few days to see if the list is changing."

He didn't answer my question—I bet his name's on the priority list. That's the second time in four days he's refused to abandon his squadron, even to save his own skin.

He really is a living definition of what a leader should be.

"Where's Camp Keithley?"

"It's next to the village of Dansalan, at the north end of Lake Lanao."

"Isn't that where Bulkeley sent the original PT-35 crew?"

"Right. If they're still there we'll re-form as a unit. Oh, and—here's one more thing."

"Yes, sir?"

"Some while back a couple of Navy seaplanes landed on the lake overnight. It's a long shot, but as Navy men, we might catch a ride on one of them, if it happens again."

That sounds like the PBYs from PatWing 10 that flew to Australia back in December. They landed on the lake and waited for the tender to arrive offshore with more fuel. I doubt they'll be back anytime soon. "Sir, were those seaplanes PBYs from Patrol Wing 10?"

"No idea, Doc. We'll eat and find a place to stretch out. The driver's agreed to take us to Camp Keithley at first light."

🐦 🐦 🐦

The bus backtracked down to Bugo, then along the coast through Cagayan and on to Iligan. There, they turned inland onto a road that wound twenty-five miles up into the mountains to Lake Lanao.

411

Charles was dozing when he was startled by Brantingham shouting at the driver, "Stop—now!"

The bus lurched to a stop behind a huge Army trailer. It had been dropped there, blocking half the road. Several soldiers rested in the nearby shade.

"Look at that!" Brantingham exclaimed.

Blocked and strapped on top of the trailer was a wood boat, PT-41. Even stripped of her weapons and torpedo tubes, she was still instantly recognizable to the RON 3 men. They poured from the bus to inspect the only survivor of their original six PT boats. But why was a seventy-seven-foot, forty-ton PT boat here, on a mountain road?

Charles stared at the boat, confused but elated. *I don't know how it got here, but it means Balog's probably still alive and kicking!*

Brantingham approached one of the soldiers. "Why is this boat sitting here, and where the hell are you taking it?"

"All I know is that it's been transferred to the Army. We were trying to move it to Lake Lanao as a patrol boat to keep the Japanese from using the lake for their seaplanes. We couldn't get it past this sharp curve, though." He paused, looking at the men who obviously cared about the boat. "We're going to have to tip it off the road right here—we're just waiting for official orders."

"I did hear talk about moving one of our boats to a mountain lake before we went to Cebu," Brantingham admitted. "Frankly, I thought it implausible, if not ridiculous, and said as much at the time. What about her crew? Where are they?"

"They stayed here all day yesterday. They actually refused to leave their boat until they were ordered to go on up to Camp Keithley."

The men's elation on finding that PT-41 had not fallen victim to Japanese ships or planes was short-lived. She was now an Army vessel, seemingly about to be abandoned or demolished. Sailors have always been sentimental about their boats and ships, and this was no exception.

It was the final confirmation that Motor Torpedo Boat Squadron 3 was now no more than words on paper.

"Let's move out," Brantingham ordered. "Nothing we can do here."

Part VI

52

Waiting

Lake Lanao, Mindanao, Philippine Islands

14 April 1942

The bus carried the heavyhearted men around the shell of PT-41 and continued the steep climb. Leaving the jungle, the road leveled onto a lush landscape with scattered fields of corn and grassland. Women worked the fields, some using *carabaos* and others using horses.

"No rice paddies," Eichelberger observed.

"I doubt we'll see any in this country," Charles replied. "We've left the Christian cross behind us." He pointed to a mosque displaying the Islamic crescent. "That priest who gave the blessing to get our boat off the coral at Bugo talked a lot about the Moros. They don't eat pork, and most of them don't like rice. They dress differently than the other islanders. Instead of the flared skirts you've seen on the women in Catholic towns, Moro women wear colorful wrap-around sheaths. The padre called their dresses *malong*s and said the black felt cap worn by the men is a *songkok*, or *kopiah*."

He paused and tilted his head toward one of the men to avoid pointing. "See that man with the white turban? That means he has made the pilgrimage to Mecca that's called the Hajj."

"When did you become a damn Moro expert?"

"In Cagayan, over dinner with that priest, back when we were at Bugo. He told me something else: These people resent Christian imperialists, both Spanish and American. Christians and Moros down here in the south manage

417

to coexist for the most part, but he said I should never wander off into the countryside alone. Outside the Christian mission towns, the western half of Mindanao is all Mohammedan."

They passed a small settlement next to the road. Women cleaned and prepared food while men lounged about, with one exception. Surrounded by scraps of metal, one man worked a grinding wheel, sharpening a long, menacing blade.

At midday the bus rolled into Dansalan. The resort town sat at the northern apex of Lake Lanao, a huge, three-sided mountain lake, twenty-two miles long and sixteen miles wide. Hotels perched near the water. Single homes, some quite luxurious, peeked through the hillside jungle. Close by was the Army's Keithley Barracks, now MTB 3's home port.

Brantingham's group joined hundreds of other American servicemen and civilians waiting at Keithley, each holding onto the slim possibility of receiving a place on a B-17 to Australia. The odds of securing an outbound seat were minuscule, even if a bomber were able to penetrate the rapidly tightening Japanese blockade. But what else could they do?

It didn't take long to locate other crewmen from PT-35 and PT-41. In the midst of handshakes, hugs, and backslaps, Balog greeted Charles with a huge embrace. "What happened to you?"

"Same question for you, John. You go first. Last I heard you were being chased by two Jap destroyers after attacking the *Kuma*."

"It wasn't easy, but we lost them. By then we had also lost communication with the 34. We ended up north of Mindanao, out of torpedoes, ammunition, and fuel. Bulkeley assumed PT-34 was either sunk or else abandoned when Cebu fell, so we had to accept that it was over. He reluctantly turned PT-41 over to the Army. I assume you came up the road from Iligan and saw for yourself how that turned out. How'd you get back here from Cebu?"

"I walked—it's a bit of a story. Can I tell you tomorrow?"

Charles and the other new arrivals luxuriated in real showers, finally able to soap off the stink of fish, sweat, and road grime.

"Man, I could stay in this hot water all day."

"Can't believe we left Cebu City only four days ago."

"That's an eternity away."

"I guess this is the end of the line."

"Looks that way."

"For now."

"Shit! Hot water's gone."

Wearing only a towel, each of the men, as instructed, neatly piled their filthy, stinking clothes on the floor at the foot of their bunks. Charles crawled into one of the three bunks in the room he shared with Eichelberger and Owen. All three men fell instantly asleep.

In the morning their clothes lay at the foot of their beds, washed and pressed by Filipino helpers. True, they were on a Pacific island filled with inhospitable if not downright hostile Moros, and they were in the center of a tightening Japanese noose. Nevertheless, hot showers, sound sleep in a real bed, and clean clothes lifted their spirits. A final surprise awaited them at morning mess.

"Hey guys! You made it!" two sailors shouted from across the room. DeVries and Napolillo ran to join their shipmates.

Through a combination of instinct and design, as MTB 3's final days approached, the surviving crewmen made their way to Lake Lanao and reunited.

"How'd you two get here from Cebu City?" Charles asked DeVries.

"We were separated when the Japs landed. We tried to meet you as planned but got cut off by the invasion. We were on our own."

Napolillo added, "We knew that Brantingham was heading for Mindanao. We couldn't get to that side of the city and follow, so we had to find our own way and meet you here. We walked south from the city, eventually finding some natives with a *banca*. For all our money and everything else in our pockets, including our cigarettes and lighters, they agreed to take us south along the Cebu Island coast, past the tip of Negros, and then across to Dapitan City."

"Over a hundred miles in an open *banca*?" Owen asked, incredulous that they were even alive.

"I made it to be around 120 miles," DeVries confirmed. "We stopped at a plantation near Dapitan and stayed for a couple of nights. The owner was a Spanish-American War veteran who liked to talk—a lot. We got here night before last."

"You do realize this is the end of the line?" Shepard injected a discordant note into their celebration. "There's too many people on the standby list at Del Monte for us to ever get a spot."

"We heard Navy seaplanes have landed on this lake."

"But not in months."

"OK, but didn't MacArthur promise to get transportation to Australia for the entire squadron?" DeVries was doing his best to maintain hope.

Regan cleared his throat. "I saw the standby list at Del Monte when Brantingham and I went into the control building yesterday. It looked to me like the top forty or fifty names were all officers. None of us were on it when we arrived. If we sailors on RON 3 are supposed to be priority passengers, Del Monte sure didn't get the word."

"Brantingham's an officer—was he on the list? He sure should have been."

"I can't say," Regan looked down.

"Can't or won't?"

Regan just shook his head.

I was right—Brantingham's a prince.

John Shambora, now angry, raised his voice. "Just how did we, and by we, I mean the whole Philippine garrison, get into this damn situation? How could the president and all those generals let tens of thousands of our soldiers get trapped on Bataan while the rest of us sit on this stinking lake, waiting for the Japs to come? It's one big FUBAR mess."

"What'd you say? Fu-bar?" DeVries asked Shambora.

"FUBAR. Fouled Up Beyond All Repair."

"I heard a more colorful translation," Regan noted, "but either way it certainly describes things perfectly. In any case, you're probably right. Bataan surrendered. Corregidor undoubtedly will. No reason to think Mindanao won't do the same."

"We weren't outfought on Bataan!" Shambora continued to vent. "Those men were starved and then they ran out of ammunition—poor bastards had no choice but surrender. It's gonna be the same here."

Charles didn't argue with Shambora. *He's right. A third of our men had malaria, a third had dysentery, and the other third had to fight and take care of the other two thirds at the same time. They never had a chance.*

"So what're we supposed to do while we wait?" Shepard asked Regan.

"I think that's it. We just wait for now. The Army here has more men than guns to give them."

"Wait. For what?" Shepard pushed, but his senior NCO had no answer.

DeVries, seated next to Napolillo, spoke quietly to Charles. "Nap and I talked yesterday about what we'd do if we got stranded here," he said. "Plans for a guerrilla resistance have already started. We'll go with them when the order to surrender comes down." He glanced at Napolillo, who nodded. "Doc, you'd be useful—want to join us?"

"A military leader from long ago, Marcus Aurelius, described how to live a noble life. He said that if you can't find a way through an obstacle, go around

420

it. Far as I know, he never said anything about giving up."

"Is that an answer?"

"Yep. If anyone tells me to surrender, I'll walk out of here. I'll never give up and I'll never surrender to the Japanese. Never." Charles looked at the two men. "When and where are these guerrillas forming up?"

Ensigns Akers and Cox arrived at Camp Keithley the next day. "Lieutenant Kelly made it to Mindanao," Cox told Brantingham. "Akers and I were already at Del Monte getting information about incoming planes when Kelly walked in. None of us were on the priority list—Bulkeley apparently thought we were dead. We're on it now, but while we're waiting, they sent the two of us to join the Navy element here and assigned Kelly to take charge of a caravan of *carabaos* forming up at Kalasungay near the Del Monte airfield. He's one unhappy officer, but he's following orders."

"How'd Kelly get here?"

"Apparently made it up as he went along, just like a lot of the guys here." Cox continued, "I do know it involved lots of walking and hiring *bancas*."

Charles thought of all the Americans fleeing to the southern island. *Visayan fishermen must be earning a good deal more ferrying soldiers and sailors across to Mindanao than they ever did by fishing.*

The next morning Brantingham assembled the squadron. "I've received orders from Commander Tisdale, the senior Navy officer in the area. We, the remnants of Squadron 3, are to form a Lake Lanao Defense Battalion."

Oh, crap. Here we go again. Whenever a flag officer sees a few sailors wandering around, he decides he needs another 'Defense Battalion.' We don't have anything beyond our pistols. What're we supposed to do—throw rocks?

Brantingham went on, "Since the Army was not successful in bringing PT-41 to the lake, our assignment is to convert some native craft into gunboats. We'll mount .30 and .50 caliber guns removed from the 41 onto large *bancas* and use them to defend the lake from Japanese aircraft, should any show up."

"Sir?" Owen asked, "Is this a serious plan?"

"Yes," was the lieutenant's unadorned answer.

It was not, to say the least, a particularly good idea. Brantingham put Bill

Johnson, Charles's good friend from PT-35, in charge of a five-man team to convert the first of three boats the Navy purchased from locals. Once the concept was proven feasible by installing and testing the first gun, the other two boats would be modified.

By evening the next day, a .30 caliber machine gun was mounted on a "putt-putt," a *banca,* so named by the Americans for the sound of its small single-cylinder engine. Regan and Johnson took the single outrigger a short distance into the lake to test their work. Brantingham, Charles, and another sailor followed in another *banca.*

"We're ready, sir," Johnson announced.

"Give her a try," Brantingham ordered.

Regan fired straight over the bow of the putt-putt into the lake. Bullets arced into the lake in a wild shotgun pattern as recoil shoved the boat backward.

"Hmm. If it was a Zeppelin, you might have hit it," Brantingham said with only a bit of sarcasm.

"Maybe. If it was real close, sir," Johnson agreed.

"Do you think you can track a plane?" Charles yelled to Johnson.

"Let me give it a try."

Johnson gave another burst of fire, starting over the bow and swinging the barrel to port as he fired. As the gun rotated perpendicular to the *banca*, the recoil rolled the *banca* over, dumping Johnson and Regan into the lake. An angry and embarrassed Bill Johnson splashed to the surface. "Damnit, Doc! You knew that was going to happen!"

Despite the seriousness of the situation, Charles was laughing too hard to reply.

"OK," said Brantingham. "We'll have to move on to Plan B."

Johnson, still in the water, asked, "OK sir. What's Plan B?"

"I have no idea," the lieutenant answered.

꙳ ꙳ ꙳

Camp Keithley was an Army post, but the ranking Navy officer wanted the sailors to contribute their share. Brantingham passed on the bad news. "MTB 3 has been loaned to the Army for general duties. I did manage to keep RON 3 intact insofar as possible. You will continue to bunk here, and I want everyone to continue reporting to Balog or Beckner, not the Army medics, for any medical issue. If and when we have surface craft to operate on the lake, you will return to Navy command. Motor Macs Richardson, Lawless, and

Hancock, fall out to the side. Balog and Beckner, you stay here too."

As the others departed, Brantingham gathered the five remaining sailors. "You five stand by for another assignment in the next several days, but I can't say any more about it. No need to brag about your seeming good fortune—this project will involve a lot of manual labor. Beckner, I need to talk to you for a minute."

"Yes, sir?" Charles asked when they were out of earshot.

"You were with Patrol Wing 10, the PBY group, before you joined MTB 3—correct?"

"Yes, sir, from June until around Christmas."

"Did you spend much time around the planes and maintenance crews?"

I'm not sure where this is heading. Full honesty is more likely to keep me out of trouble than something less. "Well, I was an independent duty corpsman, so I knew most of the men and officers fairly well."

"I'm asking more about your knowledge of the planes than the crewmen."

"At Sangley Point I helped with 'beaching' duty when we moved the PBYs up the ramp from the water. I worked on the refueling team every now and then. I helped the motor macs working on the engines and with other mechanics, but it was mainly handing them tools and parts while we talked. I was on a couple of patrols, and of course I did maintenance on the machine guns. Is there something specific you want to know?"

"No, Doc, that's enough. It's pretty much what I told Ensign Hofmann. Keep this discussion completely to yourself. Don't even talk to Balog about it. I've not been given the full details myself. Keep your mouth shut—understand?"

"Yes, sir." *Ensign Hofmann? Wasn't he the officer in charge of loading the submarines at Cebu?*

Saturday night Napolillo interrupted Charles's reading of a well-worn paperback. "Still memorizing your dictionary, Doc?"

"Hardly, Nap," Charles raised a small book that lay next to him. "I did find a couple of dime Westerns in a cabinet. They're ten years old, but at least they've got all their pages."

Napolillo flipped through one of the short novels. "Let me have them when you're finished? That's not what I'm here for though—you on any kind of duty after services tomorrow?"

"Nope."

"Want to go with DeVries and me to see what some people here are preparing to do when the Japanese Army arrives?"

"Why not?"

John Balog and Charles walked to the Sunday morning market out of curiosity. Swarms of Moros walked or boated into town to buy, sell, or trade. Most of them traveled up the lake in large *bancas* with a deck and hatch leading to a lower compartment at the stern. The marketplace exploded with color and sound when the women, jangling large metal bracelets on both arms, stepped onto the shore in their bright, patterned *malongs*.

Most of the men talked among themselves while the women covered blankets with goods for sale or trade. Charles did see one man setting up his own sales area. "John, on our bus trip here we passed a man working on a grinding wheel. Now I know what he was doing." He pointed at the intricately patterned *bolos* and *kris*. "That's what he was making from scrap steel."

"I think you're right. These daggers are impressive—look at that long, curving blade." John picked one up for closer inspection. "Wow! This edge is razor-sharp. Are you buying?"

"No, I'm happy with my own knife. Listen, I'm leaving to meet Napolillo back at the Protestant service. You're welcome to come along, or I'll catch up with you later."

"Thanks, but I'm enjoying this market. Say a prayer for me though."

After the final benediction, Napolillo led Charles to a camp outside the base perimeter. Two American soldiers stood guard over a half-dozen clustered tents and tarps. Under each shelter, sailors and soldiers worked at different projects. Napolillo introduced Charles to four men surrounding a small printing press.

"Counterfeiting?" Charles asked while examining scattered pieces of paper with images of Filipino pesos.

"Not yet, but ready to begin. We've made acceptable printing plates and formulated convincing inks from local ingredients. Two of us can backpack this whole operation to the hills when the time comes."

"What else is happening here?" Charles asked one of the men.

"That group in the far tent are working on pipe guns. Shotguns mostly. We're hoarding boxes of ammunition in another tent. Over there is our radio tent. Everything you see is something we need for resistance. It's not officially sanctioned, and we're all doing this on our own time. We guard the place from theft with two sentries during the day and four at night."

"Who's in charge?"

"None of this is officially approved, so it has no official status, and there's no commanding officer. We do have senior officers willing to assume command when the time comes. Until then, it's better for them not to be a target."

Napolillo said, "Doc, I'll be here all afternoon. Go ahead and check things out."

"I will." He turned back to the soldier. "In the hills malaria could be even more dangerous to all these people than the Japanese. What's your plan for medical care?"

"I know of at least one Army doctor and a couple of medics who agreed to join and bring medical supplies. Want to be part of this?"

"Count me in. I'll start getting my own supplies together. Will you be taking any heavy guns?"

"Shotguns, rifles, pistols, grenades, and maybe Tommy guns. We'll need to move too quickly to deal with anything heavier."

"OK. Right now, my lieutenant has me on standby for a special project, but count me in."

Returning to the market, Charles was intercepted by Eichelberger. "Doc, Balog wants you at the camp."

53

Preparing the Way

Camp Keithley, near Lake Lanao, Mindanao Island, Philippine Islands

19 April 1942

Balog met Charles outside their barracks. "It's Bill Johnson. I'm sure it's malaria, but we don't have much of a lab up here. He's been feeling bad for a couple of days. Yesterday evening he was hit with severe rigors and fever and tried to sleep it off."

"Let's go see him."

Johnson obviously felt miserable and looked worse. He was between rigors, but still sweating profusely. He wasn't yellow, yet. "Bill, how're you doing?"

"Not so well," Bill replied weakly.

"John," Charles asked Balog, "You know that old schoolhouse at the edge of base that's been resurrected as a makeshift hospital? Let's move him there."

At the schoolhouse hospital, two dozen patients lay on mats. A few were dehydrated from dysentery, but most of the others suffered in various stages of malarial illness. Bill remained conscious, but still dripped sweat and shook in spasms. "Doc?" Bill worked to focus on Charles. "Doc. How bad am I?"

Charles glanced at Balog, then returned focus to his sick friend. "Bill, I'll be honest. We've got to get your temperature down. If we can't do that, then yes, you could be in serious trouble."

An Army doctor, a captain, came over, examined Bill, and nodded at the two corpsmen. "Thanks for taking care of your buddy. You can see he's *seriously* ill."

"Yes, sir. He's already been taking quinine. Do you think he could use some Plasmochin?"

"Great idea, sailor, but we've only got quinine. It'll have to do the job."

"How about Atabrine?"

"You didn't listen!" The doctor was tired and irritable. "I'll tell you again. Quinine is the only anti-malarial we have."

"I have Atabrine I brought from Cebu."

"Then for God's sake, get it and give him a loading dose—nothing to lose at this point."

Charles ran back to the camp and returned with his precious bottle. "Billy, take this water and swallow these three pills. It's a new drug. We're going to break that fever and get you well. In the meantime, you're going to see so much of Balog and me, you'll be begging us to leave you alone."

Charles knew if it weren't for Bill Johnson getting him onto the PT boats, he would now be either dead, a Japanese prisoner, or under siege on Corregidor waiting for the inevitable. He would stay here with Johnson until his fever broke, no matter how long that took.

Balog returned the next morning. "How's he doing, Charlie?"

"Incredibly better."

"I'm feeling good," Johnson smiled at Balog.

"The Atabrine worked like a miracle," Charles said. "His temperature's staying down, and no rigors for at least six hours."

"Don't forget," Balog reminded Bill, "Malaria's the gift that keeps on giving. It'll probably return after a few weeks, or even months."

"But today I'm alive!" Bill turned to Charles, "You saved my life with those pills."

❧ ❧ ❧

During morning mess on Tuesday, 21 April, Brantingham motioned to Charles from across the chow hall. "Beckner, come with me."

"Yes, sir."

As they walked, Brantingham said, "You'll remember Ensign Hofmann when you see him. He'll only tell you what he thinks you need to know, and it's all hush-hush. I'm sure you'll figure out most of it on your own, but keep your suspicions to yourself."

Brantingham made the introduction. "Ensign Hofmann, this is the corpsman I told you about, Charles Beckner."

In full daylight, Charles could appreciate that Ensign Ross Hofmann was a young, baby-faced, clean-cut junior officer. Charles looked at Brantingham, then back at Hofmann. "I remember you, sir. From Cebu. I was one of the PT boaters loading the submarines."

"Right. You helped us load the *Sea Dragon* and *Snapper,* and now it looks like I need you again."

"Happy to help, sir. If you don't mind, how did you wind up here?"

"It's a short long story. I was a quartermaster at Cavite. After the Navy Yard bombing, I moved to Corregidor. From there I was sent to Cebu to organize a fleet of small supply boats to deliver food and ammunition to Mariveles and Corregidor."

The Filipino boat that gave the fruit to us outside the mine fields was probably one of those.

"When Cebu fell, I walked, talked, and sailed to Mindanao. I think it was your own Lieutenant Kelly that was part of our group."

"Yes. And you have a job for me, sir?"

"I'll show you. General Fort gave me use of an Army sedan. It runs, but only in second and reverse. Let's give it a try."

Hofmann took them down the west side of the lake, talking as he drove. "This is the Ganassi Road. Fifty-five miles past Ganassi, at the southern coastal town of Malabang, the Japanese are landing troops. It's probably only a matter of days before the assault on the Lanao region begins. Once they start moving up this road we won't be able to slow them down, much less stop them."

South of Dansalan, Hofmann pulled over next to the lake and pointed to a small island. It was a quarter-mile offshore and perhaps four acres in size. A sailor waited for them in a small launch. Rather than take them directly to the shore, Hofmann had the launch's pilot make a slow circumnavigation of the island.

"Doc, this is where you come in. Sometime soon two PBYs will land here before dawn. I plan to hide them from Japanese aircraft by using the coves with overhanging trees on this island. That evening they'll both leave on a mission and return the next morning. The next night they take off again and will not return." He paused and looked at Charles.

"So they're not coming here to evacuate any of us." Charles said it as a statement, not a question.

"Afraid not. What I do know is in the next week we have to prepare berthing for two PBYs and be ready to fully refuel them on consecutive days. We'll also need to ferry thirty to forty passengers back and forth from the planes to Keithley. The last PBY landed here sometime back before the Japanese landed at Davao. They waited until a seaplane tender arrived offshore, so they never had to refuel here. I haven't been able to find anyone who was involved at the time. The lieutenant here tells me you were in a PBY squadron. What can you tell me that I need to know?"

Charles hesitated, organizing his thoughts. "Sir, I'm pretty sure I know the planes that landed here in December. The first thing you should know is that the PBY is a large aircraft. It's sixty-four feet long and has a wingspan of over a hundred feet. Not only that, they're tall. The wing sits twelve feet above the waterline, and the top of the tail will be four to six feet higher, depending on her loading. Do you plan to hide them under these trees along the shore?"

"If possible."

"Then I think you'll have to cut off some lower limbs to make room to pull them against the shoreline. Even then, they won't be completely covered. Either the tail or the cockpit will stick out from the shore. Maybe you can use the branches you cut off to cover the exposed sections."

"OK. How much fuel will we need? I was told 6,000 gallons, but that's over a hundred barrels of avgas we'll have to move here."

Charles gazed over the water, calculating. "It depends on how far they're flying. If these are similar to the PBYs we had at Sangley Point, and if I'm remembering right, they hold 1,450 gallons of aviation gas in the wings. Assuming they arrive near-empty, you'll need that much for a complete refuel. You said refuel them on consecutive days, so should I assume this is a waypoint that they'll be coming back through?"

Hofmann only looked at him. No answer was an answer.

Charles continued. "OK, I'll assume they'll be empty, or nearly so, on each day. For the first refueling, you'll need around 2,900 gallons total for the two planes, and the same on the second service. That's 5,800 gallons, pretty close to your instructions. Again though, it depends on how much flying this mission requires."

Hofmann nodded. "I'll need 110 fifty-five gallon barrels."

"Yes, sir. If none is spilled and all the barrels contain good avgas. If you have all day to refuel, you can easily do it with a powered pump and one long fuel hose for each plane. If one's available, you might think about having a third pump on hand for backup."

"What else?"

Brantingham spoke up, "There's a reason Beckner commented about the fuel. Our PT boats had to deal with sabotaged avgas at Mariveles. It clogged the filters and shut down the engines at random times. That'd be fatal for these aircraft."

"I hope to hell this fuel is clean," Hofmann said. "We're trucking it up here from the Army fuel depot at Iligan City. I also have instructions to have engine oil available but they were unclear as to how much. What's your estimate?"

Charles answered, "I'm not exactly sure, sir. I seem to recall that the motor macs had to add anywhere from five to ten gallons after a ten-hour patrol. You shouldn't need much more than a full barrel of oil. If you positioned one barrel of engine oil for each plane, it'd be enough. If they need more than that, the engines probably aren't in good enough shape to get them this far anyway."

"I'll get some from Del Monte if we don't already have it here." Hofmann said as they beached the small launch on the island. "I'll give you a tour of my seaplane base. I've selected a couple of locations where we can tie down the planes. I want to know what you think of them."

Hofmann led them around the island, and the men agreed on two sites for hiding the PBYs. One could accommodate a PBY pulled in tail-first. At the other, the plane could be brought to shore nose-first. Next, they selected a staging area that could hide them from Japanese observation planes.

"Lieutenant, do you have suggestions?" Hofmann asked Brantingham.

"Even though I assume you don't want locals talking about your preparations, moving a hundred barrels of gasoline in *bancas*, one or two barrels at a time, will be impossible to keep secret. You should have a good story ready."

Hofmann looked at Charles. "Do you agree?"

"Sir," Charles said, thinking of Father Haggerty, "I think it's impossible to keep anything secret on this island. They're probably already selling tickets."

Hofmann thought a moment, then said, "We could start a rumor that we still plan bring that PT boat up the road in a week or so, and we're building a dock and base for it on this island. We're just caching the fuel here in advance. What do you think?"

"That probably works," Brantingham agreed.

Charles had his doubts, but said nothing.

Back on shore in the sedan, Brantingham asked about defensive positions. "A couple of machine guns might help if unwanted visitors show up. The .50 caliber guns and ammunition taken off PT-41 are still available."

"I thought about that too. I'll show you my idea," Hofmann replied.

Ensign Hofmann nursed the reluctant sedan up a nearby hill. From there they walked to a flat area on the crest. "This promontory is Signal Hill. What do you think of having the Army mount guns here?"

Brantingham was pleased. "It's perfect—a sweeping view of both the island and the entire lake beyond. No need to put anything on the island itself. Why ask the Army for help though? The same sailors who manned those very guns when they were on the boats are just sitting back at the camp. Can you think of someone offhand?" he asked Charles.

"Well, sir, there's me."

"Nope. You're going to be down with me when the PBYs arrive."

"Bill Johnson's recovered from his bout with malaria. He knows the .50s and shoots well. And, if he can't beg or steal a ground mount for the guns, he knows how to build one."

"Sounds good," Hofmann agreed. "I'll leave it to the sailors. But once your guns are in place I'll have the Army keep a 24/7 guard on them. I don't trust the locals."

On Thursday afternoon, 23 April, Ensigns Akers and Cox received a message from Lieutenant Kelly at Del Monte. The three officers' names had been added to the top of the priority evacuation list. A B-17 would be landing soon at Del Monte, but Akers and Cox had to be waiting at the airfield in two hours.

The officers commandeered a vehicle and driver and disappeared in a cloud of dust.

That evening Brantingham announced, "Just got a message from Del Monte. Akers, Cox, and Kelly all just left for Australia on a B-17."

"Why the hell wasn't your name on the goddamn list, Lieutenant?" Lawless, a motor mac from PT-41, demanded. "You're a damn RON 3 officer too—pardon my language, sir. If anyone should have a ticket out of here, it's you!"

Brantingham did not appear upset. "It's OK. I'd rather be with the squadron anyway."

Whether his name was on the list or not, Brantingham, the only MTB 3 officer remaining on Mindanao, stayed with his men.

54

What the Hell Are You Doing Here?

Lake Lanao, Mindanao, Philippine Islands

24 April 1942

It required four tedious trips over two days to move 122 barrels of fuel from Iligan up the twisting mountain road to the edge of Lake Lanao. From the shore *bancas* moved the barrels individually to designated staging sites on the island. Soldiers patrolled the island day and night to prevent theft and sabotage.

Charles and an Army soldier, Corporal Thomas Mitsos, fastened old tires at the shoreline of the coves where the two PBYs would tie up.

Mitsos asked, "What're these for, Doc?"

"They're called fenders, Tom. They're needed to protect the aluminum hulls of the boats that'll be docking here."

"Boats? I haven't seen any aluminum boats."

Charles was thinking of how to respond to Mitsos when Ensign Hofmann walked to the cove with a Navy lieutenant and captain in tow. "Beckner, I need you for a moment."

Charles, curious, saluted. "Sir."

Hofmann introduced him to the other officers. "This is Corpsman Beckner, one of a half-dozen PT boaters I commandeered for this mission. He was with Patrol Wing 10 when things went to hell in December and somehow wound up on the boats. While he was with the seaplane squadron, he picked up ground maintenance experience with PBYs, and he's being a great assist in

432

our preparations."

Hofmann introduced the officers, "Doc, this is Captain McGuigan, senior ship repair officer at the Cavite Navy Yard, and this is Lieutenant Bowers, an ordnance officer. I'm giving them a tour of our preparations. They might be asking you questions over the next day or two." They shook hands. War occasionally blurred formal separations of rank.

Bowers—that name's familiar. "There was a Lieutenant Bowers in charge of the demolition at Cavite on Christmas Day. Was that you, sir?"

"It was, as a matter of fact. I don't recall you being part of the squad though?"

"I was with Lieutenant Pollock, sitting on the PanAm ramp watching everything go off. It was spectacular!"

"I think we did a pretty good job," Bowers agreed with a bit of pride.

"We waited for your group on the ramp but had to leave at 0100. I'm glad you made it out, sir." *I hope that didn't sound overly critical.*

"Oh, right. We were supposed to travel to Mariveles with you at midnight. Plans changed. Turned out we had our own truck. A lot of plans changed— it was a damn chaotic night. I'm sure you've seen your share of unexpected changes since then."

"More than I can count, sir."

Ensign Hofmann brought them back to the problem at hand. "I could only find two powered launches, so I've arranged for motorized Moro *bancas* to help us tow the PBYs in and out of the coves."

Hofmann turned to continue the tour for Lieutenant Bowers and Captain McGuigan, dismissing Charles, "Thank you, Doc. I'll let you get back to work."

Interesting. Every senior Navy officer around Ensign Hofmann acquiesces to his instructions without pulling rank. I wonder if Bowers and McGuigan are hanging around on the chance of getting a ride out of here in one of these PBYs.

❧ ❧ ❧

The preparations on the island were hidden from high-altitude Japanese bombers, but "Photo Joe" was a greater concern. The small Japanese plane flew over the lake at low elevation twice a day when the weather was reasonable. Local speculation was that he flew from a small airfield at Malabang on the coast southwest of Lake Lanao. The flight pattern suggested his mission was monitoring the airstrip at Del Monte rather than Lake Lanao itself, but efforts were taken to obscure their work during Photo Joe's flights.

On the other hand, it was impossible to conceal their activities from the local population. Colorful groups of villagers stood on the shore each day, watching the sailors and soldiers moving supplies to the island.

Besides the *bancas* used to transfer fuel and equipment, several unused *bancas* were tied to the shore. Hofmann rented or purchased them to move passengers from the island to the mainland and back while the planes were being serviced. Their previous owners now watched with curiosity to see how they'd be used.

By sundown on Monday, 27 April, everything was as ready as it could be. Fuel and oil barrels were positioned at each cove. Hoses, fuel pumps, and oil funnels stood ready. Tie-down ropes waited at each berthing site.

Ensign Hofmann organized teams to guide the planes to the island. "We'll use two *bancas*, one for each PBY. Once the planes are on the water, we'll exchange codes and bring them in with our motorized boats and secure them under the trees. I have the signal codes through Commander Tisdale and will share them when the time comes."

"Will that be tonight, sir?" Tom Mitsos inquired.

"I'll let you know. I'm leaving ten men from the bomber squadron to rotate as sentries at the island and guards for the guns on Signal Hill. The rest of you should go back to camp and store up some sleep. One more thing, every one of you stay in your barracks on standby. I don't want to have to go hunting you people down when it's time."

Tuesday morning, 28 April, Charles sat down at breakfast mess, his rations one slice of SPAM, a cup of porridge, and what was offered as coffee.

Charles sniffed his cup and placed it back on the table without tasting the weird-smelling fluid. "What *is* this? and how do you manage to swallow it?" he asked the table.

"It's roasted grain, mostly," Lawless answered. "It's better than nothing."

"No—" Charles countered. "It's worse than nothing!" After months of keeping his emotions corked up, this last indignity blew out the stopper of Charles's self-control. "Damnit! It's not the cooks' fault—but someone ordered them to give us this crap and tell us it's coffee. That's pure and simple deception— it's another way of *lying* to us!" His voice rose. "The brass still say that a U.S. invasion fleet will be here in days when we know damn well that's bullshit too! It's no secret that Japanese troops are grouping on the north, west, and south coasts of Mindanao and will overrun this place in a matter of days—"

He stood up, in a red rage, almost shouting. "I just want the admirals, the generals, and our goddamn president, all to admit the damn truth! And the truth is, THIS IS NOT COFFEE! They could at least admit that much to us! And while they're admitting this wretched liquid isn't coffee, they should admit to everyone here that THERE'S NO HOPE IN HELL OF HOLDING THIS ISLAND AGAINST THE JAPANESE!"

He sat abruptly, slamming the cup down and splashing the not-coffee all over the table.

Charles's uncharacteristic outburst silenced every man in the hall.

Bill Johnson, who'd just stood up to leave for his post on Signal Hill, smiled at Charles and said, "Nice to see you're human, Doc. You've always been calm and confident before, but I guess that's how you corpsmen are trained. What you said is the truth, all right. But it's also the truth that those pills you gave me a week ago worked a miracle—I'm as good as new. I'll tell you again, Doc, thanks for saving my life." Johnson lifted his cup in salute to Charles.

Charles nodded acknowledgement, then slumped back, pent-up emotions relieved.

Normal conversation returned to the room.

At mid-morning Ensign Hofmann assembled the six sailors on his team. "I just heard from General Fort. It's a go for tonight. I'm going to the island to check everything once more. Transportation will be here at 2300 to take you to the island. Tell nobody. Get some sleep if you can—it's going to be a long two or three days."

The moon, one day shy of full, was directly overhead when they arrived back on the island at midnight. With no further preparations needed, they sat and waited.

Hofmann, worried that the PBYs might arrive before the estimated 0500 arrival, sent out the guide boats at 0300 to be certain that they'd be waiting when the planes landed.

Around 0430 the moon slipped behind Signal Hill. A few minutes later Charles heard a distant hum. He listened for another few seconds before turning to Ensign Hofmann. "They're here, sir."

"Are you certain they're the PBYs and not Japanese aircraft?"

"Yes, sir. The PBY has a distinctive engine sound."

Within minutes the roar of four engines echoed from the hills around the lake.

Charles saw the two PBYs approach, one behind the other, and drop into the moon shadow of the mountain. Both landed on the lake. Signal lights flashed back and forth over the water.

Charles waited for the first PBY to be led to shore, nose first. The pilot shut down both engines as they reached the cove. Shore lines pulled the plane over the final yards to the truck tire fenders. With long poles men pushed limbs up and aside to clear the wings.

Tom Mitsos stood next to Charles. "Is it from your old unit?"

"Can't tell—it's painted black and there's no insignia or numbers. It's a newer model than the ones we had at Sangley Point. This one's got plexiglass bubbles instead of sliding doors for the waist guns."

Through an open cockpit window the pilot talked to the men securing the lines. "I know that voice," Charles told Mitsos.

A Navy officer emerged halfway from the nose hatch.

Commander Neale?!

Lieutenant Commander Edgar Neale looked at Charles with both confusion and surprise. "Doc! What the hell are you doing here?"

55

Reunion

Lake Lanao, Mindanao Island, Philippine Islands

0530 hours, 29 April 1942

It seemed a lifetime ago that Charles last talked to Edgar Neale, his VP-102 commander at Olongapo.

"What am I doing here, sir?" Charles laughed, repeating Neale's question. "Seems I was the only one they could find who'd actually seen a PBY up close. I've been helping Ensign Hofmann prepare for your arrival."

"But, if you didn't ship out on the *Maréchal Joffre*, you should have been with Bridget's group on Bataan. How did you get here?" Neale was truly curious.

"I was with Tom Pollock during the Christmas demolition of the Navy Yard and Sangley Point. After we trucked to Mariveles, I was assigned to the Navy Corregidor Beach Defense unit. In January I joined PT Boat Squadron 3 as a gunner and corpsman. We brought MacArthur down here from Corregidor in March. I was at Cebu City when we lost our last boat, so I made my way here. There's more, but that's it in a nutshell."

"What unit are you with now?"

"Good question, sir. Bridget had command of the PatWing 10 men at Mariveles, but I was sent to an ad hoc group on Corregidor with verbal orders only. I had TAD orders for PT Squadron 3. I was helping prepare a resistance organization here when I was pulled to help prepare this island for your stopover. I have no idea where the Navy has me officially attached right now."

While Charles summarized his past four months to Neale, the plane's pilot joined them. Tom Pollock, just as surprised and a bit looser with his emotions than Neale, vigorously shook Charles's hand. "Doc! Good to see you. Are any of the other men with you?"

Neale interrupted the reunion. He was not the sentimental sort and needed to settle this unexpected wrinkle efficiently. "Tom, after we left, Beckner says he was sent TAD to the PT boaters—that same group MacArthur wants us to bring back, if possible. Since the squadron he was sent to no longer exists, I'm assuming that brings him back to PatWing 10. Sound reasonable to you?"

"Perfectly," Pollock smiled. Like others, he had assumed that after Bataan surrendered, their left-behind squadron mates were all either dead or Japanese prisoners of war. Finding Charles alive and well on Mindanao gave hope that others might also have escaped from Bataan.

Neale looked back at Charles. "OK then, that's settled. You're in Patrol Wing 10 again. You'll be flight crew on the return tomorrow night. I think we can find room."

"Yes, sir!" *Great! I'm not physically on the plane yet, but he did say "I think"!*

A realization hit. *Wait—what about Balog and the rest? I can't go and leave them behind, can I? Damn. I felt so good for a moment, and now I'm sick to my stomach just thinking of flying out of here while leaving John, Bill, and all the rest here.*

Hofmann had been waiting at the other cove but came searching for the officer in overall charge of the mission. "Commander Neale, I'm Ensign Ross Hofmann. I believe we've met before."

"Yes, I do remember you. How much of the Navy is there, here on Mindanao?"

"It's mostly some PT boaters, along with a few stragglers who made it here from Cebu."

"I sure was glad to see you guys flashing the codes when we landed. Our briefing in Darwin told us that the Japs were landing in force on Mindanao, but that you 'probably' still held the lake. Thanks for showing up."

"The lake's still ours—but only for a few more days."

Neale nodded, "We left Perth two days ago and had to fly through bad weather in and out of Darwin. Before we leave tonight, my pilots could use a hot meal and at least a short nap."

"No problem, sir. That's being taken care of. Also, I've got three machinist's mates from the PT boats here to help your crew service the engines and refuel. Tomorrow we'll have day accommodations for male and female passengers. If you'd like to clean up and rest, I'll stay on top of things here."

Dawn was breaking, and Photo Joe would soon make his morning run over the lake, but camouflaging branches now covered exposed sections of both planes. Motor macs crawled over the engines, looking for leaks and adding oil. Charles worked with the soldiers to pump and filter aviation gas into wing tanks. By early afternoon both PBYs were serviced and ready for final check by their crews.

Charles casually asked one of the PBY crewmen who had stayed on the island, "Where're you going tonight?"

"Corregidor. I assumed you knew. We'll offload the supplies and come back with every man and woman we can cram into these planes."

Maybe some nurses?

When the crewmen finished servicing the aircraft, the temperature was near 100 degrees. Dripping sweat, they sought relief in the breeze near the island's shore.

Charles joined crewmen from his previous time with PatWing 10, swapping information and stories while waiting for the pilots to return.

"It's too goddamn hot to nap," one crewman complained.

Charles glanced at him mischievously. "If you're not going to sleep anyway, come with me and I'll show you something you can tell your kids about someday."

Charles led them to the western edge of the island, held out a pair of borrowed binoculars, and pointed to the opposite shore. "Look."

"What the hell?"

It seemed an entire Moro village had come to see what they could of the PBYs and their passengers. It was a social event. Men wearing one or more of the long, threatening knives sat on their heels, madly chewing. Women stood in colorful garb, enjoying the novelty of the day. They chattered loudly, occasionally gesticulating toward the island. For those unaccustomed to the Moros, it was unsettling, if not alarming.

"What're they all doing there, Doc?"

"Just watching us."

"What's that they're chewing?"

"Betel nuts. It's a moderate stimulant, apparently addictive. Turns their teeth black."

"Are they going to do anything or just watch us?"

"Probably just stay and watch. What would you do if you were them? We're the best entertainment they've had in months."

ʕ•ᴥ ʕ•ᴥ ʕ•ᴥ

Edgar Neale could be reasonable, but Charles recalled his reputation as a "hard ass with a short temper" and knew better than to ask him directly if they were bringing back nurses from Corregidor. When the pilots returned to the island, Charles stayed close to Hofmann. *I'll eavesdrop and maybe learn something.*

"I visited Army headquarters. The intel's not good," Hofmann told Neale. "First, our position here is unstable. A Japanese amphibious force unloaded on the southwest Mindanao coast at Parang, then moved twenty-two miles up the coast to Malabang. They're holding there, presumably regrouping before a major push in this direction. From Malabang, it's only an eighteen-mile drive to the south end of this lake. A few Filipino units are harassing them, but I doubt that'll slow them down. Another force is moving up from Digos. It'll take only a day longer for them to get here."

"Will the Army still hold the lake through tomorrow?"

"They'll have to, won't they?" Hofmann paused. "I also have an update from Corregidor. An hour ago we received bad news. Probably because it's the Emperor's birthday, the Japanese began non-stop bombing and shelling of Corregidor at dawn—fires and smoke everywhere. There's been no sign of them letting up. We don't even know if the docks are still usable to ferry ashore the ammunition and bring you the passengers."

"If it comes to it, we can dump the supplies and let the passengers swim to us."

"Do you have the passenger list?"

"I only know there're supposed to be fifty-four passengers. MacArthur prioritized certain men who'll help him organize the counteroffensive to retake the islands. Those'll be at the top of the list. Wainwright and others helped him make up the list. We'll load whoever they bring us until we're full."

Neale's next comment made Charles groan inwardly. "We know there are dozens of nurses on Corregidor, and we can't take them all. I'm not even sure if we'll get any of them."

Even assuming Tillie was moved to Corregidor before Bataan surrendered, her odds for evacuation are still slim.

440

❧ ❧ ❧

At 1715, on schedule, Photo Joe made his flight over the lake, his final sortie of the day. At 1815, crews removed the camouflage from both planes and cast off from their island berths. Neale continued on Plane No. 1 with Pollock piloting. Two small boats pulled the plane backwards from the cove and turned its nose towards the open lake. Pollock warmed the engines while Neale contacted Plane No. 7, confirming it too had left its berth and was ready to taxi to their takeoff position on the lake. The pitch-black seaplanes lifted from the lake at 1845 on Wednesday, 29 April.

56

The Nurses

Lake Lanao, Mindanao Island, Philippine Islands

0530 hours, Thursday, 30 April 1942

None of the island crew returned to Camp Keithley that night. The moon, barely visible through the clouds, disappeared behind the mountaintop at 0500. Assuming the mission proceeded as planned, the two PBYs would arrive in the darkest hours before dawn. The flight to Corregidor was a daring mission to a besieged garrison surrounded by heavy Japanese forces. All were aware of the distinct possibility that one or both PBYs might fail to return. The men waiting on the island felt the weight of mission success or failure on their shoulders as much as did the actual flight crews.

John Balog rode to the lake that afternoon with the pilots and now sat on the shore with Charles, Thomas Mitsos, and two other soldiers. "I suspect this'll be our last contact with the outside before the Japs overrun the place," Mitsos said. "What are you Navy guys going to do?"

"Do I have a choice?" Balog retorted. "Let me turn that around. When that happens, what choice do any of us have? Command is already preparing for a general surrender."

"Tom's already made his choice," Charles answered for Mitsos. "You're going to the hills with the guerrillas, aren't you, Tom?"

"Definitely," Mitsos agreed. "No way can the Japs occupy this entire island. We'll just be where they aren't, use our radios to pass information about their movements to Australia, and pester the hell out of them until General

MacArthur comes back and kicks their sorry asses back into the sea." He paused, glancing sideways at Charles. "Doc, what do you mean, I'm going? You said you're coming with us—"

Balog also noticed the troubled look on Charles's face. "Charlie—what's wrong?"

I wanted to put this off, but it's time to tell him. "These PBYs are from my old squadron, Patrol Wing 10. Lieutenant Commander Neale, the mission commander, was my squadron commander back at Olongapo. When they got here yesterday morning, he told me I'm leaving with them for Australia—as flight crew. It's not certain—it's only if they can squeeze me on board. I think he feels bad about all the men left at Bataan when the last of the wing's planes flew to Australia. Bringing me back might be some small compensation."

"Charlie," Balog exclaimed, "you're the luckiest goddamn sonofabitch alive! There's going to be some truly pissed-off senior officers when they find out that a lowly sailor flew out on that plane!"

"I don't feel lucky—I feel terrible. We should be leaving together."

"Don't worry. We'll all get there somehow. Eventually." He was silent for a moment. "But hey, since you're leaving, can you do me a favor?"

"Of course." Charles had trouble getting the words out.

"Mail this for me when you get to Darwin." Balog pulled a crumpled letter from his pocket and handed it to Charles.

I'll put this with the three letters I got from Martino on that last visit to the hospital in Cebu.

Low clouds diffused the predawn light. Boats waited offshore, ready to signal the planes and bring them back to the island. Hofmann checked his watch for the hundredth time. Neale said that if weather conditions kept them from landing on the lake, they would land in the ocean and wait for daylight to fly into Lanao.

"I hear engines," Mitsos said.

"It's a PBY," Charles announced, "but it sounds like it's only one plane."

A minute later, the plane dropped to a smooth, powered landing and taxied to the flashing signals. Boats and eager hands pulled the PBY into the same cove it left from the evening before. It was Plane No. 1, piloted by Tom Pollock. At the cove, Commander Neale gave a thumbs-up from the cockpit.

There was no sign of the No. 7 plane piloted by Lieutenant Deede.

While Pollock and Neale conferred with Hofmann, Charles watched the passengers exit through the hatch like sardines spilling from a tin. *I didn't know so many people could cram into a PBY. Wow—they're gaunt and pale. Everyone here's so deeply tanned that I'd forgotten what living in the tunnels can do to a person.*

It hadn't been only the lack of sunlight in the Malinta Tunnel complex. The unrelenting stress of living in crowded tunnels under continuous shelling and bombing destroyed any sense of confidence they might have had. Sunken eyes flitted nervously above unsmiling lips. Clambering from the waist hatch, the passengers' trembling hands reached for anything stable. Those helping them from the plane realized hygiene had been abandoned on the Rock.

Charles recognized Commander Bridget leaving the plane. Having obviously survived the fighting and made it from Mariveles to Corregidor, now he too was here on Mindanao. Charles waved, but Bridget didn't see him. After Bridget, a nurse looked around nervously before climbing through the hatch. The next two, also nurses, stoically stared straight ahead. He watched for a familiar face or a flash of red hair as seven more nurses exited the PBY and came to shore.

No Tillie.

The last passengers from Pollock's PBY were still making it to shore when the roar of another plane echoed across the lake. Lieutenant Deede, piloting PBY No. 7, dropped through the clouds and landed on the glass-smooth lake. Charles's hopes lifted. *I'll bet the nurses were divided between the two planes.*

Balog trailed along with Charles to the other landing cove and was first to recognize an officer crawling from the plane. "Charles! Look who's here!" He waved at Lieutenant DeLong emerging through the hatch. Balog ran to greet him. Charles kept back, still trying to swallow his disappointment that Tillie hadn't been among the ten nurses from the first plane.

Charles's thrill of seeing DeLong and Bridget among the evacuees was tempered by the absence of any other MTB 3 or PatWing 10 sailors. Prioritizations for evacuation assumed commissioned officers, even newly minted Navy ensigns and Army second lieutenants, were more valuable to the war effort than any enlisted man or NCO.

It's not right! The people in Washington don't know what it's like to be in a war zone. Even I've seen enough to know that without experienced NCOs, the military will grind to a halt. Without them, a PBY would never get off the water, and a PT boat would never leave the dock. The decision-making sons of bitches in Washington don't understand that!

Charles returned his attention to the emerging passengers.

Nine more nurses stepped out of Plane No. 7.

Still no Tillie.

Dejectedly watching the women step onto the island, Charles realized he knew one of them, a dark-haired nurse. *What was her name!?* "Trish!" he called and ran to her.

Trish turned toward Charles and gazed at him with the same shell-shocked eyes as the other passengers. "I'm the corpsman who visited the jungle hospital," he reminded her. *No recognition.* "You had to explain 'Dark Irish' to me."

Her eyes widened in recognition. "Yes, yes. You were looking for that Navy nurse —Tillie?"

"I'm still looking for her. Do you know what happened to her?"

"I know she moved to Corregidor. Most of us did. When I left last night, there was no time for goodbyes. Fortunately, the Japanese stopped shelling an hour before the plane landed, then everything happened so fast. They pulled a group of us out and took us straight to the dock. The pilot was yelling 'Hurry, hurry!' even though some were too weak to move any faster and had to be lifted through the hatch."

Without thinking, Charles said, "You look healthy compared to most of them—I mean, considering what you've been through."

Trish looked at the ground for a moment, then back at Charles. "I do believe they sent the sickest nurses, but a couple of us are still pretty healthy."

Charles waited for her to go on. "Truth is, I think I'm here because I was a close friend of a high-ranking Army officer—and that's why my name made the list. I'll have to live with that every time I think of those nurses left back there."

"What'll happen to Tillie and the other nurses now?" Charles asked.

"A submarine made it in last week. I know it took five or six nurses when it left. Maybe Tillie was one of them, but I can't truthfully tell you if she was or wasn't on it. It's so grim there—as I was leaving, some of the girls stuffed letters in my pocket. Tillie wasn't one of them. I'm sorry."

"That's OK. She already told me what I should do if something happened to her."

"What was that?"

"Never, ever forget!"

Charles walked back to rejoin the crew setting up to refuel PBY No. 1.

57

Almost

Lake Lanao, Mindanao Island, Philippine Islands

1700 hours, 30 April 1942

Take-off time for Australia was set for 1830. By 1700, all passengers and flight crews were back on the island. Showers, clean clothes, food, and a few hours of sleep improved the nurses' appearance and mood, but occasional bursts of guilt-ridden tears for friends left behind continued.

Charles watched the passengers crawl back into PBY No. 1. The plane crew captain carefully squeezed each passenger into position with jigsaw puzzle efficiency, assigning nurses to the aft compartments. Keeping the heavier men forward would lower the nose and help the plane rise to the step during takeoff.

Charles trotted over to the cove where passengers for Plane No. 7 were starting to board. Six soldiers brought back from Corregidor had been replaced by men from Mindanao deemed to be higher on the priority evacuation list. He scanned the faces waiting to board, recognizing Lieutenant Brantingham.

Charles ran over to say goodbye to the man for whom he had developed such tremendous respect.

"Best of luck, sir. It was a privilege to serve with you." Charles saluted.

"Thank you, Doc. You served well in RON 3. I have little doubt our paths will cross again. Godspeed."

And with that farewell, Brantingham disappeared through the hatch.

Charles ran back to Plane No. 1.

Immediately, Commander Neale waved him over.

"Beckner."

"Yes, sir."

"You're leaving with us. I sent a message to Commander Tisdale—you're officially returned to PatWing 10. Get aboard."

"Yes, sir. What about Balog?" Charles put his hand on John's shoulder. "He's a Navy corpsman and senior to me. He's also been here on the ground supporting this mission."

Neale had no time for sentimental reflection or debate about his already overloaded aircraft. "Sorry. You're in PatWing 10. He's not."

Charles hesitated. *How can I leave John and the other PT boaters? They've been part of my life for the past, what, three or four months? Is that all it's been? Seems like years.*

"John?"

"Yes?"

"Are you going to the mountains with the other guerrilla fighters, when it comes to that?"

"Charlie, you know me. I follow orders."

"With or without you, those men are going to need all the quinine and atabrine you can gather." He removed his medical kit from his belt. "You know where the rest of my stuff is. Make sure it gets to the right people. Throw it in the lake before you let the Japanese have it."

"Will do."

"Here," Charles passed his .45 pistol, along with two clips of ammunition, to John. "They won't let me leave with this. If no one else needs it, give it to that soldier, Tom Mitsos, for the resistance group."

"They're letting you take your knife?"

"Didn't ask," Charles patted the butt end of the large Hospital Corps Knife. "If this plane doesn't make it all the way to Australia, my knife might be the only thing that keeps me alive."

The two men stared at each other, a thousand unspoken words passing between them. After another embrace, this one quick, John shoved Charles towards the airplane.

Climbing aboard the PBY, a childhood memory flashed into Charles's mind. He was in the wagon, talking with his father after the pitchfork confrontation in the stable. He remembered his father's words:

"*… if it's pretty clear that the situation is impossible and you're going to lose the fight, then you have to avoid it or put it off by any means you can.*"

"You mean, just run away?" Charles had asked.

"So to speak," his father had replied. *"You have to survive, Charles. Even though it might take a long time, eventually you'll be able to even the score."*

Charles was pleased to find his favorite location, the nose compartment, not yet occupied. Behind the cockpit, the Navy captain, Joe McGuigan, sat

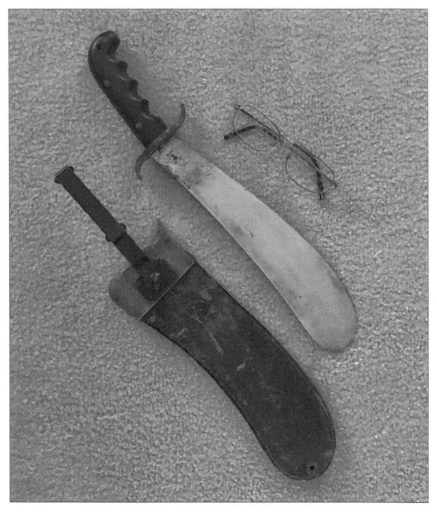

M-1904 Hospital Corps Knife, adopted in 1915 for use by USMC Naval Hospital Corpsmen serving in the field with Marines. In 1942 it was replaced by a much less elegant design that was similarly functional but cheaper to mass-produce.

on the navigation table. Farther back, Commander Bridget sat next to Army Colonel Stewart Wood. The floor in every section was covered with passengers, nurses aft and men forward. Pollock was in his seat, and Bounds, the Navy Aviation Pilot, beside him.

Neale leaned into the cockpit. "Ensign Hofmann just told me the launch that was going to pull us out has a busted engine. He hired a Moro boat to do it."

Charles overheard the conversation. *Those putt-putts don't have a lot of power.*

Charles stood from the nose hatch in the light breeze, watching the owner of the *banca* make more than a dozen passes to get a line secured between his boat and the PBY. The bow lines were slacked, and the tiny single putt-putt pulled at the nose of the giant PBY. When it was pointing into the lake, the bow lines were cast loose.

Things were going well.

Until they didn't.

First, a gust of wind stopped all movement.

Another gust pushed at the plane's broad vertical tail, twisting the PBY sideways and creating an angle between the putt-putt's towline and the airplane.

With its engine putt-putting faster, the *banca* pulled the PBY, still at an angle, into the lake. Charles watched the Moro stare into the lake water to his side.

Charles followed the Moro's look, shocked by what he saw.

He pointed at the putt-putt and yelled to Pollock, "We're being pulled onto rocks!"

Pollock looked past Charles. "What rocks?"

"They're goddamn underwater rocks! I can see them from here!"

Neale, seeing Charles in some sort of argument with the pilots, yelled, "Get back in, Doc!"

"They're right there, ten yards off—" Charles kept pointing, but was again interrupted.

"Beckner! Sit your ass down, now!" Neale yelled his order.

"Yes, sir," Charles said helplessly, crouching lower, but staying high enough to watch the *banca*. The Moro looked back at Charles with a wild, betel-stained, toothy grin.

Pulling out his *kris* knife with its razor-sharp, curving blade, the Moro slashed the tow rope and departed as fast as his putt-putt could move.

Pollock had started the engines just as the plane shuddered, with a rending sound coming from the hull. Realizing the plane had struck something and might be taking on water, Pollock prepared for a cold-engine takeoff.

In the back of the PBY nurses were already standing in inches of water. Three nurses tried to stuff clothes in the largest hole and hold them in place by standing on them, but their efforts were futile. "Water's pouring in!" they yelled from the aft compartment.

"Here we go!" Pollock said, putting his hand on the throttles.

"Don't take off!" came a yell from Commander Francis Bridget. Crawling forward, he met Neale, who was coming aft to evaluate the damage.

"Don't try to take off!" Bridget said. "Too much water on board—it's already knee-deep. With this load we'll never get off the lake."

Neale turned and, pushing his way by bodies, yelled to the cockpit, "Abort take-off! We're sinking! Beach her!"

Pollock gunned the engines and pointed the PBY back to the island cove. With the plane wallowing low in the water, he cut the engines at just the right moment, leaving enough momentum to beach the nose but not so hard as to damage the hull.

Ensign Hofmann had watched the whole disaster from shore. He jumped onto the nose of the plane just in time for the plane's abrupt stop on the car-tire bumpers to knock him back onto the rocky edge. He stood up, bleeding from a nasty cut over his eye.

Water in the aft compartment was now waist high.

People shouted and called for help. It was mostly the nurses who remained quiet and calm. After all, for months they had been dealing with life and death. Mostly death.

Small boats, two at a time, transferred the passengers to shore within minutes. Deede, after barely getting his heavy plane off the water, circled overhead, waiting for Pollock to take off and join him. Instead, he saw light signals coming from the island. The flashing code, from Pollock, said "Go on. Go on."

The wet, disappointed passengers listened to Plane No. 7's engines fade into silence. Though disappointed, all were uniformed military men and women, trained to meet adversity head on. There was no wailing and gnashing of teeth.

"Sorry, Doc," Tom Mitsos said.

"Thanks. It was an empty feeling, listening to that other plane leave, but I'm OK now."

Watching the full moon rising above the mountain ridge, Charles recalled a passage from *Meditations*. "Nothing befalls a man except what is in his nature to endure."

He turned to Mitsos. "Well, Tom, looks like I'm joining your guerrilla army after all."

58

Never Give Up

Lake Lanao, Mindanao Island, Philippine Islands

1800 hours, 30 April 1942

When the men on shore realized the plane was sinking, all of them jumped to help.

Four sailors swam with empty fuel barrels to the tail of the plane and lashed them in place with rope. simultaneously, four soldiers fashioned a raft from more empty drums, piled it high with blankets, and wedged it under the starboard wing. After all the passengers were evacuated, the crew began stripping the plane to save radios and other usable equipment and to reduce weight to slow her sinking.

The PBY finally stabilized in the water but floated so low that only an inch or two of the waist gun blisters poked above the surface. The bilge pump had failed, so the crew began bailing with buckets.

Hofmann quickly grasped the situation. Wiping blood from his eye, he told Neale, "Hand bailing's not going to work. I'll get two soldiers to rig the fuel pumps to drain water from the hull."

On shore, Tom Mitsos stripped to his shorts. "Permission to make an inspection, sir?" he asked the officers.

"Go ahead, corporal," Neale replied, surprised that an Army man appeared so confident evaluating a seaplane, especially one nearly sunk in the cove.

Mitsos swam to the hatch and disappeared inside. After a minute, he came back through the hatch and dove under the plane's hull several times. Finally, he returned to shore. "There's one big L-shaped hole in the back, just behind that ledge."

"We call that ledge the 'step,'" Pollock interjected.

"OK, sir. The step. Anyways, the tear is at least eighteen inches on a side. That was the only large hole I could find. There's a section where the bottom of the hull turns upward at a sharp angle."

"That's called the 'chine.'" Bounds took his turn educating Mitsos in Naval construction terms.

"Right. Anyway, it's caved in, but the seam is intact as far as I can tell. There are smaller holes toward the front but no other big holes I could find. Until that hole is repaired, all your bailing is just goat roping."

"Thank you, corporal," Neale said, unable to resist a smile at the military slang for any useless activity.

He turned to Hofmann. "The water itself is not doing any immediate damage. PBYs are boats after all. As far as I can tell, her wing, engines, and critical mechanical controls are all undamaged and above water. If we can patch the hull enough to hold together for takeoff, there's no reason we can't fly her all the way to Darwin."

"You're right," Pollock agreed. "I'm kicking myself though. Before we left Perth, I tried to find more muslin and marine glue in case we needed it for something like this, but no luck. All we have is the small emergency package we routinely carry. I guess I should have looked harder."

"Not your fault."

"What can I do to help?" Hofmann asked Neale.

"Do you think you can find a larger pump? We're going to need something bigger than those fuel pumps."

"I'll go back to Keithley and find something."

While Neale and Hofmann talked, Charles took a small field bandage from the personal first-aid kit on his belt and wrapped it around Hofmann's head, stopping the bleeding. "This is all I kept with me. You better have this gash taken care of back at the base, sir. It could use some stitches."

"Later," Hofmann said as he and Neale left for Keithley.

PBYs were designed and constructed as "boats that fly." The hull was divided into watertight compartments, separated by hatches with watertight doors, all now closed.

Hofmann found a donkey pump at the base and sent it back to the island. Charles and Lawless set it up in the navigation compartment, pumping as a team.

"I don't think the water level has dropped at all," Charles noted, panting after after a strenuous half hour of pumping.

"You're right," Lawless agreed.

A quick inspection revealed the bulkhead door between the navigation and mechanic's compartments was warped. Water was flowing in as fast as the two could pump it out. While Charles and Lawless pondered this problem, Pollock stuck his head in the hatch. "Not much progress?"

"No, sir. Bulkhead door's sprung. It's coming in from the next compartment as fast as we can pump it out."

"Keep trying. We've plugged most of the small holes but couldn't get our muslin patch to stick on the large one. We're pulling a blanket under the hull. If water pressure seals it tight against the skin, then we should be able to make some headway."

The blanket did slow the flow of water. That, and the arrival of a gasoline-powered pump from Camp Keithley, yielded success. Steadily, the PBY rose in the water. By 0330 the waist compartment was relatively dry and the gun blisters were completely above water.

Then the gasoline-powered pump gave out a loud *clunk* and stopped, as if to say, "There, I've done my job."

Pollock, in charge of the plane crew while Neale was at Camp Keithley, gathered all the men remaining on the island. "I think we've done all we can for the moment. Everyone, including me, is exhausted. Continue rotating men on the donkey pump and set a watch on the waterline. If water rises more than an inch, wake me. Let's get some sleep."

A few hours later in full daylight Commander Bridget stood over Pollock, gently shaking him awake. "Good morning, Lieutenant. I came to tell you that Colonel Wood and I are moving the nurses and other passengers to Del Monte. We've requested a B-17 for evacuation. You don't have much time here—the Japanese are advancing and already approaching the south end of the lake. In the next few hours you'll have to sink or destroy the plane and get the hell out yourself. If we find that B-17 is on its way, I'll try to send word in time for you to get there."

"Thanks." Pollock looked at the Navy captain who had returned with Bridget. "Good morning, sir. You were one of our passengers, I think?"

"I was. I'm Joe McGuigan, from Cavite. I'd like to help if possible."

"Captain McGuigan, if you think you can help, I'm all open to suggestions.

You were at the Navy Yard, you say?"

"Yes—in fact, I was a ship repair officer before things fell apart. How bad is the damage?"

"Those submerged rocks holed us in several places. The largest is a right-angle rip in the aluminum, about eighteen inches on a side. We've plugged most of the smaller holes, but the big one is giving us trouble. The crash blanket slowed the water enough for us to get her higher in the water. Do you want to have a look?"

McGuigan took a flashlight and entered through the nose hatch. He methodically examined the entire hull from bow to stern.

After five minutes, he returned to the navigation compartment and motioned Pollock to follow him to the shore. "Besides the holes, the chine's dented, but I don't think it's lost much structural integrity. The holes in the mechanic's compartment are between the second, third, and fourth stringers, outboard of the keel on the port side. One stringer is broken, but it can be repaired. The smaller hole, nearest the keel, is also repairable."

"What about the large hole?"

"A bit more difficult—it's a single large rip in the skin. The edges are clean and sharp though. That will help."

"So it can be fixed?"

"Sure."

"Really?"

"What I'd like to do is put the plane on a ramp and bring her ashore. After that I'll cut some proper aluminum to the correct size and shape and rivet it in place."

"Sir." Pollock said with exasperation, "You know this plane's not coming on shore, and we don't have any of those things."

McGuigan took no offense at Pollock's outburst. "Sorry, I was being facetious of course. We can't do any of that, but maybe we can improvise. Do you want me to give it a try?"

"Just tell me how we can help."

"I see the waist guns are already gone. Strip everything else you haven't already taken out. That includes blankets, oxygen gear, all spare food, and ammunition. Leave nothing but your code books and navigation gear."

"She's pretty clean already, but if we don't need it to fly, consider it gone."

"Do you have muslin and marine glue?"

"Only a little."

Hofmann had returned to the island and now joined the discussion. "I might be able to scavenge some things back at the camp. What else do you need?"

"As I said, it's a clean rip in the skin. All we have to do is fix it well enough to hold until you get her up on the step. Then, most of the stress will be removed from the damaged area until you land. I brought some hand tools and lumber with me, but it's going to take more. We need something that will work as a temporary patch." McGuigan looked at Hofmann, "Can you find us some thick rubber sheeting?"

"I'll try."

"Also a piece of thin metal sheet, I don't care what kind of metal. And bring back some blankets. Do we have any packed parachutes?"

"We should. How about spit and baling wire?" Hofmann retorted.

"That too."

John Balog had remained on the island, knowing there could be cuts and smashed fingers if they tried to make repairs. "Damned sorry, Charlie! Here's your gun back."

"Keep it, John. She can't take off with that hole, but one of the passengers was a Navy captain who knows something about repairing ships. He's going to see if he can fix things well enough to get us airborne. I can't tell what Commander Neale is thinking. He sometimes keeps things to himself, like our Lieutenant Kelly."

"I get that picture."

"Pollock, the pilot, has no doubts she can be repaired and fly back to Australia. He keeps saying she'll be airborne by the end of the day. In fact, you might want to think about hanging around for a while in case he's right."

"I think I can take waving goodbye to you once more."

Two motor macs had the gasoline-powered pump running again, and it was keeping water inside the hull at a workable level. McGuigan stripped to his skivvies. Despite being a Navy captain, senior to everyone else on the small island, he led the repair crew into the water himself. With McGuigan giving instruction, Mitsos and three other soldiers rotated two at a time, working underwater for as long as they could hold their breath. Throughout the process, McGuigan intermittently dove underwater to check the work, afterward giving the men compliments and encouragement.

After repeated dives under the oily water, a filthy, slimy McGuigan finally waded to shore. "The blanket you strung under the hull is not a watertight seal, but it slowed the flow of water enough for us to try and repair the big tear. While we wait for Hofmann to bring us what he was able to locate, will you have some of your men cut a dozen straight limbs or small tree trunks? I need them one-and-a-half to two inches in diameter and six or seven feet long. Also have them bring me one slightly larger tree trunk the same length but four or five inches in diameter. I'll use those to fashion stiffeners for the patches and reinforcement for the crossmembers."

Pollock selected a work party of four men, giving the additional strict instructions, "Do *NOT* cut any betel tree branches—not even a small one. Two nights ago, someone used betel tree branches for camouflage. It caused a major confrontation with the local Moro leader. We paid him off and promised that no more betel trees would be damaged."

Charles had a passing thought. *I wonder if Magellan was killed because he cut down a betel tree?*

John Lewis, machinist's mate from PT-35, had earlier been given charge of the military motor pool maintenance shop at Camp Keithley. Hearing of the damaged plane, he threw together things he thought might be useful and sent a truck with two-by-fours, planks, saws, drills, screws, and hammers to the island.

McGuigan did much of the labor himself. The sheet metal he asked for never appeared, so he improvised. Two hours later he reported to Pollock. "I plugged the smaller, inboard hole by laying a double thickness of canvas covered with marine glue between the stringers, extending it well beyond the two main cross members. I fitted a thick piece of wood over that patch and fixed it in place with two-inch braces every three inches. It's a pretty solid repair."

"And the large hole?"

"That's a bigger challenge, but I'm going to try."

Over the next hours, the captain emerged from the water several times to retrieve some piece of material or to fashion a needed part from the wood he had requested. Finally, he waded to shore, dried off, and updated Pollock and his anxious crew.

"The whole area around this section was badly battered, complicating a repair. We stuffed a square of sponge rubber from the back of a parachute harness between the stringers and covered it with a thin board forced under the cross members. I braced that with a two-inch board. I fit sections of that tree you cut down between two sections of stringers, covering both patches."

"Sounds like a strong repair."

"I hope it's enough to keep the bracing from springing out on takeoff."

"You hope?" Pollock raised one eyebrow.

"Yes. I hope—it was the best I could do with what we have. Let's take off the blanket and see how much she leaks."

"I thought you fixed the hole."

"It's not a completely watertight patch. It's going to leak a bit. We'll see how it does with the blanket off."

With the blanket removed, the patch partially held, but it leaked, more than "a bit." The men replaced the blanket and lashed it tightly around the hull. They would have to fly to Australia wrapped in a blanket.

The gasoline-powered pump failed a second time. A machinist's mate determined it was a thrown rod. "It's completely FUBAR! Irreparable. Nothing more than junk now." The newly popularized acronym was proving to be an accurate and prevalent description of current events.

Charles and Lawless returned to working the donkey pump in the center compartment. With the repairs in place, short bursts of bailing every fifteen minutes was sufficient to keep the water level down.

The eastern mountain slopes would be in daylight for perhaps two more hours, but they could not wait for the cover of darkness. It was time to leave. The repairs would hold long enough for the PBY to get airborne.

Or they would not.

59

Last Chance

Lake Lanao, Mindanao Island, Philippine Islands

1800 hours, 1 May 1942

Commander Neale gathered his crew for a short briefing. They included Pollock, Bounds, Ferara, Gassett, Drexel, Donahue—and Beckner.

Neale began, "Captain McGuigan admits he couldn't manage a proper repair, but with the materials and tools available, it's the best he can do. Four thousand Japanese troops are just down the road, so it's now or never. We are going to fly this thing to Australia."

"Speaking for the crew, sir," Chief Machinist's Mate Ferara spoke up, "If you and the lieutenant are ready to fly this plane, so are we. Some of us have a girl waiting for us back in Perth."

"What about Commander Bridget?" Charles asked, "And the nurses?"

"Bridget's still waiting at Del Monte for confirmation that a B-17 is on its way. Before leaving here, he told me that even if we somehow repaired her he doubted she could get off the water with a full load. He has assumed responsibility for the nurses and is staying with them. If an evacuation plane doesn't make it to Del Monte, they will in all probability surrender to the Japanese. Still, he thinks it's the best option, all things considered."

"Then good luck to him, sir."

"Captain McGuigan and Ensign Hofmann are coming with us. Except for them, we'd be sinking this plane in the middle of the lake right now. One more thing—"

"Quiet!" Machinist's Mate Lawless, against all protocol, interrupted Neale and held up his hand for silence. Neale scowled but said nothing.

In the silence, they heard the unmistakable growl of trucks and mechanized artillery.

Neale announced what they all now knew, "The Japanese have made it past Ganassi and are advancing up the west lake road. By dawn, our little island will be occupied Japanese territory. Let's go."

"I'm glad you're coming, Captain," Pollock grinned at McGuigan as they entered the hatch, one behind the other. "If you wanted to stay here, I'd be suspicious of those repairs you did."

"You've heard the saying 'between a rock and a hard place'?" Captain McGuigan was not smiling.

"Lieutenant Pollock?" Avoiding Edgar Neale, Charles made a request to Pollock. "I'm glad to be back with PatWing 10, sir. Shouldn't we offer Corpsman Balog a seat? He's been working with us all day and taking care of cuts and other injuries during the repairs."

"I'll ask Neale."

"Yes, sir, but one more thing?" Charles pressed his case, "When the PT squadron delivered General MacArthur to this island, he made a clear promise to us, that's all of the PT boat men, that we would be brought out if the opportunity arose. Besides Balog and myself, there's three others right here, Hancock, Richardson, and Lawless. They're all PT Squadron 3 crewmen."

Pollock nodded. "We were told about the PT boaters." He spoke quietly to Neale.

The four sailors were added to the official passenger manifest.

Charles watched several soldiers who'd helped McGuigan repair the PBY ask Neale if they could come along too, only to receive an emphatic "NO!" *I wonder why he did that after letting the sailors board. Is he simply minimizing weight? Maybe it was because of MacArthur's instructions regarding the PT boaters. Perhaps he had orders from General Sharp not to evacuate any Army men?*

Unless Neale explains it later, I'll probably never know his reasoning.

ฅ ฅ ฅ

The crew took their stations. Most of the passengers sat in the navigation compartment, behind the cockpit, in order to shift weight forward and help the PBY rise to the step quicker. Above the men crowded behind the cockpit, the flight engineer's feet dangled from his seat in the tower. Charles was disappointed to see the nose compartment already occupied, so he took a position in the waist, next to the starboard gun blister. The PBY-4s back at Sangley Point and Olongapo had sliding hatches for the waist guns. This newer version had Plexiglas blisters that were hinged and rotated upward, and Charles could keep an eye on those rocks.

In addition to sending pumps and materiel, Hofmann had somehow found a larger U.S. military launch to pull them from the cove and keep the plane far from the dangerous shoals.

Loaded PBYs normally use maximum engine power and as much as 4,000 feet of open lake or ocean to rise from the water. It's more than a matter of horsepower and wing lift—it's a tug-of-war with the water. Fluid physics create suction on the hull, fighting against the skyward lift of the wing.

Pollock taxied the plane away from shore for takeoff, added power, and pointed the plane towards the downwind end of the lake. From there they would have a long runway into the light wind. The aluminum hull reverberated with the pounding of small waves with the increased speed.

Without warning, the blanket covering the exterior of the hull lost suction and blew loose. A taut rope banged against the side of the plane. From the gun blister Charles could see the blanket, still tethered to the end of the rope, flapping against the tail control surfaces. Charles felt wetness at his feet and looked down and watched water rise to his ankles in only a few seconds. *The patch failed!*

Shocked faces stared at the incoming gush of lake water. "We're filling with water back here!" someone shouted.

How ironic. After dodging Japanese bombs and bullets for the last five months, I'm going to drown in a goddamn lake. I don't want to drown!

Hearing the shouts and glancing back to see for himself water in the navigation compartment, options flashed through Pollock's mind. He could still try to take off, or he could try to beach his plane. He was not positioned for an upwind take-off, and even if he could get full power from the cold engines, there might already be so much water on board it'd be impossible to get the craft airborne.

Rather than waste time weighing the odds, Pollock pushed the controls to full throttle.

Charles admired Pollock's decisiveness. *Good! We've no choice anyway. The Japs are already here. Nobody on board wants to go back.*

What followed was probably the longest takeoff ever attempted by a PBY. With more than 2,000 horsepower vibrating the plane and waves pounding against the aluminum hull, the PBY rose partially from the lake water. Suction and the weight of thousands of gallons of water inside the cabin held it back. Every muscle tensed, crewmen and passengers alike willed the plane to rise.

Each knew it was literally do, or die.

Finally, Charles felt them move to the step. The banging of waves diminished, the vibration lessened, and water stopped rising in the compartment. It felt more like flying, but the plane was still skimming on the water. Gaining speed, the PBY finally rose a few feet clear of the lake. Sloshing water and the blanket flopping on his rudder were almost more than Pollock could manage.

He held the big plane in the air and flying more or less straight, but to Bill Johnson watching from his gun position on Signal Hill, it looked more like a wounded duck limping toward the shore.

The low altitude, shifting water, and hampered tail controls still made it nearly impossible for Pollock to bank or turn. Looking to the cockpit, Charles could see Pollock's head locked forward as he fought for control of the plane. *What's he staring at?*

He leaned into the open waist blister, squinting into the airstream and recoiled in shock. They were rushing straight into the mountainside.

Charles always knew there would come a time when events beyond control would determine his fate.

Well, I said I didn't want to drown. At least crashing into that mountain will be a quick death.

Lieutenant Neale knew he could fly the plane no better than Pollock. Still he shouted, "Clear that damn mountain!"

Chief Machinist's Mate Ferara, the plane captain, ran back to the waist compartment, seeing the vibrating rope stretched taut across the open gun blister. He looked about, not finding what he needed. "We have to cut the damned rope!" he yelled at Charles.

"OK—" Charles pulled the Corpsman's knife from his belt. With a single swift thrust of the heavy knife, the rope separated, and the blanket fluttered away. *Glad I kept the blade sharp.*

Charles again looked forward. *Might have been too late—*

The dark mountain was seconds away, the plane still headed directly for Signal Hill.

In the cockpit, freed from the interference of the blanket on the tail surfaces and with water streaming from the hull, Pollock began the gentlest turn possible.

"Don't stall it, Tom," Neale said.

"It's gonna be close—"

Sensing the plane banking, Ferara said the exact same words to Charles.

Neither of them even attempted to brace themselves. If they survived the initial crash, the full load of avgas assured a hellish conflagration would consume what was left.

Greenery flashed by, just below them. Charles felt or heard, he couldn't be sure which, the first slap of trees on the bottom of the hull.

Too bad Father Haggerty's not here with a blessing.

The slapping stopped, and Charles saw the treetops receding. Pollock kept circling, needing to gain enough altitude to cross the mountains surrounding the lake.

Charles saw a sailor on a hill waving his cap wildly at the PBY. *That's Bill Johnson, manning those .50 cal machine guns from PT-41.*

Ensign Hofmann watched an agitated Commander Neale poke Pollock in the shoulder and point to the south end of the lake.

Hofmann stepped up to the cockpit and yelled into Neale's ear, "Problem?"

"Japanese plane—there, at one o'clock."

Hofmann looked at the enemy aircraft, then leaned to Neale's ear again and yelled, "It's Photo Joe. He's probably returning from a reconnaissance flight over Del Monte. If you ignore him, I'm pretty sure he'll do the same."

Photo Joe, dependable as ever, continued straight on and disappeared over the southern mountain ridge.

They left Lake Lanao and crossed Mindanao to the northwest, away from Japanese forces. Once over open ocean, Pollock banked the plane back towards Darwin. They were still in enemy airspace, but at night it was unlikely that any Japanese aircraft would detect a dark PBY flying low over an equally dark ocean.

McGuigan inspected his failed patch. He repositioned some of the timber reinforcements, stomping to wedge them back into place. He then shrugged to the watching men. It might hold when they landed. Or it might not.

The passengers and two crewmen gathered in the middle compartment below the tower, making themselves as comfortable as possible. Bounds stayed in the tower above them.

Charles looked around, his spirits lifted by the presence of these men. The four PT boaters were his solid comrades, of course. Neale, Pollock, and two other PBY crewmen he knew from his PatWing 10 days at Sangley Point and Olongapo.

No one tried to talk. A PBY in flight is a noisy beast. Shouting in someone's ear was possible, but absent an emergency, conversation simply wasn't worth the effort. The men mostly stared at the cabin wall or at their feet, occasionally glancing at one another.

Charles and John Balog exchanged nods.

It's not all that long ago I left Mom and Dad, Mary, and Jim in Princeton. At the same time, I feel like I've been part of an epic Greek poem. I've traveled more than time and miles, and it's all changed me. I'll never be that farm boy again.

He closed his eyes and let images flow through his mind. *Great Lakes, San Diego, Mare Island, Cañacao Hospital, PatWing 10, PT Squadron 3, MacArthur's evacuation, the exhausting, anxious walk across Cebu Island, and preparations for guerrilla resistance on Mindanao.*

Faces appeared. Susan the librarian in San Diego. Martin the bookish Jew and his best friend at the Corps School.

Tillie. Of course, Tillie. I remember the day we first talked on the Mare Island Hospital ward. Just by befriending me, you risked violating those damn nonfraternization rules. Tillie, wherever you are, I hope you are safe. I have not forgotten our mutual pledge. If I make it through this war and you don't, I will never forget your face and friendship. I know you will keep that same promise if I don't make it.

If neither of us survive—then thank you for being the friend I needed during these times.

If both of us survive this war, maybe we can start over as civilians. No nonfraternization rules out there.

ॐ ॐ ॐ

With dawn's light, everyone awoke.

Darwin, destroyed by the February Japanese bombing, had only a few houses and service buildings still standing.

It didn't look like much.

It looked like Paradise.

Pollock, exhausted and sleep-deprived, misjudged his altitude and cut the power too soon. Dropping to the water like a rock, the plane bounced three times, popping rivets along the hull. The patch bulged and leaked but held.

Pollock taxied the PBY straight to a small, shallow-water wooden pier.

Bounds shut down the engines. No victorious cheer broke the silence. By the thinnest possible margin, they had escaped.

The Philippine Islands now belonged to the Japanese, but Charles's war was not over.

He had survived, and he would fight again.

Epilogue

Charles Beckner

Charles and John Balog exchanged a silent hug yet one more time. There were also goodbyes with the other three MTB 3 sailors, Lawless, Hancock, and Richardson. Following breakfast and a short nap, the crew, including Charles, took off and flew straight west to the new PatWing 10 base on the Swan River near Perth, Australia.

This time Pollock landed smoothly and taxied the plane straight onto a sand beach.

Charles Beckner, probably in Perth, Australia, in 1942.

After a short stint with VP-101, Charles returned to independent duty as corpsman on the seaplane tender USS *Heron*. He was reassigned to HEDRON (Headquarters Squadron, Pacific Navy) in 1943.

In April 1944 Charles was with the 1st Marines for the assault on Okinawa. He was wounded three times, the last requiring transfer to the US hospital on Guam for surgery. Jim Beckner had joined the Navy and was at this time a crewman on the destroyer USS *Calhoun*, supporting the battle for Okinawa from offshore. On 6 April four kamikaze planes struck and sank the *Calhoun*. Jim suffered multiple wounds and was also transported to Guam for surgery. He and Charles were among 3,000 wounded or sick sailors and soldiers being cared for in hundreds of hastily constructed huts on Guam.

The war was long over before the brothers learned they had been within shouting distance of each other for those few days.

Charles Beckner with his father, Lee Beckner, in Lima, Ohio, 1958.

Charles recovered and rejoined his unit on Okinawa. After Japan's surrender, he traveled with the 1st Marines to China for six months to oversee the repatriation of 650,000 Japanese soldiers and civilians.

Charles's return to the United States in March of 1946 was anti-climactic. With celebrations of victory long over, ex-soldiers and sailors were returning to work and establishing families. Charles married Mary Carolyn Martin in November of that year, and they had their first child, Barbara (the author's wife), in 1948.

Charles continued his Navy career with postings on the East Coast, Alaska, Hawaii, and, finally, Southern California.

Chief Warrant Officer 4 Beckner was the ranking non-commissioned officer in the Navy when, after thirty-one years of service, he personally cancelled his scheduled retirement parade and ceremony, turned off his office light, closed the door, and quietly walked away.

And yes, he retired in his beloved San Diego.

Charles Conrad Beckner died on 17 February 2009 and was interred at Arlington National Cemetery with Full Military Honors.

Interment of Charles Beckner with Full Military Honors,
Arlington National Cemetery, 2009.

Commander Frank Bridget

Commander Frank Bridget led the group of twenty-five survivors from the aborted PBY mission to the Del Monte Army Airfield. Arriving mid-morning, Bridget was told that a B-17 had been dispatched from Darwin and was on its way to pick them up. His group included Lieutenant DeLong, Army Colonel Wood, the ten nurses, and about a dozen others.

By the next morning, the bomber was seriously overdue, with no further contact from the plane nor from Darwin. As the day wore on with no word of the rescue plan, the group began to shrink, with many, including Lieutenant DeLong, going separate ways, each hoping to find their own path to Australia. That evening Bridget and Wood accepted the fact that, for whatever reason, the bomber would not arrive. They moved the ten nurses and three civilian women from Del Monte, moving about Mindanao for the next nine days. Finally, out of options, Bridget and Wood surrendered their group to the Japanese.

The Japanese transferred the ten Army nurses and three civilian women to a civilian internment camp in Manila.

Bridget and Wood were sent to POW camps on Luzon. Stewart Wood survived the war, but Frank Bridget died in captivity.

There is a parallel story to their saga. Three days after Bridget's group left Del Monte, a B-24 bomber landed there with instructions to evacuate the twenty-five people from the missed PBY flight. It is unknown if that bomber left Del Monte empty or with a load of passengers. What is known is that the B-24 never returned to Darwin, apparently crashing into the sea.

Lieutenant John D. Bulkeley

After returning to the States in 1942, Lieutenant Commander Bulkeley toured to raise war bonds. He met Joseph Kennedy during this time and was instrumental in recruiting Lieutenant John F. Kennedy into the Navy's Motor Torpedo Boat Training Center in Rhode Island. In 1944 he led PT boats and minesweepers in clearing a lane to Utah Beach in the Normandy D-Day Invasion. During the Korean War Bulkeley was given command of Destroyer Division 132.

President Roosevelt awarded John Bulkeley the Medal of Honor "For extraordinary heroism, distinguished service, and conspicuous gallantry above and beyond the call of duty as commander of Motor Torpedo Boat Squadron 3."

Charles Beckner with Admiral John Bulkeley at MTB 3 Reunion, San Diego, California.

In the 1960s cold war, as Commander, Clarksville Base, Tennessee, Bulkeley continued the audacity he demonstrated as commander of MTB 3. To test the alertness of his fully armed Marine base perimeter guards, Bulkeley donned a ninja suit, blackened his face, and after darkness endeavored to penetrate the classified area undetected.

Admiral John Bulkeley retired in 1968 but was recalled to active duty in a retired-retained status to command the Navy's Board of Inspection and Survey.

He retired after fifty-five years of Navy service and in 1996 was interred with Full Military Honors in Arlington National Cemetery.

Chief Pharmacist's Mate John Xavier Balog

After reaching Australia, John Balog was assigned to the Submarine Stores Section in Perth. By then the war was in high gear, and Charles had probably moved to the USS *Heron*. To the author's best knowledge, the two corpsmen never reunited. During the war, John's family received an official report that he was "missing in action" but soon received another that his status had been changed to "safe." John met Noreen Dale in Western Australia, and they married on 16 November 1946.

John Balog died in Ashland, Oregon, in 1973.

Lieutenant Robert Kelly

Lieutenant Robert Kelly returned to the Pacific to command Motor Torpedo Boat Squadron 9 from 1943-44, earning another Silver Star for his actions during the New Georgia and Bougainville Campaigns. He commanded the destroyer *Irwin* during the 1945 battle of Okinawa. He retired from the U.S. Navy in 1961 with the rank of captain. Robert Bolling Kelly was interred in Arlington National Cemetery in 1989.

Lieutenant Vincent Schumacher and PT-32

The submarine USS *Permit* did arrive on schedule at Tagawayan on 13 March. PT-32 was no longer seaworthy, having only one working engine and leaking badly. On top of that, the submarine brought word that a Japanese warship blocked the channel to Iloilo. After scuttling PT-32, Lieutenant Schumacher and the rest of his crew were taken aboard the *Permit*.

After reaching Corregidor, most of the PT crewmen were taken off to make room for a group of enlisted men, causing much resentment. In fact, the soldiers were codebreakers, men who could not be allowed to be captured by the Japanese. Schumacher remained aboard. Soon after departing Corregidor, Japanese located and repeatedly depth-charged *Permit* for thirty hours. The submarine finally reached Australia a month after departing Tagawayan. Schumacher joined the submarine service and continued fighting in the Pacific, earning a second Silver Star.

Schumacher retired from the Navy in 1968 after a distinguished career.

Lieutenant Edward DeLong and Ensign Bond Murray

DeLong had to leave the *Trabajador* for Corregidor in April. Once the two PBYs landed at Corregidor the night of 29 April, DeLong was assigned passage on Pollock's aircraft. After the plane was damaged on Lake Lanao and the rescue bomber failed to show at Del Monte, DeLong apparently returned to Dansalan where he joined up with two other RON 3 men, one of them Ensign Bond Murray.

Determined to find their own way to Australia, they embarked with a simple plan: to work their way to the western coast of Mindanao near Illana Bay, steal a boat, and sail 1,500 miles through Japanese-controlled seas to Australia. They would travel by night, hug the shoreline whenever possible, and hop from one island to the next, all the way to Australia.

It would be hugely risky, but surrendering to the Japanese was not an acceptable option.

They had a brief encounter with Iliff Richardson, who declined to join them. From this point, the story is less well documented, but enough facts are known to make some reasonable assumptions. DeLong and Murray made it to the coast undetected, acquired a small boat, and set sail into the Celebes Sea. After following the coast of Mindanao to its southernmost point, they headed due south along a string of islands and islets toward the Celebes.

On 2 July 1942, after traveling through rough seas some 450 miles in an open boat, they were captured by Japanese troops on Bangka Island, five miles short of the Celebes Peninsula. They were unceremoniously executed and buried in a common grave.

In 1947 a forensic expert made a positive identification based on dental charts and records. Their remains were reinterred in the U.S. Cemetery at Barrackpore, India, and their status changed from "Missing in Action" to "Killed in Action."

On 1 June 1949, both gentlemen were reinterred at Arlington National Cemetery.

Ensign Iliff Richardson

When the Japanese captured Cebu, Richardson headed to Leyte, then on to Tacloban, but the Japanese had already taken the Del Monte airfield. With a group of eleven men, mostly Army Air Corps, he attempted to sail to Australia in a large native outrigger.

After traveling about 200 miles, the boat sank in a storm on 18 May. Richardson swam towards shore for nineteen hours before being rescued by Filipino fishermen. He eventually joined the Philippine guerrilla forces on Leyte. A former ham radio operator, he set up a radio network across Leyte and on Samar.

Richardson was picked up by a U.S. destroyer during the Battle of Leyte in 1944. Made an Army Intelligence major by Douglas MacArthur, Richardson held simultaneous commissions in the Army and Navy.

When he filed for his back pay, he was given four notices of courts-martial for drawing pay from both the Army and Navy. Admiral Ernest King intervened and personally apologized.

After the war, Richardson married Coma Noel and worked as a businessman in Houston, Texas. He served as technical advisor on several Hollywood films.

Richardson's contemporary account of MTB 3 was typed in a hut on a Japanese-occupied island. The original document suffered from water and decay during the war but can be viewed in the National Museum of the Pacific War Digital Archive. In 1945 Ira Wolfert, Pulitzer Prize-winning war correspondent and author, published Richardson's memoirs as a book, *An American Guerrilla in the Philippines*.

Ensign William Plant, Quartermaster William Dean, and Machinist's Mate Rudolph Ballough

Separated from the other crewmen of PT-31 after the destruction of their boat during the Subic Bay raid on the night on 19 January 1942, the three men were captured by Japanese troops.

The two enlisted men were executed on the spot.

Ensign Plant was held prisoner for the next two years. Late in 1944 Plant was among the many who died while being moved on Japanese prisoner vessels, the so-called "Hell Ships." He could have been on the *Enoura Maru* when it sank after being attacked by Allied planes, or he might have died later along with many others while being transported under incredibly barbaric conditions on the *Brazil Maru*.

Ensign Barron Chandler, Boatswain's Mate Jesse Clark, Machinist's Mate Velt Hunter, Torpedoman John Martino, and Quartermaster Albert Ross

When Corregidor surrendered, Chandler was still a patient in the tunnel hospital and taken prisoner. Clark, Hunter, Martino, and Ross were still hospitalized in Cebu and taken prisoner when it fell.

All five men survived the war.

The Bataan Nurses

As noted in the foreword, Mary Tallulah Finian (Tillie) is the only fictional uniformed person in this book. She is a composite of several courageous and capable military nurses assigned to the P.I. in 1942. The nurses who surrendered with Commander Bridget on Mindanao eventually joined other captured nurses at Manila. Sixty-six Army and eleven Navy nurses shouldered internment camp hardships as they cared for other POWs through the war. When Luzon was liberated in February 1945, every nurse had survived.

The Army and Navy nurses on Luzon were the first American women to see combat. Their bravery and commitment to duty paved the way for today's female sailors, soldiers, and airmen.

The story of the Bataan nurses is recorded in the book We Band of Angels by Elizabeth M. Norman.

Father Edward Haggerty

Arriving on Mindanao in 1936, Edward Haggerty had by 1942 grown the Ateneo de Cagayan from one small building with a hundred students to five large buildings with more than a thousand students. After the Japanese occupied Cagayan de Oro, the padre initially tried to maintain a friendly relationship with the Japanese command while maintaining contact with the guerrilla forces. Within weeks he could no longer safely remain in Cagayan and left to join the American-Filipino resistance.

Father Haggerty, referred to as that "guerrilla priest" in Japanese communications, continued assisting the resistance until the Allies returned to Leyte in 1944. In December of that year he became seriously ill with malaria. The commander of the thousands of American and Filipino guerrillas throughout the islands, Colonel Wendell Fertig, sent this message to General MacArthur: "Father Haggerty seriously ill at . . . Request plane pick him up . . . The Padre has been my firm support."

Shortly thereafter, a PBY landed in a nearby bay and took the Guerrilla Padre aboard, lifting off the water for the first leg of his trip home to the United States.

Father Haggerty documented his experience as a WW II guerrilla in his fascinating, but long out-of-print 1946 memoir, *Guerrilla Padre in Mindanao*.

Seaman 1st Class William Johnson

After Bill Johnson watched the second PBY struggle and finally lift off Lake Lanao, he returned to Camp Keithley. Told there would be a court martial after the war for anyone failing to surrender when ordered, he reluctantly obeyed.

Bill escaped on 4 July 1942 while still on Mindanao. He was a radioman with Fertig's guerrillas until Leyte was liberated.

After a short stint selling cars and insurance following the war, Bill resumed his education and became a dentist.

On 6 April 1997, he wrote this letter to Charles:

Hi!

If you are the corpsman that attended me at Camp Keithley back in the early days of 1942 I want to salute you, you saved my life. . . [At] Lake Lanao I must have been inoculated with the bug. I don't know where or when you appeared, but I do know that you were there and tried to help me. I was getting in pretty bad shape.

If I remember right you had me on up to 60 grains of quinine . . I was beginning to have black out periods. I can remember you saying, "Johnny, if we can't get something else to try you're going to die" . . . You said 'Wait,' and you went into another room and when you came back you had three tablets of atabrine. Those tablets broke the temperature and saved my life.

I never saw you after that, but I want to tell you that when you took off in that PBY, I was up on Signal Hill overlooking the island where the PBY was repaired . . manning the twin fifties taken from off one of the PTs. . .

If this story rings a bell, then I want to take this opportunity to thank you for what you did for me so long ago.

Bill Johnson

AUTHOR'S NOTE: MALARIA AND DENGUE FEVER IN THE PHILIPPINE ISLANDS IN WW II

Malaria was a significant medical problem in the Pacific Theater during World War II.

U.S. forces incurred 113,256 cases, causing 3,310,800 sick days and ninety deaths. Malaria is transmitted by the tiny *Anopheles minimus flavirostris* mosquito, and the malaria parasite *Plasmodium falciparum* is the most lethal form of human malaria.

In 1930 the US Army performed a malaria reconnaissance throughout the Philippine Islands. Corregidor was found to be relatively free of malaria. In contrast, Bataan harbored a large reservoir of disease, with a prevalence of three percent in the flat east coastal plain and more in the foothills. Limay, Lamao, Cabcaben, Mariveles, Sisiman, Bagac, and the many smaller barrios along the East Road on Bataan had high infestations.

The malaria parasite is introduced into the bloodstream when the female mosquito feeds on a human host. It then travels to the liver and divides in a new stage of growth. By the time symptoms appear, the illness has spread beyond the liver, with trillions of the parasites throughout the body. An infected soldier or sailor is incapacitated by repeated shaking chills, high fever, profound sweats, and a disabling malaise for at least a week with the initial infection. Relapse is common, even after treatment with antimalarials. Chronic illness or malnutrition increases susceptibility to the disease.

War plans in the Philippines considered the problem of malaria. The government made an effort to control the mosquito population by attacking breeding locations, providing mosquito netting for beds, and using quinine prophylaxis for those most at risk. Funding restrictions prevented widespread application of these measures, and the risk of contracting malaria in the Bataan foothills remained high, even for healthy troops.

Standard malaria treatment in 1941 was two grams of quinine sulfate daily for five days followed by thirty micrograms of plasmochin naphthoate daily for a week. Mepacrine (Atabrine) was an acceptable synthetic substitute for quinine, but at the time both mepacrine and plasmochin were so limited in availability in the Philippines that most often the only treatment available was simple quinine.

Relapses were common and required retreatment with more quinine.

By August 1941 the availability of quinine itself was threatened. The Dutch had long dominated the world's production of quinine, using as a raw source the cinchona bark from their East Indies territories and shipping it back to Holland for processing. When Germany occupied the Netherlands, the availability of quinine for the Allies was severely curtailed. If the Japanese occupied the Dutch East Indies, the primary source of cinchona bark would also be lost. Production of the synthetic alternative, mepacrine, was being ramped up, but supplies were slow to reach the Philippine Islands. Besides its limited availability, mepacrine was not a perfect quinine substitute, and its side effects led many troops to resist taking it unless they were already sick with malaria. Bitter tasting, mepacrine appeared to impart its own sickly yellow hue to the skin. Troops taking the drug as a preventive treatment for malaria often experienced headaches, nausea, and vomiting, and many swallowed it only under direct threat from their commanders.

Dengue fever is a virus spread to people through the bite of an infected *Aedes aegypti* mosquito. Nausea, vomiting, and severe eye, muscle, joint, and bone pain are common symptoms. Severe dengue can be life-threatening within a few hours. There is no effective antiviral drug for dengue fever. A commercial vaccine was not released until 2015.

During 1942-1945, around 80,000 U.S. military men were hospitalized for dengue in the Pacific Theater. A hospitalization averaged seven days, and most required another seven to ten days of convalescence before return to duty.

Bibliography

Books

Borneman, Walter R. *MacArthur At War: World War II in the Pacific*. Little Brown, 2016.

Breuer, William. *Devil Boats: The PT War Against Japan*. Presidio Press, 1987.

Bulkley, Robert J. *At Close Quarters: PT Boats in the United States Navy*. Naval Institute Press, 1962.

Chun, Victor. *American PT Boats in World War II*. Schiffer Military/Aviation History Books, 1997.

Clayton, Steven D. *Conspicuous Gallantry: Motor Torpedo Boat Squadron Three*. Unpublished Manuscript, 2004.

Creed, Roscoe. *PBY: The Catalina Flying Boat*. Airlife Publishing, Ltd., 1986.

Crocker, Mel. *Black Cats and Dumbos: WWII's Fighting BPYs*. TAB Books, 1987.

Dorny, Louis B. *US Navy PBY Catalina Units of The Pacific War*. Osprey Publishing, 2007.

Doyle, David. *PT Boats in Action*. Squadron Signal Publications, 2010.

Fessler, Diane B. *No Time for Fear*. Michigan State Press, 1996.

Gordon, John. *Fighting for MacArthur: The Navy and Marine Corps' Desperate Defense of the Philippines*. Naval Institute Press, 2011.

Gugliotta, Bobette. *Pigboat 39: An American Sub Goes to War*. The University Press of Kentucky, 1984.

Haggerty, Edward. *Guerrilla Padre In Mindanao*. Longmans, Green and Co., Inc., 1946.

Herman, Jan K. *Battle Station Sick Bay: Navy Medicine in World War II*. Naval Institute Press, 1987.

Hersey, John. *Men on Bataan*. Alfred Knopf, 1943.

Hofmann, Ross E. *Escape from Bataan*. McFarland and Company, Inc. 2016.

Keegan, John. *The Face of Battle*. Viking Press, 1976.

MacArthur, Douglas. *Reminiscences*. McGraw Hill, 1964.

Mellnik, Steve. *Philippine Diary/1939-1945*. Van Nostrand Reinhold, 1969.

Messimer, Dwight R. *In the hands of Fate: The Story of Patrol Wing Ten 8 December 1941-11 May 1942*. Naval Institute Press, 1985.

Monahan, Evelyn M and Neidel-Greenlee, Rosemary. *All This Hell: U.S. Nurses Imprisoned by the Japanese*. University Press of Kentucky, 2000.

Morris, Eric. *Corregidor: The American Alamo of World War II*. Copper Square Press, 2000.

——. *Corregidor: The End of the Line*. Stein and Day, 1981.

Norman, Elizabeth M. *We Band of Angels: The Untold Story of the American Women Trapped on Bataan*. Random House, 2013.

Polmar, Norman and Morison, Samuel L. *PT Boats at War: World War II to Vietnam*. MBI Publishing, 1999.

Tomblin, Barbara B. *Nightingales: The Army Nurse Corps in World War II*. University Press of Kentucky, 1996.

Williams, Greg H. *The Last Days of the Asiatic Fleet*. McFarland, 2018.

Wolfert, Ira. *American Guerrilla in the Philippines*. Simon and Schuster, 1945.

Worthen, Dennis B. *Pharmacy in World War II*. Dennis Worthen, 2013.

Letters

Jack Brady to 'Mother, Dad, & Ed'. 1 Feb 1942. 'In the field, Philippine Islands'.

Charles Beckner to James Beckner. 28 May 1941. Cavite, Philippine Islands.

Charles Beckner to James Beckner. April 1945. Okinawa, Japan.

Charles Beckner to James Beckner. 16 April 1945. Okinawa, Japan.

Bill Johnson to Charles Beckner. 6 April 1997.

Thomas F. Pollock to Thomas Mitsos. 18 December 1998. Monrovia, CA.

Thomas F. Pollock to Thomas Mitsos. 14 January 1999. Monrovia, CA.

Thomas F. Pollock to Charles Beckner. 20 January 1999. Monrovia, CA.

Thomas F. Pollock to 'the Army People who helped save the PBY.' 29 January 1999, Monrovia, CA.

Thomas Mitsos to Thomas Pollock. 12 March 1999. New Port Richey, FL.

Primary Accounts:

Richardson, Iliff. *Iliff Richardson Document.* Circa 1942. National Museum of the Pacific War.

Pollock, Thomas F. *Operation – Flight Gridiron 27 April – 3 May 1942.* Undated T. Pollock Papers.

Bernatitus, Ann. *Oral History.* Navy Bureau of Medicine and Surgery. 1994.

Personal interviews

CWO4 Charles Conrad Beckner, USN. Numerous conversations 1971-2009.

LCDR Clyde "Cash" Barber, USN. 2016.

Barbara Paradies King. 2018.